Supply Chain Performance

Supply Chain Performance

Collaboration, Alignment and Coordination

Edited by
Valérie Botta-Genoulaz
Jean-Pierre Campagne
Daniel Llerena
Claude Pellegrin

iSTE

WILEY

First published 2010 in Great Britain and the United States by ISTE Ltd and John Wiley & Sons, Inc.

ISTE Ltd
27-37 St George's Road
London SW19 4EU
UK

John Wiley & Sons, Inc.
111 River Street
Hoboken, NJ 07030
USA

www.iste.co.uk

www.wiley.com

Library of Congress Cataloging-in-Publication Data

Supply chain performance : collaboration, alignment, and coordination / edited by Valérie Botta-Genoulaz ... [et al.].
   p. cm.
 Includes bibliographical references and index.
 ISBN 978-1-84821-219-0
 1. Business logistics. 2. Delivery of goods--Management. I. Botta-Genoulaz, Valérie.
 HD38.5.S89616 2010
 658.7--dc22

                                                                      2010018195

British Library Cataloguing-in-Publication Data
A CIP record for this book is available from the British Library
ISBN 978-1-84821-219-0

Printed and bound in Great Britain by CPI Antony Rowe, Chippenham and Eastbourne.

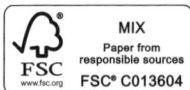

MIX
Paper from
responsible sources
FSC
www.fsc.org   FSC® C013604

Table of Contents

Introduction

This book is the result of studies conducted during two research projects supported by the Research Cluster GOSPI of the Rhône-Alpes region (France): COPILOTES (2003-2006) and COPILOTES2 (2006-2009). More than 50 researchers from seven research laboratories and six practitioners from four companies participated in these two projects.

Our work is based on the initial hypothesis that the industrial performance of a company depends strongly on its ability to strengthen its relationships with its partners (contractors, suppliers or providers and customers), to integrate its information systems and decision processes, and to synchronize product flows and activities.

In the first project, COPILOTES, we proposed approaches and developed tools to help companies assess their contribution to the performance of each supply chain (SC) to which they belong. This has encouraged them to rethink their organization and initiate new relationships with their partners, focusing on collaboration, coordination, synchronization, and information exchange. The characterization of the overall performance of a SC, the formalization of industrial practices and the evaluation of their impacts on performance have been at the heart of this project, as has the analysis of information exchanged and the value added by these exchanges. The major contributions of this research project are available at www.copilotes.eu/.

The second project, COPILOTE 2, has pursued this research by focusing on the design of decision and information systems that ensure efficient management based on collaborative practices and sharing of information between companies. We have also analyzed the behavior of participants in a SC, as well as the impact of that behavior in terms of collaborative and information-sharing (IS) practices. As most

Introduction written by Valérie BOTTA-GENOULAZ, Jean-Pierre CAMPAGNE, Daniel LLERENA and Claude PELLEGRIN.

SCs are composed of autonomous agents with their own objectives, this may cause biases in both collaborative practices and shared information, affecting local and global performance. Mechanisms of coordination, inter-organizational strategic alignment and strategic behavior have been the key focus of this second project.

The management of dependencies between members of a supply-chain is an aim common to both research projects. According to Malone and Crowston [MAL 99], using a resource produced by another entity, using the same resource in multiple entities, or collectively producing a single resource from multiple entities, constitutes three basic dependencies. These dependencies – flow dependency, sharing dependency and fit dependency – require coordination. For these authors, coordination is "the act of managing dependencies between entities and the joint effort of entities working together towards mutually defined goals" [MAL 94]. This book aims to deal with supply-chain coordination mechanisms: IS, information systems alignment, cooperation, collaboration, integration, etc. However, as Arshinder et al. [ARS 08] argue, despite the consensus on Malone and Crowston's definition in the supply-chain literature, there are various perspectives on how to link the concepts of collaboration, cooperation, information systems alignment, integration, and supply-chain (SC) coordination. In this book we therefore adopt Arshinder et al.'s broad perspective on SC coordination, which has the advantage of including more elaborate coordination frameworks (for example, Simatupang et al.'s taxonomy of coordination modes in a supply-chain [SIM 02]). Based on their approach [ARS 08], we consider the following premises:

– "SC coordination" is a term encompassing cooperation (joint operation), collaboration (working jointly), and integration (combining into an integral whole). It also involves information systems alignment (jointly expanding the information structure beyond the boundaries of each supply-chain member).

– These elements (cooperation, collaboration, information systems alignment, integration) are complementary to each other. They constitute coordination mechanisms to manage interdependencies among supply-chain members.

– The use of these coordination mechanisms depends on complexity and uncertainty: the complexity of supply-chain activities for which efforts are required in order to achieve common goals; the uncertainty and complexity of decision-making regarding logistics operations; uncertainty on the behavior of supply-chain members due to entities that are separated in a supply-chain; etc.

– The value of SC coordination can be captured through control variables that measure the improvement of SC performances and need to be shared between SC members.

The question of the value of SC coordination is at the very core of this book. A need for coordination mechanisms arises from interdependencies between the activities of SC members, and this need differs depending on sources of complexity and uncertainty. This book therefore addresses, from different points of view, the question of the extent to which or the conditions under which these mechanisms positively affect performance. Figure A.1 uses Arshinder *et al.*'s framework to portray the three parts of this book and to highlight the variety of methodologies used.

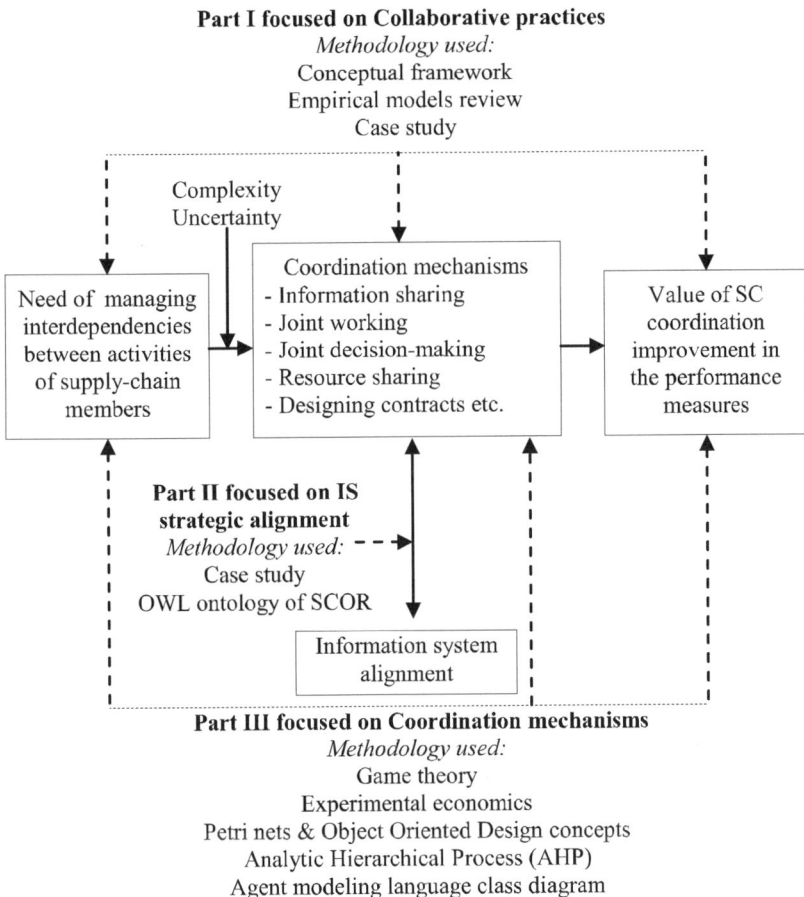

Part I focused on Collaborative practices
Methodology used:
Conceptual framework
Empirical models review
Case study

Complexity
Uncertainty

Need of managing interdependencies between activities of supply-chain members

Coordination mechanisms
- Information sharing
- Joint working
- Joint decision-making
- Resource sharing
- Designing contracts etc.

Value of SC coordination improvement in the performance measures

Part II focused on IS strategic alignment
Methodology used:
Case study
OWL ontology of SCOR

Information system alignment

Part III focused on Coordination mechanisms
Methodology used:
Game theory
Experimental economics
Petri nets & Object Oriented Design concepts
Analytic Hierarchical Process (AHP)
Agent modeling language class diagram

Figure A.1 *Synthesis of Parts 1, 2 and 3 of the book*

Part I

The three chapters in Part I of this book focus on the collaborative practices in SCs. By this we mean the practices that enable independent members of the same SC to work jointly to plan and execute operations when they consider that this collaborative effort has an impact on actual performance [SIM 05]. As Whipple and Russell point out, "collaboration is a very broad and encompassing term" [WHI 07]. Therefore, Part 1 does not address the concept of collaboration but only the range of collaborative practices and their relationships to performance. What are these practices? Moreover, since IS is a core practice, what is the nature of the information that can be shared between a focal firm and customers or suppliers? What are the impacts of these practices on SC performance?

Chapter 1 questions the models, called SC collaboration–performance models, which empirically test the effects of collaborative practices on SC performance. Two main questions frame the debate: How can we recognize a model linking SC collaboration and performance? And how can we compare SC collaboration–performance models? These questions start from the problem examined by Ho *et al.* [HO 02] of weaknesses in empirical research on the relationship between SC management practices and performance.

Discussing SC collaboration–performance models in light of Ho *et al.*'s recommendations, the authors propose two research directions. First, according to [HO 02], they clarify the meaning of the "SC collaboration" construct, i.e. the range of collaborative practices likely to be used for the definition of its measurement scale. From existing categorizations of collaborative practices, they propose a framework that highlights types of collaborative practices prioritized according to the organizational and decision-making levels committed in the relationship. Second, taking the SC collaboration–performance model as a unit of analysis, the authors widen Ho *et al.*'s analysis of the modeling approaches by using the concept of "fit" (fit as moderation, fit as mediation, fit as matching, fit as co-variation, fit as gestalts, and fit as profile deviation) as developed by Venkatraman [VEN 89]. They show the relevance of these functional forms of "fit" for describing and categorizing the modeling approaches of SC collaboration–performance models. They then use this categorization in a systematic review of empirical papers referring explicitly to the relationship between collaborative practices and performance. This review also proves that it is possible to extend Venkatraman's complexity scale of "fit" models to the SC collaboration–performance models. A so-called contingency chart emerges, that allows us to compare SC collaboration–performance models in two dimensions: the complexity of laws of relations between the model variables, and the level of organizational commitment in collaboration that the SC collaboration construct reflects.

Chapter 2 focuses on information-sharing practices. The authors adopt the point of view of a focal firm that has several suppliers and several customers, and that seeks to qualify its organizational configuration (context, strategic objectives and organizational capabilities) and its downstream and upstream information-sharing practices (nature of shared information and exchange mechanism). The framework enables managers of the focal firm to study the conditions and impact of IS and collaborative processes on the functioning and dynamics of each entity in a supply chain. This questioning framework is structured on four levels (theoretical constructs, empirical constructs, attributes, and questions). This in turn is based on two main theoretical constructs, organization configuration and information-sharing practice. The theoretical construct "organization configuration" is composed of three empirical constructs that qualify the internal and external environment and objectives, the product offering, and the SC configuration. The theoretical construct "information-sharing practice" considers six categories of information to be shared, both downstream and upstream and, for each category, the direction of the sharing, either from the focal firm to the partner (supplier or customer), or from the partner to the focal firm. Each type of shared information is qualified by content (level of aggregation, business departments concerned by its use, application component that records it and perceived impact on the performance). It is also qualified by the process that characterizes the exchange (temporal characteristics, origin of the exchange, application component from which the information is extracted, communication technology used for the exchange, and contracting parameters). In conclusion, the authors present two analyses based on this questioning framework and drawn from enquiries conducted within the COPILOTES and COPILOTES2 projects.

Nowadays, companies increasingly face the need to evaluate the impact of their SC management practices, not only for their regular stakeholders (shareholders, employees, suppliers and customers), but also for the external stakeholders representing "civil society", like local residents, non-governmental organizations, customer associations, etc. Consequently, the evaluation system must integrate performance assessment on the economy, environment and society in order to highlight the interactions between these three dimensions. Chapter 3 addresses this issue by considering collaborative practices and sustainable practices together. For this purpose, the authors work in three stages:

– First, they propose a generalized model of industrial performance, encompassing three dimensions: economic, environmental and social. The economic performance is analyzed in terms of five criteria (responsiveness, reliability, flexibility, quality and financial) and the indicators are classified according to their application area (upstream, downstream or transverse) and their orientation (customer *versus* business). Based on the literature, the environmental criteria cover five areas (environmental management, resource management, pollution, danger and natural environment) and the social criteria another five areas (working conditions, human rights, societal commitments, customers and good business practices).

– In the second stage, the authors build two tools: the first one characterizes the collaborative practices and the second one the sustainable practices of a company. In both models, a practice refers to a well-identified process and is characterized by a degree on a maturity scale and a decisional level where the practice is engaged. In addition, the collaborative practice model integrates a third dimension to take into account a behavior (proactive *versus* reactive) of the company in the use of collaborative practice.

– In the third stage, the authors propose a two-step approach to identify existing correlations between collaborative effort and economic performance, and then to analyze existing relationships between performance and sustainable practices. An application of this approach to the analysis of environmental impacts concludes the chapter.

Part II

Part II emphasizes the inter-organizational alignment between business and information systems at strategic and operational level. According to Henderson *et al.*'s strategic alignment model (SAM) [HEN 93], companies continuously make co-alignments between four domains (business strategy, IT strategy, organization, and IT infrastructure) in order to optimize their performance. However, SC coordination implies the extension of this alignment to the inter-organizational level. How can this alignment be achieved? Part II considers this question from two different perspectives.

Chapter 4 looks at how companies embedded in the same SCs adapt their information systems to reach their strategic goals in respect of their suppliers and customers. The main idea of the chapter is to extend the SAM to the inter-organizational level. The authors use this extended framework as a heuristic device to question the inter-organizational alignment and to better understand the factors and connection modes that companies can set up to operationalize their alignment. The methodology used is a single case study that describes the dynamics of alignments occurring in a jewelry SC during a radio frequency identification (RFID) implementation project between a middle-sized retailer and its supplier, a logistics service provider. The case study describes the project from 2006 to 2009 highlighting the main participants, their expectations, the physical processes and their transformations during the project, the information flows, and the IT infrastructure that supports it. For the analysis of RFID implementation, the authors adapted and completed an existing framework and plotted a map that emphasizes the different routes of intra- and inter-organizational strategic alignments. This analysis highlighted three characteristics of the complexity of inter-organizational alignment. First, several alignments, and not only one strategic alignment, progressively take place during the implementation project. Second, these alignments have to cross the classical horizontal SC associated with the product and the vertical SC related to the RFID tags. Finally, this study shows the interactions between different types of alignment in the SC, with each intra-organizational alignment affecting the other intra-organizational alignments of partners in the same SC.

Chapter 5 also addresses the question of inter-organizational alignment, but at a finely detailed level. The authors refer to the SAM by considering that alignment of knowledge is a central focus for strategic alignment because knowledge on information systems is represented in a variety of ways (databases or collections of documents, emails and XML schemas, etc.). Therefore, at an abstract level, the interoperability and cooperation of information systems require mechanisms that ensure a *semantic integration*, i.e. mechanisms that allow for comparison and recognition of the resemblances and differences between the various concepts treated. The concept of ontology is a way to meet this challenge of knowledge interoperability. Ontology may be defined as "a formal explicit specification of a shared conceptualization" and the purpose of this chapter is to study how the transmission of information in ontologies facilitates collaboration in a SC. The solution developed by the authors consists in using the well-known SCOR model. This model provides a terminology and standardized processes enabling a general description of SCs and their translation into process maps, as well as a transformation of the textual model of the SCOR model into ontology.

Part III

Part III of this book pays particular attention to the question of coordination between members of the same SC. SC are distributed decision systems with local and autonomous decision makers, so SC coordination is a "pattern of decision-making and communication among a set of actors who perform tasks to achieve a goal" [MAL 97]. The usual goal of coordination is to reduce overall SC costs and to share the savings or the individual participants' benefits [SIM 00]. In other words, SC performances are directly linked to the coordination mechanisms used. In Part III, five chapters analyze the impacts of different coordination mechanisms – such as information-sharing processes – on performance and/or the determinants of these mechanisms that allow for increasing performance, such as trust or risk-aversion attitudes.

In Chapter 6, the coordination mechanism analyzed concerns the sharing of information about demand forecasts in a two-echelon supply chain (a retailer and a supplier). Using a strategic modeling approach, i.e. game theory, the first objective of this chapter is to analyze SC managers' decision-making in order to assess their potential impacts on the local performance of each participant, as well as on the overall performance of the SC. Game theory offers insights enabling us to anticipate the behavior of rational participants when confronted with conflicting situations, or with cooperative or power relationships, in a context of IS. The participants' different strategies are defined according to this analytical approach, and Nash equilibriums are determined according to the actors' rational optimizing behavior. An example of a strategy is whether or not to send a truthful forecast (for the retailer) and whether or not to trust the retailer's forecast (for the supplier).

A second added value of this chapter consists of highlighting the strong complementarity between the analytical approach and behavioral game theory, i.e. a theory of strategic interactions that is rooted in real human behaviors. Using experimental economics methodology, this chapter aims to go beyond theoretical conclusions by experimentally studying the real behaviors of strategic interactions among participants. Here, the scientific challenge consists:

(i) of testing and assessing a model in a controlled environment; but also

(ii) of identifying typical patterns of human behavior in a given context, which could introduce some innovations into the theoretical models in use.

Our results show that subjects do not follow the theoretical predictions: retailers try to induce suppliers to produce more than the optimal level corresponding to a low demand on the final market, and suppliers do not trust the forecasts transmitted by their retailer. These results open new perspectives on dynamic strategies that evolve over time, and emphasize the need to change the hypotheses used in the analytical models. They also highlight the need to represent in more detail the trust/confidence mechanisms among participants, so that potential behaviors can be differentiated by considering relationship factors.

Firms in modern SCs seek to increase their competitive edge by employing new strategies such as re-centering some of their activities by outsourcing, so their vulnerabilities tend to increase, especially in the current, uncertain environment. Chapter 7 takes into account the operational risks induced by these strategies and introduces a particular coordination mechanism among SC partners as a risk-mitigation action in supply chains, i.e. a supplier selection mechanism to enhance the purchasing policy of the manufacturer.

Based on a global model of a SC with several suppliers and one manufacturer, the authors show how coordination among SC partners can be used as a global mitigation action to reduce a set of SC risks. Examples of such risks include demand fluctuations and uncertainties in the supplier's production capacities impacting inventory levels, backorder costs, and demand fill rate as quality of service. The coordination mechanism studied here is based on an iterative procedure for supplier selection, while the Analytic Hierarchy Process (AHP) method is used to take several criteria (costs, quality and lead time) into account inside the supplier selection mechanism. For modeling and simulation purposes, the petri net and object oriented design framework are used. In fact, this framework is generic enough to easily integrate intra- or inter-partner mitigation actions as well as the individual behavior of each SC partner. The simulations performed with this coordination model show that it is able to keep the total cost of the system and the back-order cost of the manufacturer low even when the uncertainties increase. Moreover, the coordination mechanism is able to reach high demand fill rates (calculated as the fraction of demand immediately filled by the inventory on hand), even for high uncertainties. The use of the coordination mechanism can improve the fill rate by more than 5% when compared to a model without a coordination mechanism. Now that the framework is set, other criteria and coordination mechanisms can be implemented and tested to measure how these mechanisms contribute to reducing the level of risks in SCs.

Chapter 8 is a joint effort by researchers in management and computer scientists towards an understanding of the role and the impacts of trust in SC. It explores the loop between the strengthening or weakening of trust and the effect of this trust on the performance of SCs. Trust is considered a necessary antecedent of information sharing in SCs, where information sharing has always been seen as beneficial, i.e. reducing costs, improving service levels and reducing lead times and stock-outs.

After an exhaustive literature review on trust in organizational and inter-organizational relationships, this chapter presents a trust model based on 15 criteria, with measurement scales, in order to elaborate an aggregated criterion of trust in a SC relationship and to analyze the links between this trust's criteria, IS and the potentially increased performance of the SC.

Based on this model of trust, a simulation model based on a multi-agent architecture is proposed in order to evaluate the performance of a supply chain, taking into account the level of trust between participants in the chain. This simulation will make the connection between level of trust and level of performance by analyzing IS between the companies (the type of information shared depends on the level of trust and trustworthiness of behavior between the partners). The trust simulation model is validated with a case study, the MIT beer game, which is an example of SC management that has attracted much attention from academic researchers. Multiple rounds of experiments are conducted with different scenarios, focusing on the "behaviors of trust" of agents in the SC. The main finding is that, in a SC, the level of trust directly affects the level and quality of IS, which improves performance by reducing lead time and enabling companies to anticipate variations in market demand.

In the current competitive market context, companies should increase their reactivity through collaboration with the other members of their SC. This collaboration usually involves IS among the members of the SC. Several kinds of information may be shared. Basically, upstream information (lead time, supplier capacities, etc.) is distinguished from downstream information (demand, demand forecasts, etc.) and IS may concern both of information types.

Chapter 9 studies the impact of lead time IS (i.e. upstream) and demand IS (i.e. downstream) in three different SC contexts. The impact of both lead time IS and centralized decision-making is investigated for the first two SCs (one SC with stock in the distribution centre, another without). For the third SC, replenishment policies with three different levels of demand IS (no IS, slow IS and instantaneous IS) are compared. In the first two studies, a warehouse storing products in order to deliver them to several retailers is considered. The various scenarios considered allow us to conclude that lead time IS has considerable impacts in all the cases studied. This kind of IS positively or negatively affects the performance, depending mainly on the type of behavior of the end customer (backorder, i.e. patient customer, or stock-out, i.e. the customer does not come back). It is also affected by the cost of stock-outs, the number of retailers and the type of lead time. Moreover, final demand IS does not always incur savings since it may also require lead time IS. In other words, final demand IS only has a positive impact when the lead time information is also shared. In the third SC context, three replenishment policies, where two of them use downstream IS, are compared: optimization without IS, point-to-point IS and instantaneous IS.

Coordination in SCs also concerns the individual strategic decision on what ordering strategy to use. Indeed, every order placed by a firm not only depends on the firm's state (e.g. inventory level, products currently shipped from suppliers, etc.) and replenishment policy, but also on the state and ordering policy of its clients and suppliers. Strategic decisions on what ordering strategy to use must therefore take account not only of the internal constraints of the company, but also of the constraints imposed by the rest of the SC.

In Chapter 10, the coordination of replenishment policies in a SC is analyzed using game theory, which allows for the study of decisions made by companies when they take other companies' decisions into account. More particularly, the strategic decisions are the three replenishment policies analyzed in Chapter 9. In this setting, the interactions between the replenishment policies of two firms can be analyzed as a non-cooperative static game in which the strategic decisions of companies affect each company's payoff. The nine combinations (i.e. 3^2 combinations of the three policies) are numerically simulated and evaluated in terms of average inventory and backorder costs.

In addition to using game theory to study the multiple effects of the choices made by the different companies, this chapter investigates the impact of two parameters of these companies that may also impact on their choice of a replenishment policy. These parameters are the corporate decision makers' attitude towards risk and the importance given by these decision-makers to the service delivered to their clients. These two parameters are integrated into an original decision criterion, which takes the risk of loss into account.

The main results of this chapter show that information sharing (slowly or instantaneously) is not always the best strategy for firms. The specification of a firm's decision criteria – which account for the performances of joint strategies in terms of inventory holding, backorder costs, and their strategic behaviors supported by game theory tools – shows that firms benefit from information sharing in real time only when market demand is weakly volatile.

Acknowledgments

We thank Liz Libbrecht for the quality of her proof-reading. Her reactivity and diligence have largely contributed to the accomplishment of this book. Special thanks also to Daniel Brissaud, Head of the Cluster GOSPI (Rhône-Alps Region, France), which supported the project this book is based on.

Bibliography

[GRU 95] GRUBER T.R., "Toward principles for the design of ontologies used for knowledge sharing", *International Journal of Human Computer Studies*, vol. 43, no. 5, 1995, pp. 907-928.

[HEN 93] HENDERSON J.C., VENKATRAMAN N., "Strategic alignment: leveraging information technology for transforming organizations", *IBM Systems Journal*, vol. 38, no. 2/3, 1993, pp. 472-484.

[HO 02] HO D.C.K., AU K.F., NEWTON E., "Empirical research on supply chain management: a critical review and recommendations", *International Journal of Production Research*, vol. 40, no. 17, 2002, pp. 4415-4430.

[MAL 94] MALONE T. W., CROWSTON K., "The interdisciplinary study of coordination", *ACM Computing Surveys*, vol. 26, no. 1, pp. 87-120.

[MAL 99] MALONE T., CROWSTON K, LEE J., PENTLAND B., DELLAROCAS C., WYNER G., QUIMBY J., OSBORN C., BERNSTEIN A., HERMAN G., KLEIN M., O'DONNELL E., "Tools for inventing organizations: Toward a handbook of organizational processes", *Management Science*, vol. 45, no. 3, 1999, pp. 425-443.

[SIM 02] SIMATUPANG T.M., WRIGHT A.C., SRIDHARAN R., "The knowledge of coordination for supply chain integration", *Business Process Management Journal*, vol. 8, no. 3, pp. 289-308.

[SIM 05] SIMATUPANG T.M., SRIDHARAN R, "An integrative framework for supply chain collaboration", *International Journal of Logistics Management*, 2005, vol. 16, no. 2, pp. 257-274.

[VEN 89] VENKATRAMAN N., "The concept of fit in strategy research: toward verbal and statistical correspondence", *Academy of Management Review*, vol. 14, 1989, pp. 423–444.

[WHI 07] WHIPPLE J.M., RUSSELL D., "Building supply chain collaboration: a typology of collaborative approaches", *International Journal of Logistics Management*, vol. 18, no. 2, 2007, pp. 174-196.

PART I

Focus on Collaborative Practices

Chapter 1

Modeling the SC Collaboration–Performance Relationship in Empirical Research

1.1. Introduction: the SC collaboration–performance relationship in question

In the debate on the conceptualization of supply chain management (SCM) in empirical research, collaboration appears as a core element of the SCM construct (see the critical review on the SCM construct in [HO 02]). Although a dominant rhetoric in SCM claims that increased collaboration among supply chain stakeholders leads to enhanced performance, empirical research does not provide clear support for the hypothesis of a positive relationship between the two [BAG 05, FAW 02, HIN 02, KUL 04, STA 99, SWI 07, VER 06].

From a theoretical point of view, this instability of the effects on performance of collaborative practices in supply chains (denoted "SC collaboration" hereafter), should not come as a surprise. As Corsten and Felde [COR 05] point out, economic theory gives examples of contexts where collaboration has negative outcomes. According to Williamson's cost transaction theory [WIL 85], when collaboration is based on assets co-specialization, the cost of the co-specialization and the partner's vulnerability to opportunism can seriously affect the expected long-term performance. Dyer and Singh's relational view of the firm [DYE 98] likewise claims that inter-firm collaboration can be a source of competitive advantage but may also give rise to *precarious collaboration* [SIN 96] in some contexts. For

---

Chapter written by Claude PELLEGRIN, Valérie BOTTA-GENOULAZ and Jean-Pierre CAMPAGNE.

instance, in a turbulent environment, a close relationship with one customer limits the opportunities of economies of scale and increases risks. Lastly, apart from these economic explanations related to the context of collaboration, a firm's behavioral approaches can also explain the unsuccessful implementation of collaboration or insufficient efforts in this respect (see, for instance, references in [FAW 08]).

In this chapter we turn away from theoretical debate on the barriers of inter-firm collaboration to focus on empirical research on the SC collaboration–performance relationship. In order to highlight some critical choices for empirical research, and thereby explain why certain findings are relatively unstable and non-cumulative, we take those models that link SC collaboration to performance, as a unit of analysis in empirical research.

In 2002, Ho *et al.* [HO 02] addressed the problem of some weaknesses of empirical research on the relationship between SCM practices and performance, and made two main recommendations. First, they proposed to remove all ambiguity from the content domain of the SCM construct by developing conceptual models that encompass the three core elements of SCM, i.e. value creation, integration of key business processes and collaboration. Second, they emphasized differences in terms of research focus and analytical methods. For this purpose they designed a typology distinguishing different approaches to modeling the SCM practice–performance relationship.

A careful examination of these two recommendations offers two research directions for studying the models underlying empirical research on the relationship between SC collaboration and performance. Each of these directions is developed in section 1.1. Together, they are then used as a basis to specify the objectives and structure of this chapter.

1.1.1. *How to recognize a model linking SC collaboration to performance*

As noted above, we use the term "SC collaboration" to denote the range of collaborative practices. Removing any ambiguity in the content of the SC collaboration construct is essential for empirical research on the link between SC collaboration and performance. However, as Whipple and Russell [WHI 07, p. 177] point out, "collaboration is a very broad and encompassing term and thus requires more specific, in-depth analysis and categorization" (see also [BAR 04]). This remark stresses the need to clarify the range of collaborative practices encompassed in the term SC collaboration, i.e. the range of collaborative practices considered in the measurement scale items of the SC collaboration construct. We provide such clarification in section 1.2.1.

Clarifying the measurement scale of the SC collaboration construct is, however, insufficient in empirical research to recognize a model that actually tests the outcomes of collaborative practices. Consider the following examples: the first is adapted from a study by Vickery *et al.* [VIC 03] and the second from a study by Swink *et al.* [SWI 07]. Both test the effects of an integrative supply chain strategy on performance and at first glance neither of them seems to seek empirical evidence for the SC collaboration–performance relationship.

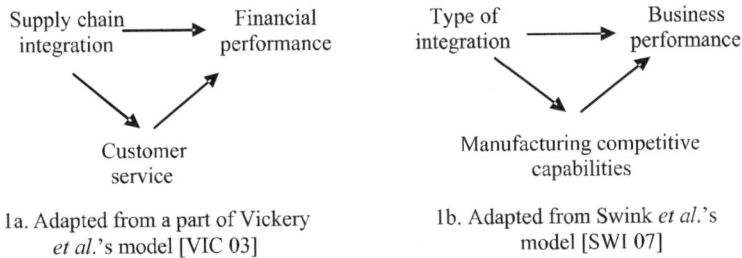

1a. Adapted from a part of Vickery *et al.*'s model [VIC 03]

1b. Adapted from Swink *et al.*'s model [SWI 07]

Figure 1.1. *Two models testing the effects of supply chain integration on performance*

In their model, for the measurement of the "supply-chain integration" construct, Vickery *et al.* use a "meta-scale" combining items related to supplier partnering, closer customer relations and cross-functional teams. By contrast, Swink *et al.* keep the four constructs separate (corporate strategy integration, product–process technology integration, strategic customer integration and strategic supplier integration). This choice of conceptualization allows them to separately test the effect of the variables denoted "strategic customer/supplier integration" on performance. Moreover, since the measurement scales of these constructs refer explicitly to collaborative practices, we can consider that Swink *et al.*'s model contributes to empirical research on the effects of SC collaboration on performance. Conversely, the conceptualization used by Vickery *et al.* does not isolate hypotheses on the relationship between collaboration and performance, although it also refers to collaborative practices (closer customer relations and cross-functional team).

A first lesson can be learned from these examples: "collaboration" is not the keyword that enables us to recognize an empirical study testing the effect of SC collaboration on performance. In particular, the concept of integration can refer to collaborative practices and, in this case, a careful examination of the measurement scale of constructs used in the model is necessary. In our first approach, provided that we define the range S of collaborative practices (problem addressed below), the following definition can be given:

DEFINITION 1.1: A SC collaboration–performance model is a model in which at least one relationship tested is of the (K → Performance) type, where K is a multidimensional construct such that at least one item in one dimension of K explicitly refers to the range S of collaborative practices.

It is easy to recognize SC collaboration–performance models in the presence of a path diagram and/or a list of hypotheses (see EXAMPLE 1.1 below). It is sufficient to highlight a hypothesis of the (K → Performance) type where the measurement scale of K refers to a set of collaborative practices (for instance, information sharing or structural collaboration). In some cases, however (see EXAMPLE 1.2 below), only the examination of analytical procedures ensures the recognition of an SC collaboration–performance model.

EXAMPLE 1.1: Stank *et al.* [STA 01] present the following path diagram (see Figure 1.2) where hypothesis H2 posits that: external collaboration has a positive influence on logistical service performance outcomes.

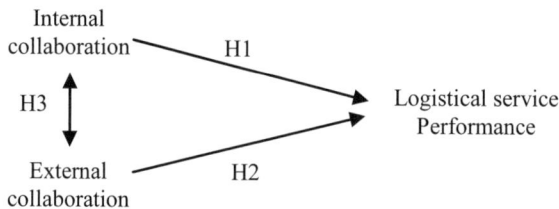

Figure 1.2. *Stank et al.'s model [STA 01]*

In the questionnaire used to measure external collaboration, some items concern collaborative practices: operational information sharing, performance measure sharing, and common supply chain arrangements under principles of shared risks and rewards. According to DEFINITION 1.1, Stank *et al.*'s model is obviously a SC collaboration–performance model.

EXAMPLE 1.2: In their European survey, Bagchi *et al.* [BAG 05] capture the notion of collaboration with key suppliers/carriers or key customers through a construct labeled "inter-firm integration" comprising four dimensions: feedback seeking, decision-making, replenishment (for suppliers only), and supply-chain relations.

In Figure 1.3, the inter-firm integration construct has dimensions that do not directly pertain to information sharing or other collaborative practices. An examination of the operationalization of Bagchi *et al.*'s model shows that the construct labeled "Feedback seeking" concerns information sharing and that, among items measuring the "Decision-making" construct, one of them refers to the degree of suppliers' involvement in decisions pertaining to inventory management. However, the authors present neither a diagram, nor a list of hypotheses.

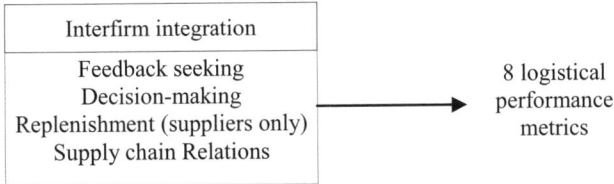

Figure 1.3. *Adapted from Bagchi et al.'s model [BAG 05]*

In this case, examination of analytical procedures is required to recognize models of (K → Performance) type. In fact, Bagchi *et al.* carry out multiple regressions with the eight performance metrics as dependent variables and with the predictor variables. Since they select the predictor variables according to their incremental contribution to the coefficient of determination, they prove many significant relationships of the (K → Logistical performance metric) type, where K refers to the use of collaborative practices.

1.1.2. *In search of an appropriate perspective for modeling the SC collaboration–performance relationship*

In their second recommendation for empirical research in SCM, Ho *et al.* emphasize modeling approaches. They stress the need to model "not only SCM practices and their impacts on performance, but also the effects of inter-organizational contextual factors on the functioning of SCM practices" [HO 02, p. 4424], recommending the following path diagram:

Contextual factors → SCM practices → Performance.

We will now discuss some analytical and conceptual problems arising from this proposal. Thus, by widening the analysis of modeling approaches, we propose new baselines for the study of empirical research on the relationship between collaborative practices and performance.

1.1.2.1. How to address the issue of context in the model

Ho *et al.* suggest that contextual factors are *moderators* of the effectiveness of SCM practices, i.e. they affect the strength of the relationship between SCM practices and performance. However, analytically the path diagram (Contextual factors → SCM practices → Performance) means that SCM practices are a *mediator* variable between context and performance. In their seminal paper, Baron and Kenny [BAR 86] contend that a mediator (SCM practices) represents the generative mechanism through which a predictor (Contextual factors) influences an outcome variable (Performance). Since the terms moderator and mediator cannot be used interchangeably [BAR 86, CAR 03], there is a need for further distinction between the two in such conceptual models.

As various authors have pointed out, contextual factors and attributes of collaboration are often *moderators* of the relationship between collaborative practices in SCM and performance. For instance, plant size is a moderator of the relationship between integration and performance in [SWI 07]. In [COR 05], trust and dependence are moderators of the relationship between supplier collaboration practices and performance. A moderating variable reduces or enhances the influence of these practices on performance, and failure to consider it in empirical research may obscure the causality between collaboration and performance.

Another situation occurs when a third variable M works as a *mediator* of the collaboration–performance relationship. For instance, Salvador *et al.* [SAL 01] prove that, under special conditions, the impact of collaboration on suppliers and customers can be either completely or partially mediated by "internal practices" (see also [STA 01]). For this purpose, the authors consider a causal path from "collaboration" to the mediator M (internal practices) and from M to "performance". They also test the hypothesis of a direct impact of collaboration on performance. In other cases, the variable "collaboration" can be a mediator between other constructs and performance. For instance, in the model proposed by Paulraj *et al.* [PAU 08, p. 55], the construct labeled "inter-organizational communication", i.e. external collaboration, "fully mediates the relationship between information technology and supplier performance" and "only partially mediates the relationship between information technology and buyer performance". We see that here "collaboration" plays a complex mediating role in the links between independent variables and performance.

Ho *et al.*'s proposal thus raises a question: should we use moderators and/or mediators when modeling the relationship between a system of practices and performance? Moreover, if we call the different variables (SC collaboration, performance, other variables) whose relationships with each other are of interest in a SC collaboration–performance model *units of model*, will moderation or mediation be the only types of relationships that we have to consider in the units of the model? We address this issue in the following section.

1.1.2.2. What are the laws of the relationship among units of the model?

This question refers to a well-known and recurrent issue raised by pioneer organizational researchers in the methodology of contingency analysis [DRA 85, FRY 87, PRE 01, VEN 84, VEN 89, VEN 90a]. According to Fry *et al.* [FRY 87, p. 119], the laws of relationship that we set out to test are "lawful statements that express an association, linkage, or connection between two or more units" of a model. The contingency theorists have provided significant insight into the idea of a law of relationship, with the concept of *fit*. A key idea of contingency theory is that successful performance is the result of a proper "fit", also denoted as the "*alignment*", of endogenous design variables with exogenous context variables. Endogenous design variables can, for instance, be choice of collaborative practices, or level of internal and external integration and exogenous context variables includeorganizational size, environmental uncertainty, available information technology, etc. In other words, if it is a "*fit*" between variables (we refer to the collaborative practices) that determines the performance, then empirical research seeks "to specify the effects of performance that are attributable to fit" [VEN 89, p. 430].

Contingency theory thus offers a new way to investigate empirical research on the SC collaboration–performance relationship: *which are the observable types of fit between variables in empirical research?* In his seminal paper, Venkatraman [VEN 89] provides a rich classificatory framework to perform this investigation: *fit as moderation, fit as mediation, fit as matching, fit as gestalts, fit as profile deviation, and fit as co-variation.* In the following sections, we will apply these six perspectives as a device for analyzing empirical research on the SC collaboration–performance relationship.

1.1.3. *Structure of the chapter*

The above discussion stresses the need to clarify the characteristics of empirical models linking collaborative practices and performance. Which conceptualization of collaboration do the models portray? What should the content of the range S of collaborative practices be if we want to recognize without ambiguity a model that empirically tests the relationship between SC collaboration and performance? What is the modeling approach used to link collaborative practices and performance? In particular, what are the observable *types of fit*, in Venkatraman's sense, between variables?

In section 1.2 we discuss a framework enabling the comparison of empirical research that investigates the relationship between SC collaboration and performance. First, from existing categorizations of collaborative practices, we clarify the meaning of the SC collaboration construct, i.e. the range S of collaborative practices likely to be used for the definition of its measurement scale. Then, taking the SC collaboration–performance model as a unit of analysis, we discuss, as in [HO 02], different modeling approaches (individual *versus* aggregated collaborative practices, different aspects of firms' performance) and the different ways (moderation, mediation, matching, gestalts, profile deviation and covariation) in which conceptual variables may account for differences when testing such a relationship.

In section 1.3 we use this contingency framework as an analytical device to review empirical papers referring explicitly to the SC collaboration–performance relationship. Based on this analysis of selected papers, we then build a contingency chart, consisting of the 2D mapping of models that empirically test the linkage between collaborative practices and performance.

The conclusion summarizes the findings of this study in two main lessons that highlight some critical choices for a contingency view of empirical research on the SC collaboration–performance relationship.

1.2. Analyzing the SC collaboration–performance link in empirical research

This section presents the two dimensions of the analytical device chosen to analyze the SC collaboration–performance models (DEFINITION 1.1). We first focus on the SC collaboration construct and then propose a contingency framework to categorize the modeling approaches of the SC collaboration–performance relationship.

1.2.1. *Clarifying the range S of collaborative practices for the measurement of the SC collaboration construct*

Clarifying the range S of collaborative practices in the supply chain is essential to make the definition of the SC collaboration–performance model operative (see DEFINITION 1.1). This deliberate focus on practices is justified by the choice of the unit of analysis: models that seek empirical evidence of the link between collaboration and performance. Thus, the very core of the recognition of such a model is the evidence of practices in the measurement scale of constructs pertaining to SC collaboration. This recognition commonly relies on an existing categorization. A categorization of collaborative practices carries a model of supply chain collaboration, however, and this model conveys a vision of supply chain performance. It is therefore important to elucidate the different layers in a categorization of collaborative practices: the practices (i.e. the layer of collaborative evidence), the model supporting the categorization, and the performance vision underlying this model.

In the following, categorizations of collaborative practices existing in the literature on SCM are discussed in section 1.2.1.1. From the main existing typology, a framework is then presented that highlights the relationships between categories of collaborative practices underlying the collaboration model and performance (section 1.2.1.2). Finally, we question the relevance of this framework for the recognition of the SC collaboration construct in empirical research (section 1.2.1.3).

1.2.1.1. *Categorizations of collaborative practices*

With the exception of Whipple and Russell's typology [WHI 07], the categorization of collaborative practices has just been a by-product of research on SC collaboration. Two types of classification appear in the literature and both reflect the idea of different levels or intensity in the collaboration. They differ in rationale, however, justifying the difference of collaboration intensity and methodological underpinnings of their development.

1.2.1.1.1. Information exchange practices *versus* structural collaboration practices

A first type of categorization posits that collaboration engages the partners in information–integration efforts, and that collaboration oriented towards integration requires more sophisticated and structural devices than collaboration anchored only in information exchange. Grounded in the literature but not empirical research, this categorization classifies collaborative practices in two broad groups according to their supposed closeness to either information exchange or process integration. For example, Kulp, Lee and Ofek [KUL 04] use the term "information–integration practices" to indicate a continuum from practices of *information exchange* (sharing of information on demand, level of inventory, etc.) to more structural practices aimed at *collaborative planning*. The former focuses on the transfer of relevant information between the parties, while the latter searches for the synchronization of operations with transfer of responsibility on ordering, inventory replenishment or reverse logistics mechanisms, for instance.

Vereecke and Muylle [VER 06] likewise consider that the exchange of information constitutes a basic form of collaboration. The intensity of collaboration depends on the level of embodiment of this information exchange in systems geared towards process integration. They first distinguish the group of data-sharing practices (called *information exchange*, as in [KUL 04]). These practices are designed to avoid the "bullwhip effect" (due to distortion of information), to reduce inventory excesses and to improve the response speed. A second group, called *structural collaboration*, includes all collaborative practices based on structural devices enabling the integration of processes between partners: ECR (efficient consumer response), VMI (vendor managed inventory), CR (continuous replenishment), CPFR (collaborative planning, forecasting, and replenishment), Kanban systems, plant co-location, reverse logistics systems, etc.

1.2.1.1.2. The contribution of Whipple and Russell's typology [WHI 07]

A second approach to the categorization of collaborative practices rests on the premise that collaboration is an *organizational model* [BOW 03] that can be deployed at various organizational and decision-making levels (operational, tactical and strategic). The nature of the collaborative relationships and practices related to these relationships evolve according to the organizational (or decisional) level (operational, tactical and strategic) concerned. For example, the CPFR implementation model developed by Skjoett-Larsen *et al.* [SKJ 03] consists of three gradual levels, depending on the degree of partners' involvement towards process integration. A higher degree entails a stronger interaction between partners, more sophistication in the information technology used, and more commitment of organizational levels. In contrast, Skjoett-Larsen *et al.* only consider the practice of CPFR. Whipple and Russell's typology [WHI 07] is actually the only categorization that is theoretically founded. It was developed through a "grounded theory" approach (see [GLA 67, STR 94]) from interviews with 21 managers from six different manufacturing firms. It distinguishes three types of collaborative practices at three organizational levels:

– Practices pertaining to *collaborative transaction management* (type I) focus on coordination of information on a short-term horizon by the way data are exchanged at operational level. The authors give the examples of scorecard collaboration and VMI.

– Practices pertaining to *collaborative event management* (type II) focus on the execution of tactical plans for avoiding medium-term horizon supply chain disruptions by way of collaborative decision-making processes associated with specific events. The authors suggest initial CPFR – i.e. without generation of an order forecast – event collaborations (promotions and new product introductions).

– Practices pertaining to *collaborative process management* (type III) focus on long-term improvement plans at strategic level to fully realize integrated processes. The typical example is advanced CPFR with generation of order forecasts, without necessarily an automatic conversion of sales forecasts to order forecasts.

In their thorough analysis, the authors differentiate each type of collaborative practice according to 10 characteristics. Five attributes concern the supplier/customer relationship: the focus of the collaboration; focus of the collaboration process; expected return on this type of collaborative relationship; focus of information; and knowledge level committed in the relationship (from explicit knowledge to a high level of tacit knowledge). Four are related to the decision-making process that supports interaction between the partners: organizational level concerned by the collaboration (operational, tactical, strategic); people engaged in the interaction; degree of involvement in decision-making (individual, departmental, social or relational network); and time horizon. The last distinctive trait is the technology configuration to manage this type of practice (see [WHI 07], Table II, p. 180 for a detailed explanation of each of these characteristics).

1.2.1.2. Types of collaborative practices and their relationship to performance: a framework from the firm's resource-based view

In the conclusion of their exploratory study, Whipple and Russell suggest that their typology defines "three distinct levels or types of collaboration", which means that *each type of practice would also be a level of commitment in collaboration.* Here we propose to develop a conceptual framework that posits a link between the types of collaborative practices (in the sense of Whipple and Russell's typology), the levels of commitment in collaboration, and the competencies and capabilities that each level of commitment in collaboration requires. To explain this link, we first need to point out the supply-chain integration framework developed by Michigan State University and summarized by Bowersox, Cross and Stank [BOW 03], and its link with the relational perspective of the resource-based view (RBV) of the firm [BAR 91, DYE 98, KAN 94, TAK 01, WER 84].

According to Bowersox *et al.*, the gain of positional advantages and performance differentials via cross-enterprise collaboration is the result of three levels of *processes*: the *leadership process* at the strategic level; the *planning and control process* at the tactical level; and the *integrated operations process* at the operational level. Each of these processes requires *core competencies* to drive competitive advantage. Each of these competencies is itself supported by *capabilities*, i.e. the ability to concretely combine resources, physical and knowledge-based assets to conceive and implement the collaboration strategy. Without being exhaustive (see [BOW 03] for developments), the following examples illustrate this framework:

– At the strategic level, the *leadership process* provides the dependency and collaboration principles to which the partners agree. It requires *relational integration competency* to ensure the persistence and development of these principles between partners over time. This relational competency is based on a bundle of capabilities and resources, for example the ability to clarify shared responsibility between the partners, the development of policies for conflict resolution, etc. According to Dyer and Singh [DYE 98], the synergistic combination of these capabilities with specific assets and resources enables the realization of relational rents, i.e. "a supernormal profit jointly generated in an exchange relationship".

– At the tactical level, the *planning and control process* uses information and measurement systems to plan and control the operations requiring collaboration. Among required competencies, Bowersox *et al.* highlight, for instance, the need to maintain an information system able to support various operational configurations adapted to each market segment. This competency is supported by different capabilities on information management, internal communication, etc.

– At the operational level, the *integrated operations process* ensures the coordination required for order fulfillment and replenishment across the supply chain. In this model, customer integration, internal integration and material/service supplier integration are the three competencies required. The customer integration competency, for example, rests on the ability to develop specific programs that continuously match customer expectations, in order to adapt the operational process to unplanned customer requirements or to deal with unexpected events.

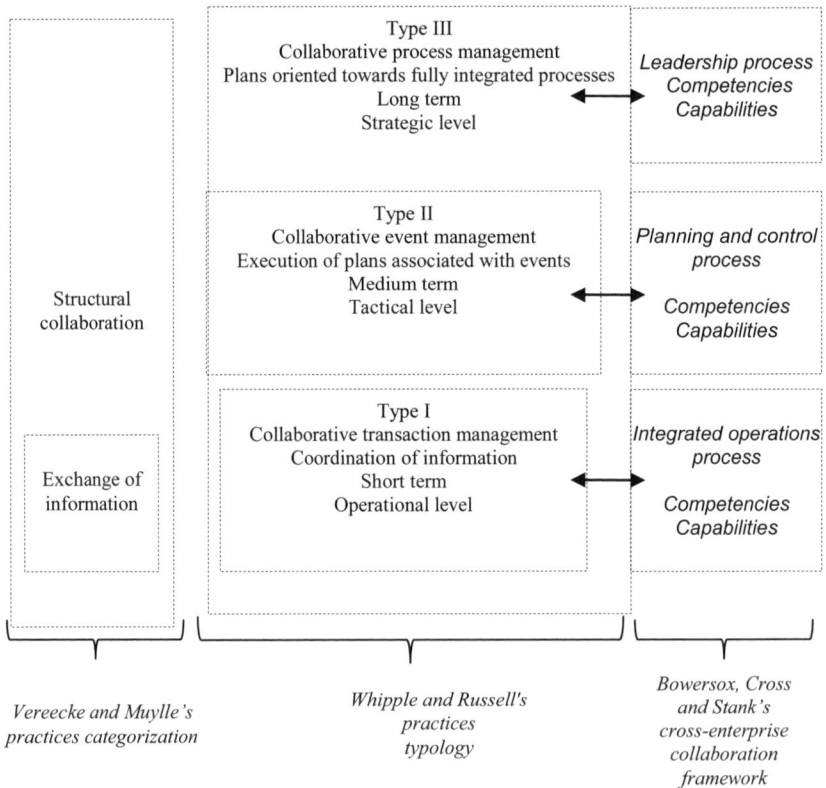

Figure 1.4. *A framework linking types of collaborative practice categorizations and Bowersox et al.'s cross-enterprise collaboration model*

Figure 1.4 draws a parallel between Whipple and Russell's typology and Bowersox *et al.*'s cross-enterprise collaboration framework: each type (I, II and III) of collaborative practice corresponds to each level of processes, competencies and capabilities defined above. It includes Vereecke and Muylle's model, which shares a common categorization thread with Whipple and Russell's typology: the evolution of practices towards more integrated processes between the partners. It also shows differences in focus between the two, however. For example, the VMI, a type I practice in Whipple and Russell's typology, is a structural collaboration in Vereecke and Muylle's categorization. In fact, Whipple and Russell's typology does not take the level of process integration required by some information exchange practices into account.

Figure 1.4 highlights the different layers of a categorization of collaborative practices: the types of practices, i.e. the layer of collaborative evidence used in the measurement scale of the SC collaboration construct, and the organizational and performance models that support the categorization. At each level, collaborative practices appear as a layer of collaborative evidence, and these practices are supported by capabilities at different levels of organizational process. These capabilities are intangibles that both deploy and link various complex bundles of resources, skills and knowledge to manage relationships with suppliers or customers. Such idiosyncratic competencies are at the very centre of competitive advantage for the RBV [COA 02, PEN 59, TEE 97]. Hence this conceptual framework, grounded in the RBV theory of the firm, establishes a link between two hierarchies:

– types of collaborative practices prioritized according to the organizational and decision-making levels committed in the relationship;

– a hierarchy of competencies and capabilities that underlies the positional advantages and performance differentials of the firm via cross-enterprise collaboration.

1.2.1.3. Measurement scales of the SC collaboration construct in the light of categorizations

The above categorization framework (see Figure 1.4) may first be used prospectively in an empirical study to design a measurement scale of the SC collaboration construct. Such a measurement scale is generally based on factors such as: "Please estimate the degree of involvement of key suppliers/customers in such a collaborative practice on a five-point or seven-point scale ranging from x to y". In this case, Figure 1.4 works as a decision-support tool for the choice of types of collaborative practices that have to be included in the questionnaire. Table 1.1 gives some examples drawn from empirical research using such measurement scales.

Table 1.1 shows the relevance of this categorization framework in capturing collaborative practices in a questionnaire and ensuring the representativeness of practices. It is worth noting, however, that the use of categorizations (including Figure 1.4 and Table 1.1) in the design of a questionnaire can entail problems. For example, should we consider information exchange on sales promotions as a type I practice with or without structural collaboration, or a type II practice? It obviously depends on the context of the exchange: informal exchange, or exchange according to a pre-specified agreement requiring a structural device, or a joint decision at a strategic level operating under principles of shared risk and reward. Only knowledge about the context and about the means and ends of the practice allows the type of practice to be defined. This example points out the difficulty of capturing the nature of collaborative practices when designing a questionnaire in empirical research pertaining to the SC collaboration–performance relationship. It highlights the need to use broad categories that take the means and ends of practices into account in the wording of questions.

Type 1 information exchange of at operational level	Upstream	[STA 01]: operational information, performance measures
		[SIM 04]: promotional events, demand forecast, POS data, price changes, inventory holding costs, on-hand inventory levels, inventory policy, supply disruptions, order status or order tracking, delivery schedules
		[CHA 07] Order schedule, order delivery, information sharing
	Downstream	[STA 99]: on special promotions, pricing changes, stocking instructions for new products, removal dates of discontinued products, shipment (delivery) problems
		[STA 01]: operational information, performance measures
		[KUL 04]: consumer needs, store inventory levels, warehouse inventory levels
Type 1 structural collaboration at operational level	Upstream	[SAN 07]: real-time sharing of operations information, real-time sharing of cross-functional processes
		[CHA 07]: interactive demand forecasting
		[SWI 07]: real-time production schedule
	Downstream	[KUL 04]: VMI
		[CHA 07]: interactive demand forecasting
		[SWI 07]: real-time production schedule

Type 2 collaborative events management enlarged to tactical collaboration	Upstream	[SAN 07]: engagement in collaborative planning [SIM 04]: joint plan on product assortment, joint plan on promotional events, joint decision on availability level, joint decision on inventory requirements, joint decision on optimal order quantity [PAU 08]: face-to-face planning/communication
	Downstream	[STA 99]: information about events or changes that may affect the other party, to solicit customer input for planning logistics strategy [SIM 04]: joint plan on product assortment, joint plan on promotional events, joint decision on availability level, joint decision on inventory requirements, joint decision on optimal order quantity GIM 05]: work team for the implementation and development of continuous replenishment program or other ECR practice, joint planning to anticipate and resolve operative problems [PAU 08]: face-to-face planning/communication
Type 3 collaborative process management enlarged to collaboration at strategic level	Upstream	[COR 05]: working closely in technology development, process development, target costing, project planning [BAG 05]: collaboration with supplier in R&D
	Downstream	[KUL 04]: collaboration to develop new products and services, joint development of reverse logistics systems [GIM 05]: joint development of logistics processes, joint establishment of objectives, joint development of the understanding of responsibilities, joint decisions about ways to improve cost efficiencies [FYN 05]: production system tailored to meet the requirement of the customer, collaboration for significant investments in tooling and equipment

Table 1.1. *Examples of practices used in measurement scales of the SC collaboration construct*

Figure 1.4 and Table 1.1 may also be used retrospectively for the analysis of a model that tests the relationship between collaborative practices and performance. Given such empirical research, this categorization is a tool to facilitate the understanding of the following questions:

– What is the organizational model (and hence, the performance model) underlying the measurement scale of the SC collaboration construct?

– To what extent does the model make an exhaustive account of different types of collaborative practices or of different levels of organizational commitment in collaboration (operations process, planning and control process, strategic collaboration)?

These issues are one dimension of the analytical device used in section 1.3 to review empirical papers referring explicitly to the relationship between collaborative practices and performance.

1.2.2. *The SC collaboration–performance model as a unit of analysis*

In our comments on Ho *et al.*'s proposition concerning the effects of contextual factors on the functioning of SCM practices (section 1.1.2), we emphasized the need to widen the analysis of the modeling approaches used to test the link between collaborative practices and performance. To enrich the modeling of this link, we suggested considering how to link together or associate different units of the model (predictor variables, context variables, collaboration structure variables, outcome variables, etc.). Then, to account for these laws of relationship among units of the model, we put forward a contingency framework and, more particularly, the concept of "fit" as developed by Venkatraman [VEN 89]. Finally, we explained how Ho *et al.*'s typology [HO 02] and Venkatraman's contingency view provide a way to categorize the modeling approaches used to test the relationship between collaborative practices and performance. In the following two sections we focus on the concept of fit in SC collaboration–performance models in order to show the relevance of this perspective for differentiating such models.

1.2.2.1. *In search of modeling approaches for testing the relationship between practices and performance*

In 2002, Ho *et al.* proposed a typology based on how collaborative practices (individually, collectively, relatively or by inter-relationships) affect performance. As outlined above, they also proposed to take the context in the model into account. Venkatraman's contribution provides explicit functional forms for the interrelationship between context, practice and performance.

1.2.2.1.1. A first approach to modeling approaches: Ho *et al.*'s typology

A SC collaborative practice–performance relationship (DEFINITION 1.1) is a special case of a SCM practice–performance relationship. It therefore suffices to adapt Ho *et al.*'s categorization to SC collaboration–performance models:

– *type 1 model* tests the relationship between an individual SC collaborative practice and a particular aspect of performance outcomes;

– *type 2 model* tests the relationship between individual as well as aggregated SC collaborative practices and a particular aspect of performance outcomes;

– *type 3 model* seeks to study the relative strength of the impact of each SC collaborative practice on a particular aspect of a firm's performance;

– *type 4 model* tests both the inter-relationships between various SC collaborative practices and their impacts on performance outcomes.

As mentioned above, however, this typology neglects other variables likely to directly or partially influence the performance variable.

1.2.2.1.2. Venkatraman's concept of "fit" applied to the SC collaboration–performance model

One of the important concepts of contingency theory is that successful performance results from a proper alignment of endogenous design variables (related to organization) and exogenous context variables (such as environmental uncertainty, organizational size, etc.). In general, contingency models are designed to highlight the combination of variables (at least one independent variable with other variables) that improves performance. In order words, *the effect of performance is attributable to the fit between variables* and the differences in performance attributable to fit can be seen in an empirical test [VEN 89]. The important contribution of Venkatraman's paper was to identify six functional forms of fit.

The first three – fit as moderation, fit as mediation, and fit as matching – concern situations where "two constructs are co-aligned, and can best be understood in terms of pairwise co-alignments among individual dimensions that represent two constructs" [VEN 90b, p. 2]. Venkatraman termed these forms of co-alignment a "reductionist perspective" because such approaches to co-alignment focuses on pairs of isolated variables rather than on complex patterns of inter-related variables.

The following three – fit as gestalts, fit as profile deviation, and fit as co-variation – fall into the systems perspective [VAN 85] or holistic perspective [VEN 90b] of the co-alignment because they highlight the holistic nature and multiple variables of co-alignment. In these cases, empirical research aims to test the overall effectiveness of co-alignment on performance [DRA 85, PRE 01]. As pointed out by Venkatraman, each perspective "implies distinct theoretical meanings and requires the use of specific analytical schemes".

In the following, we show the relevance of this conceptual framework for differentiating the SC collaboration–performance models.

1.2.2.2. The reductionist perspective of fit in SC collaboration–performance models

According to [VEN 90b], a SC collaboration–performance model falls under the reductionist perspective if it explains performance through the interaction between pairs of contextual and structural characteristics pertaining to collaboration. In the following sub-section we discuss three functional forms of understanding *contingency*: moderation, mediation and matching.

1.2.2.2.1. Fit as moderation in SC collaboration–performance models

A *moderator* is a qualitative or quantitative variable (Z) that affects the *form* and/or *strength* of the relationship between an independent or predictor variable (X) and a dependent or criterion variable (Y). It means that the impact of the independent variable (X) on the dependent variable (Y) varies across the different levels of moderator (Z): "when" or "for whom" the independent variable X most strongly (or weakly) causes the dependent variable Y [BAR 86, WU 08]. As illustrated in Figure 1.5, however, the distinction between a moderation affecting the form of a relationship and a moderation affecting its strength has both conceptual and analytical implications.

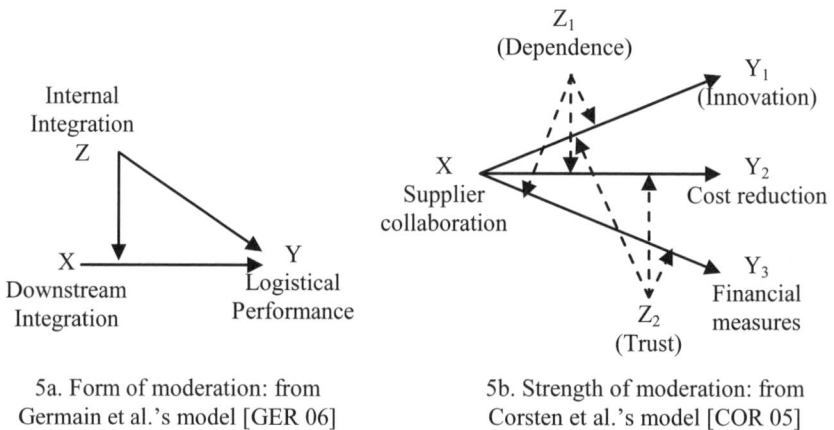

5a. Form of moderation: from   5b. Strength of moderation: from
Germain et al.'s model [GER 06]   Corsten et al.'s model [COR 05]

Figure 1.5. *Two models of fit as moderation*

In Figure 1.5a, the authors specify that internal (Z) and downstream (X) integration interact in predicting logistical performance (Y). Their hypotheses reflects the form of moderation: internal integration affects the relationship between downstream integration and logistical performance, in addition to the fact that internal integration and downstream integration impact performance. One of their contributions is indeed to show that logistical performance is predicted by internal or downstream integration, but the lack of internal integration may reduce or even negate the impact of external integration (i.e. collaboration) on performance [GER 06].

In Figure 1.5b, the authors posit that the impact of supplier collaboration on performance outcomes differs across the level of dependence (Z_1) and trust (Z_2). They prove, for instance, that trust and dependence enhance the effect of collaboration on the buyer's innovation level, and that the effect of collaboration on financial performance is stronger under conditions of low trust compared to high trust [COR 05]. Z_1 and Z_2 therefore affect the ($X \rightarrow Y_i$) relations but, unlike the previous case (form of moderation), testing the link between Z_1 (Z_2) and Y_i (for i = 1, 2, 3) would be meaningless.

According to Venkatraman [VEN 89, p. 424], we can say that, in both cases that "the fit between the predictor (X as downstream integration or supplier collaboration) and the moderator (Z as internal integration or dependence, or trust) is the primary determinant of the criterion variable" (the performance, Y). However, *when the moderation affects the form of relation (X $\rightarrow$ Y), this fit is an interaction between X and Z (a new variable called X*Z), which jointly determines the performance Y*. A common way (but not the only one) to test the relation (X $\rightarrow$ Y) is to use a multiple regression analysis with or without a dummy variable, according to the scale types of variables X and Z (nominal, ordinal, interval and ratio). For example, in Figure 1.5a the moderation effect can be written as follows:

$$Y = a_o + a_1X + a_2Z + e \qquad\qquad [1.1]$$

$$Y = a_o + a_1X + a_2Z + a_3X{*}Z + e \qquad\qquad [1.2]$$

The coefficient a_3 represents the synergistic effect of variables X and Z working together, over and above their separate effect; the moderation effect of Z (internal integration) is supported if coefficient a_3 differs significantly from zero.

When the moderation affects the strength of relation (X $\rightarrow$ Y), the fit results from a splitting of the domain of X into subgroups based on different levels of the moderator variable (Z). The moderation effect is tested using subgroup analysis and, depending on the scale types of variables X and Z, a multiple regression analysis by subgroups or ANOVA (analysis of variance) could be used.

1.2.2.2.2. Fit as mediation in SC collaboration–performance models

A qualitative or quantitative variable (Z) functions as a *mediator* (see Figure 1.6) to the extent that variations in levels of the independent or predictor variable (X) significantly account for variations in variable (Z), and variations in variable (Z)

significantly account for variations in the dependent or criterion variable (Y) [BAR 86].

Figure 1.6 shows that the independent variable X (external collaboration, for example) causes an intervening variable Z (internal collaboration in the example), which in turn causes the performance variable (Y). A direct impact of the external collaboration (X) on the dependent variable (Y) is, however, possible. If the relation between the independent variable (X) and dependent variable (Y) is no longer statistically different from zero when the paths (a) and (b) are controlled, then the mediation is said to be *complete*. If the effect is reduced only when paths (a) and (b) are controlled, the mediation is *partial*.

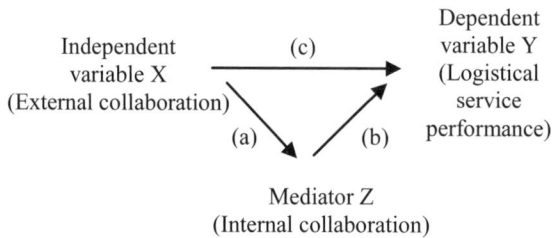

Figure 1.6. *Example of a fit as mediation (mediation effect)*

Note that in empirical research this mediation effect is assumed to exist. Hence, by design, the model is expected to empirically test all potential effects of mediation. For example, Figure 1.6 is only a special case of Stank *et al.*'s model depicted in Figure 1.2, where (see Figure 1.2, section 1.1.1.) the hypothesis (H3) cannot determine *a priori* whether internal or external collaboration is the mediating variable. The choice of methods to test path models involving mediating variables is therefore critical when designing such a model. Although the analytical issues are outside the scope of this chapter, analytical consideration for model design is discussed below.

Consider Figure 1.6, Baron and Kenny's method [BAR 86], the historical approach developed in the 1980s, helps us to understand the search for a mediation effect in an empirical research. This method consists of four steps:

– step 1: regression of Y on X ($Y = b_1 + cX + $ error e_1) and testing the regression coefficient (c) for significance in order to ensure the existence of an impact to mediate between X and Y;

– step 2: regression of Z on X ($Z = b_2 + aX + $ error e_2) and testing the regression coefficient (a) for significance;

– step 3: regression of Y on X and Z ($Y = b_3 + bX + c'Z + $ error e_3) and testing the regression coefficient (b) for significance when X is under control;

– step 4: in order to ensure the existence of a complete mediation (or partial respectively) by Z, testing that c' is null (respectively $c' < c$) when Z is under control.

A simple adjustment of steps 3 and 4 (replace X with Z and Z with X) allows us to test whether external collaboration (X) is the mediator or not.

Although this causal step approach is conceptually attractive, it presents some analytical limits for the testing of path models involving mediating variables (low type I error rate and low statistical power). Many other approaches to analyzing mediating variables have consequently been developed (see the seminal paper [BAR 86] and, for example, [MAC 02, WU 08] for recent developments). Structural equation modeling is the most widespread method. One of the advantages of this method is "to provide goodness-of-fit indices to assist in assessing the viability of the hypothesized model" [WU 08, p. 387]. Figure 1.7 illustrates this point from Stank *et al.*'s model [STA 01] presented in Figure 1.2.

Initial model design (no *a priori* hypothesis on the mediator)

H1: Internal collaboration has a positive influence on logistical service performance outcomes

H2: External collaboration has a positive influence on logistical service performance outcomes

H3: Internal collaboration and External collaboration are positively related

Results of hypothesis testing (see Stank et al.'s model depicted in Figure 1.2)

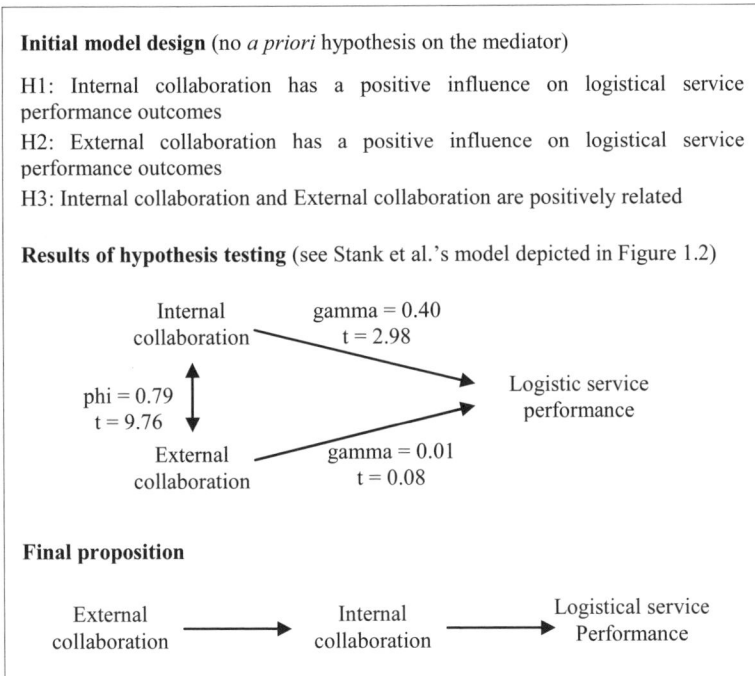

Internal collaboration — gamma = 0.40, t = 2.98

phi = 0.79, t = 9.76

External collaboration — gamma = 0.01, t = 0.08

Logistic service performance

Final proposition

External collaboration → Internal collaboration → Logistical service Performance

---

Figure 1.7. *Mediation test using structural equation modeling (adapted from [STA 01])*

The hypothesized model does not specify a mediator *a priori*. The results show that internal and external collaboration are significantly correlated (standardized correlation factor phi = 0.79, t-value = 9.76) and that internal collaboration influences performance positively (standardized correlation factor gamma = 0.40, t-value = 2.98). External collaboration and performance outcomes are, however, not correlated (standardized correlation factor gamma = 0.01, t-value = 0.0). Finally, Stank *et al.*'s empirical research suggests that internal collaboration is a mediator of the relationship between external collaboration and performance. Figure 1.7 thus shows how the structural equation modeling approach can be used for assessing the extent to which a mediation model fits the data.

1.2.2.2.3. Fit as matching in SC collaboration–performance models

The term *fit as matching* is invoked in empirical research when the study considers the interaction between two variables and develops a measure of their fit without reference to a criterion variable – unlike the previous two, moderation and mediation. The assessment of the effect of this fit on a set of criterion variables is possible but is subsequent to the measure of the fit as matching. Therefore, in SC collaboration–performance models, the fit as matching effect cannot concern the relationship between collaboration and performance.

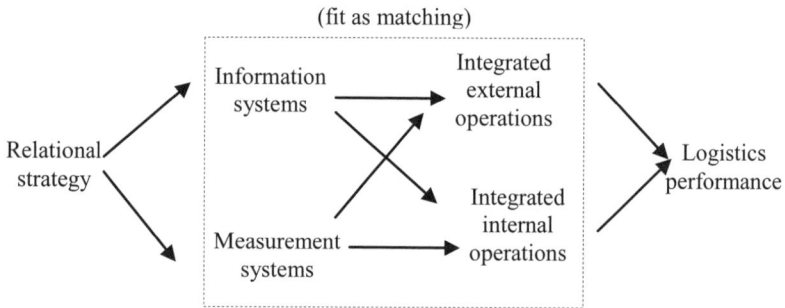

Figure 1.8. *"Fit as matching" in Rodriguez et al.'s model [ROD 04]*

In Figure 1.8, for example, a part of the model developed by Rodriguez *et al.* [ROD 04] empirically tests "the relationship between high levels of information systems and high levels of internal and external operations integration, as well as between measurement systems and internal and external operations integration". The "fit as matching" between level of information systems (or measurement systems) and level of integrated internal operations (or integrated external operations) is measured. The authors then test the impact of integrated internal or external operations on logistics performance.

1.2.2.3. *Systems approach of fit in SC collaboration–performance models*

In the previous approaches, fit was based on bivariate relationships: pairs of factors pertaining to the context and/or structure of collaboration interact to explain performance. In contrast, the systems approach seeks to characterize *patterns of consistency* among dimensions of the organization (for instance, context of collaboration, structure of measurement, information systems, etc.), each pattern corresponding to equally effective alternative designs. According to Venkatraman, the systems approach of fit entails three functional forms: *fit as co-variation, fit as profile deviation*, and *fit as gestalt*. Below we discuss their how they account for SC collaboration–performance models in empirical research.

1.2.2.3.1. Fit as co-variation in SC collaboration–performance models

Fit as co-variation assumes that, first, there exists a pattern of co-variation between a set of theoretically related variables and, second, this unobservable construct is positively related to performance. The central idea is that the better the cohesion among the variables constituting this pattern (unobservable construct), the better the performance [DRA 85]. The design of this higher-order construct confronts researchers with the identification and development of measurement scales. The critical issue, however, is to prove that, first, the dimensions of the SC collaboration construct "complement and reinforce each other in terms of enhanced relationships" [FYN 05, p. 342] and, second, this internal consistency has, in turn, an effect on performance. Therefore, specifying and testing fit as covariation imply hard analytical issues that we will illustrate with an example (for the basic principles of the operationalization, see [VEN 86, p. 436] and [FYN 05, p. 346] for recent references).

Below we consider the SC collaboration–performance model developed by Fynes *et al.* [FYN 05] as a noticeable illustration of this approach. The originality of this model is in examining the performance of supply chain collaboration in terms of quality. The authors consider several facets of quality performance (design quality, conformance quality and customer satisfaction) and hypothesize that design quality and conformance quality are antecedents of customer satisfaction. For the sake of clarity, however, we simplify the performance construct in Figure 1.9.

In the "fit" model, the original idea is to encapsulate, in one higher-order construct (named the SC relationship quality), six dimensions pertaining to collaborative practices and to characteristics of relationships. Two dimensions account for information exchange practices (communication) and structural collaboration practices (cooperation), one concerns the level of commitment in collaboration (commitment), and the three others (adaptation, interdependence and trust) qualify the nature of relationships with the partners. In this way, the latent construct (SC relationship quality) is assumed to reflect the internal co-alignment among the six observable first-order factors.

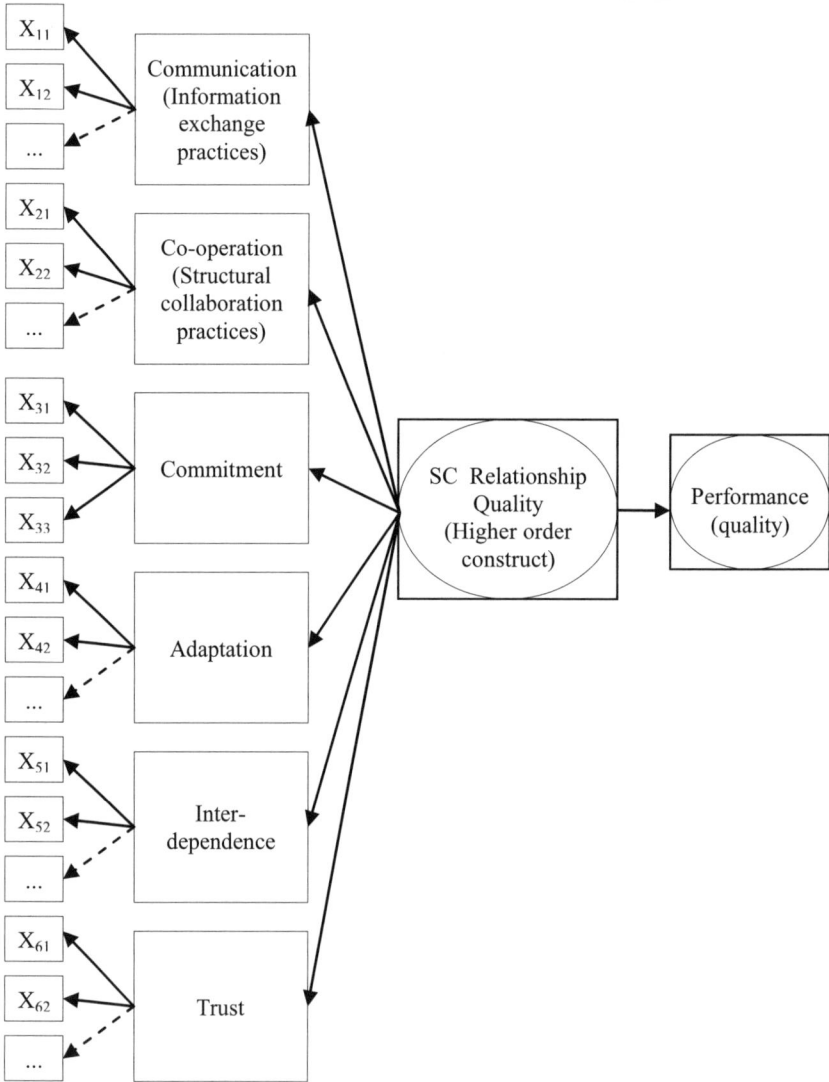

Figure 1.9. *Fit as co-variation: a simplified version of Fynes et al.'s model [FYN 05]*

Figure 1.9 highlights the central idea of the functional form "fit as co-variation". If the internal consistency is high, the six variable factors should all significantly contribute to determining the variable representing SC relationship quality. In turn, the SC relationship quality, i.e. a pattern of co-variation between a set of six factors, will then serve as a direct determinant of performance (provided the fit is statistically acceptable).

From an analytical point of view, the main problem is a well-known dilema in sociological research. Figure 1.9 reflects the internal consistency of the six dimensions of the SC collaboration as a second-order factor model: the model assumes that performance depends on a higher-order construct (named SC relationship quality), which subsumes both the dimensions of collaboration and consistency of these dimensions. An alternative model, called the "first-order factor model", would be to specify the direct effects each dimension has on performance.

A central question is whether the second-order factor model proves superior to the first-order factor model. As noted above, discussions about the criteria used to test this proposition are outside the scope of this chapter (see [VEN 89, VEN 90a]). Another analytical issue that we only point out arises from structural equation modeling analysis, which is the tool commonly used. The advantage of this approach is to simultaneously estimate the measurement scales (construct reliability, convergent validity and discriminant validity) and the structural models used to determine whether the hypotheses are supported. The choice of fit indices available to the researcher when he or she assesses whether a specified model "fits" the data or not, is open to debate. We refer to Fynes *et al.* [FYN 05, p. 346] for an illustration of this problem in the case of SC collaboration–performance models, and to Hooper *et al.*'s guideline [HOO 08] for the selection of appropriate fit indices.

1.2.2.3.2. Fit as profile deviation in SC collaboration–performance models

Fit as profile deviation is based on "the degree of adherence to an externally specified profile" [VEN 89, p. 433]. It therefore presupposes: (1) the building of a conceptual linkage between *context* and *structure* (or environment and strategy, depending on the focus of the study), i.e. a set of dimensions consistently representing the structure for a particular context; and (2) the specification of an "ideal" profile along these dimensions for this particular context. The adjective "ideal" means that such a profile reflects a high level of alignment between context and structure along the considered dimensions and that this high level of co-alignment is positively related to performance. Conversely, a deviation from this ideal profile denotes "a weakness in the co-alignment resulting in a negative effect on performance" [VEN 89, p. 433].

To understand the critical issues that this perspective raises for empirical research on SC collaboration–performance models, we can draw on a series of papers by Simatupang and Sridharan [SIM 02, SIM 04, SIM 05]. Consider a *context of cooperation* between retailing and supplying companies and, for this particular context, the *coordination structure* expounded by Simatupang and Sridharan in [SIM 05]. This structure devoted to management of the retailer–supplier link integrates three dimensions of collaborative practices – namely, information sharing, decision synchronization and incentive alignment – that, according to the authors, constitute "three enablers of collaboration". Two main assumptions underlie this conceptual model: a) these three dimensions of collaborative practices are required to enable the partners to achieve better overall performance; and b) the overall performance depends on the degree to which the partners are involved in each of the dimensions (information sharing, decision synchronization and incentive alignment). Consequently, if we define a measurement scale for each dimension of collaborative practices and performance criteria, then empirical research makes it possible to:

– compare, along the three dimensions, the profile of different respondents drawn from a sample of pairs (retailers, supplier) involved in a collaborative relationship;

– relate a profile to a level of performance on each criterion and develop, using an appropriate statistical device (see [DRA 85], SIM 04]), a profile ("ideal profile") that can serve as a benchmark for assessing a profile deviation.

In [SIM 04], Simatupang and Sridharan report an empirical study of this nature in which they benchmark the profile of collaborative practices and operational performance. Their approach is consistent with a fit system perspective since they seek to establish "patterns of collaborative achievement", i.e. to show how profiles using collaborative practices contribute to the achievement of performance. Figure 1.10 is a simplified adaptation of their approach.

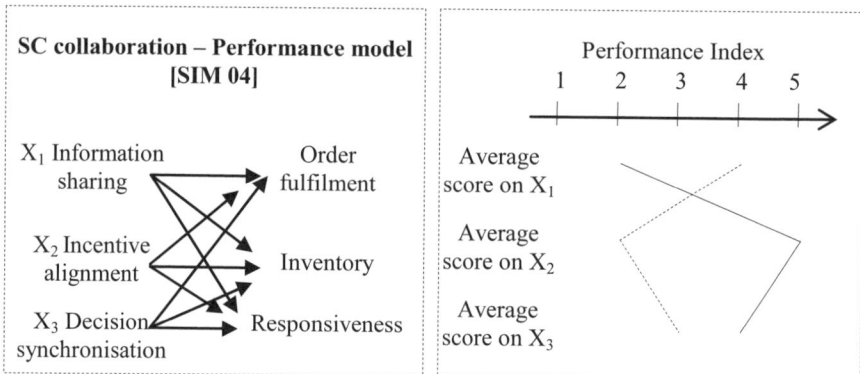

Figure 1.10. *Simatupang and Sridharan's model as a "profile deviation" model*

The left side of Figure 1.10 gives the model used by the authors. For each dimension X_1, X_2 and X_3 of collaboration, the measurement scale refers to the extent to which respondents (retailer and supplier) use the range of explicit collaborative practices pertaining to this dimension. The performance is measured as the degree to which the respondents perceive better order fulfillment, inventory and responsiveness because of collaborative practices. On the right side of Figure 1.10, we use the *collaboration index* and *the performance index* developed by Simatupang and Sridharan. For a dimension X_i, the collaboration index represents the average of the scores obtained by a respondent. For each respondent, the performance index is the average of fulfillment, inventory and responsiveness perceived. The right side of Figure 1.10 thus illustrates the profile deviation between two respondents.

This example shows that "fit as profile deviation" is a relevant category for classifying SC collaboration–performance models. Above all, it highlights the prerequisite for implementing such an approach: the identification of pattern of achievement of performance, i.e., a conceptual model consisting of dimensions of supply chain collaboration with a high internal consistency and related to supply chain performance.

1.2.2.3.3. Fit as gestalt in SC collaboration–performance models

The fit as gestalt approach is based on the search for archetypes, i.e. a small number of "recurring clusters" whose components are related to each other in ways that yield a coherent set [MIL 81]. This recurring cluster concept is close to that of pattern of achievement of performance defined above. Generally, in contingency theory this is not the case because the fit as gestalt is not anchored to a performance criterion. Obviously, this difference does not hold in the case of SC collaboration–performance models since the recurrent clusters obtained are assumed to be related to levels of performance.

For example, Simatupang and Sridharan [SIM 04] use the model described in the previous section to identify four "gestalts" linking collaboration to performance by crossing two criteria: the level (low *versus* high) of collaboration index (C) and the level (low *versus* high) of performance index (P). They thus obtain four coherent patterns of performance achievement through the involvement in collaborative practices: underrating collaboration (C: low, P: low); efficient collaboration (C: low, P: high); prospective collaboration (C: high, P: low), and synergistic collaboration (C: high, P: high).

The identification of the pattern of achievement of performance that underlies Simatupang *et al.*'s model (left side of Figure 1.10) thus leads to two functional forms of fit: fit as gestalt (described above) and fit as profile deviation (right side of

Figure 1.10). Given this closeness, the categorization proposed in the following section does not distinguish between them.

1.3. Towards a categorization of empirical studies on the SC collaboration–performance linkage

The previous section provides an analytical device for identifying and categorizing the SC collaboration–performance models. First, Figure 1.4 and Table 1.1 show the extent to which a model takes into consideration different types of collaborative practices and different levels of organizational commitment in collaboration. Second, the contingency framework developed above provides a way to categorize the modeling approaches through functional forms of fit among variables of the model. In this section we use this device to review empirical papers referring explicitly to the relationship between collaborative practices and performance.

We first explain the methodology used to identify relevant papers and the main characteristics of SC collaboration–performance models (section 1.3.1). We then build a map that allows us to compare the models according to the level of organizational commitment underlying the relationship between collaborative practices and performance: operational level (collaboration in the operations process); tactical or structural level (collaboration committing the planning and control process); and strategic level (strategic collaboration). Finally (section 1.3.2), we propose a "contingency chart" that categorizes the models according to the coupling between this level of organizational commitment in collaboration, and the complexity of laws of relationships (type of fit, for example) that are used to specify the effects of performance.

1.3.1. *Paper selection methodology and its characteristics*

1.3.1.1. *Selection*

In order to select empirical papers that contribute to understanding the linkage between collaborative practices and performance, we used EBSCOHost with Business Source Premier to make a systematic search for articles published from 1999 to 2008 that included the words "collaboration", "supply chain" and "performance" in the title or the abstract. In order to obtain a first list of empirical papers, we classified the 90 papers selected in this search in four groups: "conceptual", "analytical/simulation", "case study", and "empirical". We then sought to capture empirical research that refers to "integration" rather than "collaboration" (see discussion in section 1.1.1). We therefore used the recent literature review by Fabbes-Costes *et al.* [FAB 08] on empirical research linking supply chain integration and performance. We then sorted the 38 papers selected by these authors according to the following criteria: 1) empirical research in which the operationalization of the "integration" construct explicitly refers to collaborative practices in the sense defined in section 1.2.1; and 2) the dependent variable refers to performance indicators irrespective of the scope of performance (logistical measures, various improvement indicators, financial performance, etc.). This two-step review process allowed us to select 16 papers, each referring to SC collaboration–performance models in the sense of DEFINITION 1.1.

A first descriptive analysis was undertaken according seven topics: general purpose; what about "more a rhetoric than a reality?"; the scope of collaborative practices taken into account for the operationalization of "collaboration" or "integration" constructs; the data collection; the predictor, moderator or mediator variables used; the "performance" construct; and the main findings. Table 1.2, which was extracted from this analysis, summarizes information about the context of each study (type and size of focal firms in data sample, "upstream" and/or "downstream" collaboration considered in data collection). It includes the facets of the SC collaboration construct embedded in the model underlying the empirical research, and the performance measures used.

1.3.1.2. *Characteristics of selected empirical researches*

Although each of the 16 selected papers refers to empirical research testing the linkage between collaborative practices and performance, the studies differ significantly in terms of sample frames, facets of collaboration considered in the construct intended to represent collaborative practices, and the variables used for assessing performance (see Table 1.2).

1.3.1.2.1. The sample frames (Table 1.3)

The sample frames differ significantly in terms of sample size, industry, focus on type of firms (manufacturing firms or mix of manufacturing/wholesale/retailing firms), and direction of collaboration (upstream, downstream, or up- and downstream). Quite logically, four out of five small sized samples focus on a single industry and the fifth one relates to a single country, while the large samples mainly concern empirical research on the performance of both upstream and downstream collaboration practices in a wide range of industries. These "demographic" variables of the empirical research population have to be taken into account when comparing findings from different studies. For example, can we compare empirical research from the food industry [STA 99], food and consumer packaged goods [KUL 04], Spanish food, perfumery and detergents industry [GIM 05], Irish electronic industry [FYN 05] and American package printing industry [VAC 08]?

Authors	Focal firms, context, up/downstream collaboration	Facets of the SC collaboration construct Performance variables
Stank *et al.* 1999 [STA 99]	Suppliers (manufacturers, wholesale distributors) of food industry; 47 usable responses; downstream	SC coordination construct entailing: information sharing + use of communication technology + features of inter-firm partnership + use of performance monitoring Absolute logistical measures + performance relative to competitors
Stank *et al.* 2001 [STA 01]	306 firms (manufacturers, wholesale, retailers) in North America; up and downstream	Internal and External collaboration as a dimension of SC integration Logistical measures + capabilities to meet anticipated dates, to modify order size, etc.
Simatupang *et al.* 2004 [SIM 04]	76 New Zealand firms (29 manufacturers, 9 distributors, 38 retailers); up and downstream	Collaboration as a coordination structure entailing information sharing, decision synchronization and incentive alignment. Purpose: to benchmark the profile of collaborative practices Three indicators of logistical performance
Kulp *et al.* 2004 [KUL 04]	54 divisions in food and consumer packaged goods manufacturing firms; downstream	A structure of information integration entailing information sharing and structural collaboration Profit margins in industry
Rodrigues *et al.* 2004 [ROD 04]	284 managers: 258 manufacturers, 23 retailers, 3 in wholesale/ distribution; up and downstream	SC integration construct portraying collaboration as relational strategy, as management structure including information system (IS) and measurement systems, and integrated (internal or external) operations Logistics performance (6 indicators)
Bagchi *et al.* 2005 [BAG 05]	149 manufacturers in Europe (Nordic 48%, UK 24%, Germany 17%); 9 industries; up and downstream	Inter-firm integration construct captures collaboration through 4 scales: feedback seeking, decision-making, replenishment (for suppliers only), and supply-chain relations Eight logistical indicators
Gimenez *et al.* 2005 [GIM 05]	64 manufacturing firms in the Spanish food, perfumery and detergents sector; downstream	A 8-item scale construct labeled "external integration" Service improvement, costs and stock-out reductions
Corsten *et al.* 2005 [COR 05]	135 members of a purchasing association in different industries; upstream	Collaboration as a joint action in buyer–supplier relationships for technology development, process development, target costing, project planning Buyer performance on innovation, cost and finance

Fynes et al. 2005 [FYN 05]	202 companies in the electronics sector in the Republic of Ireland; downstream	A construct SC relationship quality including communication, cooperation, commitment, adaptation, interdependence, and trust Three indicators of SC relationship quality
Germain et al. 2006 [GER 06]	152 manufacturing firms or strategic business units; wide range of industries; downstream	Collaborative practices embedded in 2 constructs: downstream integration and internal integration Logistics performance mediating financial measures
Vereecke et al. 2006 [VER 06]	374 European manufacturing firms; up and downstream	Information exchange and structural collaboration performance: 17 logistical indicators
Sanders 2007 [SAN 07]	245 strategic business units (SBU) of large manufacturing firms in wide range of industries; upstream collaboration	Intra- and inter-organizational collaboration including items about information sharing and structural collaboration Improvements in cost, product quality improvement, new product introduction time, delivery speed
Chang Won Lee et al. 2007 [CHA 07]	122 various firms practicing SCM in the Midwest region; up and downstream	Integration construct referring to customer linkage, supplier linkage and internal linkage Cost containment and logistical reliability variables
Swink et al. 2007 [SWI 07]	224 manufacturing plant managers; diversity of industries, plant sizes, and process types; up and downstream	SCM integration construct: strategic customer and supplier integration, product–process technology integration, corporate strategy integration Manufacturing competitive capabilities + business performance (market performance, customer satisfaction)
Vachon et al. 2008 [VAC 08]	84 plants in North American package printing industry; up and downstream	Two 5-item scales capture the use of collaborative environmental practices Thirteen perceptual measures towards manufacturing and environmental performance
Paulraj et al. 2008 [PAU 08]	221 informants with strategic position in US manufacturing firms (medium to large firms); up and downstream	A construct labeled "inter-organizational communication": 5 items related to information sharing, 1 to structural collaboration practices Logistical performance for buyer (7 indicators) and supplier (7 indicators)

Table 1.2. *Context, facets of the SC collaboration construct and measures of performance in selected papers*

Characteristic	Modalities	Distribution	References
Sample size S	S < 100	5	[GIM 05, KUL 04, SIM 04, STA 99, VAC 08]
	100 < S < 200	4	[BAG 05, CHA 07, COR 05, GER 06]
	S > 200	7	[FYN 05, PAU 08, ROD 04, SAN 07, STA 01, SWI 07, VER 06]
Industry	Single industry	5	[FYN 05, GIM 05, KUL 04, STA 99, VAC 08]
	Mixed industries	11	[BAG 05, CHA 07, COR 05, GER 06, PAU 08, ROD 04, SAN 07, SIM 04, STA 01, SWI 07, VER 06]
Type of firms	Only manufacturing	10	[BAG 05, FYN 05, GER 06, GIM 05, KUL 04, PAU 08, SAN 07, SWI 07, VAC 08, VER 06]
	Manufacturing and distribution	6	[CHA 07, COR 05, ROD 04, STA 99, STA 01, SIM 04]
Direction of collaboration	Only upstream	2	[COR 05, SAN 07]
	Upstream and downstream	9	[BAG 05, CHA 07, PAU 08, ROD 04, SIM 04, STA 01, SWI 07, VAC 08, VER 06]
	Only downstream	5	[FYN 05, GER 06, GIM 05, KUL 04, STA 99]

Table 1.3. *Characteristics of sample frames*

1.3.1.2.2. Conceptualization of the SC collaboration construct

The conceptualization of the SC collaboration construct is an even more important characteristic of such empirical research. The question is how collaborative practices are embedded in the measurement scale of a higher-order latent construct encompassing the concept of supply chain collaboration. A thorough analysis of the papers presented in Table 1.2 leads us to identify three perspectives: SC integration, SC coordination and supplier–customer relationship.

– For half of the empirical studies (eight out of 16), collaborative practices appear in the measurement scale of a first- or second-order construct related to SC integration. External collaboration practices are viewed as one dimension of SC integration or inter-firm integration [BAG 05, CHA 07, GER 06, GIM 05, STA 01], or as a part of a structure of information integration [KUL 04]. In addition, others give a strategic dimension to SC integration and, in this case, collaborative practices are one element of the deployment of this strategy: a relational strategy aiming for SC integration [ROD 04], or collaboration as a type of strategic integration at the manufacturing plant level [SWI 07].

– A second group of conceptualizations (two out of 16) connects collaboration to the concept of SC coordination. For example, collaborative practices are considered as basic elements of information sharing, decision synchronization and incentive alignment, which together constitute a structure of coordination [SIM 04]. In [STA 99], collaborative practices are a part of inter-firm supply chain coordination processes characterized by effective communication, information exchange, "partnering" and performance monitoring.

– A third group (six out of 16) considers collaborative practices only as a joint action in the management of supplier–customer relationships [COR 05, SAN 07, VAC 08, VER 06]. Two studies go further by including these practices in a relationship management system ([FYN 05] and [PAU 05]).

1.3.1.2.3. Performance as a dependent variable

Unsurprisingly, almost all selected papers use logistics and/or manufacturing indicators in the measurement scale of the dependent variable for assessing the degree of performance improvement due to collaborative practices. These variables obviously concern various areas:

– service performance: [BAG 05, CHA 07, GER 06, GIM 05, KUL 04, ROD 04, SAN 07, SIM 04, STA 99, STA 01, VAC 08, VER 06];

– cost containment variables: [BAG 05, CHA 07, COR 05, GIM 05, ROD 04, SAN 07, STA 99, VER 06];

– manufacturing indicators: [PAU 08, SWI 07, VAC 08, VER 06];

– quality (customer satisfaction, design, conformance, product quality improvement): [FYN 05, PAU 08, SAN 07, SWI 07, VAC 08, VER 06];

– environmental performance: [VAC 08].

Generally, these logistics and manufacturing indicators assess absolute performance improvements for the focal firm. In some cases, however, the performance is measured in relation to competitors [KUL 04, STA 99], or the scale measures the degree to which the chain members (not only the focal firm) achieve better logistical performance [SIM 04].

The dependent variable seldom refers to indicators pertaining to business or financial performance. When the measurement scale assesses an improvement in business performance, the indicators seek to measure the effect of collaboration on market performance (growth rate, market share) [SWI 07], innovation [COR 05], or new product introduction time [SAN 07]. Only three studies (out of 16) consider the financial performance:

– improvement of return on assets and return on sales in [COR 05] and [GER 06];

– profit growth in [KUL 04] and [GER 06].

In conclusion, it is worth noting that, with the exception of [KUL 04] and [FYN 05], the performance variables are seldom used as intermediate variables. [KUL 04] considers, for example, that information sharing and structural collaboration first improve intermediate performance in terms of retailer or manufacturer stockouts and wholesale price and, second, positively effect the firm's profitability (profit margins) through these intermediate measures. Furthermore, they control for other variables (holding cost, distribution cost, etc.) likely to affect the manufacturer's profit margins through this intermediate performance. In this way, not only is the impact of collaboration on performance mediated by intermediate performance variables, but the indirect effect of covariate variables is also taken into account. Fynes *et al.* [FYN 05] likewise mediate the impact of the supply chain relationships' quality on customer satisfaction through two intermediate performance variables: namely design quality and conformance quality. It therefore seems necessary for future research to examine the impact of collaboration on performance, by taking into consideration the effect on dependent variables not only of potential intermediate performance variables but also of variables that may affect the relation between intermediate performance and dependent variables.

1.3.2. *Comparing empirical research according to the level of organizational commitment in collaboration*

Bowersox *et al.*'s framework (see section 1.2.1.2 and Figure 1.4) identifies three key processes that combine to create and deliver value in cross-enterprise collaboration. First, each of these processes corresponds to an organizational level of commitment in collaboration; second, each requires specific competencies supported by capabilities; and third, the firm selectively deploys these competencies and capabilities to obtain positional advantages and performance differentials via collaboration [BOW 03].

We can therefore expect that an empirical research seeking to test the link between collaboration and performance refers to different organizational levels of commitment in collaboration. A way to compare the selected papers is to project the SC collaboration–performance models that underlie the empirical research onto Figure 1.4. Figure 1.11 plots the 16 selected papers according to whether they incorporate a strategic vision of the collaboration; take into account a structure (information system, measurement system or relationship management system) devoted to coordination and collaboration control; or else focus on collaborative practices aimed at integrating the operational processes.

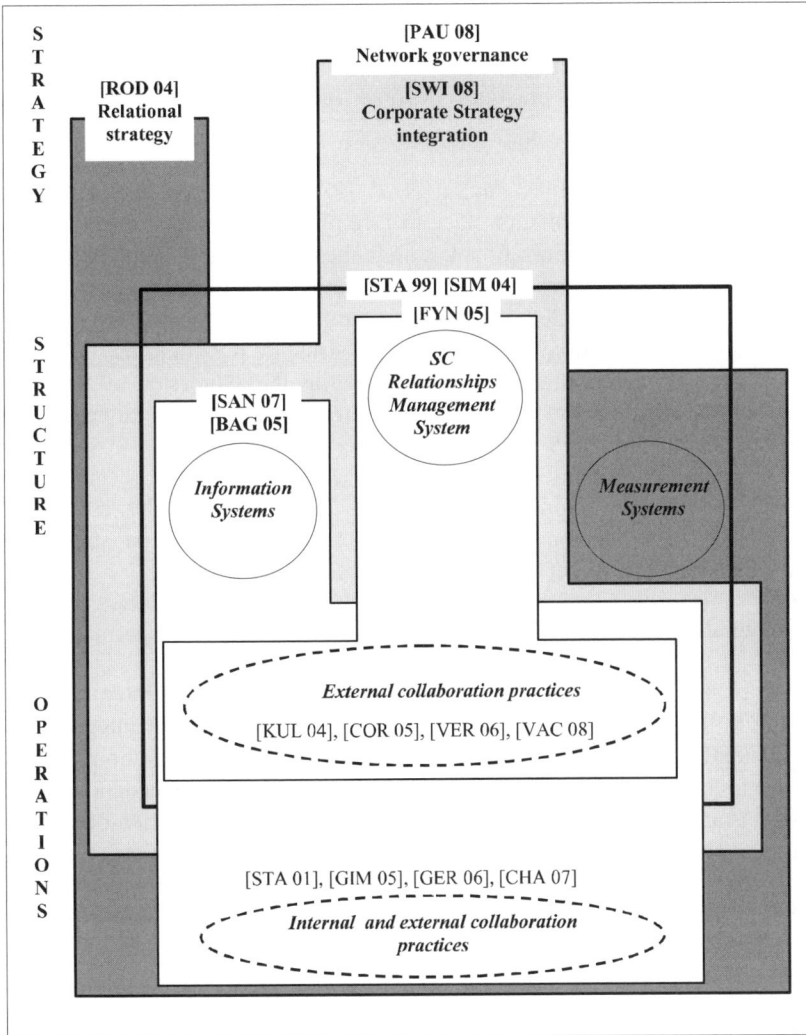

Figure 1.11. *SC collaboration–performance models and organizational level of commitment in collaboration*

1.3.2.1. *Models incorporating a strategic vision of collaboration*

Figure 1.11 emphasizes three papers that reflect the strategic dimension of supply chain collaboration. Rodriguez *et al.* [ROD 04] portray the relationship between SC collaboration and performance as a double mediation effect:

Relational strategy → Structural choices → SC collaboration → Performance

A relational strategy (i.e. a set of processes aiming to create a shared vision of collaboration between partners) promotes the development and maintenance of information and measurement systems. This, in turn, positively influences internal and external collaborative practices devoted to the integration of operational processes.

From a similar perspective, Paulraj *et al.* [PAU 08] encompass collaborative practices (exchange of information, face-to-face planning/communication, etc.) in a construct called "inter-organizational communication". They then highlight its strategic importance by considering it as a relational competency based on two dimensions: a strategy oriented towards long-term relationships and governance of the buyers/suppliers network, and the choice of structure regarding the information system. The collaborative practices are thus seen as the expression of a relational competency that mediates the links between strategic and structural key antecedents and performance.

Unlike the previous models, Swink *et al.* [SWI 07] consider collaborative practices with customers or suppliers not as a mediator between strategy and performance, but as the direct expression of an integration strategy:

Integration strategy → Plant's competitive capabilities → Performance

More precisely, they define integration strategy as a set of strategic activities pertaining to four dimensions. Two dimensions (strategic customer integration and strategic supplier integration) explicitly refer to strategic collaboration. They are focused on sharing information and knowledge for a better understanding of the expectations and preferences of customers and for a better exploitation of suppliers' capabilities. The third dimension (corporate strategy integration) reflects the process of acquiring and sharing knowledge pertaining to business and manufacturing strategies. Finally, the forth dimension (product–process technology integration) concerns the co-development of products or processes. The central idea of this conceptual framework is that these four axes of strategic activities integrate strategic information and knowledge from outside the walls of a manufacturing plant and enable the development of the plant's competitive capabilities, which, in turn, affects the market performance and customer satisfaction.

1.3.2.2. Models focused on a structure devoted to collaboration

In Figure 1.11, five models highlight the structural level of collaboration: [BAG 05, FYN 05, SAN 07, SIM 04, STA 99]. To various degrees they share the idea that collaboration spans the boundaries of the organization; that it therefore requires a specific management structure, and that the existence of such a specific structure is a determinant of performance.

For Simatupang and Sridharan [SIM 04], this structure devoted to collaboration constitutes a key choice of organization design. It entails five elements: a performance measurement system; an information system attached to information sharing; an incentive alignment system; a structure to ensure the decision synchronization between the chain members; and integrated operational processes. In 1999, Stank *et al.* [STA 99] investigated the impact of such an inter-firm coordination structure on logistics performance. In addition to an information-sharing policy between the partners, the proposed structure included an inter-firm partnership management system, an information structure based on Electronic Data Intercahnge (EDI), and a performance-monitoring system.

Although the Bagchi *et al.*'s survey [BAG 05] assesses the impact of supply chain integration on logistical indicators, it aims to understand the reality of supply chain integration in European firms first. A careful examination of the measurement scales used in the model shows that SC collaboration is viewed as an information management system aimed at involving suppliers and/or customers in committees/teams/task forces for feedback-seeking, joint decision-making, and replenishment policies in different areas (R&D, procurement, etc.). Their model therefore focuses more on the structure based on information systems to achieve integration than on the operational reality of collaborative practices. In Sanders' model [SAN 07] we also find this emphasis on the information system as a driver of performance. Sanders even considers that external collaboration practices do not directly influence performance and have just a mediating role in the relation between an organizational use of e-business technologies and organizational performance.

Finally, for Fynes *et al.* [FYN 05], as discussed in section 1.2.2.3.1 and Figure 1.9, collaborative practices constitute only two dimensions, namely communication and cooperation, of a multi-dimensional system to manage the quality of relationships in the supply chain.

1.3.2.3. Models focused on the operational level of collaborative practices

The bottom of Figure 1.11 shows the SC collaboration–performance models (eight out of 16) that consider just the operational dimension of collaboration. A recurrent issue is the inter-relationship between internal and external collaboration.

Indeed, we can expect that a relative degree of achievement in intra-organizational collaboration is necessary before an advantage can be gained from collaboration with external partners. The assumptions regarding either the relative impact of internal and external collaboration on performance, or the mediation relationship between internal and external linkage are therefore central to several models: [CHA 07, GER 06, GIM 05, STA 01]. The findings do not, however, present a high degree of stability. For example, Stank *et al.* [STA 01] show that internal collaboration improves delivery speed, dependability, responsiveness, flexibility and overall customer satisfaction, while the relationship between external collaboration and logistics service lacks empirical support. In contrast, Gimenez *et al.* [GIM 05] find that external integration positively influences performance while the internal integration in the logistics-production interface has no clearly positive effect on logistics performance. Obviously, these ambiguous findings call for careful consideration of the characteristics of the sample frame (see Table 1.3), of the scales used for measuring internal or external linkage, and of the type of analysis to which the theoretical model is subjected (structural equation modeling in [GER 06, GIM 05, STA 01], and multiple linear regression analyses in [CHA 07]).

Finally, four empirical researches [COR 05, KUL 04, VAC 08, VER 06], focus exclusively on the link between external collaboration practices and performance without referring to the internal collaboration practices, or strategy and structures that foster collaboration. Their originality actually lies in the choice of context, or in a specificity of modeling. For example, the objective of Vereecke *et al.* [VER 06] is to use the data of the 2001 International Manufacturing Strategy Survey in Europe to obtain industry-based empirical results on collaboration practices. Accordingly, they focus on two broad classes of practices that can be identified from this survey: information sharing and structural collaboration understood as a co-location of plan; and use of kanban or consignment stock/VMI practices. The choice of context is also central in [VAC 08] because the authors emphasize environmental collaborative activities (joint environmental goal-setting, shared environmental planning, pollution or other environmental impact reduction policies). The originality of [KUL 04] and [COR 05] lie in the modeling intent. As noted above, [KUL 04] stresses the mediation of intermediate performance variables in the impact of collaboration on the manufacturer's profitability (see section 1.1.3.2.2). [COR 05] specifically examines the moderation effects of trust and dependence on the benefits of collaboration (see Figure 1.5).

1.3.3. *A contingency chart of SC collaboration–performance models*

Figure 1.11 shows to what extent empirical research reflects the consideration of different organizational levels: the strategic dimension of collaboration, the structural devices (information system, measurement system, etc.) devoted to the management of collaborative relationships, or the operational level where collaborative practices are performed. This hierarchy of organizational commitment in collaboration therefore constitutes a (vertical) dimension along which the SC collaboration performance models can be classified.

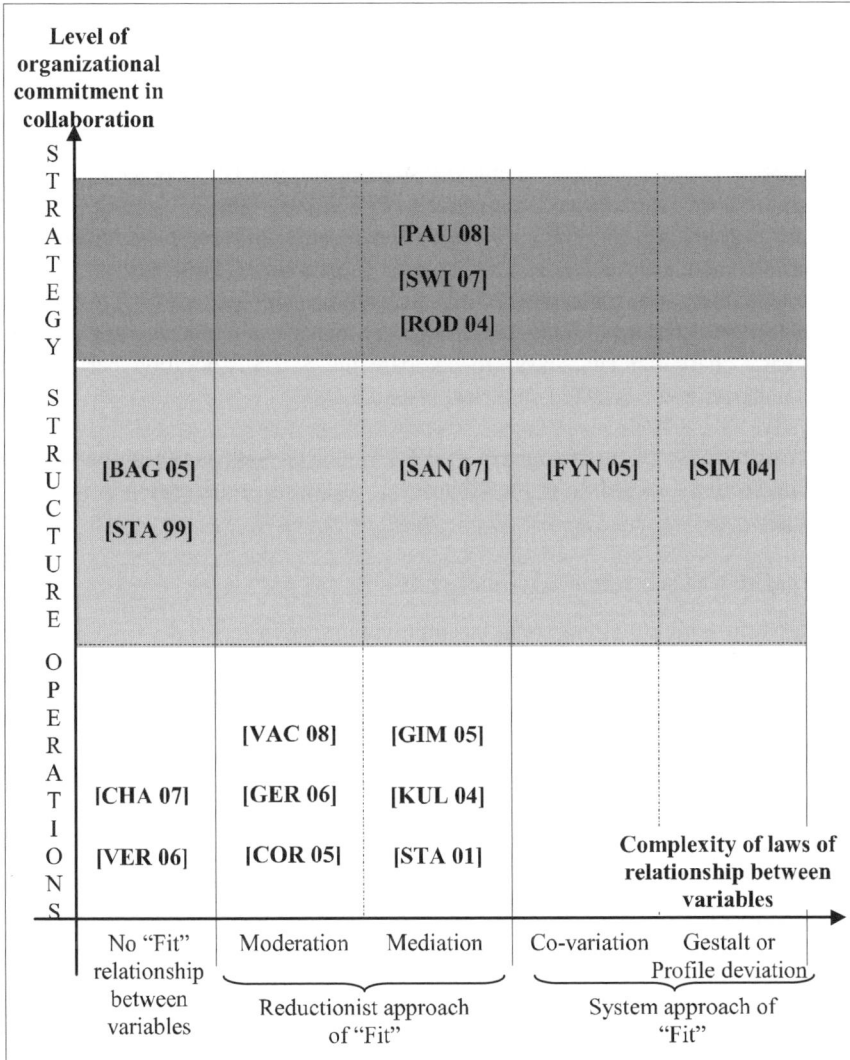

Figure 1.12. *A contingency chart comparing SC collaboration–performance models*

Section 1.2.2 has moreover emphasized some specific functional forms of co-alignment (called "fit") between variables in SC collaboration–performance models. Following [VEN 90a], we have distinguished two perspectives of co-alignment, depending on the complexity of co-alignment conceptualization: the reductionist perspective when the model examines the performance impact of pairwise interactions or alignments and the system approach when the model retains the holistic nature of co-alignment. We have then shown the relevance of certain functional forms of fit for specifying the theoretical relationships between model variables. Of course, some models do not pertain to any of these forms of fit: they are of the (K → Performance) type, where K is a 1D variable referring to SC collaboration. Building on this complexity scale of fit models [VEN 89, p. 124], we propose another (horizontal) dimension to classify the SC collaboration–performance models. This choice is based on increasingly complex relationships between the model variables: no "fit" relationship between variables; reductionist approach (moderation, mediation) of fit; and system approach of fit (co-variation, profile deviation/gestalt). Figure 1.12, based on these two dimensions, provides a contingency chart that enables us to compare the SC collaboration–performance models underlying the selected empirical research.

For the purpose of this comparison, the 16 selected models are grouped in the following sections according to the complexity of laws of relationship between the variables.

1.3.3.1. *Models with a system approach of fit*

It is worth noting that empirical research is missing in the upper right corner of Figure 1.12: none of the models that incorporate a strategic vision of collaboration assumes a system approach of fit. The only models that seek to identify *patterns of consistency* likely to constitute *forms of achievement* of performance focus on a specific structure devoted to the management of collaboration. These two models, [SIM 04] and [FYN 05], have been extensively developed in section 1.2.2.3. In Simatupang *et al.*'s model [SIM 04], a coordination structure entailing five elements devoted to management and control of collaboration is used to benchmark the profile of collaborative practices and operational performance (see section 1.2.2.3.2) and to identify four gestalts relating to collaboration and performance by crossing a collaboration index with a performance index (see section 1.2.2.3.3). Similarly, as shown in section 1.2.2.3.1, [FYN 05] is an exemplary illustration of fit as co-variation: performance is directly related to a cohesive pattern of six variables reflecting a quality management system of supplier relationships.

1.3.3.2. *Models with a reductionist approach to fit*

Irrespective of the organizational level at which the collaboration is considered, these models relate performance to moderating or mediating effects between pairs of variables, rather than to internal consistency of multiple variables pertaining to collaboration.

A recurrent question is whether external collaboration is a direct antecedent of performance, an antecedent of other variables influencing performance, or a mediator of the relationship between other variables and performance. As noted in section 1.3.2.1, [ROD 04] posits performance as an outcome of appropriate alignment between strategy, structure, and collaborative processes, and this fit is a double mediation effect: strategy → structural choices → collaborative practices → performance. For Paulraj *et al.* [PAU 08], collaboration also functions as a mediating variable between a governance strategy of buyer–supplier relationships and performance. In [SAN 07], the model does not consider the strategic level of collaboration, but collaborative practices play a similar mediating role between a structural device devoted to collaboration and performance: the impact of the use of e-business technologies on performance is mediated by inter- and intra-organizational collaboration. Note that Sanders' conceptual model does not hypothesize a direct relationship of extra-organizational collaboration (external collaboration) on performance but only a relationship mediated by intra-organizational (internal) collaboration. Similarly, this issue of a one- or two-way mediated relationship between external and internal collaboration is central in empirical research (see [GER 06, GIM 05, STA 01]) focused on the operational level of collaboration rather than the strategic or tactical levels. However, empirical research does not provide a clear support on the mediation effect between internal and external collaboration. While findings in [STA 01] and [SAN 07] support the hypothesis of a relationship of the (external collaboration → internal collaboration → performance) type, [GER 06] shows that internal collaboration is, above all, a moderator of the relationship between external collaboration and performance. As pointed out in section 1.2.1, a further explanation of these unstable findings involves clarifying the measurement scales of constructs of internal and external collaboration.

Another noticeable mediation effect concerns the use of intermediate performance variables in [SWI 07] and [KUL 04]. For example, in [SWI 07], the impact of collaboration on business performance is mediated by manufacturing-based competitive capabilities. This is consistent with Bowersox *et al.*'s framework (section 1.2.1.2 and Figure 1.4): capabilities are seen as the *generative means* by which collaboration affects business performance. Kulp *et al.* [KUL 04] adopt a similar view (see section 1.1.3.2.2) when they hypothesize the mediating role of wholesale prices and stockouts between collaboration and profitability.

Finally, Figure 1.12 takes into account fit as moderation in SC collaboration–performance models through [GER 06] and [COR 05], already cited in Figure 1.5 and [VAC 08]. Recall that a moderation effect enriches a model by proposing variables (called moderators) that affect the form or strength of the relationship between collaboration and performance (see section 1.2.2.2.1). For example, [COR 05] posits that the effects of supplier collaboration on buyer performance are influenced by trust and dependence as well as firm size, stability of demand and age of relationship. Similarly, when Vachon *et al.* [VAC 08] examine the impact of environmental collaborative activities on manufacturing performance, they control the moderator effect of several variables, such as plant size, parent company size, reinvestment rate, average age of a key piece of process technology, supplier base, and customer concentration.

1.3.3.2.1. Models without fit relationships between variables

While a fit model empirically tests a *contingent* proposition, i.e. *a conditional association of two or more independent variables* with a performance outcome, a model without fit relationships hypothesizes a *congruent* proposition, i.e. *an unconditional association among variables* [DRA 85, p. 514]. Such SC collaboration–performance models do not take the inter-relationships between variables into account; they examine the relationships between individual or aggregated practices pertaining to collaboration and particular aspects of performance. Therefore, they are never type 4 models in Ho *et al.*'s terminology (see section 1.2.2.1.1) but type 1, 2 or 3 models. As reported in [HO 02], a basic modeling approach is:

> *Performance(i) = f(Facet$_j$)*, where performance(i) is a particular measure for i= 1,2,…, n and Facet$_j$ is a particular facet of collaboration for j = 1,2,…, m.

For example, in [CHA 07], three facets of collaboration are modeled by three constructs: supplier linkage, customer linkage and internal linkage. The corresponding measurement scales relate to different collaborative practices: information sharing with customers and suppliers, practices of strategic and operational involvement with suppliers, and various devices favoring internal collaboration. Thus, three performance constructs (cost-containment, logistic reliability and overall performance) lead us to test nine hypotheses on the influence of each of three types of linkage on each of three performance measures.

The most common form of these models aims at studying the *relative impact* of different facets of collaboration on particular aspects of performance:

> *Performance(i) = f(Facet$_1$, Facet$_2$, …, Facet$_m$)*, where performance(i) is a particular measure for i= 1,2,…, n and Facet$_j$ is a particular facet of collaboration.

For example, [STA 99] identifies four facets of an inter-firm coordination structure: information-sharing, use of technology for communication, particular aspects of inter-firm partnership, and use of performance monitoring. This study develops measurement scales for each of these four constructs. It then uses hierarchical regression analyses and ANOVA to test the relative strength of each of the four facets of an inter-firm coordination structure on each of 16 key logistical measures. In an in-depth study of the state of supply chain integration in European manufacturing firms, [BAG 05] uses a similar idea to establish whether increasing levels of the intensity of supply chain integration affects their logistic performance. Eight logistical indicators are chosen. Simple and multiple regression analyses are carried out to study the relative impact of various facets of collaboration (collaboration with suppliers in inventory control, procurement, production, R&D, or supply design, etc.) on each indicator.

Finally, [VER 06] presents an original approach to compare the relative impact of supplier–customer collaboration on performance improvement. First, the authors use a factor analysis to highlight two types of collaboration (information exchange and/or structural collaboration) and six performance variables (cost, flexibility, quality, delivery, procurement and time to market). For each type of supplier/customer collaboration (information exchange or structural collaboration), the authors split the sample into four categories, depending on the level (low/high) of collaboration with suppliers and the level (low/high) of collaboration with customers. It should be noted that these categories resulting from use are obtained not by a cluster analysis as in "fit as gestalt", but by using "the median as cut-off value to distinguish low and high levels of collaboration" [VER 06, p. 1186]. An analysis of variance (one-way ANOVA) thus allows us to compare the impact of collaboration per performance variable and per information exchange (or structural collaboration) category.

1.4. Summary and conclusion

Based on the problem addressed by Ho *et al.* [HO 02] concerning weaknesses of empirical research, we have highlighted two main issues: *how we can recognize a model linking SC collaboration and performance; and how we can compare SC collaboration–performance models.*

The first issue requires the conceptualization of collaboration, that is the design of the measurement scale of the SC collaboration construct. For this purpose we established a framework based on a RBV of the firm's performance, linking Whipple and Russell's typology and Bowersox *et al.*'s cross-enterprise collaboration model. This categorization helps us to understand the extent to which a model makes an exhaustive account of different types of collaborative practices and, above all, of different levels of organizational commitment in collaboration. Clearly, it is a decision-support tool for the design of a questionnaire seeking to capture a representation of collaborative practices. Since Bowersox *et al.*'s model emphasizes the performance model that supports the categorization, it stresses the need for consistency between the organizational levels reflected in the SC collaboration construct and choice of performance variables aimed at measuring the impact of collaboration.

The second issue relates to the existence of a conceptual framework favoring the comparison of modeling approaches. It raises the question of a meta-model taking into account the possible *laws of relationship among units of SC collaboration–performance models*, i.e. how the units of models (SC collaboration construct, performance variables and other variables) are linked or associated. For this purpose, we borrowed the concept of fit developed by contingency theorists and the six functional forms of fit identified by Venkatraman: *fit as moderation, fit as mediation, fit as matching, fit as co-variation, fit as gestalts, and fit as profile deviation*. We then showed the relevance of these functional forms of fit for describing and categorizing the modeling approaches of SC collaboration–performance models. To this end, we first illustrated and discussed each of these functional forms in the case of SC collaboration–performance models, and then used this categorization in a systematic review of empirical papers referring explicitly to the relationship between collaborative practices and performance. This review also proved that it was possible to extend Venkatraman's complexity scale of fit models to the SC collaboration–performance models. A *contingency chart* (Figure 1.12) thus emerged that allowed us to compare SC collaboration–performance models according two dimensions: the complexity of laws of relations between the model variables, and the level of organizational commitment in collaboration that the SC collaboration construct reflects.

In conclusion, we highlight two lessons regarding critical choices for modeling the SC collaboration–performance relationship:

– The first concerns the conceptualization of the SC collaboration construct. It takes the form of two questions: What are the organizational model and performance model that underlie the measurement scale of the SC collaboration construct? To what extent does the model make an exhaustive account of different types of collaborative practices, or of different levels of organizational commitment in collaboration (operations process, planning and control process, strategic collaboration)?

– The second is drawn from Figure 1.12. This contingency chart highlights empty boxes. In particular, it calls for empirical research applying the fit as gestalt or fit as co-variation perspectives to SC collaboration–performance models. How might a firm achieve performance by fitting, *into a cohesive whole*, a set of variables pertaining to collaboration strategy, structural devices devoted to collaboration, and collaborative practices that ensure the integration of operational processes? The question remains open in empirical research.

1.5. Bibliography

[BAG 05] BAGCHI P.K., HA B.C., SKJOETT-LARSEN, T., SOERENSEN, L.B., "Supply chain integration: a European survey", *The International Journal of Logistics Management*, vol. 16, no. 2, 2005, pp. 275-94.

[BAR 86] BARON R.M., KENNY D.A., "The moderator-mediator variable distinction in social psychological research: conceptual, strategic, and statistical considerations", *Journal of Personality and Social Psychology*, vol. 51, no. 6, 1986, pp. 1173–1182.

[BAR 91] BARNEY J., "Firm resources and sustained competitive advantage", *Journal of Management*, vol. 17, no. 1, 1991, pp. 99–120.

[BAR 04] BARRATT M., "Understanding the meaning of collaboration in the supply chain", *Supply Chain Management: An International Journal*, vol. 9, no. 1, 2004, pp. 30-42.

[BOW 03] BOWERSOX D.J., CLOSS D.J., STANK T.P., "How to master cross-enterprise collaboration", *Supply Chain Management Review*, July/August, 2003, pp. 18-27.

[CAR 03] CACERES R.C., VANHAMME J., "Les processus modérateurs et médiateurs: distinction conceptuelle, aspects analytiques et illustrations", *Recherche et Applications en Marketing*, vol. 18, no. 2, 2003, pp. 67-100.

[CHA 07] CHANG WON LEE, IK-WHAN G. KWON, SEVERANCE D., "Relationship between supply chain performance and degree of linkage among supplier, internal integration, and customer", *Supply Chain Management: An International Journal*, vol. 12, no. 6, 2007, pp. 444-452.

[COA 02] COATES T.T., MCDERMOTT C.M., "An exploratory analysis of new competencies: a resource based view perspective", *Journal of Operations Management*, vol. 20, no. 5, 2002, pp. 435–450.

[COR 05] CORSTEN D., FELDE J., "Exploring the performance effects of key-supplier collaboration. An empirical investigation into Swiss buyer-supplier relationships", *International Journal of Physical Distribution & Logistics Management*, vol. 35, no. 6, 2005, pp. 445-461.

[DAY 94] DAY G.S., "The capabilities of market-driven organizations", *Journal of Marketing*, vol. 58, 1994, pp. 37-52.

[DRA 85], DRAZIN R., VAN DE VEN A. H., "An examination of alternative forms of fit in contingency theory", *Administrative Science Quarterly*, vol. 30, 1985, pp. 514-539.

[DYE 98] DYER J.H., SINGH H., "The relational view: Cooperative strategy and source of interorganizational competitive advantage", *Academy of Management Review*, vol. 23, no. 4, 1998, pp. 660-679.

[FAB 08] FABBES-COSTES N., JAHRE M., "Supply chain integration and performance: a review of the evidence", *The International Journal of Logistics Management*, vol. 19, no. 2, 2008, pp. 130-154.

[FAW 02] FAWCETT S.E., MAGNAN G.M., "The rhetoric and reality of supply chain integration", *International Journal of Physical Distribution & Logistics Management*, vol. 32, no. 5, 2002, pp. 339-61.

[FAW 08] FAWCETT S.E., MAGNAN G.M., MCCARTER M.W., "A three-stage implementation model for supply chain collaboration", *Journal of Business Logistics*, vol. 29, no. 1, 2008, pp. 93-112.

[FRY 87] FRY L.W., SMITH D.A., "Congruence, contingency, and theory building", *Academy of Management Review*, vol. 12, no. 1, 1987, pp. 117-132.

[FYN 05] FYNES B, VOSS C., DE BURCA S., "The impact of supply chain relationship quality on quality performance", *International Journal of Production Economics*, vol. 96, 2005, pp. 339-354.

[GER 06] GERMAIN R., IYER K.N., "The interaction of internal and downstream integration and its association with performance", *Journal of Business Logistics*, vol. 27, no. 2, 2006, pp. 29-52.

[GIM 05] GIMENEZ C., VENTURA, E., "Logistics-production, logistics-marketing and external integration: their impact on performance", *International Journal of Operations and Production Management*, vol. 25, no. 1, 2005, pp. 20-38.

[GLA 67] GLASER B.G., STRAUSS A., *The Discovery of Grounded Theory: Strategies for Qualitative Research*, Aldine, Chicago, 1967.

[HIN 02] HINES P., SILVI R., BARTOLINI M., "Demand chain management: an integrative approach in automotive retailing", *Journal of Operations Management*, vol. 20, no. 6, 2002, pp.707-728.

[HO 02] HO D.C.K., AU K.F., NEWTON E., "Empirical research on supply chain management: a critical review and recommendations", *International Journal of Production Research.*, vol. 40, no. 17, 2002, pp. 4415-4430.

[HOO 08] HOOPER D., COUGHLAN J., MULLEN M. R., "Structural equation modelling for determining model fit", *Electronic Journal of Business Research Methods*, vol. 6, no. 1, 2008, pp. 53-59.

[KAN 94] KANTER R.M., "Collaborative advantage", *Harvard Business Review*, vol 74, no. 4, 1994, pp. 96-108.

[KUL 04] KULP S.C., LEE H.L., OFEK E., "Manufacturer benefits from information integration with retail customers", *Management Science*, vol. 50, no. 4, 2004, pp. 431-444.

[MAC 02] MACKINNON D.P., LOCKWOOD C.M., HOFFMAN J.M., WEST, S.G., SHEETS V., "A comparison of methods to test mediation and other intervening variable effects", *Psychological Methods*, vol. 7, no. 1, 2002, pp. 83-104.

[MIL 81], MILLER D., "Toward a new contingency approach: the search for organizational gestalts", *Journal of Management Studies*, vol. 18, no. 1, 1981, pp. 1-26.

[PAU 08] PAULRAJ A, LADO A.A., INJAZZ J. CHEN I.J., "Inter-organizational communication as a relational competency: Antecedents and performance outcomes in collaborative buyer–supplier relationships", *Journal of Operations Management*, vol. 26, 2008, pp. 45–64.

[PEN 59] PENROSE E.T., *The Theory of the Growth of the Firm*, Basil Blackwell, London, 1959.

[PRE 01] PRESCOTT C. E., "The concept of fit in organizational research", *International Journal of Organization Theory & Behavior*, vol. 4, no. 3 & 4, 2001, pp. 287-306.

[ROD 04] RODRIGUEZ A.M., STANK T.P., LYNCH D.F., "Linking strategy. structure, process, and performance in integrated logistics", *Journal of Business Logistics,* vol. 25, no. 2, 2004, pp. 65-94.

[SAL 01] SALVADOR F., FORZA C., RUNGTUSANATHAM M., CHOI. T., "Supply chain interactions and time-related performances: an operations management perspective", *International Journal of Operations & Production Management*, vol 21, no. 4, 2001, pp. 461-475.

[SAN 07] SANDERS N.R., "An empirical study of the impact of e-business technologies on organizational collaboration and performance", *Journal of Operations Management*, vol. 25, 2007, pp. 1332–1347.

[SIM 02] SIMATUPANG T.M., SRIDHARAN R., "The collaborative supply chain, International", *Journal of Logistics Management*, vol. 13, no. 1, 2002, pp. 15-30.

[SIM 04] SIMATUPANG T.M., SRIDHARAN R., "Benchmarking supply chain collaboration: an empirical study", *Benchmarking: An International Journal*, vol. 11, no. 5, 2004, pp. 484-503.

[SIM 05] SIMATUPANG T.M., SRIDHARAN R., "An integrative framework for supply chain collaboration", *International Journal of Logistics Management*, vol. 16, no. 2, 2004, pp. 257-274.

[SIN 96] SINGH K., MITCHELL W., "Precarious collaboration: business survival after partners shut down or form new partnerships", *Strategic Management Journal*, vol. 17, no. 7, 1996, pp. 99-115.

[SKJ 03] SKJOETT-LARSEN T., THERNØE C., ANDERSEN C., "Supply chain collaboration: theoretical perspectives and empirical evidence", *International Journal of Physical Distribution & Logistics Management*, vol. 22, no. 6, 2003, pp. 531-549.

[STA 99] STANK T.P., CRUM M., ARANGO M., "Benefits of interfirm coordination in food industry supply chains", *Journal of Business Logistics*, vol. 20, no. 2, 1999, pp. 21-42.

[STA 01] STANK T.P., KELLER S.B., CLOSS, D.J., "Performance benefits of supply chain logistical integration", *Transportation Journal*, vol. 41, no. 2/3, 2001, pp. 32-46.

[STR 94] STRAUSS A., CORBIN J., *Basics of Qualitative Research: Grounded Theory, Procedures and Techniques*, Sage Publications, 1994.

[SWI 07] SWINK M., NARASIMHAN R., WANG C., "Managing beyond the factory walls: effects of four types of strategic integration on manufacturing plant performance", *Journal of Operations Management*, vol. 25, no. 1, 2007, pp. 148-64.

[TAK 01] TAKEISHI A., "Bridging inter- and intra-firm boundaries: Management of supplier involvement in automobile product development", *Strategic Management Journal*, vol. 22, no. 5, 2001, pp. 403–433.

[TEE 97] TEECE D.J., PISANO G., SHUEN A., "Dynamic capabilities and strategic management", *Strategic Management Journal*, vol. 18, no. 7, 1997, pp. 509–533.

[VAC 08] VACHON S., KLASSEN R.D., "Extending green practices across the supply chain: the impact of upstream and downstream integration", *International Journal of Operations & Production Management*, vol. 26, no. 7, 2008, pp. 795-821.

[VAN 85] VAN DE VEN A. H, DRAZIN R., "The concept of fit in contingency theory", *Research in Organizational Behaviour*, vol. 7, 1985, pp. 333-365.

[VEN 84] VENKATRAMAN N., CAMILLUS J.C., "Exploring the concept of "fit" in Strategic Management", *Academy of Management Review*, vol. 9, no. 3, 1984, pp. 513-525.

[VEN 89] VENKATRAMAN N., "The concept of fit in strategy research: toward verbal and statistical correspondence", *Academy of Management Review*, vol. 14, no. 3, 1989, pp. 423-444.

[VEN 90a] VENKATRAMAN N., "Performance implications of strategic co-alignment: a methodological perspective", *Journal of Management Studies*, vol. 27, 1990, pp. 19–41.

[VEN 90b] VENKATRAMAN N., PRESCOTT J.E., "Environment-strategy coalignment: an empirical test of its performance implications", *Strategic Management Journal*, vol. 11, 1990, pp. 1-23.

[VER 06] VEREECKE A., MUYLLE S., "Performance improvement through supply chain collaboration in Europe", *International Journal of Operations & Production Management*, vol. 26, no. 11, 2006, pp. 1176-1198.

[VIC 03] VICKERY S.K., JAYARAM J., DROGE C., CALANTONE R., "The effects of an integrative supply chain strategy on customer service and financial performance: an analysis of direct versus indirect relationships", *Journal of Operations Management*, vol. 21, no. 5, 2003, pp. 523-39.

[WER 84] WERNERFELT B., "A resource-based view of the firm", *Strategic Management Journal*, vol 5, no. 2, 1984, pp. 171-180.

[WHI 07] WHIPPLE J.M., RUSSELL D., "Building supply chain collaboration: a typology of collaborative approaches", *International Journal of Logistics Management*, vol. 18, no. 2, 2007, pp. 174-196.

[WIL 85] WILLIAMSON O. E., *The Economic Institutions of Capitalism*, The Free Press, New York, 1985.

[WU 08] WU A.D., ZUMBO B.D., "Understanding and using mediators and moderators, social", *Indicators Research*, vol. 87, no. 3, 2008, pp. 367-392.

Chapter 2

Information-sharing Practices and their Impacts on Supply Chain Performance

2.1. Introduction

To meet the strong challenges of global competition, companies are constantly in search of new ways to improve the performance of their supply chain. This organizational change requires them to strengthen coordination and collaboration mechanisms (see Chapter 1), such as information-sharing practices. The following questions must be considered:

– What is the nature of the information that can be shared with customers and suppliers?

– How can this exchange be done? Which information system can support it?

– What impact can we expect on the performance of a company? How is the performance of the whole supply chain affected?

– Are information-sharing practices dependent on the parameters or context of the organization? If so, how?

In this chapter, we propose a *conceptual framework for analyzing or "questioning" information exchange practices* that organizations implement or could implement with their supply chain partners. By highlighting the characterization of both the information content and the exchange mechanism, this

Chapter written by Valérie BOTTA-GENOULAZ and Claude PELLEGRIN.

framework allows us to investigate the relationship between companies' configurations and their information-sharing practices in order to ensure coordination within their supply chains.

An analysis of the scientific literature shows that empirical studies do not address *all* the attributes of information exchange, such as information content, exchange processes, firms' configurations, etc. Our framework, on the other hand, can serve as a reference for comparing both empirical and analytical/simulation studies of the relationship between information-sharing practices and performance.

This framework can also be of particular interest to practitioners: it can be used to model the relationships between the parameters of an organization and the nature and intensity of the collaboration with its partners, or to identify and measure the impacts of information sharing on its performance.

This chapter is organized as follows: section 2.2 contributes to the framework of questioning. After discussing the role of information and information systems (IS) in organizations, we look at how companies have gradually used information technologies (IT) and IS as support for integrating intra- and inter-organizational processes. We investigate the contribution of IT and IS collaboration to supply chain performance. Section 2.3 reviews some research studies on the impact of information sharing by emphasizing the content of shared information and the conditions of information exchange in order to provide theoretical foundations for the framework proposed in section 2.4. Section 2.5 uses two examples to illustrate analyses that can be conducted using this questioning framework. Finally, we conclude in section 2.6 by highlighting the advantages of this framework, both for researchers and for practitioners.

2.2. Role of information and IS in supply chain collaboration

The sharing of tasks within an organization creates coordination needs that have to be fulfilled in order to ensure coherence. Negotiated and organized searches for coherence involve the processing and communication of information. Most surveys show that communication problems are a major impediment to the good performance of an organization. Lack of communication or miscommunication results in coordination gaps and a lack of relevance of knowledge representations used in the organization. Information, which contributes to organizational coherence, is the basis for the functioning of organizations [REI 02]. This leads us to a practical interest in information sharing.

Individual or collective decisions are based on representations whose relevance ensures effectiveness. The consistency of multiple decisions is based on coordination where the communication of information is essential. To act effectively, the organization must have relevant representations of its environment; it must be able to interpret the signals received in order to understand the world around it (interpret to understand).

Although the environment is evolving, the organization will therefore seek to learn and to select effective responses to stimuli it receives. These learning processes presuppose the existence of devices for storing information within the organization (remember to learn). This leads us to study the devices used to manage and share information.

Section 2.2.1 introduces the notions of information and IS in and between organizations. We review the numerous application programs (modules, application components) that an information system is composed of, and propose a classification of their components. Section 2.2.2 highlights the role of IS and IT in supporting the exchange of information required for business process integration. Finally, in section 2.2.3 we highlight the contribution of IT/IS to supply chain collaboration and supply chain performance.

2.2.1. *Information and information systems*

Scientific literature is very rich in definitions of IS. Alter [ALT 96] defines an IS as an organized set of resources (hardware, software, personnel, data, procedures, etc.) which uses information IT to capture, transmit, store, retrieve, manipulate or display information used in one or more business processes. Specifically, we note that an IS is a device that allows the management of information related to the functioning of a company, for some or all stages of design, sourcing, production, distribution and sales to the company's customers.

By "system", we mean a "systematic arrangement" of the collection of information deemed relevant, and of their processing by or for the various participants likely to use such information in their activities.

By "information", we mean all data: raw or "processed" (that is, made understandable to potential users). The nature of this information can be widely diverse, depending on the extent of the IS and its fundamental objectives.

Considered originally as a matter of automation of repetitive administrative tasks, the issue of effective and efficient use of information and communication technologies has now become strategic. It concerns any organization, regardless of its size and scope of activity. The evolution of these technologies has contributed to the development of information and business management systems, with a constant expansion of the functional and decision-making scope. The first functional application have been replaced by enterprise resource planning (ERP) systems, complemented by the decision-support systems designed to conform to new optimization needs, either internally or across an organization's borders.

As noted by Robey *et al.* [ROB 00], research on IT designed to support organizational learning produces three main conclusions. First, value is produced by the creation of conceptual designs for organizational memory IS. Second, information technologies enhance organizational learning by increasing members' communication and by supporting discourse among them. Third, information technologies may both enable and disable organizational learning. They conclude that systems designed to support organizational learning aim to enhance organizational effectiveness in fundamental ways. Organizational memory can be actualized with IT, and shared cognition can be encouraged through systems that link members together while providing access to structured and unstructured data. These conclusions can be extended to organization networks, such as supply chains.

In the field of operations planning, advanced planning capabilities were added to ERP systems with the emergence of advanced planning and scheduling (APS) systems or supply chain planning (SCP) systems. Extended to several entities in the case of multinational or multi-site organizations, they can manage and optimize the supply chain. Other features have been developed to cover all activities of supply chain management at the operational level: SCEM (supply chain event management) systems, SCE (supply chain execution) systems, WMS (warehouse management system), AOM (advanced order management) systems, TMS (transportation management system). In order to support the product design process, other complementary application software packages have been proposed, such as PDM (product data management) systems and PLM (product lifecycle management) systems.

Customer relationship management (CRM), at the heart of a business' concerns, has also been developing with the emergence of CRM software, whose philosophy is to anticipate the demand for better knowledge of customer expectations. The management of partner relationships has taken advantage of new communications technologies to deploy functions of e-business (e-commerce, business-to-business, business-to-consumer, e-procurement, market-place, etc.) aiming to link the different actors of the company's business and their IS. In the field of management, the proliferation of information available in databases has made it very difficult to identify the information carrier of value. Decision support systems – or business intelligence (BI) – are then supplements to the IS in the field of data analysis and reporting. While the ERP system remains the core of a company's information system, we are witnessing an expansion of its functional area, with the addition of upstream supply chain management functions and downstream customer-relationship management functions. These extensions enable better visibility and traceability of the supply chain as a whole.

Given the diversity and abundance of current acronyms, we propose the concept of "application component" in order to ensure a pragmatic and neutral usage with regard to business software companies. An application component is a commercial software application that supports a partial generic business model and specific business processes [MIL 08b]. This cannot be taken from a partition technique of all current applications, given the heterogeneity of commercial software, their overlaps and duplicate definitions. It is based on the theory of a "generic enterprise module" in the business modeling method Generalized Enterprise Reference Architecture and Methodology (GERAM) [BER 97], and the concept of COTS ("commercial off the shelf") sometimes referred to as "on the shelf components" [ALB 02]. The higher the level of integration, the more the application architecture is the image of organizational choices (and not of data or functionality distribution). Therefore, it is the analysis of business processes that provides the best basis for the classification of features for a "universal" representation of application components, suitable for composing a supply chain information system (see Figure 2.1). This can be viewed as an extension of the system architecture for supply chain management proposed by Verwijmeren [VER 04].

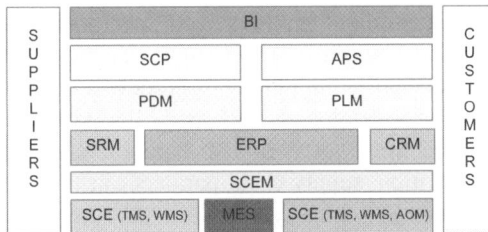

BI	Business Intelligence
APS	Advance Planning and Scheduling
SCP	Supply Chain Planning
PDM	Product Data Management
PLM	Product Lifecycle Management
SRM	Supplier Relationship Management
ERP	Enterprise Resource Planning
CRM	Customer Relationship Management
SCEM	Supply Chain Event Management
SCE	Supply Chain Execution
TMS	Transport Management System
WMS	Warehouse Management System
AOM	Advanced Order Management
MES	Manufacturing Execution System

Figure 2.1. *Software application components [MIL 08b]*

Further on in this chapter, we explore the application components affected by information that a firm can share with suppliers or customers.

2.2.2. IS and IT for information exchange and business process integration

Information sharing is a key for the integration of intra- or inter-organizational business processes. In this section, we explore the various ways that companies have successively achieved this integration.

During the 1990s, ERP systems were introduced as an approach to systems integration. ERP systems support generic processes that attempt to integrate the internal supply chain of a firm [BOT 05, BOT 07]. At intra-organizational level, this can be achieved more easily in cases where enterprises replace most of their legacy systems with ERP modules. For many years, organizations have focused on electronic data interchange (EDI) technology to improve the automation of inter-organizational business processes and supply chains. Although organizations gained significant benefits from the use of EDI, they turned to the use of the internet due to EDI limitations (e.g. high cost, inflexible technology) [STE 02].

Intra- and inter-organizational integration can also be achieved through enterprise application integration (EAI), which incorporates functionality from disparate applications and leads to cheaper, more functional and manageable IT infrastructures. Themistocleous *et al.* [THE 04] propose a framework for evaluating the portfolio of integration technologies, such as EAI, used to unify inter- and intra-organizational IS. They define two types of integration: loose and tight. Based on these two types of integration, supply chain partners can form: (a) loosely-coupled training partnerships through which information may be shared; or (b) tightly-integrated chains where there is a higher degree of process dependency. They analyze the characteristics of integration according to the system category to integrate – packaged (e.g. ERP), custom, (e.g. legacy) or e-business (e.g. e-store) – and identify seven permutations: custom-to-custom, custom-to-packaged, custom-to-e-business, packaged-to-packaged, packaged-to-e-business, e-business-to-e-business, and custom-to-packaged-to-e-business. For each of them, they analyze the most efficient technologies for system integration, i.e. for coordination.

Nowadays, economic development and collaboration between firms leads to increased information exchange between different organizations, and increasingly to real "inter-organizational IS". Inter-organizational information systems (IOIS) will function to support the different business processes from "design" to "deliver" – processes that cross the boundaries of an organization [AUB 02]. Williamson *et al.* [WIL 04] define an IOIS as a collection of IT resources, including communication networks, hardware IT applications, standards for data transmission, and human skills and experiences. It provides a framework for electronic cooperation between businesses by allowing for the processing, sharing and communication of information. Many researchers have analyzed the impact of IOIS on organizational structure and management of supply chains [HOL 95, HUM 01, WIL 04]. They show that entities in the chain develop cooperative relationships that make the whole chain more competitive. Holland concluded that IOIS reduce competition among suppliers and customers of the same chain and that this competition is now between several channels and not between several individual entities. Further development on strategic inter-organizational alignment can be found in Part II of this book.

Many authors note that developments in IS and IT, if used effectively, appear to promise the ability to significantly improve collaboration between trading partners in ways that can increase supply chain agility [WHI 05]. In the following section, we highlight the contribution of IS and IT to supply chain collaboration and supply chain performance.

2.2.3. *Contribution of IT/IS to supply chain performance*

The role of IS or IT in supply chain management or supply chain coordination has been studied extensively in the scientific literature [AKK 03, BAR 02, CHE 07, EDW 01, ENG 06, KEN 97, SAN 02, SOL 04, WIL 04]. The analysis of the use of certain application components, such as ERP or APS as the applications most frequently used by business, enable us to identify their advantages and limits as regards supply chain collaborative practices. ERP systems are recognized as an essential tool in the digitization of business processes [MIL 08a], but their scope rarely integrates upstream and downstream channel systems based on dedicated software (e.g. SRM, SCM or CRM).

The equipment of supply chain partners does not appear to have reached the level of integration desired by the participants themselves, who are aware of the needs in this area. ERP systems, meanwhile, offer companies the required level of internal functional integration to implement interdependence of business processes with external entities. Information needs relating to control and planning activities remain, however, even in the case of ERP implementation. Similarly, the analysis of the use of APS shows a low integration of the processes while the need to collaborate is shared by the participants [GRU 09]. Moreover, it shows a partial use of APS modules: preferences are given to "demand management" modules, to the detriment of those dedicated to planning and scheduling.

Some authors have also studied the importance of IT and information sharing in supply chain management.

Contingencies	Relationships within SCM	
	Focal – upstream (Trader as a buyer)	Focal – downstream (Trader as a supplier)
Asymmetry	Increase the power over the upstream firms (influence the upstream firm's business processes)	Increase the bargaining power over the downstream firm or decrease the power of downstream firms over the local firm through diffusing the IOIS to downstream firms
Reciprocity	Information sharing (facilitating virtual business network)	Information sharing, better customer service (e.g., easier purchase and product information request)
Efficiency	Reduce coordination cost*	Reduce coordination cost*
Stability	Increase focal organization's stability (e.g., by locking the suppliers)	Increase focal organization's stability (e.g., by locking the customers and building competitor's entry barrier)
Legitimacy	Increase the reputation of focal firm as well as its upstream firms	Increase the reputation of focal firm as well as its downstream firms

* Coordination cost includes: (1) the cost of searching for suppliers and buyers; (2) the cost of maintaining the relationship; (3) the transaction cost.

Figure 2.2. *IOR contingencies within SCM [HUM 01]*

Gunasekaran *et al.* [GUN 04] have carried out a large-scale literature review and have developed a framework with the objective of finding pertinent factors and useful insights related to the role and implications of IT in supply chain management. This framework highlights the role of IT in supporting the pursuit of performance in supply chains. Humphrey *et al.* [HUM 01] have reviewed the theoretical foundations for the study of inter-organizational relationships within a supply chain management context and have analyzed the contingencies of deploying IOIS. They have proposed a framework that deploys IOIS from an IOIS provider's perspective (see Figure 2.2). These authors highlight the role of information-sharing practices to ensure the reciprocity in "focal-upstream" and "focal-downstream" relationships.

As seen in the introduction of this book, Simatupang *et al.* [SIM 02] analyze the role of IT in relation to the coordination mechanisms of integrated supply chains. They propose a framework of knowledge that unifies the different modes of coordination required to integrate the supply chain processes of different partners in order to achieve chain profitability (see Figure 2.1). Information-sharing practices appear as one of the four coordination modes. Each mode has different contexts and emphasizes different cognitive processes. Information sharing coordination attempts to achieve the coherency of information, while participants cooperate with one another and follow the rules of disseminating information across borders. It attempts to make relevant, accurate and timely information available to decision makers. Simatupang *et al.* also suggest key drivers of coordination modes that have positive impacts on supply chain performance (see Figure 2.3).

Figure 2.3. *Key drivers of coordination modes [SIM 02]*

We conclude that IS and IT provide important support for collaboration in supply chains. Whatever technical method is adopted to manage integration (EDI, internet, EAI, IOIS, etc.), it appears that complementary organizational or social factors are also to be considered.

2.2.4. *Conclusion*

In this section, we have seen the role and the importance of information as an element of consistency and openness of an organization. Supply chain management often requires the integration of inter- and intra-organizational relationships and coordination of different types of flows within the entire supply chain structure. Inter-company integration and coordination via IT has become a key to improved supply chain performance. Recent advances in IT are enabling firms to effectively and inexpensively manage the coordination of the physical flow of materials as well as different types of information through a supply chain.

Recently, more attention has been given in the literature to the issue of measuring the magnitude and effectiveness of available information that logistics IS provide. Here, researchers have sought to provide frameworks to analyze the impact of collaborative practices on performance. The following section focuses on the role of the content and exchange conditions of information sharing between partners in the chain.

2.3. Role of content and conditions in information sharing

Although numerous empirical studies have investigated the impact of collaborative practices on performance (see Chapter 1), few have focused exclusively on information-sharing practices. Of those, even fewer seek to link performance with variables qualifying the "what" and the "how" of information exchange and the business conditions (environment, organization, etc.) that influence information sharing. Zhou and Benton's work [ZHO 07] is a noticeable exception, since it tests the linkages among supply chain dynamism as a proxy for the environmental conditions of exchange, information sharing, supply chain practice (namely supply chain planning, just-in-time (JIT) production, and delivery practice), and delivery performance. In this section, we review some research on the impact of information sharing by emphasizing the content of shared information and the conditions of information exchange in order to provide theoretical foundations for the questioning framework elaborated in section 2.4.

2.3.1. *Content of shared information and performance*

2.3.1.1. *Some limits of empirical research on the "what" of the exchange*

Information sharing is a key variable of empirical research on the relationship between collaboration and performance (see Table 1.1 in Chapter 1). A thorough examination of constructs used in these studies, however, shows that the content of shared information is not always explicit. Information sharing appears in some items used for the measurement of an encompassing construct (e.g. "integrated external operations" and "integrated internal operations" in [ROD 04], "feedback seeking" in [BAG 05], "communication" in [FYN 05], "supplier integration" and "customer integration" in [SWI 07]). These items, however, do not specify the content of shared information. Sometimes, the items measuring the "information-sharing" construct only refer to an information area: operational information, performance measures, best practices, and supply chain arrangements [STA 01]. When the operationalization of constructs makes this content explicit, it may not reflect all possible directions of exchange: to or from suppliers, and to or from customers.

For example, [KUL 04, GER 06, GIM 05] only consider downstream information: consumer needs, store inventory levels and warehouse inventory levels in [KUL 04]; sales forecasts, sales and stock levels in [GIM 05]; and joint sales forecast, actual sales data, and planned promotions in [GER 06]. Stank *et al.* [STA 99], however, distinguish downstream information according to the direction of exchange: special promotions, pricing changes, information on new/discontinued products, shipment problems, removals date, events and production schedules in the "to customer" case, and demand forecasts and point-of-sale demands in the "from customer" case.

As a partial conclusion, it appears that empirical research sheds limited light on the question of what information the players in the supply chain should share. This is partly due to the fragmentation of empirical research from the point of view of the variable "content". The choice of appropriate information to share for effective performance has not been a focus of research: some models only consider types of upstream information and others only types of downstream information. The effect of interactions of information types simultaneously exchanged with suppliers, customers and intermediate partners (retailers, distributors, etc.), is seldom taken into account. The framework built in section 2.4 for questioning information-sharing practices will seek to clarify all types of information exchanged and their interactions in a general supply chain structure (see Figures 2.4 and 2.5 in section 2.4).

2.3.1.2. *Inseparability between content and quality of exchange*

The question of content exchange must not be divorced from that of how well or to what extent information is exchanged. Barut *et al.* [BAR 02] apply this idea when they define a measure of the coupling between members of the supply chain. The measure, called degree of supply chain coupling (DSCC), is a two-tuple index, which takes into account both the intensity and extent to which information about demand, capacity, inventory and scheduling is shared and used by the firm in both directions of the supply chain. This allows for measuring inter-company integration and coordination via IT to improve supply chain performance.

Zhou *et al.* [ZHO 07] also address this notion of information quality, i.e. the degree to which the information exchanged between organizations meets the needs of the organizations. They propose an interesting literature review on the ways to consider this notion. Information accuracy appears as the main criterion [McC 99, McG 98, NEU 79, PET 99, SUM 95]. Other criteria are added, depending on the authors: frequency or intensity of exchange [McC 99, NEU 79, VIJ 97], and readability and accessibility of information in [PET 99].

As for Zhou *et al.* [ZHO 07], they propose two empirical constructs for the theoretical construct "information sharing", namely "information content" and "information quality". They measure information quality on nine scales corresponding to the following attributes: accuracy, availability, timeliness, internal connectivity, external connectivity, completeness, relevance, accessibility, and frequently updated information. The framework presented in section 2.4 addresses this question of content/quality of exchanged information by emphasizing attributes that, together, shape the quality. For this purpose, we have selected: the level of aggregation of the information with regard to product and time, the temporal characteristics (experience of exchange and frequency), the precise statement of the departments concerned by the use of information, and the characteristics related to the ways of recording information and that provide reliability and reliance (see section 2.4.3).

2.3.2. *Conditions of information exchange and performance*

The influence of the exchange environment on the relationship between information sharing and performance is a well-known aspect of empirical analysis. We break down these conditions of exchange into two broad categories, according to whether they relate to the intrinsic configuration of exchange (configuration parameters of the supply chain, type of business processes concerned, technological environment of the exchange, etc.) or to extrinsic influence variables (barriers or favoring factors related to the exchange environment).

2.3.2.1. *Configuration parameters influencing information sharing*

By the configuration parameters of supply chains, we mean the parameters intrinsic to the supply chain and relating to the demand, product and process characteristics, the type of industry, etc. As several researchers have shown, some supply chain configuration parameters influence the relationships between supply chain partners. Lee *et al.* [LEE 97], for example, have initiated an important stream of research on the effects of demand variability on the need for information sharing: retailer demand variability causes a bullwhip effect that can adversely affect supply chain performance and increase the need for greater supply chain coordination.

Li *et al.* [LI 06] show that supply chain management practices may be influenced by contextual factors, such as the type of industry, firm size, a firm's position in the supply chain, supply chain length, and the type of supply chain. Studies that are more interesting connect supply chain configuration, information-sharing practices and performance.

For example, Van der Vaart *et al.* [VAA 04] consider two extreme configurations in supply chains. On the one hand, supply chains have to cope with uncertainty in volume, mix and lead time. They are particularly concerned by the operations related to supplier-buyer linkages. On the other hand, supply chains are predominantly cost-driven. They focus on shared network resources, i.e. common-capacity sources in two or more supply chains or networks, but do not require high levels of integration.

Van Donk *et al.* [DON 04] call these configuration parameters "business conditions" and Welker *et al.* consider that the "business conditions, and especially their complexity determine the characteristics of supply chain linkages and influence information-sharing practices in order processing" [WEL 08, p. 708]. Welker *et al.* propose an overview of the business conditions that may influence information sharing. Drawn from a literature review of empirical research, this framework distinguishes five areas of *business conditions*:

– time elapsed from order request to delivery (delivery time);

– "order winners", i.e. the capabilities (cost, speed, reliability, quality, and flexibility) that ensure a competitive advantage;

– variety of demand and type of supply chain relationship (from regular to incidental customers);

– product and process characteristics (number of product lines, product composition, batch size, etc.);

– position of customer order decoupling point (Engineer to order, make to order, assemble to order, and make to stock).

The main finding of Welker *et al.*'s empirical research is that simple business conditions need limited information sharing and some use of standard information and communication technologies (in particular ERP). Complex business conditions, on the other hand, require greater sharing of external information and traditional forms of communication. The impact of these business conditions on information-sharing practices justifies the choice of variables characterizing the configuration and complexity of the supply chain in the questioning framework developed in section 2.4.

2.3.2.2. Environmental influence on information sharing

In empirical research analyzing the impact of collaborative practices, such as information-sharing practices on supply chain performance, environmental variables often appear as moderators of the collaboration–performance relationship. The link between environmental variables, information sharing and performance may however be more complex. In the following two sections, we discuss this point. For this purpose, we distinguish two sources of influential environmental factors in the empirical research literature: business environment and collaboration environment.

2.3.2.2.1. Influence of the business environment

The influence of the business environment on information-sharing practices rests on two theoretical pillars: contingency theory and Galbraith's information processing theory [GAL 73]. Contingency theory states that the match of strategy to environment predicts performance. On this basis, Fisher's model [FIS 97] and Lee's model [LEE 02] identify different supply chain strategies, depending on the uncertainty and turbulence of markets. These strategies have a common foundation borrowed from Galbraith's theory: as uncertainty and turbulence in the environment increase, information-processing capacity needs to increase in order to achieve superior performance. Precisely, in supply chains, sharing information among supply-chain members is one way to increase information-processing capacity.

This theoretical frame leads Zhou *et al.* [ZHO 07], for example, to investigate the influence of *business environmental dynamism* on information sharing and supply chain practices. By *environmental dynamism*, they characterize unpredictable changes in products, technologies, and demand for products in the market. For this purpose, they measure the theoretical construct of business environmental dynamism using three empirical constructs emphasizing the part of new products in the total revenue of the company and the innovation rate in products and operating processes. Data collected from 125 North American manufacturing firms show that supply chain dynamism has a significant positive influence on effective information sharing and effective supply chain practice, but that it has more influence on information sharing than supply chain practice.

Another way to understand the above theoretical framework is to consider that information sharing is a mediator between business environment, supply chain strategy and performance:

[(business environment → supply chain strategy) → information sharing] → performance

For instance, in Paulraj *et al.* [PAU 08], information sharing and other collaborative practices are embedded in a theoretical construct, namely "inter-organizational communication" equated to a relational competency. Business environment is then translated into terms of long-term relationship orientation, network governance, and IT, which together influence the choice of practices requiring information sharing for superior performance.

These considerations argue for the inclusion of variables relating to external factors (sales variability, variability of economic performance, intensity of competition, etc.) and to strategic objectives in a framework aiming (as in section 2.4) to question information-sharing practice.

2.3.2.2.2. Influence of the collaboration environment

The role of the collaboration environment, and particularly of barriers to information sharing, is a central concern in the supply chain literature. Fawcett *et al.* [FAW 08], for example, present a literature review of practices and requirements for effective supply chain collaboration. They portray a contingency framework linking driving forces, resisting forces and collaboration initiatives. Among the latter, relationship management and trust building appear as key elements for effective collaboration. Their empirical research also highlights another central element for the manager: the location of power within the supply chain. We focus below on these two influencing factors of information sharing: power and trust.

The work of Maloni and Benton [MAL 00] has been reported in a seminal paper on the role and subsequent importance of power in the supply chain. Grounded in previous, well-known classifications of power bases [FRE 59, HUN 74], their framework identifies the different bases of inter-firm power and empirically shows contrasting effects of the different sources of power upon inter-firm relationships in the supply chain. Recent studies deepen this influence of power on the supply chain. Zhao *et al.* [ZHA 08] focus on customer integration and empirically test a model that represents the relationship between customer power, relationship commitment and customer integration in a supply chain. Belaya *et al.* [BEL 09] assume that power in supply chains has two sides: negative and positive. They present a conceptual framework on how the different aspects of power can be effectively used as mechanisms to manage alignment of actions, that is coordination and alignment of interests, i.e. cooperation.

Trust is one of the parameters of supply chain information exchange most studied (see Chapter 8 for a review on the concept of trust and the effects of trust in supply chains). Trust is sometimes regarded as a barrier to information exchange [AKI 00] or a moderator of the collaboration–performance relationship [COR 05]. It is sometimes seen as a condition for exchange [FYN 05, KLE 07, SHI 07, YAN 08]. Indeed, several authors link power and trust. Dapiran *et al.* [DAP 03] ask: "Are co-operation and trust being confused with power?" Power may be seen as the antithesis of trust [KUM 98] and it undermines the trust within the relationship [MAL 97]. However, power is the way to build trust: informational power to build trust [EYU 91], and reward power to promote cooperation and generate trust in the relationship [GAS 86]. Belaya *et al.* [BEL 09] argue that "referent power" (the good power base) should be used to build trust.

These findings justify the consideration of power in our framework on information sharing in practice (section 2.4). We seek to understand how supply chain managers perceive the power influence of different stakeholders on variables that determine the supply chain performance. In line with previous reflection on the link between power and trust, in section 2.4 we consider that the variable "trust" is encapsulated in the construct "influence and power".

2.4. Conceptual framework for questioning information-sharing practices

This section presents a conceptual framework for questioning information-sharing practices in supply chains. We adopt the point of view of a focal firm (FF) in the supply chain, which has several suppliers (S), several customers (C), and possibly some intermediate partners (IP). An intermediary partner may be a third party or another entity, such as a distributor, warehouse, platform, etc., that is administered by the focal firm (see Figure 2.4).

Our conceptual framework allows for the characterization of the context of this FF and of the downstream and upstream information-sharing practices. Particular attention is paid to describing the nature of shared information and of the exchange. With this framework we are able to analyze the link between companies' configurations and information-sharing practices, so that coordination between supply-chain participants can be guaranteed. We can also study the conditions and impact of information sharing and collaborative processes on the functioning and dynamics of each entity in a supply chain.

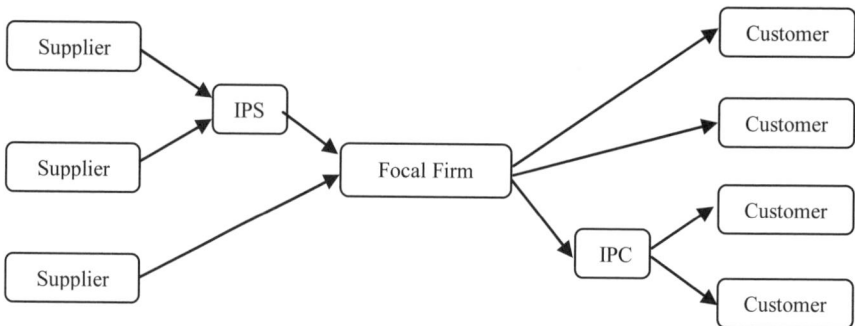

Figure 2.4. *Supply chain structure*

Specifically, the framework allows us to link:

– the firm's configurations (the general context of the focal company, its strategy, the characteristics of its product lines, supply chain, partners, organizational capabilities on which it bases its responsiveness to markets, etc.); and

– collaborative practices that are (or may be) implemented in certain key business processes (customer relationship management, forecasting, demand management, production planning, etc.) in order to ensure the coordination with supply chain partners for a better supply chain performance. These collaborative practices are characterized by their own content – the "what" – and their own process – the "how".

This framework is designed for managers seeking to account for their information-sharing practices and wanting to assess the perceived performance of their supply chain. It answers the question: "What are the actual sharing practices in my company, given its configuration?"

After introducing the business information on which the exchange is conducted (section 2.4.1), we present the structure of the questioning framework in section 2.4.2. The constructs proposed to model the firm's configuration are introduced in section 2.4.3, and those for information-sharing practices, in section 2.4.4.

2.4.1. *Nature of information to share*

Informal or formal, transactional or managerial, unidirectional or shared, internal or transverse – information sharing is the foundation of any collaborative relationship. Much of the existing research focuses on information sharing within supply chains and seeks to identify information that can be shared in order to assess the impact of the exchange and distribution of the expected gain, or to discuss technical issues raised by this exchange.

Many authors have sought to identify information that may be shared in order to improve the performance of the chain [FIA 05, FLY 10, GAO 01, LAU 04, LEE 00, LIU 03, LLE 06, RYU 09, SAH 05, SHO 01, WEL 08, YU 10]. Such information mainly concerns products, resources, inventories, times and dates, demand and sales. Some findings in the literature suggest sharing as much information as possible to increase benefits, while others have shown that the value of the exchange depends on the nature of shared information. For example, Yu *et al.* [YU 10] have concluded from their empirical study that sharing information on capacity and/or inventory only, without sharing information on demand, interferes with production at manufacturers and causes misunderstandings, which can magnify the bullwhip effect. Complementary findings on the value of information sharing are developed in Chapter 9.

Section 2.4.1.1 gives some details about the type of information shared in a supply chain: products, resources, inventories, times and dates, demand and sales. In section 2.4.1.2, we present the selection of information, which supports our questioning.

2.4.1.1. *Information description*

2.4.1.1.1. Product information

The information on products exchanged along the supply chain are specifically related to their techno-economic characteristics and their production conditions at different stages of the chain, like product structure, product specifications, bill of materials, routings, etc. Such information is therefore a questioning on the constitution of the supply chain. It might be shared between potential partners when designing or building a supply chain. The concept of production costs or logistics costs is addressed mainly in terms of impacts that cost changes may have on storage policies or production schedules.

2.4.1.1.2. Resource information

Information on resources is frequently shared in a supply chain, since the knowledge capacity of each partner in the chain directly determines its flexibility and ability to adapt to internal (failure of partner) and external (final demand) risks. Examples include resource capability, resource capacity, batch size, ordering production and shipment.

2.4.1.1.3. Inventory information

Information on inventories concerns on-hand, backlog, work-in-process, stock availability for raw materials, intermediate products or final products. They can be grouped into three categories: inventory level at each stage of the supply chain, inventory costs incurred at each stage of the process, and finally inventory parameters and policies (make-to-stock, make-to-order, assemble-to-order, or engineer-to-order) adopted by each partner. This exchange of information is often at the heart of collaborative work because it allows for the synchronization and coordination of various physical flows between business partners.

2.4.1.1.4. Information on times and dates

Production times, delivery times and due dates are the three main types of data exchanged. It is not so much the time length that is central in the information exchanges but its changes over time or the nature of the hazard that weighs on it.

Planning information completes this category, with information such as order status and production schedule.

2.4.1.1.5. Demand and sales information

This category of information is the most studied in the scientific literature, as it has a direct influence on the bullwhip effect (see Chapters 9 and 10). Concerning information on demand or sales (i.e. sales data, sales forecasts), generally two kinds of data are shared: information relating to end-market demand (sales forecast, demand characteristics, distribution parameters, and customer requirement information) and information relating to the orders from each partner in the chain (order quantity).

This second category of information represents a sort of transcript of final demand by downstream firms that integrate their own constraints and operating conditions. This information then refers to the data produced from this "translated" final demand: production and procurement planning. The value of the exchange is not so much on the information itself but more on the logic and procedures leading to the development of various plans that are communicated along the supply chain, such as order status for tracking and tracing.

2.4.1.2. Information selected for the questioning framework

Based on this review, we propose to use the framework to study six types of information to be shared both up- and downstream. For each type of information, we explain the direction of the sharing, either from the FF to the partner (supplier S or customer C) – denoted FF→S or FF→C – or from the partner to the focal firm – denoted S→FF or C→FF, as illustrated in Figure 2.5. Table 2.1 summarizes these elements.

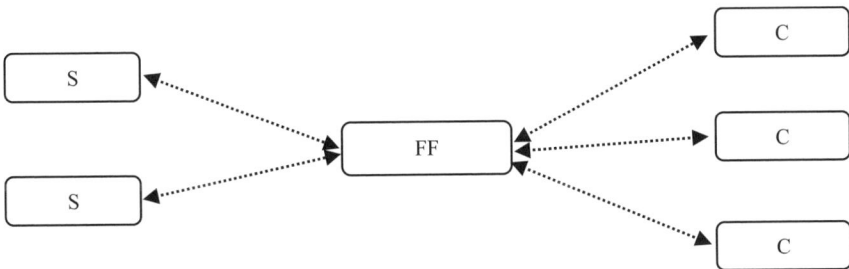

Figure 2.5. *Information exchanges in the supply chain*

Upstream information	Direction of sharing	Downstream information	Direction of sharing
Production plans	FF→S	Customer activity: customer sales and expected demand	C→FF
Production planning parameters (capacity, batch sizes, planning mode, manufacturing lead time)	S→FF	Business strategy	C→FF
Purchase request forecasts	FF→S	Customer inventory level	C→FF
Focal firm's quality procedures Supplier's quality procedures	FF→S S→FF	Delivery time, customer's required delivery	FF→C
Purchase order tracking and tracing	S→FF	Customer order tracking and tracing	FF→C
Inventory management policies: – focal firm's information: replenishment rules, safety stock, raw materials inventory level – supplier's information: safety stock, order point, finished product inventory level	FF→S S→FF	Production management policies: – focal firm's information: replenishment rules, manufacturing batch size, distribution batch size – customer's information: replenishment rules safety stock, order point, manufacturing batch size, inventory level	FF→C C→FF

Table 2.1. *Information selected for the questioning framework*

2.4.2. *Structure of the questioning framework*

The proposed framework is structured in four levels: theoretical constructs, empirical constructs, attributes, and variables (i.e. questions), as described below.

– A theoretical construct "organization configuration" qualifies the configuration of the organization studied. This construct enables us to analyze two types of issue. Those that relate: (i) to the firm's organizational capabilities, used to align its logistics operations on general strategy, i.e. supply chain capabilities (according to [GIL 99]); and (ii) to the collaboration capabilities (according to [BOW 03], given the overall objective of the framework), developed to take advantage of competitive inter-organizational collaboration. This theoretical construct is articulated with three empirical constructs:

- the empirical construct "internal and external environment and objectives" characterizes the importance of internal and external factors for the operation and competitiveness of the FF, as well as its strategic and logistic objectives;

- the empirical construct "product offering" characterizes the variability, the specificity of both products and production system of the FF;

- the empirical construct "supply-chain configuration" characterizes physical flows in terms of lead time, the partners in terms of number and influence, and the role of the FF's IS and IT.

– A theoretical construct "information-sharing practice", which qualifies the collaborative practices by a *content* and a *process* that make it possible to structure questions related to the following: the business processes concerned by the collaboration; the relationship opportunities associated with these business processes; the instrumentation of this collaboration; and the perceived performance involved in the collaboration. We focus here on 12 information-sharing practices, derived from the six natures of information identified in section 2.4.1.2., both up- and downstream from the focal company. We thereby evaluate the existence and weight of each practice (i.e. the proportion of partners with which the focal organization shares the information), and concentrate the analysis on the most accomplished relationship:

- the empirical construct "content" characterizes the information shared (the "what"): its level of aggregation, the business departments concerned by its use, the application component that records it, and its perceived impact on the performance;

- the empirical construct "process" characterizes the exchange (the "how"): its temporal characteristics (age, frequency), its originator (the focal firm or the partner), the application component from which the information is extracted, the communication technology used for the exchange, and its contracting parameters.

The linking of the construct "organization configuration" and the construct "information-sharing practice" (i.e. the variables that characterize both constructs) makes it possible to identify correlations, to explain the efficiency of some business processes, or the performance of the organization or of the supply chain.

It is also possible to identify patterns linking characteristics of the organization and information-sharing practices (see Figure 2.6). The business departments that take part in the exchange, confirmed by the application components, allow for recognition of the business processes.

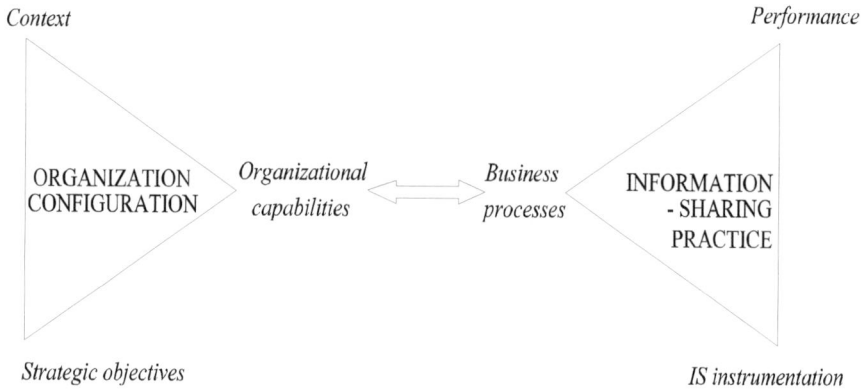

Context   *Performance*

ORGANIZATION   *Organizational*   *Business*   INFORMATION
CONFIGURATION   *capabilities*   *processes*   - SHARING
                                                               PRACTICE

Strategic objectives   *IS instrumentation*

Figure 2.6. *Model for questioning the configuration/practice relation*

In the following sections, we develop the two theoretical constructs "organization configuration" and "information-sharing practice".

2.4.3. *Theoretical construct: organization configuration*

The theoretical construct "organization configuration" is composed of three empirical constructs: internal and external environment and objectives (see Table 2.2), product offering (Table 2.3), and supply-chain configuration (Table 2.4).

Our study is limited to the strategic business unit (SBU) – the most important in terms of sales for the FF – and, in this SBU, to the two most important lines of products. For each product line, we consider the list in Table 2.3.

Importance of external factors to the operation of the focal firm's business:	– sales variability – variability of economic performance – rate of technological change – regulations – intensity of competition – forecasting difficulty
Importance of internal factors for the competitiveness of the focal firm's business:	– requires capital – needs for investment – ability to do research and development – control of regulations – knowledge of customer needs – regulation (right) of the competition – search for economy of scale
Importance of strategic objectives:	– search for low cost – search for differentiated products – search for standardized products – maintenance of position as market leader – obtaining the position of market leader – development of sales abroad – development of turnover
Importance of logistics objectives:	– obtaining low costs – security of supply – ability to respond to changes in volume of demand – ability to respond to variety of demand – rapid response to demand – offer of additional services to the product

Table 2.2. *Internal and external environment and objectives*

Importance of product variety
Degree of product specificity: tailor-made, configured to demand, customized, standard
Importance of the pull system: ETO, MTO, ATO, MTS
Average life cycle of product: <1 year, <3 years, <10 years, > 10 years.
Dominant production process: one-of-a-kind, discrete, production line, process

Table 2.3. *Product offering*

Perceived complexity of the supply chain:	– quantification of suppliers (S) – quantification of upstream intermediate partners (IPS) – quantification of customers (C) – quantification of downstream intermediate partners (IPC)
Configuration parameters of the supply chain:	– proportion of flows passing through IPS – proportion of flows passing through IPC – distribution of delivery lead time to the customers (<48h, between 48h and 1 week, between 1 week and 1 month, >1 month, >3 months) in the case of direct delivery – distribution of the delivery lead time to the customers (<48h, between 48h and 1 week, between 1 week and 1 month, >1 month, >3 months) in the case of delivery via an intermediate upstream partner – distribution of the delivery lead time of the suppliers (<48h, between 48h and 1 week, between 1 week and 1 month, >1 month, >3 months) in case of direct delivery – distribution of the delivery lead time of the suppliers (<48h, between 48h and 1 week, between 1 week and 1 month, >1 month, >3 months) in the case of delivery via an intermediate upstream partner
Influence and power:	– quantification of the partners that have an influence, a structuring power on the organization of the chain (S, IPS, C, IPC) – nature of suppliers' influence: on lead times, prices, quality – nature of IPS influence: on lead times, prices, quality – nature of customer influence: on lead times, prices, quality – nature of IPC influence: on lead times, prices, quality
Role of information systems and technologies:	– application component used by the focal firm: ERP, APS, PLM, MES, SCE, WMS, spreadsheet – distribution of upstream exchange mode: telephone, fax, email, EDI, internet, EAI, e-marketplace – distribution of downstream exchange mode: telephone, fax, email, EDI, internet, EAI, e-marketplace
Collaboration characteristics:	– numbers of partners (S, IPS, C, IPC), with which the focal firm has preferred collaboration relationships – ranking of the justification of the collaboration with S: search for economy of scale, solving production problems, solving quality problems, collaborative design, strategic inventory management – ranking of the justification of collaboration with IPS: search for economy of scale, solving production problems, collaborative product design, strategic inventory management – ranking of the justification of collaboration with C: better response to customer needs, improving understanding of customer needs, improving production planning, improving production schedule, collaborative product design – ranking of the justification of the collaboration with IPC: better response to customer needs, improving understanding of customer needs, improving production planning, improving production schedule

Table 2.4. *Supply chain configuration*

2.4.4. *Theoretical construct: information-sharing practice*

Before characterizing a specific information-sharing practice, some requirements about its importance have to be specified:

– Is this specific information shared, i.e. is the practice in process? If not, is it wished or planned?

– What is the proportion of partners with which this exchange takes place – 0%, <10%, <25%, <50%, <75%, <100%?

– What turnover percentage for the FF is made with these partners (suppliers or customers) – 0%, <10%, <25%, <50%, <75%, <100%?

As the responses can often vary, depending on the partner concerned, we propose to consider the special relationship for which the FF has facts. It seems useful to choose the partner for which this information exchange is the most *successful*, *accomplished* and *richest*, and therefore probably the one that contributes more strongly to the performance of the logistic relationship. Therefore, the analysis is performed with this selected partner.

Level of aggregation of the information:	– product aggregation: macro product lines, product lines, product reference
	– time aggregation: day, week, month, etc.
Business departments concerned by the use of the information:	– business departments concerned by its first usage: purchasing, procurement, planning, production, sales, logistics, support (human resources, computing, etc.)
	– business departments concerned by its subsequent usage: purchasing, procurement, planning, production, sales, logistics, support (human resources, computing, etc.)
IS characteristics:	– application component (by the focal firm or the partner) into which the information is recorded: ERP, BI, APS, CRM, SCE, MES, legacy system
	– way of recording: manual, automatic
	– information reliability management by the focal firm (only for received information): reliance on the information, existence of reprocessing
Impact on performance:	– perceived importance by the focal firm of the impact of the received (or sent) information on performance of the focal firm, partner or whole supply chain
	– performance indicator impacted by the focal firm: service rate, inventory costs, production cycle, product quality, logistics costs, committed costs, quality of service

Table 2.5. *Information content*

Temporal characteristics:	– age of the exchange: <1 month, <1 year, >1 year
	– frequency of the exchange: day, week, month, year (depending on the information)
Organizational and contractual characteristics:	– originator of the exchange: the focal firm or the partner
	– contracting of the exchange (information content, exchange procedures, risk management)
IS characteristics:	– application component from which the information is extracted: ERP, BI, APS, CRM, SCE, MES, legacy system
	– communication technology used for the exchange: telephone, fax, email, EDI, internet, EAI, e-marketplace
	– exchange security management (only for sent information): none, login, encryption, etc.

Table 2.6. *Exchange process*

The theoretical construct of information-sharing practice is composed of two empirical constructs: "information content", which characterizes the nature of the information, and "exchange process", which characterizes the exchange relationship. For both constructs, some questions depend on the direction of the exchange: from the FF or from the partner, and on the nature of the information.

2.5. Illustration: examples of analysis[1]

Several analyses can be performed based on the questioning framework. In the following sections, we present the results of two studies carried out under the COPILOTES and COPILOTES2 research projects in the Rhône-Alpes region of France. The first analysis illustrates its use of obtaining a map of companies based on their information-sharing practices (section 2.5.2). The second one presents a study of the influence of information sharing on perceived performance (section 2.5.3).

This regional survey was conducted by poll. Its objectives were to study the experiences and practices of firms in IS, information exchange, and collaborative practices, and to obtain a representative mapping of their practices, under which companies should be able to position themselves. Conducted on 22 companies in the Rhône-Alpes region, the survey was based on a questionnaire derived from the questioning framework, which was administered face-to-face by the project's team members. This mode of administration was linked to the questionnaire length and

---

1 We thank the Professors, Assistant Professors and PhD students who took part in these studies (in alphabetic order): X. Boucher, R. Derrouiche, F.-A. Gruat-La-Forme, D. Llerena, P.-A. Millet, G. Neubert, O. Sakka and M. Seville.

accuracy, and to the technical nature of the questions. The responses to questions were coded and analyzed using SPSS software.

Before outlining the results of our investigation, we first present an analysis of the nature of respondent firms and their perception of their strategic and logistics environment. We then describe their collaborative practices in supply chains.

2.5.1. *Sample analysis*

2.5.1.1. *Economic, strategic and logistic situation of the respondents*

The companies surveyed are mostly medium sized and belong to larger groups. They operate in various sectors and are fairly diverse. They produce mainly standard products but have a relatively wide variety of products. Their dominant production mode is the production line and they operate on both push and pull systems.

The main external factors perceived to influence the functioning of the company (in descending order of importance) are:

– variability of sales;

– competition;

– difficulties of forecasting;

– and, to a lesser extent, regulations.

Companies perceive the knowledge of customer needs as the main internal success factor. Their perceptions of their environment and its emphasis on success factors and environmental variables depend more precisely on their size and the variety of family products they offer. Indeed, it appears that very large companies are highly sensitive to both the regulatory burden and the weight of the competitive environment. Small and medium enterprises are not as strongly affected by the rules and are distributed heterogenously in terms of their perception of the weight of the competitive environment.

The strategic objectives listed by businesses as priorities are: achieving or maintaining a leadership position, followed by development of turnover. For SMEs, however, low cost and development of turnover remain the most frequently cited strategic objectives. The purpose logistics cited in the first place, whatever the size of the company, is security of supply, followed by ability to respond to changes in volume of demand.

In conclusion, the context in which respondents are involved is characterized by the pressure of the competitive environment, the difficulty of forecasting and the weight of regulations. In this environment, firms identify their knowledge of customer needs as the main success factor.

2.5.1.2. Collaborative relationships of the respondents

The number of partners with which firms enter into collaborative relationships is relatively small: on average fewer than 10 clients (60% of companies) and five suppliers (for 60% of firms), irrespective of the size of the company.

When trying to explain the number of partners with which firms forge a special relationship, we realize that the reasons for choosing the number of partners are asymmetric between customers and suppliers. The quantitative importance of the collaborative relationship with customers is partly explained by the competitive and regulatory environment, while the quantitative importance of the collaborative relationship with suppliers remains unexplained.

The analysis also suggests that one of the main factors explaining the quantitative importance of downstream collaboration (customer number) is the number of suppliers having an influence on the company and *vice versa*. This leaves us to suppose that what happens upstream in the company's supply chain is not independent of what happens downstream and *vice versa*. Thus, it seems that there is an integrated approach to the supply chain, although the sides of the chain are not subject to the same environmental constraints.

2.5.2. Mapping companies according to information-sharing practices

The sharing of information by companies in their supply chain is important, both upstream and downstream. The size of the company does not appear to have a significant relationship with the extent of information sharing in the supply chain. Note that "extreme" firms (who share all information or none) are small companies.

Seventy percent of the companies share at least half of the information mentioned in the questionnaire, while 15% of the companies share all of the information. The latter are companies that have found their knowledge of customer needs to be the key to success.

In addition, data analysis shows the main reason why upstream information sharing is an internal factor, s*earch for differentiated products*, even though we may think that, above all, it explains downstream information sharing. Similarly, the main driver of downstream information exchange is the internal factor, *search for standardized products*. This internal factor could suggest that the driver mainly explains upstream information exchange. Finally, *knowledge of customer needs* does not appear to explain much of the downstream information exchange. We can suggest here that how firms integrate the expectations of the other side of the chain may explain the differences between firms that share a lot of information and those that share less (both up- and downstream).

The main information shared downstream deals with customer activity and lead times; while that shared upstream concerns purchase request forecasts and quality procedures. The latter seem to be concentrated on one or both partners, but this seems to be less so upstream than downstream, and less marked for the main information exchanged (purchase request forecasts and quality procedures).

A thorough analysis of information exchanged by companies allows us to propose a map of the firms in the sample and to identify groups of firms. The mapping (see Figure 2.7) is obtained by multiple correspondence analysis. Dimension 1 (horizontal) represents the depth of downstream information sharing, while dimension 2 (vertical) focuses more on upstream information sharing. These dimensions are the ones on which companies differ most. Dimension 1 is the most discriminating.

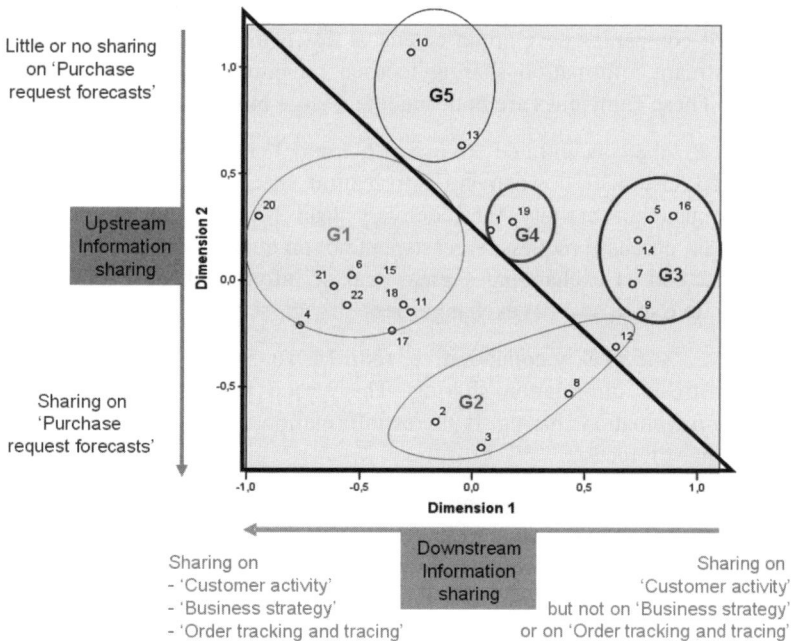

Figure 2.7. *Map of companies according to their information-sharing practices*

It appears that the reason for business groups' opposition to dimension 1 is not the sharing of customer activity in which most of them partake, but more specifically the extent of information shared downstream. Thus, the firms in Group 2 share information on customer activity, like those of Group 1, but they do not share information about business strategy or the traceability of customer orders. In reality, on this map there is an area between groups that share information on client activity and those that do not. Therefore, to groups that share information on customer activity, dimension 1 opposes those that are satisfied by this exchange and those that enhance the degree of information-sharing downstream (completing this exchange by sharing information about business strategy and order traceability).

The companies differ on dimension 2 in sharing purchase request forecast information with their partners. We thus obtain an interpretation of the mapping that allows us to better identify groups and name them:

– *Group 1*, "the collaborative" (No. 4, 6, 11,15, 17, 18, 21, 22 and 20) brings together companies that exchange information with many partners, especially on customer demand, business strategy, traceability of customer orders and also on purchase request forecast (except for No. 20) and, for most, on quality procedures. It is a group of companies developing extensive downstream information sharing, as well as upstream information sharing focused on purchase forecasts and quality procedures. These companies are both small and large businesses.

– *Group 2*, "the concentrated" (No. 8, 12, 2 and 3) is a group of companies that has a limited vision of downstream information sharing primarily based on the sharing of customer activity (and delivery lead times). They share upstream information on purchase request forecasts, but not on quality procedures, with a sub-group (No. 2 and 3) exchanging a great deal of information upstream, while the other subgroup (No. 8 and 12) exchanges less.

– *Group 3*, "the weakly collaborative" (No. 14, 16, 5, 7, 9), is opposed to Group 2 for downstream information sharing. This group has very little or even no downstream information sharing. It shares information upstream focused mainly on purchase request forecasts.

– *Group 4*, "the focus upstream" is composed of companies 1 and 19. It is a group of companies that exchange information with downstream partners, not on customer activity or business strategy, but only on traceability of customer order, delivery time and production management policies. On the other hand, these companies share upstream information on purchase request forecasts, quality procedures, production plans and inventory management policies.

– *Group 5*, "the atypical" is composed of companies 10 and 13 is a somewhat atypical group in that they do not exchange information about that which, in other companies, is the basis of sharing. Instead, they exchange downstream information on business strategy, order traceability and delivery lead times.

Yet the media and nature of IS used to exchange such information seem common to different groups of companies. The media used most are phone, fax and internet. The use of ERP systems and Excel to share information either up- or downstream is massive: 82% of companies use them. The use of ERP systems is completed, especially downstream, by heavy use of specific software components to exchange downstream information on business strategies, and upstream information on purchase request forecasts. Other application components (BI, CRM, etc; see figure 2.1), however, are poorly used.

Exchanges are sometimes contractual but not very secure. The content of the information seems to be easily editable. Contracts on upstream information focus on production plans, purchase request forecasts and inventory management policies; downstream, the contracts focus on customer activity, inventory levels and lead times. Respondents paid very little attention to the security of information sharing. When this security exists, the primary means of security is the establishment of login.

2.5.3. Influence of information sharing on perceived performance

Based on the proposed framework, it is possible to study the impact of information sharing on the performance of the focal firm (FF), the partner (S or C) or the supply chain.

In order to measure the impact of information exchange on performance, we sorted the respondents' answers into three categories: not important at all (O), of average importance (M), and of great importance (S). The details of results are presented in Tables 2.7 and 2.8 for upstream and downstream information sharing, respectively. The column Nb represents the percentage of respondents who share the given information. The figures in the nine other columns represent the distribution on the three categories (O, M, S) of the perceived impact of information sharing by the respondent, respectively on its own firm, on the partner (supplier or customer) and on the whole supply chain.

The focal firm, the supplier, the customer and the whole supply chain all benefit from the sharing of information but in different proportions. The company is seen as the most beneficial recipient of these exchanges, followed by the supply chain. On the other hand, the benefit to partners of the exchange (customer and supplier) appears to be less.

Direction of sharing	Information	Nb	Impact on the performance of:								
			the focal firm			*the supplier*			*the supply chain*		
			O	M	S	O	M	S	O	M	S
FF→S	Production plans	50%	-	28%	72%	-	45%	55%	-	45%	55%
FF→S	Purchase request forecasts	100%	-	22%	78%	-	34%	66%	-	39%	61%
S→FF	Production planning parameters	59%	-	31%	69%	7%	39%	54%	-	30%	70%
S→FF	Purchase order traceability	36%	-	25%	75%	-	25%	75%	-	22%	78%
S↔FF	Quality procedures	86%	11%	11%	78%	5%	10%	85%	10%	26%	64%
S↔FF	Inventory management policies	36%	11%	22%	67%	13%	37%	50%	14%	14%	72%

Table 2.7. *Impact of upstream information sharing on performance*

Direction of sharing	Information	Nb	Impact on the performance of:								
			the focal firm			*the customer*			*the supply chain*		
			O	M	S	O	M	S	O	M	S
FF→C	Delivery lead times	77%	-	50%	50%	-	19%	81%	6%	12%	82%
FF→C	Order traceability	64%	-	8%	92%	7%	36%	57%	-	43%	57%
C→FF	Customer activity	73%	6%	13%	81%	-	20%	80%	-	6%	94%
C→FF	Business strategy	55%	8%	8%	84%	-	16%	84%	-	19%	81%
C→FF	Customer inventory	55%	9%	-	91%	-	33%	67%	-	9%	91%
C↔FF	Production management policies	59%	-	15%	85%	-	25%	75%	-	25%	75%

Table 2.8. *Impact of downstream information sharing on performance*

More generally, we can see that the information exchanged upstream and downstream seems to have a significant impact on the focal company's perceived performance, except for delivery lead times. These exchanges mainly contribute to the improvement of the service rate and then to the inventory costs. It is primarily the information shared upstream on the quality procedures and purchase order traceability that increases product and service quality.

The information transmitted by clients impacts most strongly on the performance of the focal firm, particularly that concerning inventory levels of customers (91%). This exchange also positively impacts on the performance of the chain, but not on the client itself. The exchanges of information on business strategy and customer activity are also considered very favorable for the focal company, customer and supply chain (over 80%). Of the information received from suppliers, quality procedures have the greatest impact on both the focal firm and supplier (78% and 85% respectively). The exchange of information on the traceability of purchase orders, although less frequent, also positively affects the two parties involved (focal company and supplier) as well as the supply chain. The exchange of information on inventory management policies and production planning parameters seems less significant.

We notice a different influence concerning the two types of information that the company transmits to its customers. Communicating information to customers about the traceability of orders is considered to be very important for the company itself (92%), but much less so for the customer or the supply chain (57%). We think that this contributes to customer service, which allows the company to differentiate itself from the competition. Sharing information on the delivery lead time is deemed more important to the customer and the chain (about 81%) than to the company itself (50%). We believe that this exchange of information is so systematic and clear that firms do not perceive it as a discriminatory factor for their internal performance.

Communicating its manufacturing schedules or purchase forecasts to suppliers is deemed crucial for the focal company (72% and 78% respectively). It is important for the company to put itself in a position to better manage its supply and thus be more effective in its own activities, even if the company does not think that it improves the performance of the provider or supply chain.

Finally, information sharing in supply chains is seen as having less influence on the committed costs, i.e. logistics costs as inventory costs. The logistic goal of obtaining low costs – that respondents state is one of the main objectives – therefore seems to be achieved by an exchange of information on customer activity and purchase requirement forecasts, which impact mostly on inventory and logistic costs.

2.5.4. *Concluding remarks*

Here we have presented two examples of analyses that can be performed from enquiries based on the proposed questioning framework. The former illustrates its use to obtain a map of companies based on their information-sharing practices, while the latter presents a study of the influence of information sharing on perceived performance.

In a context in which the key success factors identified are knowledge of customer needs and forecasting difficulty, we analyzed data collected on a sample of companies whose primary goals were low costs (either strategic or logistic), security of supply and rapid response to demand. We showed that the exchange of information is primarily upstream on purchase request forecasts and quality procedures; and downstream on delivery times and customer activity.

The data analysis presented here, which is a set of interim results, has identified groups of companies that differ, depending on the size and nature of the information sharing that they have set up. We have identified two groups (the "collaborative" and "weakly collaborative") strongly opposed on the degree to which downstream information sharing should be extended. Companies that share equally little up- and downstream information (the weakly collaborative) are primarily small and medium-sized businesses, while "collaborative" companies are both large and small businesses.

In large companies, it seems that extensive information sharing is required. This could be explained by a desire to more efficiently manage the regulatory and competitive environment in which some companies appeared very sensitive.

Small and medium enterprises clearly perceive the impact of sharing information with partners in the supply chain on their performance. This sharing could be conditioned by constraints imposed by organizational, financial and human resources, and by choices companies can make in the allocation of these resources among the various activities they undertake.

2.6. Conclusion

Empirical and analytical models proposed in the literature do not take into account all of the differential elements of information-sharing practices (information content, exchange process, firm configuration, etc.); hence, the need for a framework that questions the reality of practice.

The framework proposed in this chapter allows us to examine the configuration of an organization as well as its information-sharing practices in a general supply chain structure. It allows us to measure and analyze the perceptions of the impact of these practices on a company's performance. It is expected that, by addressing collaborative practices simultaneously from up- and downstream in a supply chain, researchers will be able to better understand their scope and the activities associated with supply-chain management. This will allow them to test the antecedences and consequences of collaborative practices, such as information sharing. Furthermore, the framework makes it possible to explain the efficiency of some business processes and to identify patterns linking characteristics of the organization with information-sharing practices.

The proposed framework can also help firms[2] to understand the performance issues of collaborative practices like information sharing, by facilitating their questioning. In addition, it enables the respondent firms to evaluate their perceived supply-chain performance at several points in time. The results could provide an initial benchmark for firms in their attempts to assess their practices on a longitudinal basis. Further research should assess supply chain performance with input from other members of the chain, i.e. suppliers, shippers, consignees, service providers, customers, etc., in order to produce a shared analysis of the collaboration.

2.7. Bibliography

[AKI 00] AKINTOYE A., MCINTOSH G., FITZGERALD E., "A survey of supply chain collaboration and management in the UK construction industry", *European Journal of Purchasing & Supply Management*, vol. 6, 2000, pp. 159-168.

[AKK 03] AKKERMANS H., BOGERD P., YUCESAN E., VAN WASSENHOVE L.N., "The impact of ERP on supply chain management: exploratory finding from European Delphi study", *European Journal of Operational Research*, vol. 146, 2003, pp. 284-301.

[ALB 02] ALBERT C., BROWNSWORD L., *Evolutionary Process for Integrating COTS-Based Systems* (EPIC). CMU/SEI-2002-TR-009, 2002.

[ALT 96] ALTER S., *Information Systems: A Management Perspective*, 2nd edition, Benjamin-Cummings Publishing, Redwood City, 1996.

[AUB 02] AUBERT B.A., DUSSART A., *Systèmes d'Information Inter-entreprises*, Rapport Bourgogne du CIRANO, 2002RB-01, 2002.

[BAG 05] BAGCHI P.K., HA B.C., SKJOETT-LARSEN, T., SOERENSEN, L.B., "Supply chain integration: a European survey", *The International Journal of Logistics Management*, vol. 16, no. 2, 2005, pp. 275-94.

---

2 This questioning framework led to a computerized self-administered questionnaire, available in French at www.copilotes.eu.

[BAR 02] BARUT M., FAISST W., KANET J.J., "Measuring supply chain coupling: an information system perspective", *European Journal of Purchasing & Supply Management*, vol. 8, no. 3, 2002, pp. 161-171.

[BEL 09] BELAYA V., HANF J.H., "The two sides of power in business-to-business relationships: implications for supply chain management", *The Marketing Review*, vol. 9, no. 4, 2009, pp. 361-381

[BER 97] BERNUS P., NEMES L., "Requirements of the generic enterprise reference architecture and methodology", *A. Rev. Control*, vol. 21, 1997, pp. 125-136.

[BOT 05] BOTTA-GENOULAZ V., MILLET P.-A., "A classification for better use of ERP systems", *Computers in Industry*, vol. 56, no. 6, 2005, pp. 572-586.

[BOT 07] BOTTA-GENOULAZ V., "Les ERP: un atout pour la cohérence, un risque pour la flexibilité ?", in: G. de Terssac, I. Bazet and L. Rapp, (eds), *La Rationalisation dans les Entreprises par les Technologie Coopératives*, OCTARES Editions, MSHS-T Series, no. 5, 2007, pp.37-53.

[BOW 03] BOWERSOX D.J., CLOSS D.J, STANK T.P., "How to master cross-enterprise collaboration?", *Supply Chain Management Review*, July/August, 2003, vol. 7, no. 4, pp 18-27.

[CHE 07] CHEN M.C., YANG T., LI H.-C., "Evaluating the supply chain performance of IT-based inter-enterprise collaboration", *Information & Management*, vol. 44, 2007, pp. 524-534.

[COR 05] CORSTEN D., FELDE J., "Exploring the performance effects of key-supplier collaboration: an empirical investigation into Swiss buyer-supplier relationships", *International Journal of Physical Distribution & Logistics Management*, vol. 35, no. 6, 2005, pp. 445-461.

[DAP 03] DAPIRAN G.P., HOGARTH-SCOTT S., "Are co-operation and trust being confused with power? An analysis of food retailing in Australia and the UK", *International Journal of Retail and Distribution Management*, vol. 31, no. 5, 2003, pp. 256-267.

[DON 04] DONK (Van) D.P., VAN DER VAART J.T., "Business conditions, shared resources and integrative practices in the supply chain", *Journal of Purchasing & Supply Management*, vol. 10, 2004, pp. 107–116.

[EDW 01] EDWARDS P., PETERS M., SHARMAN G., "The effectiveness of information systems in supporting the extended supply chain", *Journal of Business Logistics*, vol. 22, no. 1, 2001, pp 1-27.

[ENG 06] ENG T.Y., "An investigation into the mediating role of cross-functional coordination on the linkage between organizational norms and SCM performance", *Industrial Marketing Management*, vol. 35, no. 6, 2006, pp. 762-773.

[EYU 91] EYUBOGLU N., ATAC O. A., "Informational power: A means for increased control in channels of distribution", *Psychology and Marketing*, vol. 8, no. 3, 1991, pp. 197-213.

[FAW 08] FAWCETT S.E., MAGNAN G.M., MCCARTER M.W., "A three-stage implementation model for supply chain collaboration", *Journal of Business Logistics*, vol. 29, no.1, 2008, pp. 93-112.

[FIA 05] FIALA P., "Information sharing in supply chains", *Omega,* vol. 33, 2005, pp. 419-423.

[FIS 97] FISHER M.L., "What is the right supply chain for your product?" *Harvard Business Review*, vol. 75, no. 2, 1997, pp.105–116.

[FLY 10] FLYNN B.B., HUO B., ZHAO X., "The impact of supply chain integration on performance: A contingency and configuration approach", *Journal of Operations Management,* vol. 28, 2010, pp. 58-71.

[FRE 59] FRENCH J. R. P., RAVEN B., "The bases of social power", in: Cartwright, D. (ed), *Studies in Social Power*, Ann Arbor, MI, University of Michigan Press, 1959, pp.150-167.

[FYN 05] FYNES B., VOSS C., SEÁN D.B., "The impact of supply chain relationship quality on quality performance, *International Journal of Production Economics*, vol. 96, no. 3, 2005, pp. 339-354.

[GAL 73] GALBRAITH J., *Designing Complex Organizations*. Addison-Wesley, MA, 1973.

[GAO 01] GAONKAR R., VISWANADHAM N., "Collaboration and information sharing in global contract manufacturing network", *Transactions on Mechatronics*, vol. 6, no. 4, 2001, pp. 366-376.

[GAS 86] GASKI J. F., "The theory of power and conflict in channels of distribution", *Journal of Marketing*, vol. 48, no. 3, 1986, pp. 9-29.

[GER 06] GERMAIN R., IYER K.N., "The interaction of internal and downstream integration and its association with performance", *Journal of Business Logistics*, 2006, vol. 27, no. 2, pp. 29-52.

[GIL 99] GILMOUR P., "A strategic audit framework to improve supply chain performance", *Journal of Business & Industrial Marketing*, vol. 14, no. 5/6, 1999, pp. 355-363.

[GIM 05] GIMENEZ C., VENTURA, E., "Logistics-production, logistics-marketing and external integration: their impact on performance", *International Journal of Operations and Production Management*, vol. 25, no. 1, 2005, pp. 20-38.

[GRU 09] GRUAT-LA-FORME F.-A., BOTTA-GENOULAZ V., CAMPAGNE J.-P., "The role of APS systems in supply chain management: a theoretical and industrial analysis", *International Journal of Logistics Systems and Management*, vol. 5, no. 3-4, 2009, pp. 356-374.

[GUN 04] GUNASEKARAN A., NGAI E.W.T, "Information systems in supply chain integration and management", *European Journal of Operational Research*, vol. 159, 2004, pp. 269-295.

[HOL 95] HOLLAND C., "Cooperative supply chain management: the impact of interorganizational IS", *Journal of Strategic Information Systems*, vol. 4, no. 2, 1995, pp. 117-133.

[HUM 01] HUMPHREYS P.K., LAI M.K., SCULLI D., "An inter-organizational information system for supply chain management", *International Journal of Production Economics*, vol. 70, 2001, pp. 245-255.

[HUN 74] HUNT S. D., NEVIN J. R., "Power in a channel of distribution: Sources and consequences", *Journal of Marketing Research*, vol. 11, no. 2, 1974, pp. 186-193.

[KEN 97] KENDALL K., "The significance of information systems research on emerging technologies: seven information technologies that promise to improve managerial effectiveness", *Decision Sciences*, vol. 28, 1997, pp. 775-792.

[KLE 07] KLEIN R., "Customization and real time information access in integrated e-business supply chain relationships", *Journal of Operations Management*, vol. 25, 2007, pp. 1366-1381.

[KUL 04] KULP S.C., LEE H.L., OFEK E., "Manufacturer benefits from information integration with retail customers", *Management Science*, vol. 50, no. 4, 2004, pp. 431–444.

[KUM 98] KUMAR N., SCHEER L. K., STEENKAMP J.B. E., "Interdependence, punitive capability, and the reciprocation of punitive actions in channel relationships", *Journal of Marketing Research*, vol. 35, no. 2, 1998, pp. 225-235.

[LAU 04] LAU J.S.K., HUANG G.Q., MAK K.L., "Impact of information sharing on inventory replenishment in divergent supply chains", *International Journal of Production Research*, vol. 42, no. 5, 2004, pp. 919-941.

[LEE 97] LEE H.L., PADMANABHAN V., WHANG S., "Information distortion in a supply chain: The bullwhip effect", *Management Science*, vol. 43, no. 4, 1997, pp. 546–558.

[LEE 00] LEE H.L., WHANG S., "Information sharing in a supply chain", *International Journal of Technology Management*, vol. 20, no. 3, 2000, pp. 373-387.

[LEE 02] LEE H.L., "Aligning supply chain strategies with product uncertainties", *California Management Review*, vol. 44, no. 3, 2002, pp. 105–119.

[LI 06] LI S., RAGU-NATHAN B., RAGU-NATHAN T.S., RAO S.S., "The impact of supply chain management practices on competitive advantage and organizational performance", *Omega*, vol. 34, no. 2, 2006, pp. 107-124.

[LIU 03] LIU E., KUMAR A., "Leveraging information sharing to increase supply chain configurability", *Proceedings of the Twenty-Fourth International Conference on Information Systems*, 2003, pp. 523-537.

[LLE 06] LLERENA D., DUVALLET J., LEMARIE S., PENZ B., (2006). "Evaluer les impacts du partage d'information: objectif, méthodologie, resultants", available at: www.copilotes.eu, accessed 27.4.10.

[MAL 97] MALONI M. J., BENTON W. C., "Supply chain partnerships: Opportunities for operations research", *European Journal of Operational Research*, vol. 101, no. 3, 1997, pp. 419-429.

[MAL 00] MALONI M. J., BENTON W. C., "Power influences in the supply chain", *Journal of Business Logistics*, vol. 21, no. 1, 2000, pp. 49-73.

[McC 99] McCORMACK K., *What Supply Chain Management Practices Relate to Superior Performance?* DRK Research Team, Boston, MA, 1998.

[McG 98] McGOWAN A., "Perceived benefits of ABCM implementation", *Accounting Horizons*, vol. 12, no. 1, 1998, pp. 31–50.

[MIL 08a] MILLET P.-A., BOTTA-GENOULAZ V., "Process alignment maturity in changing organizations", In: B. Grabot, A. Mayère, I. Bazet (eds), *ERP Systems and Organisational Change – A Socio-technical Insight*, Springer Editions, London, 2008, pp.157-180.

[MIL 08b] MILLET P.-A., Une étude de l'intégration organisationnelle et informationnelle: Application aux systèmes d'informations de type ERP, PhD Thesis, INSA-Lyon (France), 2008.

[NEU 79] NEUMANN S., SEGEV E., "A case study of user evaluation of information characteristics for systems improvement", *Information and Management*, vol. 2, 1979, pp. 271–278.

[PAU 08] PAULRAJ A., LADO A.A., CHEN I.J., "Inter-organizational communication as a relational competency: Antecedents and performance outcomes in collaborative buyer–supplier relationships", *Journal of Operations Management*, vol. 26, no. 1, 2008, pp. 45-64.

[PET 99] PETERSEN K., *The Effect of Information Quality on Supply Chain Performance: an Inter-organizational Information System Perspective*, Michigan State University, MI, 1999.

[REI 02] REIX, R., *Systèmes d'Information et Management des Organisations*, Vuibert, Paris, 2002.

[ROB 00] ROBEY D., BOUDREAU M.C., ROSE G.M., "Information technology and organizational learning: a review and assessment of research", *Accounting, Management and Information Technologies*, vol. 10, no. 2, 2000, pp. 125-155.

[ROD 04] RODRIGUEZ A.M., STANK T.P., LYNCH D.F. "Linking strategy, structure, process, and performance in integrated logistics", *Journal of Business Logistics*, vol. 25, no. 2, 2004, pp. 65-94.

[RYU 09] RYU S.-J., TSUKISHIMA T., ONARI H., "A study on evaluation of demand information-sharing methods in supply chain", *International Journal of Production Economics*, vol. 120, no. 1, 2009, pp. 162-175.

[SAH 05] SAHIN F., ROBINSON E. P., "Information sharing and coordination in make-to-order supply chain", *Journal of Operations Management*, vol. 23, no. 6, 2005, pp. 579-598.

[SAN 02] SANDERS N.R., PREMUS R., "IT applications in supply chain organizations: a link between competitive priorities and organizational benefits", *Journal of Business Logistics*, vol. 23, no. 1, 2002, pp.65-83.

[SHI 07] SHIN S.K., ISHMAN M., SANDERS G.L., "An empirical investigation of socio-cultural factors of information sharing in China", *Information & Management*, vol. 44, 2007, pp. 165-174.

[SHO 01] SHORE, B., "Information sharing in global supply chain systems", *Journal of Global Information Technology Management*, vol. 4, no. 3, 2001, pp. 27-50.

[SIM 02] SIMATUPANG T. M., WRIGHT A. C., SRIDHARAN R., "The knowledge of coordination for supply chain integration", *Business Process Management Journal*, vol. 8, no. 3, 2002, pp. 289-308.

[SOL 04] SOLIMAN K.S., JANZ B.D., "An exploratory study to identify the critical factors affecting the decision to establish internet-based inter-organizational information systems", *Information & Management*, vol. 41, no. 6, 2004, pp. 697-706.

[STA 99] STANK T.P., CRUM M., ARANGO M., "Benefits of interfirm coordination in food industry supply chains", *Journal of Business Logistics*, vol. 20, no. 2, 1999, pp. 21-42.

[STA 01] STANK T.P., KELLER S.B. AND CLOSS, D.J., "Performance benefits of supply chain logistical integration", *Transportation Journal*, vol. 41, no. 2/3, 2001, pp. 32-46.

[STE 02] STEFANSSON G., "Business-to-business data sharing: A source for integration of supply chains", *International Journal of Production Economics*, vol. 75, 2002, pp. 135-146.

[SUM 95] SUM C., YANG K., ANG J., QUECK S., "An analysis of material requirements planning benefits using alternating conditional expectation", *Journal of Operations Management*, vol. 13, no. 1, 1995, pp. 35–48.

[SWI 07] SWINK M., NARASIMHAN R., WANG C., "Managing beyond the factory walls: effects of four types of strategic integration on manufacturing plant performance", *Journal of Operations Management*, vol. 25, no. 1, 2007, pp. 148-64.

[THE 04] THEMISTOCLEOUS M., IRANI Z., LOVE P.E.D., "Evaluating the integration of supply chain information systems: A case study", *European Journal of Operational Research*, vol. 159, no. 2, 2004, pp. 393-405.

[VAA 04] VAART (Van der) J.T., DONK (Van) D.P., "Buyer focus: Evaluation of a new concept for supply chain integration", *International Journal of Production Economics*, 2004, vol. 92, no. 1, pp. 21–30.

[VER 04] VERWIJMEREN M., "Software component architecture in supply chain management", *Computers in Industry*, vol. 53, 2004, pp. 165-178.

[VIJ 97] VIJAYASARATHY L., ROBEY D., "The effect of EDI on market channel relationship in retailing", *Information and Management*, vol. 33, no. 2, 1997, pp. 73–86.

[WEL 08] WELKER G. A., VAART (Van der) T., DONK (Van) D. P., "The influence of business conditions on supply chain information-sharing mechanisms: A study among supply chain links of SMEs", *International Journal of Production Economics*, vol. 113, 2008, pp. 706–720.

[WHI 05] WHITE A., DANIEL E.M., MOHDZAIN M., "The role of emergent information technologies and systems in enabling supply chain agility", *International Journal of Information Management*, vol. 25, no. 5, 2005, pp. 396-410

[WIL 04] WILLIAMSON E.A., HARRISON D.K., JORDAN M., "Information systems development within supply chain management", *International Journal of Information Management*, vol. 24, no. 5, 2004, pp. 375-385.

[YAN 08] YANG J., WANG J., WONG C.Y., LAI K.-H., "Relational stability and alliance performance in supply chain", *International Journal of Management Science, Omega*, vol. 36, 2008, pp. 600-608.

[YU 10] YU M.-M., TING S.-C., CHEN M.-C., "Evaluating the cross-efficiency of information sharing in supply chains", *Expert Systems with Applications*, vol. 37, no. 4, 2010, pp. 2891-2897.

[ZHA 08] ZHAO X., HUO B., FLYNN B. B., YEUNG J. H. Y., "The impact of power and relationship commitment on the integration between manufacturers and customers in a supply chain", *Journal of Operations Management*, vol. 26, no. 3, 2008, pp. 368–388.

[ZHO 07] ZHOU H., BENTON Jr. W.C., "Supply chain practice and information sharing", *Journal of Operations Management*, vol. 25, no. 6, 2007, pp. 1348-1365.

Chapter 3

Modeling and Evaluation of Industrial Practices' Impacts on Performance

3.1. Objectives

Measuring the impacts of industrial practices on performance requires us first to characterize this performance. It obviously has an economic dimension, but the environmental and social impacts are increasingly relevant as well. In this chapter we focus on collaborative and sustainable practices in industry.

To measure the impacts of these practices on company performance, we first propose a generalized model of industrial performance, of three dimensions: economic, environmental and social.

The second part of the chapter is devoted to the presentation of two models designed, respectively:

– to characterize and assess the collaborative practices of a company; and

– to characterize and classify its sustainable practices.

Finally, we analyze relationships between supply chain practices and economic or global performances.

Chapter written by France-Anne GRUAT LA FORME, Émilie BAUMANN-CHARDINE, Jean-Pierre CAMPAGNE and Valérie BOTTA-GENOULAZ.

3.2. Characterization of global performance

An increasing number of companies can be characterized by the simultaneous satisfaction of several performance goals. At the same time they are subjected to external pressures, pertaining mainly to the concept of sustainable development.

In 1987, for first time the Brundtland Report of the worldwide Commission on the Environment and Development mentioned the aim of "sustainable development". It defined this term as "a development which satisfies our needs without compromising future generations and the satisfaction of their own needs" [BRU 87].

Concretely, this means that companies need to take steps to create value not only for shareholders but also for their customers, their workers and society in general. This vision of a multi-criteria or global performance, and the search for a balance between the economic, social and environmental dimensions [CDJ 04], seems to be a new performance challenge.

Sustainable development requires that companies develop all three dimensions: environmental, social and economic. This concept is known as corporate social responsibility (CSR), several definitions of which are found in the literature:

– the World Board of Firms for Sustainable Development suggests that "Corporate Social Responsibility represents the commitment to contribute to sustainable economic development, by working with workers, their family, the local authorities and society as a whole to improve the quality of life" [WBC 00];

– the European Commission defines CSR as the voluntary integration by companies of social and environmental concerns into their business activities and their relationships with stakeholders [EUR 01].

These two definitions highlight two common points, namely, commitment/volunteerism and the relevance of the stakeholders:

– *commitment/volunteerism*: judging by environmental and social recommendations, it is not mandatory for companies today to develop CSR practices;

– *the stakeholders*: are defined by [FRE 84] as "a group or a person who is able to influence or to be influenced by the activity of the firm".

It seems here that the CSR field is very wide, even nebulous, in its definition and especially in the identification of stakeholders. Several typologies do nevertheless exist, which help to delimit the concept. Usually we can differentiate between the internal company stakeholders who are directly involved in the economic process (like shareholders, workers, suppliers, customers, competitors, etc.), and the external stakeholders who represent "civil society" (like local residents, non-governmental organizations, customers' associations, etc.).

Note that CSR enables companies to balance or integrate economic growth, environmental factors and social concerns while responding to shareholders' and stakeholders' expectations. Today, CSR in worldwide companies is translated into the concept of global performance.

[REY 03] defines the global performance of a company as a combination of economic, social and environmental performance (see Figure 3.1).

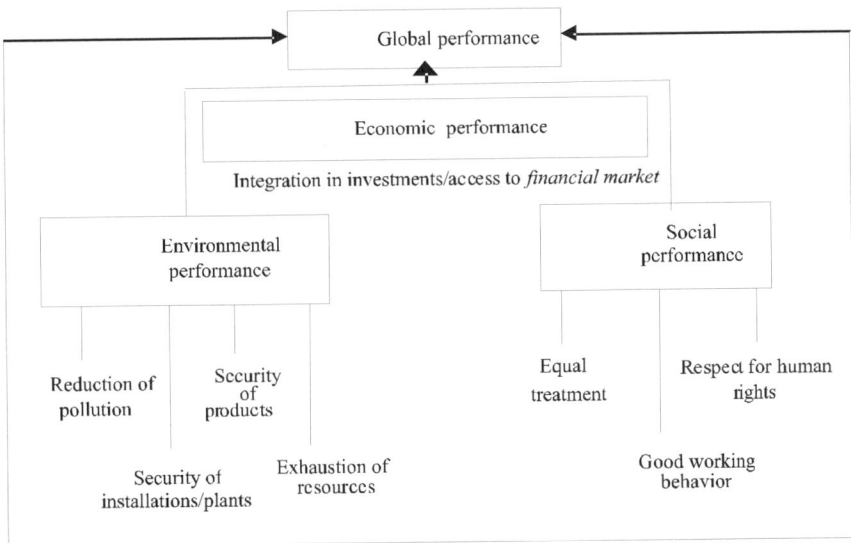

Figure 3.1. *Global performance [REY 03]*

Current policies, which tend to promote sustainable development in many fields, involve manufacturers and encourage them to think about the environmental and social impacts of their activities. The whole supply chain is concerned, from product design to product recycling, because of its numerous impacts (water use, energy consumption, waste production, etc.).

For a long time, companies' performance was reduced to measurement. As a result, they were driven by management control. [ARD 86] describes management control as a system in which companies use tools such as financial accounting, management accounting, and so on to plan, budget for, engage in and follow implemented plans of action to reach their objectives, expressed in terms of a single criterion: costs.

In the 1980s, cost criteria were not enough anymore; new objectives appeared in the form of quality, defined by way of customer satisfaction, lead time and availability. This was the birth of multi-criteria performance. Management started to integrate multi-criteria performance and to consider the company's relationships between itself and its suppliers and distributors. In this context, indicators were implemented at each level (strategic, tactical and operational) to express performance.

Nowadays, companies are subjected to external pressures, notably related to the concept of sustainable development. A company should envisage its solvency in terms of development for all the stakeholders, whether they are direct or indirect. In concrete terms, a company should make improvements by creating value for its shareholders, customers, workers and society as a whole. This means seeking a balance between the economic, environmental and social dimensions.

To illustrate this evolution, we emphasize the advantages of sustainable development indicators. The European Environment Agency [EEA 99] notes three major uses of environmental indicators:

– to supply information on environmental problems, allowing policy makers to prioritize issues;

– to support policy development and optimize the assignment of resources to addressing priority issues;

– to effectively monitor the effects of policy responses.

In generic terms, these could equally be applied to social and economic indicators [WAR 02].

The measurement of performance and the dissemination of information on it can be seen as an integral feedback loop within management systems, ultimately aimed at achieving the goals of sustainable development. [GUI 01] adds that the main uses of global performance are:

– as an input to strategic planning, decision-making, project and program design for companies and/or their partners;

– as a source of information for monitoring, evaluation and impact analysis;

– as a source of information for reporting; and

– as a process to raise awareness about sustainable development issues.

Most studies on supply chain management and CSR consider green supply chain management to be the concept of minimizing the ecological footprint of a product/service during its lifecycle. This lifecycle consists of design [GHE 05], purchase, production, logistics [SCH 05] and recycling [BEA 05]. Nevertheless, the term "ecological footprint" focuses only on environmental impacts.

Moreover, most studies propose 1D assessment systems relating to the economic, environmental or social dimensions. We believe, on the other hand, that global performance has to be measured with a 3D model that includes performance assessment of the economy, the environment and society, to show the interactions between all three dimensions.

3.2.1. *Economic performance*

We propose to characterize economic performance through five dimensions: responsiveness, reliability, flexibility, quality and finances. These are based on indicators linked to specific areas of the supply chain: upstream, downstream or transverse. These indicators are classified in two categories: key success factors or KSI, which are customer oriented; and key performance indicators or KPI, which are business oriented:

– KSF reflects a level of performance directly perceived by customers and represent a strategic challenge for a company. A company can assess its competitiveness compared to its performance on the KSF.

– KSI are linked to the performance of the company or supply chain and contribute directly or indirectly to the performance of KSF. The performance of KPI is not directly perceptible by the client [GAR 01, SCC, 08].

The indicators used to build this model are summarized in Table 3.1. In this model, an indicator of performance is characterized by:

– *a type*: KSI and KPI;

– *a scope*: upstream, downstream, internal or transverse;

– *a nature*: reliability, reactivity, flexibility, quality and financial.

		Upstream part of the supply chain	**Internal part of supply chain**	**Downstream part of supply chain**	**Cross-supply chain**
Customers facing indicators: KPI	*Reliability*	– order fill rate			
	Quality	– product quality			
	Reactivity	– order fulfillment lead time – customer query time			
	Flexibility	– flexibility of service system to meet customer need			
	Financial	– sale price – profit margin			
Company facing indicators: KSI	*Reliability*	– on-time delivery – forecast accuracy – delivery plan adherence	– on time production – production plan adherence	– on-time supplier performance – inventory accuracy – stock out probability – sourcing plan adherence	– reverse plan adherence
	Quality	– production quality		– supplier quality performance	
	Reactivity	– delivery lead time	– production cycle time	– source cycle time – supplier response time	– design cycle time – reverse cycle time – development cycle time – total supply chain cycle time
	Flexibility	– upside delivery flexibility	– production flexibility – volume flexibility	– downside capacity flexibility	– mix product flexibility
	Financial	– delivery cost – inventory cost	– production cost – resources utilization rate – inventory cost	– purchasing cost – replenishment cost – inventory cost	– total supply cost – total cash-flow time – reverse logistic cost – design product cost

Table 3.1. *Economic performance indicators*

3.2.2. *Environmental performance*

Environmental performance represents the compatibility between the company's business and the preservation of ecosystems.

The ISO 14031 standard [AFN 99] defines environmental indicators as specific terms providing information on the company's environmental performance. These indicators measure interactions between companies and the environment [HEN 08]. Indicators can be broken down as followed [AFN 99]:

– environmental performance indicators (EPIs), which include:

- management performance indicators (MPIs) providing information on management efforts to influence the company's environmental performance;

- operational performance indicators (OPIs) providing information on environmental performance connected with company exploitations;

– environmental conditions indicators (ECIs), which provide information on local, regional, national or global environmental conditions.

In the scientific literature, we found some contributions focused on MPIs. [OLS 01] present the [EUR 97] classification of MPIs: environmental investments; running costs pertaining to environmental protection (fees, personnel expenses, fines, energy, maintenance); the number of employees with specific environmental tasks; the number of reported incidents; and the degree of compliance with regulations. [TAM 04] propose a system called "green construction assessment" for environmental management in Hong Kong's construction industry. This system includes six criteria to measure environmental performance: management's involvement; training; investments; the environmental management program; research and development; and environmental planning. [WAR 02] divides environmental performance indicators into four categories describing:

– environmental conditions at the site;

– environmental loadings due to productive activity at the site;

– the system of environmental management;

– environmental achievements.

Research has also been undertaken on OPIs. The Global Reporting Initiative, created in 1997 with the aim of improving the quality and rigor of sustainable development reporting, suggested six criteria to classify environmental indicators [GRI 00]:

– the reduction of materials consumption;

– the reduction of direct and indirect energy consumption;

– the reduction of emissions, effluents and wastes, in particular greenhouse gas impact;

– the optimization of transport; the selection of products/services;

– compliance.

[LAM 00] has developed an accounting model that fits with sustainable development and emphasizes the management of recycling, waste, water consumption, electricity consumption, transport and biodiversity. [BAR 03] suggest an assessment method for technical and economic performance in production cycles. They proposed the evaluation of cleaner production innovations through nine criteria, for example the efficiency of utilization of raw materials and energy; the amount of auxiliary materials used; and water intensity.

[RAO 06] has built a questionnaire to test how the indicators correlate with environmental performance of small to medium enterprises in six industrial sectors in the Philippines. To do so, they selected a set of environmental indicators divided up according to impact. There are both internal indicators and external indicators.

Another type of classification is proposed by the European Environment Agency [EEA 99], based on the following matters of concern:

– What is happening to the environment and to humans? (Descriptive indicators).

– Does it matter? (Performance indicators).

– Are we improving? (Efficiency indicators).

– Are we on the whole better off? (Total welfare indicators).

In addition to these indicator lists, we also find several performance assessment models in the literature. These are presented below.

[KRA 05] have proposed a standardized set of sustainability indicators for companies, covering all the main aspects of sustainable development. Indicators are grouped into three sustainability sub-indices and finally merged into an overall indicator of a company's performance (ICSD). The G score method, proposed by [JUN 01], consists of five categories: general environmental management, input, process, output, and outcome. G score is a measure of company environmental performance based on a voluntary environment, health and safety report. It is calculated by aggregating the points of the above five categories. [HER 07] have developed an analytical tool called COMPLIMENT, which provides detailed information on the overall environmental impact of a company. COMPLIMENT integrates parts of three tools: lifecycle assessment, multi-criteria analysis and environmental performance indicators.

Some authors, notably [CHA 01] and [GAS 04], focus their research on the ecological footprint and the quantitative land and water requirements to sustain a living standard into infinity, thereby assuming certain efficiency improvements.

[HEN 08] have shown first that the importance of the measurement of EPIs is associated with companies that have a more active environmental strategy, ISO 14001-compliant companies, larger companies and public companies. They have also established that the global use of EPIs is also associated with a more active environmental strategy, ISO 14001 compliance, larger companies and public companies.

Recently, [SIN 09] have proposed an overview of sustainability assessment methodologies. They have also compiled information related to sustainability indices formulation strategy, scaling, normalization, weighting and aggregation methodology. [PER 08] have emphasized the role of the uncertainty of measurements, indicators and indices in the evaluation of environmental performance. [MOL 09] have recapitulated studies relating to the impact of the environment on company performance.

In their studies on supply chain management, [ZHU 04] and [ZHU 08] have worked on the correlations between green supply chain performance indicators and green practices. They have tested the influence of quality management and just-in-time on these connections. [VAC 08], using archival data from *The Global Competitiveness Report (2004–2005)* [POR 04], and the *2005 Environmental Sustainability Index* [EST 05], have conducted a statistical assessment of the linkage between supply chain strength, generally defined as the number and quality of the suppliers and customers in a country, and the three dimensions of sustainable development. [MIN 05] has presented an environmental indicator set specifically for the tomato ketchup chain. [TSO 08] have proposed a new approach: how alternative supply chain scenarios match environmental principles applicable to supply chain design and operation. For these purposes, six groups of EPI have been proposed and the authors have developed a model for solving the multi-criteria decision-making problem.

In Table 3.2 we sum up the various environmental criteria found in the literature. From these contributions, we identify five environmental criteria (represented by the superscript numbers), defined as: environmental management (1), resources (2), pollution (3), dangerousness (4) and natural environment (5).

[EUR 01]	Environmental investments[1] Environmental expenses[1] Workers implication[1] Compliance[1]
[TAM 04]	Management involvement[1] Training[1] Investments[1] Environmental management program[1] Research and development[1]
[WAR 02]	Environmental conditions[1] Environmental loadings[1] The system of environmental management[1] Environmental achievements[1]
[GRI 00]	Raw materials[2, 4] Energy[2] Emissions[3], effluents[3] and wastes[2,4] Transport[3] Compliance[1] Products and services[2,4]
[LAM 00]	Recycling[2] Wastes [2,4] Water[2] Electricity[3] Transport[3] Biodiversity[5]
[BAR 03]	Raw materials[2,4] Energy[2] Auxiliary materials[2,4] Water used[2] Waterborne emissions[3] Atmospheric emissions from the production cycle[3] Atmospheric emissions from the energy cycle[3] Hazardous and toxic wastes[4] Solid waste[2]
[RAO 06]	Materials[2,4] Energy[2] Water[2] Waste[2,4]

[KRA 05]	Total energy consumption[2]
	Bought-in energy consumption per unit of production (UP)[2]
	Coal consumption per UP[2]
	Fuel oil consumption per UP[2]
	Gas consumption per UP[2]
	Water consumption per UP[2]
	Consumption of chlorinated hydrocarbons per UP[2]
	Production mass
	Air emissions per UP[3]
	CO_2 emissions per UP[3]
	NOx emissions (calculated as NO_2) per UP[3]
	SO_2 emissions per UP[3]
	Dust emissions per UP[3]
	Emissions of Volatile organic compound (VOC) per UP[3]
	Wastewater per UP[3]
	Chemical oxygen demand (COD) emissions into surface waters per UP[3]
	Emissions of heavy metals into surface waters per UP[3]
	Lead, chromium, copper and nickel per UP[3]
	Zinc per UP[3]
	Waste for recycling and disposal per UP[2]
	Waste for recycling per UP[2]
	Hazardous waste for disposal per UP[4]
	Waste for disposal per UP[2]
[JUN 01]	General environment management[1]
	Input: material[2]
	Input: energy[2]
	Process/operation[1]
	Output: desirable output[2]
	Output: undesirable output[3,4]
	Outcome: financial outcome[1]
	Outcome: non-financial outcome[1]
[CHA 01]	Materials consumption[2]
	Energy use[2]
	Passenger transport[3]
	Freight transport[3]
	Water use[2]
	Built (degraded) land[5]

Table 3.2. *The environmental criteria in the literature*

3.2.3. *Social performance*

Social performance concerns the social consequences of the company's activity, for all stakeholders.

Contributions on social dimension assessment are rare, extremely recent and largely concentrated on public health.

Some researchers, who are interested in social dimension assessment, have considered applying the lifecycle assessment (LCA) method. [GAU 05] has suggested extending the most widely used LCA tool for the purpose of sustainable development. He proposes the measurement of corporate social and environmental performance with the extended lifecycle assessment method. [DRE 06] have developed a methodology of social lifecycle impact assessment. Social LCA aims at making it easier for companies to conduct business in a socially responsible manner, by providing information about the potential social impacts on people caused by activities in the lifecycle of their product. [LAB 06] have proposed a procedure of calculation of the social impact indicator based on the lifecycle impact assessment, and have tested it on the process industry in South Africa. [BEN 07] have developed a methodology for social lifecycle assessment in the case of the North American tomato sector. [GRI 07] has proposed a guideline to describe a methodology of a product-related social lifecycle assessment, and a list of social indicators. Moreover, several companies, for instance BASF, Procter & Gamble and Deutsche Telekom, are working with company-specific tools to collect data on social aspects [GRI 06].

Other researchers have envisaged social dimension assessment from other points of view. [HUT 08] have reviewed metrics, indicators and frameworks of social impacts and initiatives relative to their ability to evaluate the social sustainability of supply chains. They propose four indicator groups – equity in work, healthcare, safety, and philanthropy – and explore the relationship between business decision-making and social sustainability. [GRI 00] and [CON 08] focus on a methodology for CSR reporting: assuring a representative diversity of indicators across stakeholders, scales, sites and performance issues. In particular, they have developed social indicators. [GRI 00] proposes a social distribution by main subject:

– labor practices and decent working conditions, including employment practices, labor/management relations practices, occupational health and safety practices, etc.;

– human rights investment and procurement practices, including non-discriminatory practices, freedom of association and collective bargaining practices, child labor practices, etc.;

– indigenous rights, including society community practices, corruption, public policy, etc.;

– product responsibility, including customer health and safety practices, product and service labeling practices, marketing communications practices, etc.

Finally, the future social responsibility standard, the ISO 26000 [AFN 08], has been based on the integration of sustainable development into business strategy. It presents an operational framework of CSR through six spheres concerning the social dimension: human rights, work relations and conditions, the environment, good business practices, customer issues, and social commitment.

Table 3.3 sums up the various social criteria found in the literature. From these studies, we have identified five social criteria (represented by the superscript number), which are: working conditions (1), human rights (2), societal commitments (3), customers (4), and good business practices (5).

[GAU 05]	Taking the employees into consideration[2] Quality, health and safety at work[1] Relations with contractual stakeholders[5] Relations with various other stakeholders[5]
[LAB 06]	Health[3] Education[3] Environment[3] Housing/living conditions[3] Security/crime[3] Facilities and services[4] Population characteristics[3] Community characteristics[3] Economy welfare/employment[3]
[BEN 07]	Human rights[2] Work conditions[1] Health and safety[1] Cultural aspects[3] Governance[5] Socio-economic repercussions[3] Value and impacts of the product[4]
[GRI 07]	Safe and healthy working conditions[1] Freedom of association, right to collective bargaining and workers' participation[2] Equality of opportunity, treatment and fair interaction[2] Abolition of forced labor[2]

	Abolition of child labor[2]
	Adequate remuneration[1]
	Adequate working time[1]
	Employment security[1]
	Social security[1]
	Professional development[1]
	Job satisfaction[1]
	Safe and healthy living conditions[3]
	Respect of human rights[2]
	Respect of indigenous rights[2]
	Community engagement[3]
	Maintaining and improving social and economic opportunities[3]
	Public commitments to sustainability issues[3]
	Prevention of unjustifiable risks[3]
	Employment creation[3]
	Vocational training[3]
	Anti-corruption efforts and non-interference in sensitive political issues[5]
	Social and environmental minimum standards for suppliers and cooperation partners[5]
	Contribution to the national economy and stable economic development[5]
	Contribution to the national budget[5]
	Prevention and mitigation of armed conflicts[5]
	Transparent business information[5]
	Protection of intellectual property rights[4]
	Protection of the user's/consumer's health and safety[4]
	Quality of product or service[4]
	Fair competition and marketing practices[4,5]
	Complete and understandable product information[4]
	Protection of user's/consumer's privacy[4]
	Enhancing the user's/consumer's social and economic possibilities[4]
[HUT 08]	Equity in work[2]
	Healthcare[1]
	Security[1]
	Philanthropy[3]
[GRI 00]	Labor practices and decent work[1]
	Human rights[2]
	Indigenous rights[3]
	Product responsibility[4]

[CON 08]	Working conditions/health and safety[1]
	Employee opportunities and relations[2]
	Internal communications[1]
	Community relationships[3]
[AFN 09]	Human rights[2]
	Work relations and conditions[1]
	Environment[3]
	Good business practices[5]
	Customer's issues[4]
	Social commitment[3]

Table 3.3. *The social criteria in literature*

3.3. Characterization models for supply chain practices

To characterize practices in supply-chain management, we have developed two models: the first one to characterize collaborative practices and the second one to characterize sustainable practices. In both models, a practice refers to a given process and is characterized by:

– its maturity;

– its managerial dimension.

In addition, the collaborative practice model integrates a third dimension to take into account the origin of a management practice.

3.3.1. *A characterization model for collaborative practices*

3.3.1.1. *Processes and collaborative practices*

From a literature review, we have identified 10 processes from which some collaborative practices can be implemented. These processes are described and defined as follows:

– *customer-driven supply chain* means the knowledge that the company has about the customers' demand and the real impact of this information in its organization and mode of functioning;

– *transport and distribution* means the activities connected to the transportation and storing of finished products, from the company to the customer, and the associated management rules;

– *demand-driven sales planning* means the knowledge that the company has about the customers' demand, and the real impact of this information on its organization and mode of functioning;

– *lean manufacturing* concerns all of the operations proposed to improve and optimize the efficiency of the company's production;

– *supplier collaboration* concerns the level of collaboration and integration of the suppliers in the company's purchasing of its components or raw materials;

– *supply logistics* concerns the activities connected to the traffic and storing of components or raw materials, from the supplier to the stocks of the focus company, and the associated management rules;

– *integrated supply chain management* concerns the integration of activities and characteristics of suppliers and customers in the organization and mode of functioning of the focus company;

– *reverse logistics* concerns the activities bound to the reverse logistics, from customers to the company and from the company to its suppliers;

– *product design* concerns the activities from the phase of design to the phase of commercialization of new products;

– *product development and product evolution* concerns the activities of modification and evolution until the commercialization of the existing products.

3.3.1.2. *Perimeter and intensity of the collaborative practices*

Based on various studies [THI 03], we have identified two main dimensions, or axes, to define the maturity of the relationship between partners:

– the first dimension concerns the stability of the collaborative relationship: this relationship can be occasional or, on the contrary, regular, planed and organized;

– the second dimension concerns the extent of the relationship between the supply chain partners. Depending on the process, the perimeter of the collaborative relationship can be limited to the internal entities of the company, or it can be larger and involve external partners, such as suppliers or customers.

From these two dimensions, "stability" and "extent", and for each collaborative practice, we have established four levels of maturity in order to characterize and measure the intensity of the collaborative relationship. The generic axis characterizing the four levels is proposed in Figure 3.2. Depending on the practice, the position of the four levels 1, 2, 3 and 4 can differ. For example, for some practices it is not relevant to define level 1 at the intersection of the two axes because this never happens. On the contrary, sometimes it is not useful to define the highest level (4) for a "regular relationship" and "with all of the main supply chain partners", because this performance level cannot be reached by any company.

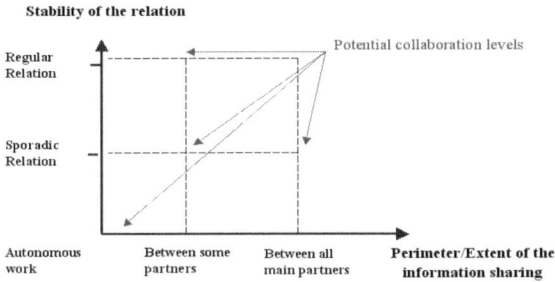

Figure 3.2. *Maturity axis of a collaborative practice*

3.3.1.3. *Decisional level*

We have studied these processes and collaborative practices on decisional dimensions, such as strategy and organization (or strategic dimension), planning (or tactical dimension) and product flows (or operational dimension). Depending on the decisional level, the horizon can be one month or one year (at the strategic level) or one hour or minute (at the operational level).

Based on all of the notions described in Table 3.1, we propose a 3D model as shown in Figure 3.3. The first axis lists the 10 relevant processes of the supply-chain management (downstream, inside, upstream and transverse part of the supply chain). The second axis allows us to study these processes on various dimensions, such as strategy and organization, planning and product flows. For each process and each dimension, two intentions are distinguished: reactive and proactive. Collaborative practices are also defined. For each collaborative practice, the third axis distinguishes four levels of intensity and extent in the relationship between the entities concerned by the shared information.

3.3.1.4. *Proactive and reactive collaboration relationship*

We have identified two categories of collaborative practices. When a company takes the information and constraints given by its supply-chain partners into account it has "reactive" behavior (reactive collaboration). When this company diffuses information across the supply chain, we consider that it has pro-active behavior (pro-active collaboration).

A reactive collaborative practice is engaged in when the company activates a collaborative relationship after a stimulus by its partner in order to improve local and global performance. This stimulus can be information, data or a request, and is considered an input for the collaborative action. We consider that the company is reactive when its collaborative reaction improves the performance of the whole supply chain. For example, to be reactive, a company can integrate an external constraint or modify its process following a remark by a partner.

A proactive collaboration practice is strongly linked to the notion of anticipation, exchange or sharing of information. Thus, the company will be proactive if it anticipates its collaborative action with its partners.

Perimeter	Process	Dimension					
		Strategy and organization		Planning		Product flow	
		Intentions		Intentions		Intentions	
		Proactive	Reactive	Proactive	Reactive	Proactive	Reactive
Downstream	Customer-driven supply chain	Collaborative Practice	Collaborative Practice	-	-	-	-
	Transport and distribution						
	Demand-driven sales planning						
Internal	Lean manufacturing	For each of these practices four maturity levels are proposed					
Upstream	Supplier collaboration						
	Supply logistics						
Transverse	Integrated supply-chain management						
	Reverse logistics						
	Product design						
	Product development and evolution						

Figure 3.3. *Collaborative practices characterization model*

From this model, a company can:

– describe, model and analyze its collaborative practices;

– compare its collaborative practices with the collaborative attitudes of other companies that have some similar characteristics.

3.3.1.5. *Example of collaborative practices*

As an example of those collaborative relationships, the proactive and reactive collaborative practices for the process – supply logistic – are allocated to the following three dimensions: strategy and organization, planning, and product flow.

A company shows reactive collaborative behavior when:

– on the strategic level, it considers its suppliers' strategy and constraints when devising its own supply and inventories strategy;

– on the tactical level, it includes its suppliers' constraints in its replenishment planning;

– on the operational level, it is able to provide information about its product flow at its suppliers' request.

A company shows pro-active collaborative behavior when:

– on the strategic level, the company informs its suppliers about its sourcing strategy, goals or stakes, in order to improve the supply performance;

– on the tactical level, the company shares its projected supply planning with its suppliers in order to validate it with them;

– on the operational level, the company systematically shares information on its inventories with its suppliers in order to synchronize and optimize the supply flow.

As an example of the collaboration maturity associated with each collaborative practice, the four levels of the maturity lever for the *supply logistic* process are the following:

– *level 1*: the company does not inform its suppliers of its sourcing strategy, goals or stakes;

– *level 2*: *ad hoc*, and for some key suppliers the company announces information related to its sourcing strategy, goals or stakes in order to improve the supply performance;

– *level 3*: the company announces information related to its sourcing strategy, goals or stakes regularly and for some key suppliers in order to improve the supply performance;

– *level 4*: the company announces information related to its sourcing strategy, goals or stakes regularly and for all of its key suppliers in order to improve the supply performance.

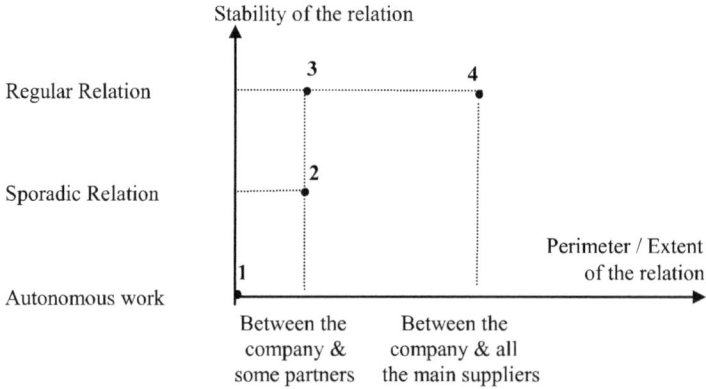

Figure 3.4. *Illustration of the maturity levels for the supply logistics process*

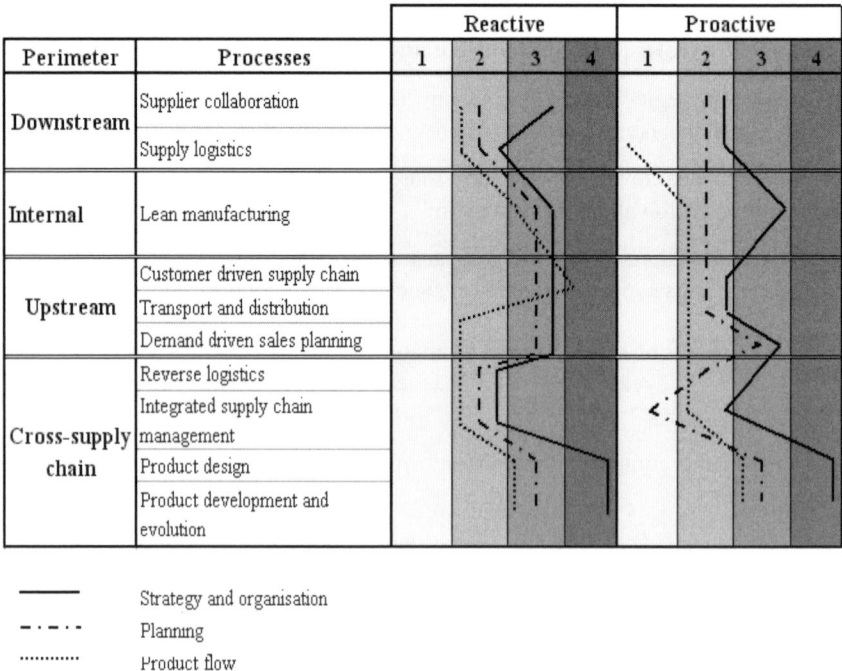

		Reactive				Proactive			
Perimeter	Processes	1	2	3	4	1	2	3	4
Downstream	Supplier collaboration								
	Supply logistics								
Internal	Lean manufacturing								
Upstream	Customer driven supply chain								
	Transport and distribution								
	Demand driven sales planning								
Cross-supply chain	Reverse logistics								
	Integrated supply chain management								
	Product design								
	Product development and evolution								

———— Strategy and organisation

— · — · · Planning

············ Product flow

Figure 3.5. *Collaborative profile of the industrial case study*

This framework or model can be applied by a company. Figure 3.5 is an illustration of the collaborative profile that we can obtain for an industrial company. This profile can evolve year after year and these changes can be analyzed by the company.

3.3.2. *A characterization model for sustainable practices*

3.3.2.1. *Processes and sustainable development practices*

Many standards relating to the modeling or the characterization of the supply chain are built around the identification of processes.

We rely on five standards to identify the main processes and sub-processes characterizing supply chain management:

– the SCOR (supply-chain operations reference) model [SCC 08] has been developed and distributed by the Supply Chain Council. It defines an approach, models and indicators to represent, diagnose and assess the supply chain;

– the Cooper model [COO 97] presents the supply chain as eight processes. It is at the crossroads between business processes and standard duties defined as "silos" in company organization;

– EVALOG [GAL 07] is a logistics guide that centers its analysis on six themes. Four are like processes: customer relationships, supplier relationships, production, and product development. The two others concern company strategy and its organization;

– [POR 90] presents the supply chain as five primary activities: inbound logistics, operations, outbound logistics, marketing and sales, service; and four support activities are identified: company infrastructure, human resources management, technology development and procurement;

– [ASL 05] suggests a catalog of measures and steps for improvement. It serves to characterize the supply chain (as is) through 200 questions along 11 main lines of enquiry. From these elements of characterization, auditors analyze the company situation in the supply chain and put forward some recommendations, which allow for an improvement (to be made).

From these five standards, we characterize the supply chain as discussed in the following sub-sections.

Realization processes			
	Up	In	Down
SCOR	Source	Make	Deliver
	Return		
Cooper	– product development and commercialization – supplier relationship management	– manufacturing flow management	– customer relationship management – customer service management – fulfillment
	Returns		
EVALOG	– product development	– production planning and capacity	– customers relationships
	Suppliers relationships		
Porter	– procurement – inbound logistics	– operations	– marketing and sales – outbound logistics
	Service		
ASLOG	– product design – source – procurement	– production	– distribution – sales
	Maintenances and returns		
Synthesis	– product design – source – procurement	– make	– marketing and sales – deliver
	Return		

Figure 3.6. *Processes in standards*

3.3.2.1.1. Realization processes

Design and develop products/services: Refer to actions related to prototyping and design for a new product/service (total design), and to actions related to evolutions and changes of existing products/services (partial design) from the commercialization phase to the industrialization phase:

– organize the design;

– select the raw materials;

– select the manufacturing processes;

– design the labeling;

– design the packaging;

– anticipate the product/service's end of life.

Procure: Refer to actions related to the purchasing of components or raw materials by the considered company:

– select the suppliers;

– manage supplier's relationships.

Source: Refer to actions related to the movement and storage of components or raw materials, from the supplier to the stocks of the considered company, and to the management of associated business rules:

– organize the delivery of components or raw materials;

– receive and stock components or raw materials;

– receive correct shipping documents;

– organize the procurement;

– validate the payment of components or raw materials.

Produce: Refer to operations for improving and optimizing the efficiency of the manufacturing activities of the considered company.

Deliver: Refer to actions related to the movement and storage of end products/services from the company to its customer, and the associated business rules. Organize the delivery of end products/services:

– organize the delivery of end products/services;

– consolidate orders;

– build load;

– select route;

– select carriers and means of transport;

– send end products/services;

– package end products/services.

Sell: Refer to the weight or the importance attached to customers in the organization and running of the considered company:

– explore;

– meet customers' needs;

– assess customers' satisfaction;

– manage the activities schedule of demand.

Return: Refer to actions related to the reverse logistics, from customers to the considered company or from the company to the suppliers. These returns concern the products/services that are faulty or recoverable (e.g. recyclable):

– organize returns;

– collect products/services;

– sort out products/services;

– store products/services;

– deliver products/services;

– process products/services.

3.3.2.1.2. Management processes

Management processes require the following:

– *plan*: refer to actions related to the activity supply chain planning;

– *define company strategy*: refer to actions related to the establishment, maintenance and enforcement of decisions of the considered supply chain;

– *manage risks*: refer to actions related to the identification, coordination and management of risks of the considered supply chain;

– *collaborate with partners*: refer to actions related to collaboration in the considered supply chain;

– *manage the quality*: refer to actions related to management of the product/service quality in the considered supply chain.

3.3.2.1.3. Enabling processes

The enabling processes are:

– *manage human resources and organization*: refer to actions related to human resources in the considered supply chain;

– *manage financial resources*: refer to actions related to the management of financial resources in the considered supply chain;

– *manage stocks*: refer to actions related to the inventory strategy and to the plan of total inventory levels (including raw material, work in process, finished and purchased finished goods) including replenishment models, ownership, product mix, and stocking locations, both inter- and intra-company;

– *manage capital assets*: refer to actions related to the acquisition, preservation and disposition of an organization's capital assets in the considered supply chain;

– *manage maintenance*: refer to actions related to the management of maintenance in the considered supply chain;

– *manage juridical issues*: refer to actions related to the identification and respect of regulatory documentation and process standards set by external entities in the considered supply chain;

– *manage information systems and data*: refer to actions pertaining to the collection, integration and preservation of data and to the management of information systems in the considered supply chain.

3.3.2.1.4. Measurement processes

Measurement of the performance of processes and sub-processes is studied through the impacts of supply chain practices on the three performance dimensions.

3.3.2.2. *Degrees of maturity of sustainable practices*

In order to assess the degree of practices' implementation, we propose a scale with four degrees from zero to three where zero corresponds to a non-deployment and three to a regular and full deployment of the practice (see Table 3.4).

Degrees	**Interpretation**
0	This practice is not deployed or not much
1	This practice is deployed occasionally and only for some products/services
2	This practice is deployed regularly and only for some products/services
3	This practice is deployed regularly and for all products/services

Table 3.4. *Degrees and interpretation of levels of implementation*

3.3.2.3. Decisional levels of sustainable practices

Perimeter	Processes	Decision level		
		Strategic	Tactical	Operational
Up	Product design	Sustainable practice	Sustainable practice	Sustainable practice
Up	Source	-	-	-
Up	Procurement			
Internal	Make	For all processes and for each given sustainable practice, three decision levels are proposed		
Down	Marketing and sales			
Down	Deliver			
Transverse	Return			

Table 3.5. *Examples of sustainable practices by decision level*

3.3.2.4. Example of sustainable practices

As an example of sustainable relationships, the sustainable practices for the process – *supply logistic* – are allocated among the three dimensions: *strategy and organization, planning* and *product flow*. A company develops a sustainable behavior when:

– on the strategic level it considers environmental and social dimensions in its suppliers' selection;

– on the tactical level it organizes and rationalizes suppliers' rounds;

– on the operational level it demands that its suppliers send security certificates by email.

3.4. Characterization of relationships between practices and their impacts on performance

We have designed a global performance of supply chain (GPSC) assessment model according to the following characteristics.

It is articulated around several supply chain management practices (P_k) with which a degree of implementation is associated, $W(P_k)$. We propose to consider a four-level scale for this implementation, from zero to three (see Table 3.4). Each supply chain management practice is associated with a supply chain process (design, source, produce, deliver, etc.).

The aim of the GPSC assessment model is to measure the impacts of each practice on the three dimensions: economy, environment and society (see Figure 3.7). For each dimension, five criteria have been identified in the literature. Several sub-criteria, characterized by performance indicators, compose each criterion (see Figure 3.14).

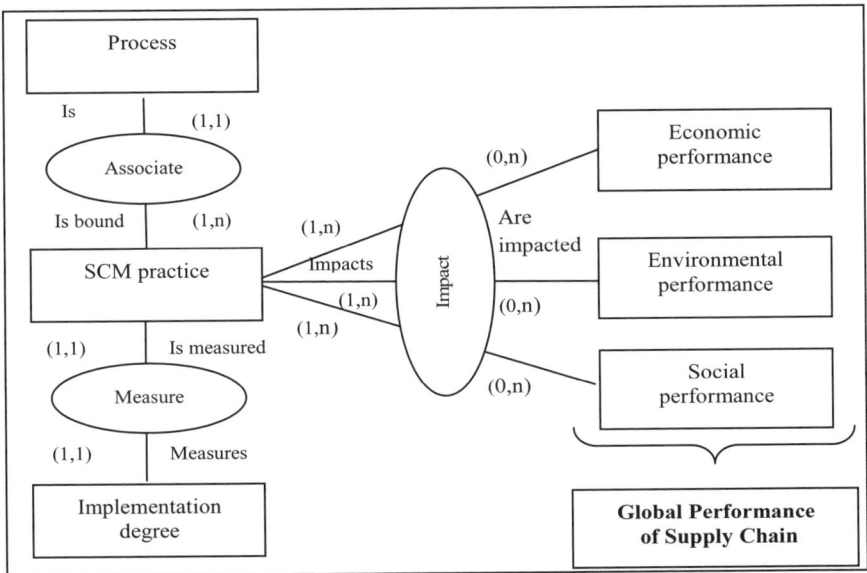

Figure 3.7. *Structure of the SCGP model*

3.4.1. *Relationships between collaborative practices and economic performance*

We have identified the potential correlations between the collaborative practices and their impacts on the performance of the supply chain, as described in Table 3.6.

Practices – KPI		Perimeter				Nature				
KPI – Practices		Up	Intern.	Down	Trans.	Flexib.	React.	Quality	Fiability	Finance
Collaborative Practices / Perimeter	Upstream	yes	no	no	yes	yes*		yes	yes* / yes	yes
	Internal	no	yes	no	yes	yes*	yes*	yes*	yes*	**yes**
	Down	no	no	yes	yes		yes*		yes*	yes
	Transverse	no	no	no	yes	yes* / yes				yes
Managerial Level	Strategic	-	-	-	-	-	yes	yes	-	yes
	Tactical	-	-	-	-	-	yes	-	yes	-
	Operational	-	-	-	-	-	yes	-	-	-

Table 3.6. *Potential links between collaborative practices and economic performance*

"Yes" means that we have identified some correlations between some collaborative practices and some key performance indicators.

"No" means that there are no links between the collaborative practice and the performance indicator.

"-" means that no significant link has been identified between the collaborative practice and the performance indicator.

"*" means that a trend is observed for some processes.

To characterize the perceived performance level of a company, we cross-compare the stability and extent of its satisfaction. We consider four satisfaction levels (see Figure 3.8).

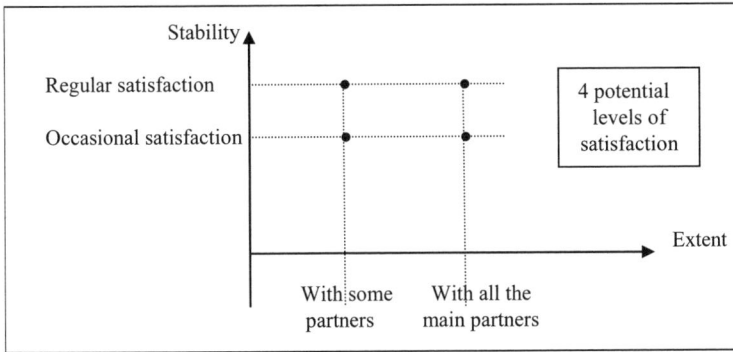

Figure 3.8. *Satisfaction level of perceived performance*

For example, for the – *on-time delivery* – indicator, the four levels are defined as follows:

– *level 1*: the company is not satisfied with the performance level attained regarding the reliability of its delivery activity;

– *level 2*: occasionally and for some distributors, the company is satisfied with the performance level attained regarding the reliability of its delivery;

– *level 3*: regularly and for some distributors the company is satisfied with the performance level attained regarding the reliability of its delivery;

– *level 4*: regularly and for all of its main distributors the company is satisfied with the performance level attained regarding the reliability of its delivery relation between collaborative practices and performance indicators.

3.4.1.1. *Perceived performance evaluation*

From the collaborative-oriented performance model (see Table 3.1), we aim at obtaining the collaborative-oriented performance profile of a company. For each indicator proposed in this model, the company has to establish its position on one of the four levels of perceived performance. Moreover, we have associated a rank for each indicator according to the estimated criticality regarding the company's performance:

– we consider that a performance indicator belongs to rank A when it is essential for the company's competitiveness;

– we consider that a performance indicator belongs to rank B when it is important for the company but not essential to its performance.

The perceived performance of a company can be modeled as in Figure 3.9.

KPI : Reactivity
4
3
2
1
Upstream
Internal
Upstream
Transverse

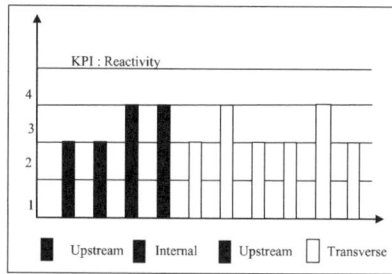

Figure 3.9. *Example of performance profile*

The performance can be synthesized as shown in Figure 3.10.

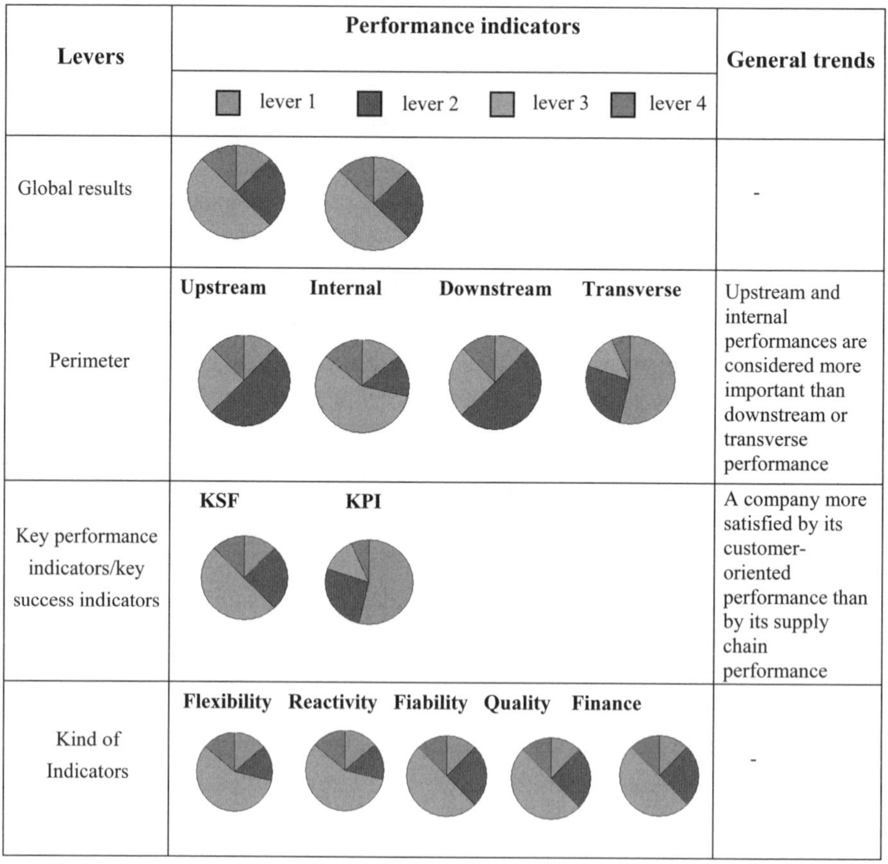

Levers
Performance indicators
General trends
lever 1
lever 2
lever 3
lever 4
Global results
-
Perimeter
Upstream
Internal
Downstream
Transverse
Upstream and internal performances are considered more important than downstream or transverse performance
Key performance indicators/key success indicators
KSF
KPI
A company more satisfied by its customer-oriented performance than by its supply chain performance
Kind of Indicators
Flexibility
Reactivity
Fiability
Quality
Finance
-

Figure 3.10. *Synthesis of a company's performance*

3.4.1.2. Relationship between performance and collaborative practices

We have defined a matrix to link the collaborative practices and the performance indicators. The main goal is to highlight some potential impacts of collaborative efforts on the different aspects of the supply chain performance (see Table 3.1).

From this matrix, a company is able to identify the collaborative practices to introduce, according to the type of performance it needs to improve (see Figure 3.11):

– which kind of performance has to be improved (reactivity, reliability, quality, flexibility, cost)? (level 1);

– which perimeter of the supply chain is concerned (downstream part, inside part, upstream part of the supply chain)? (level 2);

– which indicator, in particular, do we want to improve? (level 3).

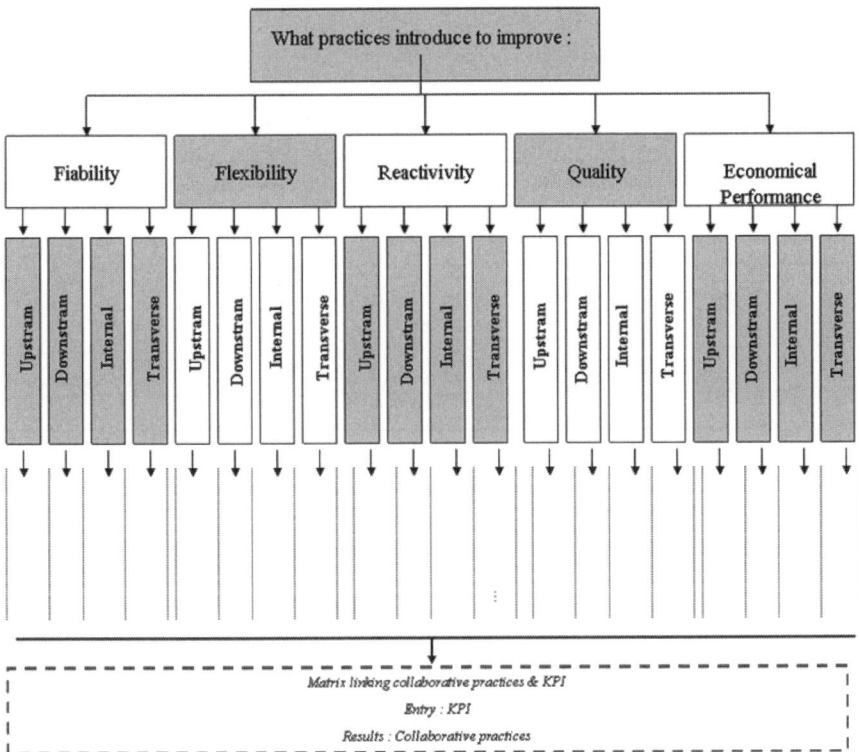

Figure 3.11. *Which collaborative practice for which performance indicator*

– identify and understand the consequences, impacts and benefits of some collaborative practices that a company can manage with its partners across the supply chain (see Figure 3.12). This analysis can be structured in various dimensions:

- the perimeter on which the collaborative practice is based (level 1);

- the process associated with the collaborative practice (level 2);

- the managerial dimension (level 3)?

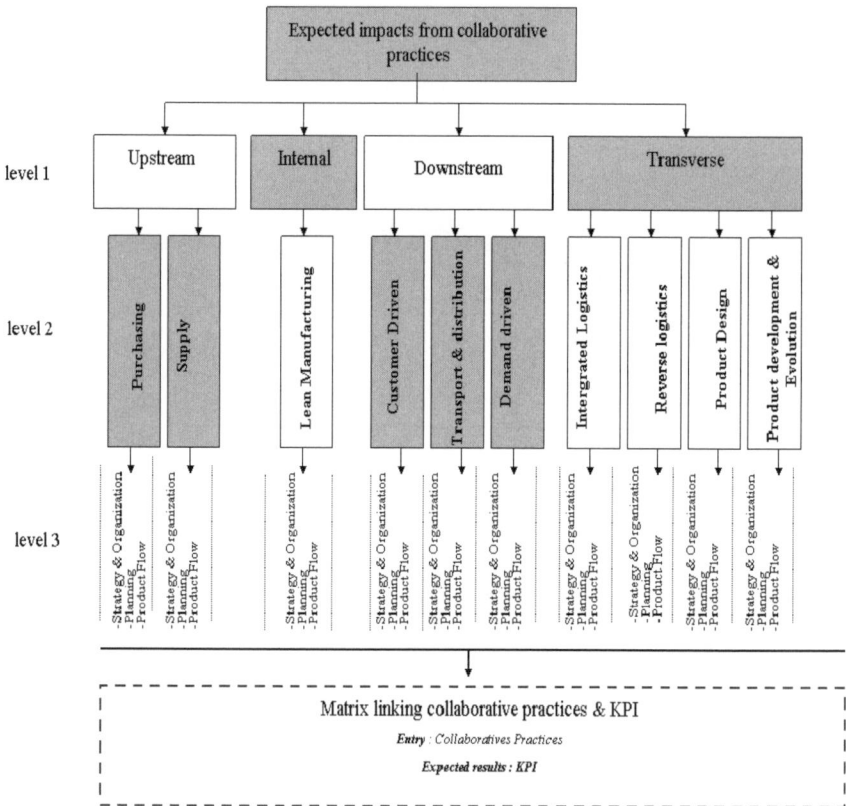

Figure 3.12. *Which performance impacts to expect for various collaborative practices*

After informing the collaboration characterization model and collaboration-oriented performance model, a company can juxtapose them to obtain some initial results on its situation. We consider that a company can be confronted with three different cases (see Figure 3.13):

– *Scenario 1*: the perceived performance related to indicator X is consistent with the levels reached for most associated collaborative practices. A way to improve the performance of the indicator X could be through an increase at the collaborative practices level.

– *Scenario 2*: the perceived performance related to indicator X is below the levels reached for most associated collaborative practices. In others words, collaborative efforts do not seem to bear fruit. For example, the reason for this ineffectiveness could be explained by the context or information system, which does not efficiently support the collaborative actions across the supply chain.

– *Scenario 3*: the perceived performance related to indicator X is superior to the levels reached for most associated collaborative practices. For example, this situation can be explained for some non-strategic indicators when the company's requirement is not high.

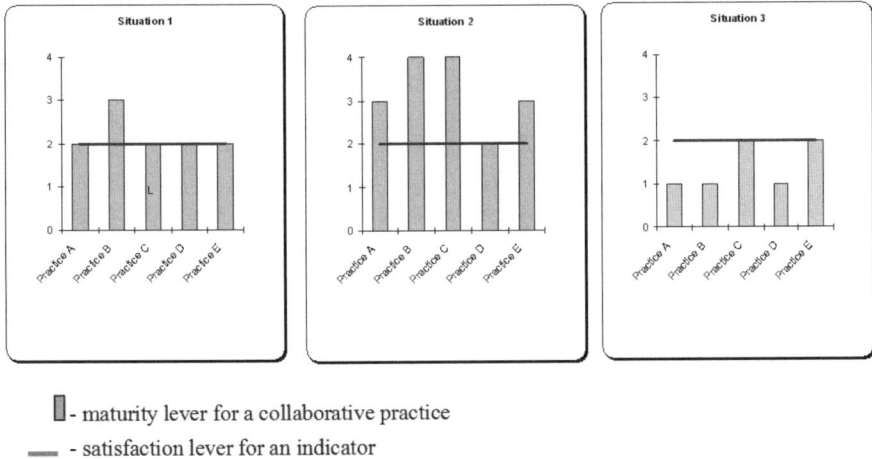

$\blacksquare$ - maturity lever for a collaborative practice
— - satisfaction lever for an indicator

Figure 3.13. *Some potential situations for collaborative performance evaluation*

When a company considers the levels of its perceived performance and collaborative maturity level, it can analyze its collaborative behavior, evaluate efficiency and underline some areas for improvement. Nevertheless, note that a context model could be useful before analyzing certain results, such as those relating to the company's environment for example.

3.4.2. *Relationships between sustainable practices and global performance*

The identification of sustainable development criteria, sub-criteria and indicators constitutes a requirement for the definition of the GPSC characterization and measurement model.

We propose to measure the GPSC in four steps (see Figure 3.14). The three dimensions of sustainable development are broken down into five criteria, which in turn are subdivided into sub-criteria.

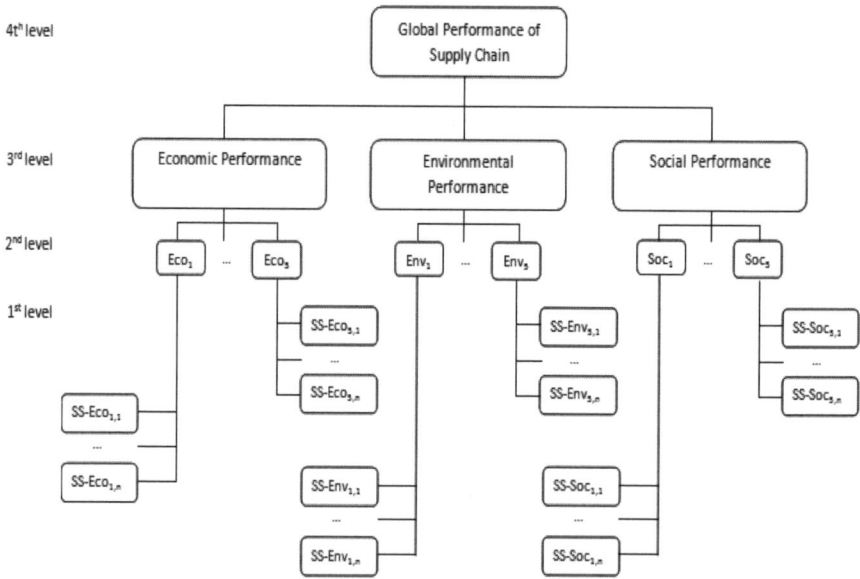

Figure 3.14. *Tree of supply-chain global performance model*

In the first step: Let SC-Eco$_{ij}$ denote the jth sub-criterion of the ith economic criterion respectively. SC-Env$_{ij}$ and SC-Soc$_{ij}$ are defined similarly for the environmental and social criteria. Each practice (P_k) positively or negatively influences one or more sub-criteria of each dimension, or has no impact.

Impact $(P_k, SC\text{-}Eco_{i,j}) \in \{-1 ; 0 ; 1\}$ $\forall k\ i =$ criteria i from 1 to 5   [3.1]

$j =$ sub-criteria of i j from 1 to n$_i$

Impact $(P_k, SC\text{-}Env_{i,j}) \in \{-1 ; 0 ; 1\}$ $\forall k$ $i =$ criteria i from 1 to 5   [3.2]

$j =$ sub-criteria of i j from 1 to n_i

Impact $(P_k, SC\text{-}Soc_{i,j}) \in \{-1 ; 0 ; 1\}$ $\forall k$ $i =$ criteria i from 1 to 5   [3.3]

$j =$ sub-criteria of i j from 1 to n_i

As we measure the impacts according to the degree of implementation of practices, the impacts are weighted. For each practice k:

Weighted impact $(P_k, SC\text{-}Eco_{i,j}) =$ Impact $(P_k, SC\text{-}Eco_{i,j})*W_p$ [3.4]

$-3 <$ Impact $(P_k, SC\text{-}Eco_{i,j}) < 3$

Weighted impact $(Pk, SC\text{-}Envi,j) =$ Impact $(Pk, SC\text{-}Envi,j)*W_p$ [3.5]

$-3 <$ Impact $(Pk, SC\text{-}Envi,j) < 3$

Weighted impact $(P_k, SC\text{-}Soc_{i,j}) =$ Impact $(P_k, SC\text{-}Soc_{i,j})*W_p$ [3.6]

$-3 <$ Impact $(P_k, SC\text{-}Soc_{i,j}) < 3$

In the second step: When we aggregate the sub-criteria on the criterion level we agree to compensate for impacts between them. For example, a company that implements a practice that improves the percentage of renewable energy while reducing the percentage of recyclable outputs has a neutral performance on the resources" criterion.

We define *Perf (P_k, Eco_i)* as the criterion performance of the practice P_k on the ith economic criterion Eco_i as:

$$Perf(P_k, Eco_i) =$$

$$\frac{1}{N(Eco_i)} \sum_{j=1}^{N(Eco_i)} [Impact(P_k, SC - Eco_{i,j}) \times W(P_k)]$$ [3.7]

$$\forall k$$

Perf (P_k, Env_i) and *Perf (P_k, Soc_i)* are defined similarly for the environmental and social criteria:

$$Perf(P_k, Env_i) =$$

$$\frac{1}{N(Env_i)} \sum_{j=1}^{N(Env_i)} [Impact(P_k, SC - Env_{i,j}) \times W(P_k)] \tag{3.8}$$

$$\forall k$$

$$Perf(P_k, Soc_i) =$$

$$\frac{1}{N(Soc_i)} \sum_{j=1}^{N(Soc_i)} [Impact(P_k, SC - Soc_{i,j}) \times W(P_k)] \tag{3.9}$$

$$\forall k$$

In the third step: Each dimension – economic, environmental and social – is composed of five criteria. We measure their performance on each practice k, respectively $Eco(P_k)$, $Env(P_k)$ and $Soc(P_k)$, as:

$$\text{Eco}(P_k) = \sum_{i=1}^{5} Perf(P_k, Eco_i) \quad \forall k \ \text{-5<Perf}(P_k, Eco_i)\text{<5} \tag{3.10}$$

$$\text{Env}(P_k) = \sum_{i=1}^{5} Perf(P_k, Env_i) \quad \forall k$$
$$\text{-5<Perf}(P_k, Env_i)\text{<5} \tag{3.11}$$

$$\text{Soc}(P_k) = \sum_{i=1}^{5} Perf(P_k, Soc_i) \quad \forall k$$
$$\text{-5<Perf}((P_k, Soc_i)\text{<5} \tag{3.12}$$

In the fourth step: The fourth level represents the global performance, denoted by a trinity. The trinity is made up of the economic, environmental and social performances, either weighted or not.

The GPSC model enables us to analyze the links between practices and the performance target of sustainable development for a company. In this section we present an illustration of the use of the GPSC model in two fictive cases: Company A and Company B.

3.4.2.1. *The measurement of global performance*

Global performance of companies A and B

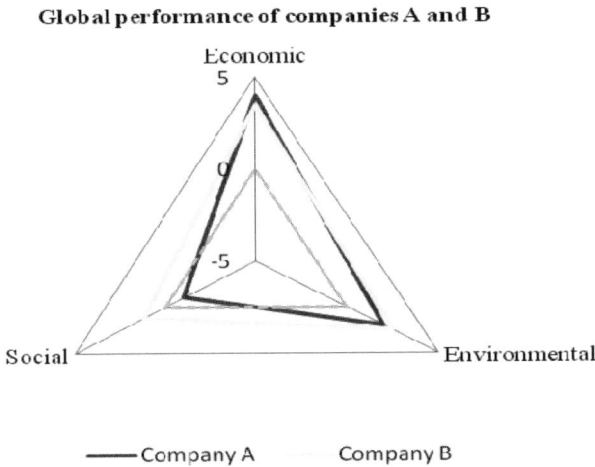

Figure 3.15. *The measure of global performance*

Performance	Company A	Company B
Economic	4	3.5
Environmental	2	2.5
Social	-1	1.25

Table 3.7. *The measure of global performance*

The results of the GPSC assessment model of two companies are presented in Figure 3.15 and Table 3.7.

The measure of global performance highlights the fact that the activities of the two companies have mainly positive impacts on the economic dimension. These companies' survival is guaranteed.

The environmental impact is also positive for these two companies. They have probably developed environmental strategies to reduce their environmental impact.

Regarding the third dimension, the activity of Company A has negative impacts on the social dimension, whereas the activity of Company B has positive impacts, although this remains the least-developed dimension in relation to the other two.

3.4.2.2. *Impacts of a given supply chain management practice*

We propose to analyze the impacts of P4, which is the assessment of the performance of suppliers in the two companies (see Table 3.8).

	Company A	Company B
Global performance of P4		
Economic performance of P4		
Environmental performance of P4		
Social performance of P4		

Table 3.8. *Impacts of practice P4*

The supply chain management practice P4 positively affects the economic and environmental dimensions of Company A and negatively affects its social dimension. The analysis of economic impacts emphasizes that criteria 2, 4 and 5 reach the maximum performance. The analysis of environmental impacts shows that criteria 2, 4 and 5 reach the maximum performance but that criterion 1 has a negative performance, i.e. a negative impact on the environment. The analysis of social impacts shows that only criterion 1 has a neutral impact. The other criteria negatively influence the social dimension.

The supply chain management practice P4 impacts positively on the economic and social dimensions and negatively on the environmental dimension of Company B. The first three economic criteria produce very good results. The analysis of environmental impacts shows that only criterion 2 positively influences environmental protection, that criterion 5 has a neutral impact, and that the other three criteria negatively influence the environmental performance. Company B seems to concentrate its efforts on the social dimension, since the implementation of practice P4 positively influences all the social criteria.

3.4.2.3. *Impacts of a given sustainable criterion*

Table 3.9. *Impacts of sustainable criteria*

The GPSC assessment model enables a company to act on a given sustainable criterion. In fact, from a sample of companies we establish links between supply chain management practices and sustainable criteria (see Table 3.9). For example, if a company wants to improve environmental criterion 1, its managers should concentrate their efforts on practices P3 and P6.

3.5. Conclusion

Nowadays, the performance of a supply chain has to be analyzed globally by simultaneously considering three dimensions: economic, environmental and societal. This performance obviously depends on the managerial practices of companies in the supply chain, particularly their collaborative and sustainable practices.

To analyze the impact of these practices on the global performance, we have first characterized this performance by proposing an analysis framework for the above three dimensions of industrial performance, and by defining performance indicators or components for each dimension: economic, environmental and societal.

In the second phase, we have characterized these managerial practices by associating each of them with a given process and managerial level, and by proposing a mono- or bi-directional framework to measure the degree of maturity of these practices. The proactive or reactive nature of collaborative practices has furthermore been highlighted.

Finally, we have proposed two successive steps: the first to identify existing correlations between collaborative efforts and economic performance; and the second to analyze existing relationships between performance and sustainable practices. An application of this approach to the analysis of environmental impacts concludes this chapter.

3.6. Bibliography

[AFN 99] AFNOR, *ISO 14031:1999 Environmental Management – Environmental Performance Evaluation - Guidelines*, International Standardization Organization, 1999.

[AFN 08] AFNOR, *Lignes Directrices Relatives à la Responsabilité Sociétale* – French translation of, CD ISO 26000, 12 December 2008.

[ARD 86] ARDOIN J.L., MICHEL D., SCHMIDT J., *Le Contrôle de Gestion*, Publi-Union, 1986.

[ASL 05] ASSOCIATION FRANCAISE POUR LA LOGISTIQUE, *Référentiel de Performance Logistique*, Edition no. 4.2, 2005, available online www.aslog.org, accessed 27.4.10.

[BAR 03] BARBIROLI G., RAGGI A., "A method for evaluating the overall technical and economic performance of environmental innovations in production cycles", *Journal of Cleaner Production*, vol. 11, 2003, pp. 365-374.

[BEA 05] BEAULIEU M., ROY J., "Structure de gouvernance des filières à rebours: deux cas québécois", *Logistique & Management*, vol. 13, no. 1, 2005, pp. 79-88.

[BEN 07] BENOIT C., PARENT J., KUENZI I., REVERET J-P., "Developing a methodology for social life cycle assessment: The North American Tomato's CSR Case", *Governance and Life Cycle Analysis, Opportunities for Going Beyond ISO-LCA*, September 27-28, 2007

[BRU 87] BRUNDTLAND G., *Our Common Future: The World Commission on Environment and Development*, Oxford University Press, 1987

[CDJ 04] CDJ: Centre des Jeunes Dirigeants d'Entreprises, *Le Guide de la Performance Globale*, Editions d'Organisation, Paris, 2004

[CHA 01] CHAMBERS N., LEWIS K., Ecological Footprint Analysis: Towards a Sustainability Indicator for Business, *ACCA Research Paper*, vol. 65, Glasgow, Scotland, 2001.

[CON 08] O'CONNOR M., SPANGENBERG J.H., "A methodology for CSR reporting: assuring a representative diversity of indicators across stakeholders, scales, sites and performance issues", *Journal of Cleaner Production*, vol.16, 2008, pp. 1399-1415.

[COO 97] COOPER M.C., LAMBERT D.M., PAGH J.D., "Supply chain management: More than a new name for logistics", *International Journal of Logistics Management*, vol. 8, no. 1, 1997, pp. 1-13.

[DRE 06] DREYER L.C., HAUSCHILD M.Z., SCHIERBECK J., "A framework for social life cycle impact assessment", *International Journal LCA*, vol. 11, no. 2, 2006, pp. 88-97.

[EEA 99] EUROPEAN ENVIRONMENT AGENCY, *Environmental Indicators: Typology and Overview*. EEA, Copenhagen, Denmark, 1999.

[EST 05] ESTY D., LEVY M., SREBOTNJAK T., DE SHERBININ A., 2005 *Environmental Sustainability Index*, New Haven: Yale Center for Environmental Law and Policy, and Palisades NY: Center for International Earth Science Information Network (CIESIN), Columbia University, 408 pages, 2005. Available at http://www.yale.edu/esi

[EUR 97] EUROPEAN GREEN TABLE, *Environmental Performance Indicators in Industry. Report 5: Practical Experiences with Developing EPIs in 12 Companies*, Oslo, Norway, March 1997.

[EUR 01] EUROPEAN COMMISSION, *The Green Guide* (le Livre Vert, Promouvoir un cadre européen pour la responsabilité sociale des entreprise), Office des Publications Officielles des Communautés Européennes, 2001

[FRE 84] FREEMAN R. E., *Strategic Management: A Stakeholder Approach*, Pitman, 1984

[GAL 07] GALIA, *Global Evalog: Guide de l'évaluation Logistique dans l'Industrie Automobile*, 2007, available online http://www.galia.com, accessed 27.4.2010.

[GAR 01] GARIBALDI G., *L'Analyse Stratégique, Comment Concevoir les Choix Stratégiques en Situation Concurrentielle*, Les Editions d'Organisation, 2001

[GAS 04] GASSNER J., NARODOSLAWSKY, M., "Sustainable economy and their application to Austria", *International Journal of Environmental Sustainable Development*, 2004, vol. 3, no. 2, pp. 120–144.

[GAU 05] GAUTHIER C., "Measuring corporate social and environmental performance: The extended life-cycle assessment", *Journal of Business Ethics*, vol. 59, 2005, pp. 199–206.

[GHE 05] GHERRA S., "Développement durable, supply chain management et stratégie: les cas de l'éco-conception", *Logistique & Management*, vol. 13, no. 1, 2005, pp. 37-48.

[GRI 00] GRI : GLOBAL REPORTING INITIATIVE, *Sustainability Reporting Guidelines*, GRI, Version 3.0, 2000-2006

[GRI 06] GRIEßHAMMER R., BENOIT C., DREYER L.C., FLYSJO A., MANHART A., MAZIJN B., METHOT A-L., WEIDEMA B., "Feasibility study: Integration of social aspects into LCA", *May, Discussion Paper from UNEP-SETAC Task Force Integration of Social Aspects in LCA* meetings in Bologna (January 2005), Lille (May 2005) and Brussels (November 2005), Freiburg, Germany, 2006

[GRI 07] GRIEßHAMMER R., BUCHERT M., GENSCH C-O., HOCHFELD C., MANHART A., REISCH L, RÜDENAUER I., *PROSA: Product Sustainability Assessment Guideline*, Öko-Institut e.V., Institute for Applied Ecology, Freiburg, 2007.

[GRU 07] GRUAT-LA-FORME F.A., Modèle d'évaluation de performance d'une chaîne logistique: application à une entreprise de l'ameublement, Doctorate Thesis, Institut National des Sciences Appliquées de Lyon, 2007.

[GUI 01] GUIJT I., MOISEEV A PRESCOTT-ALLEN R., IUCN *Resource Kit for Sustainability Assessment*, IUCN-The World Conservation Union, Gland, Switzerland, 2001.

[HEN 08] HENRI J-F., JOURNEAULT M., "Environmental performance indicators: An empirical study of Canadian manufacturing firms", *Journal of Environmental Management*, vol. 87, 2008, pp. 165-176

[HER 07] HERMANN G.B., KROEZE C., JAWJIT W., "Assessing environmental performance by combining life cycle assessment, multi-criteria analysis and environmental performance indicators", *Journal of Cleaner Production*, vol. 15, 2007, pp. 1787-1796

[HUT 08] HUTCHINS M.J., SUTHERLAND J.W., "An exploration of measures of social sustainability and their application to supply chain decisions" *Journal of Cleaner Production*, vol. 16, 2008, pp. 1688–1698

[JUN 01] JUNG E.J., KIM J.S., RHEE S.K., "The measurement of corporate environmental performance and its application to the analysis of efficiency in oil industry", *Journal of Cleaner Production*, vol. 9, 2001, pp. 551–563

[KRA 05] KRAJNC D, GLAVIC P., "A model for integrated assessment of sustainable development", *Conservation and Recycling*, vol. 43, 2005, pp. 189–208

[LAB 06] LABUSCHAGNE C., BRENT A.C., "Social indicators for sustainable project and technology life cycle management in the process industry", *International Journal LCA*, vol. 11, 2006, no. 1, pp. 3-15

[LAM 00] LAMBERTON G., "Accounting for sustainable development – A case study of city farm", *Critical Perspectives on Accounting*, vol. 11, 2000, pp. 583–605

[MIN 05] MINTCHEVA V., "Indicators for environmental policy integration in the food supply chain (the case of the tomato ketchup supply chain and the integrated product policy)", *Journal of Cleaner Production*, vol. 13, 2005, pp. 717-731

[MOL 09] MOLINA-AZORÍN J.F., CLAVER-CORTE' S.E., PEREIRA-MOLINER J., JOSE' TARI J., "Environmental practices and firm performance: an empirical analysis in the Spanish hotel industry", *Journal of Cleaner Production*, vol. 17, 2009, pp. 516–524.

[OLS 01] OLSTHOORN X., TYTECA D., WEHRMEYER W., WAGNER M., "Environmental indicators for business: a review of the literature and standardization methods", *Journal of Cleaner Production*, vol. 9, 2001, pp. 453–463.

[PER 08] PERETTO E., CANZIANI R., MARCHESI R., BUTELLI P., "Environmental performance, indicators and measurement uncertainty in EMS context: a case study", *Journal of Cleaner Production*, vol. 16, 2008, pp. 517-530.

[POR 90] PORTER M., *The Competitive Advantage of Nations*, Harvard Business Review, 1990.

[POR 04] PORTER M., SCHWAB K., SALA-I-MARTIN X., LOPEZ-CLAROS A., *The Global Competitiveness Report (2004-2005)*, Palgrave Macmillan, 2004.

[RAO 06] RAO P., LA O' CASTILLO O., INTAL Jr P., SAJID A., "Environmental indicators for small and medium enterprises in the Philippines: An empirical research", *Journal of Cleaner Production*, vol. 14, 2006, pp. 505-515.

[REY 03] REYNAUD E., "Développement durable et entreprise: vers une relation symbiotique", *Journée AIMS*, Atelier développement durable, ESSCA Angers, France, 2003.

[SCC 08] SUPPLY CHAIN COUNCIL, *Supply Chain Operations Reference Model: Overview of SCOR, Version 9.0*, SCC, document available for SCC members, 2008.

[SCH 05] SCHMIDT J., "Le développement d'une logistique en accord avec le développement durable", *Logistique & Management*, vol. 13, no. 1, 2005, pp. 31-36.

[SIN 09] SINGH R.K., MURTY H.R., GUPTA S.K., DIKSHIT A.K., "An overview of sustainability assessment methodologies", *Ecological Indicators*, vol. 9, 2009, pp. 189-212.

[TAM 04] TAM C.M., TAM W.Y., TSUI W.S., "Green construction assessment for environmental management in the construction industry of Hong Kong", *International Journal of Project Management*, vol. 22, 2004, pp. 563–571.

[THI 03] THIERRY C., Gestion des chaînes logistiques: modèles et mise en œuvre pour l'aide à la décision moyen terme, Mémoire d'HDR, University of Toulouse II le Mirail, 2003, available at: www.univ-valenciennes.fr/GDR-MACS/hdr/memoire_habilitation _CT.pdf, accessed 27.4.10.

[TSO 08] TSOULFAS G.T., PAPPIS C.P., "A model for supply chains environmental performance analysis and decision making", *Journal of Cleaner Production*, vol. 16, 2008, pp. 1647–1657.

[VAC 08] VACHON S., MAO Z., "Linking supply chain strength to sustainable development: a country-level analysis", *Journal of Cleaner Production*, vol. 16, 2008, pp. 1552–1560.

[WAR 02] WARHURST A., Sustainability Indicators and Sustainability Performance Management. Final Report of MMSD Project (Mining, Minerals and Sustainable Development) of the International Institute for Environment and Development, IIED and WBCSD, 2002

[WBC 04] WBCSD: World Business Council for Sustainable Development, *Issue Management Tool: Strategic Challenges for Business in the Use of Corporate Responsibility Codes, Standards, and Frameworks*, WBCSD, October 2004, available online   http://www.wbcsd.org/web/publications/accountability-codes.pdf,   accessed 27.4.10.

[ZHU 04] ZHU K., SARKIS J., "Relationships between operational practices and performance among early adopters of green supply chain management practices in Chinese manufacturing enterprises", *Journal of Operations Management*, vol. 22, 2004, pp. 265–289.

[ZHU 08] ZHU K., SARKIS J., LAI K-H., "Confirmation of a measurement model for green supply chain management practices implementation", *International Journal of Production Economics*, vol. 111, 2008, pp. 261–273.

PART II

Focus on Strategic Alignment
of Information Systems

Chapter 4

Inter-organizational Strategic Alignments in a Jewelry Supply Chain using RFID: a Case Study

4.1. Introduction

In today's world, globalization and technological innovations call for improved organizational adaptability and more flexible and advanced systems in manufacturing, logistics, engineering, and information and process technology [MOM 02]. In order to improve their performance, firms are outsourcing their non-core competency activities and focusing on their own business.

Obviously, this dilemma of internalization/externalization of activities leads to an increasing dependency of businesses and greater complexity of supply chains. In this context, the objective of supply chain management (SCM) is to increase the financial and operational performance of each partner and of the global supply chain. By enabling a closer relationship between all supply chain partners, SCM achieves cost reductions and revenue enhancements, as well as flexibility in dealing with uncertainties in supply and demand [BOW 00, LEE 97]. SCM is based on the integration of key business processes, from end user through to original suppliers that provide products, services and information, and thus added value for customers and other stakeholders [LAM 98]. Two IT and information systems (IS) supporting the organization and its partners up- and downstream have been recognized as critical factors in the improvement of SCM [KOH 06, NEU 04]. As Gunasekaran

Chapter written by Carine DOMINGUEZ, Blandine AGERON, Gilles NEUBERT and Ishraf ZAOUI.

and Ngai [GUN 04b] have pointed out, it is currently impossible to achieve an effective supply chain without IT/IS. Since suppliers are located all over the world, it is essential to integrate activities both inside and outside of an organization. This requires an integrated IS and IT for sharing and supporting information on various value-adding activities along the supply chain. IS/IT is like a nerve system for SCM [GUN 04b].

Based on a literature review, Avison *et al.* [AVI 04] suggest that firms cannot be competitive or successful if their business and IS/IT strategies are not aligned. Most research has focused on strategic alignment as a standalone problem, i.e. between one company's strategy and its own IS, often based on the strategic alignment model (SAM) developed by Henderson and Venkatraman [HEN 93]. So far, this question has not been extended to the inter-organizational level: how do companies, embedded in the same supply chain, adapt their IS to reach their strategic goals in respect of their suppliers and customers? To explore this question of inter-organizational alignment, we undertook a single case study of a jewelry supply chain. This case study focuses on the relationships set up between a middle-sized retailer and its supplier, a logistics service provider. The longitudinal description of the project from 2006 to date highlights the main participants, their expectations, the physical processes and their transformations during the project, the information flows, and the IT infrastructure that supports radio frequency identification (RFID).

The results highlight the main difficulties observed during the pilot and implementation phases, as well as the evolving benefits that the retailer and its supplier were seeking. We used the SAM to design different routes of intra- and inter-organizational strategic alignments between the two supply-chain partners. These alignments were particularly complex as they included a large number of partners and concerned two different supply chains: jewelry and RFID tags. Finally, we found that these alignments were incremental and resulted from the interactions of both intra- and inter-organizational alignments. In fact, each intra-organizational alignment was inter-related and impacted on those of the partners. The quality of "local" alignments (intra-organizational alignment) impacted on the global supply chain (inter-organizational alignment).

The remainder of this chapter is organized as follows. First, we review past research on IT as a key issue in supply chain performance, on strategic alignment in supply chains based on the SAM and on RFID technology. We then describe the research methodology and the case study that we analyzed. Finally, we discuss our results and the implications of our work for further research on inter-organizational strategic alignment.

4.2. IT as a key issue for supply chain performance

4.2.1. *Coordination and integration: two key words for SCM*

SCM is based on the integration of key business processes, from end user through to the original suppliers that provide products, services and information, and thus add value for customers and other stakeholders [LAM 98]. One of the main features of SCM is that vertical-process integration from suppliers to customers can be performed through inter-firm strategic alliances. This collaboration between partners has been discussed extensively in the strategic management literature [BOW 00, GIL 98, HAN 97] . It is often defined as two or more companies working together to create a competitive advantage and higher profits than can be achieved by acting alone [SIM 05]. In this context, many firms are changing their organization to break down both intra- and inter-company barriers for improved integration of their activities. The concept of integration can be approached from different perspectives (functional, business process, IS, etc.) but always aims to shift from local management to system management. From the literature, it emerges that integration can support business processes at two different levels [ROM 03]: intra-company and inter-company.

To meet the objective of global performance in the supply chain companies need to work as a team, with all areas of the business properly integrated. This leads them to adopt a new, more collaborative way of managing relationships with their partners. Collaboration, coordination and integration have become key words for supply chain performance. In order to achieve this, various coordination mechanisms can be identified [ARS 08]:

– supply chain contracts (buyback, revenue sharing, quantity flexibility, quantity discounts);

– IT (email, internet, electronic data interchange (EDI), enterprise resource planning (ERP));

– information sharing (demand, inventory, lead time, production schedule, capacity, cost);

– joint decision-making (cost consideration, replenishment, forecasting, ordering).

It is interesting to note that information plays a major role in the coordination of supply chains and performance improvement. More precisely, the correct IT is key to improving a firm's supply chain performance. While it is difficult to evaluate the direct impact of IT on supply chain performances [GUN 01, GUN 04b], many authors have proposed frameworks and empirical studies, as shown in the following overview.

4.2.2. *IT: one essential enabler of supply chain integration*

The importance of IT in supply chains has been an area of discussion since companies started to deal with multiple suppliers and/or customers worldwide. The geographic and cultural distance between all of the supply chain partners requires IT integration if the problem of organizational density is to be tackled (see Figure 4.1).

The influence of IT on supply chains has been highlighted by Byrd and Davidson [BYR 03], who state that three main antecedents impact firm's performance:

– the IT department's technical quality, i.e. the technical value of the products and services that are rendered by the department compared to the IT departments of the firm's nearest competitors;

– the IT plan utilization that is linked to IT applications across many activities, which integrate the functions of organizations either with each other or with external entities such as customers and suppliers;

– top management's support for IT, which reflects the importance that the top executives place on IT.

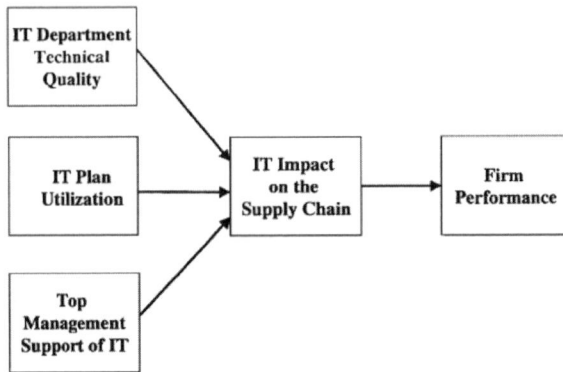

Figure 4.1. *Antecedent of IT impact on firm performance [BYR 03]*

More recently, Li *et al.* [LI 09] proposed a model where supply chain integration bridges IT implementation and supply chain performance. In their framework they distinguish two kinds of IT impact on supply chain performance: direct and indirect (see Figure 4.2).

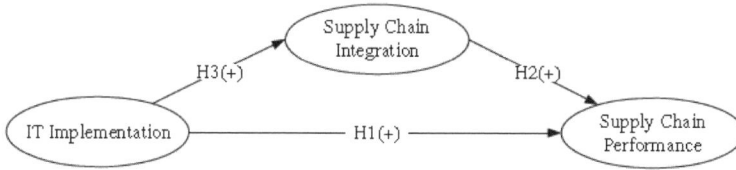

Figure 4.2. *Direct and indirect impact of IT on supply chain performance [LI 09]*

With direct impact, implementation of technologies such as EDI, bar coding, automatic identification and data capture, open standards and unique identification codes improve supply chain performance [LI 09].

Indirect impact is based on the hypothesis that IT has a positive effect on integration and that integration has a positive effect on performance. The constituent elements of supply chain integration are:

– strategies for optimizing logistics system resources based on design for logistics;

– an understanding of market trends, accuracy of demand forecasting, and accuracy and adaptability of SCM planning;

– control and tracking of inventory: accuracy and visibility or process standardization and visibility.

Even if there is no comprehensive framework available on the application of IT for achieving an effective supply chain, Gunasekaran and Ngai [GUN 04b] have proposed such a framework based on a literature review. They have identified the major components of IT-enabled supply chains, comprising six main areas: (1) strategic planning, (2) virtual enterprise, (3) e-commerce, (4) infrastructure, (5), knowledge and IT management, and (6) implementation of IT.

4.3. Strategic alignment in a supply chain

In this section we discuss the question of alignment practice in the context of a supply chain. We have opted for SAM as the central model to examine integration and performance in the supply chain because this model is still relevant in both academic and professional literature.

4.3.1. *The strategic alignment model*

Henderson and Venkatraman [HEN 93] built the SAM on two propositions. First, the economic performance of a company depends on the strategic fit between strategy and the organizational and technological infrastructures that are deployed. Second, strategic alignment relies on a dynamic process of adjustment between strategy and functional integration (organization and IT infrastructure).

The SAM aims to understand the dynamic fit between four domains (see Figure 4.3): business strategy, IT strategy, organization, and IT infrastructure. The company makes continuous co-alignments between these four domains in order to optimize its performance.

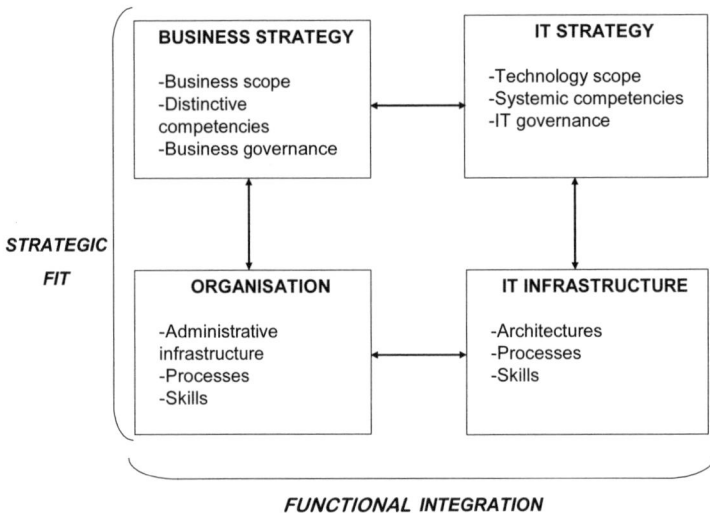

Figure 4.3. *SAM [HEN 93]*

Even if the SAM appears to be the reference in strategic alignment, it has been widely criticized. Ciborra [CIB 97] argues that alignment is not the correct way to consider organizations that are predominantly driven by improvisation and tinkering with the resources at hand. Smaczny [SMA 01] contends that alignment, as a geometrical and mechanical approach, is not the appropriate paradigm by which to manage IT in today's organizations. Finally, Palmer and Markus [PAL 00] – based on a basic alignment model and strategy descriptors – show that there is no connection between fit and performance.

Other authors have, on the contrary, defended the SAM. Lederer and Mendelow [LED 89] suggest that alignment increases the likelihood of developing systems more critical to the organization, and of obtaining top management support for IS. Besides this, the application and analysis of alignment will facilitate a more competitive and profitable organization [GAL 91].

These discussions on the "capacity" of the model to tackle the role of IT in business performance are interesting. We agree that one single model is unlikely to be able to explain the relationship between IT, environment, structure, feasibility, managerial beliefs and performance [COL 07]. Nevertheless, we believe that new orientations have to be taken into consideration, as Fimbel proposes [FIM 07]. We argue that we have to discuss not only the fact that organizations have adopted some technologies, but also the levels of IT use in both supplier and buyer organizations. We follow the recommendation of Gallien [GAL 04] and Sledgianowski and Lufman [SLE 05], who argue that the alignment issue has to be extended and integrated on an enterprise-wide basis in a supply-chain perspective.

To further our understanding of performance in the supply chain, we suggest extending the SAM to the inter-organizational level (see Figure 4.4).

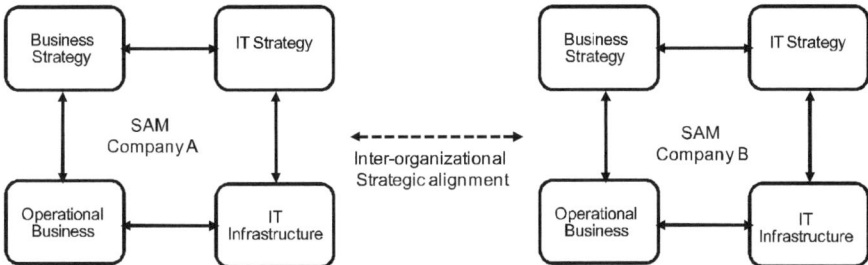

Figure 4.4. *SAM extended to the inter-organizational level*

This model highlights key questions that are still unresolved [AVI 04]. First, it points out the link between the capacity of companies to align themselves and their level of performance. Second, it emphasizes how companies become aligned with one another. Finally, it stresses how alignment can be measured. Nevertheless, trying to give answers to these questions can lead to a better understanding of the factors and connection modes that companies can set up to operationalize their alignment.

4.3.2. *Strategic alignment and performance in the supply chain*

The measurement of alignment is one of the most important concerns in business because of the impact business-IT alignment has on performance. The more closely IT investments are aligned with the business, the greater the business value generated. Several approaches have been used to assess alignment. Based on the classification of Miles and Snow [MIL 78], they have proposed three different corporate strategies according to the type of IT used (communication, e-commerce, e-intelligence, e-collaboration):

– *prospectors* are companies that are looking for new markets and innovations in the technological field;

– *defenders* are focused on costs and aim to maintain their market share in a stable environment;

– *analyzers* try to adopt an intermediary position between cost orientation and risky investments.

Despite a large volume of literature on IT alignment (for a literature review, see [CHA 07]), few authors have examined this measurement of alignment in the supply chain context. This lack of attention to inter-organizational context can be explained by the fact that alignment is merely an engineering formal structure process alignment. It therefore totally ignores business partnerships and the increased need for collaboration in the context of distributed supply sources. McDonald [MAC 91] has developed a model in which he examines the external impacts of alignment on customers, suppliers and markets. Similarly, Henderson and Vankatraman [HEN 93] recognize that alignment must be both internal and external to organizations. They suggest that organizations must align their business and IT strategies with industry and technology forces. Based on this recommendation, Rey and Neely [REY 08] have extended Venkatraman's test of co-alignment in the context of the inter-organizational relationship. By capturing successful contractual relationships between supply-chain partners, they observe that effective cooperation relies on business partners' needs to align their performance measures [KAP 06, YEU 06]. They conclude that alignment of performance measures of inter-organizational relationships depends on the fit between the contract's objectives and partners' objectives.

Others concepts have been developed to explain the level of alignment: modularity and integrality [VOO 06]. Concerning the concept of modularity, three main dimensions have been observed: product modularity, process modularity and supply chain modularity. Contrary to modularity, integrality is determined by the degree of proximity of elements. This classification shows that there are several factors that can be considered, apart from technology itself, to understand the level of integrality or proximity in a supply chain. Supply chain modularity, moreover, refers to whether certain supply functions or tasks are carried out by a single organization or not. It determines who does what – the allocation of labor – and to how different participants interact with each other. Of course, the nature of products also influences the level of integrality in a supply chain. Depending on the industry, the degree of component independence or product modularity can affect a firm's sourcing strategy. Finally, modularity can be summarized by the degree of autonomy of parties involved and their type of coordination. The concept of modular production networks can be used to specify combinations of different degrees of geographic, organizational, cultural and electronic proximity.

4.4. RFID

In this section we present RFID technology, its benefits and the issues around it. We then discuss this technology in the context of supply-chains.

4.4.1. *RFID technology*

RFID technology is derived from World War II-era techniques used to enable aircraft to identify themselves to other friendly aircraft and commanders on the ground. The technology was developed in manufacturing automation. From 1998 to 2003, the leadership of RFID for retail initiatives was concentrated at Massachusetts Institute of Technology (MIT), where the Auto-ID Center was established in 1999. In late 2003, the Auto-ID Center at MIT officially closed and transferred its intellectual property to Electronic Product Code Global (EPC Global standards only relate to the deployment of RFID in the supply chain).

The technology drew more attention when both Wal-Mart and the US Department of Defense mandated their top suppliers to adopt RFID technology.

4.4.2. *The benefits and problems with RFID*

RFID provides multiple benefits for the supply chain. It adds value along the entire supply chain, related logistical operations and business relationships, to enable more effective business process design.

A firm has to justify initial investments in the technology, but the benefits are very often intangible. To derive benefits from RFID, it is important for companies to integrate RFID data into their business processes. They must also develop feedback so that new sources of information lead to more efficient processes and decision making.

Despite these benefits, RFID technology still raises some technical issues. The first concern is overlapping: signals from one reader can interfere with signals from another reader when their physical coverage overlaps or when readers are reading many tags in the same field. From a supply chain perspective, several major technical challenges exist for firms wishing to initiate RFID programs to create significant economic value. Today, as suppliers struggle to implement RFID solutions, they are just beginning to grapple with the issue of how to integrate new RFID with existing enterprise data.

4.4.3. RFID in supply chains

4.4.3.1. Applications

The applications of RFID are wide, including the manufacturing and distribution of numerous physical goods. RFID can be used in distribution centers where it can read tags and automatically update inventory quantities as tagged cases and pallets are brought in. This can free up manual labor at various otherwise labor-intensive steps: quantity check-in, reception process, printing, receiving checklists, and comparing incoming product lists with purchase orders.

In the supply chain context, RFID provides a means of tracking supplier items from the supplier through the distribution network to the point of consumption [NIE 07].

Fosso-Wamba et al. [FOS 07] have identified the four main processes that can be directly concerned with or affected by RFID:

– storage and replenishment: the inventory location system will automatically adjust its quantity each time the storage driver drops off a load at that location;

– order filling: pickers do not have to manually update inventory databases;

– shipping: RFID could streamline shipping operations by registering products as cases are transferred onto trailers;

– product and asset tracking: tracking systems can generate alerts in the case of delays and ensure timely delivery, removing the need to deploy human labor for handling and inspection. With increased information visibility throughout the supply chain, retailers will be able to respond more efficiently to problematic and exceptional handling cases.

More precisely, Angels [ANG 05] explain that in retail supply chains the role of RFID is to streamline inventory management by providing views of product shipments and inventory with a high level of detail (data on product location, product characteristics and product inventory level).

4.4.3.2. Benefits for the supply chain

In order to benefit completely from RFID, companies should choose the appropriate RFID technology. To do so, several factors need to be taken into account: 1) the needs of a firm's corporate environment; 2) the needs of its trading partners; and 3) the needs of the industry to which the firm belongs [ANG 05]. On the other hand, the implementation of RFID technology raises IT infrastructure issues, such as data collection and usage. Many firms have to invest in new hardware and software before implementing RFID technology. Some experts recommend setting up a pilot project to test RFID technology and observing required business process changes.

The major benefits of RFID implementation will come from solutions across the whole supply chain. Nevertheless, taking all the partners into account is difficult because of disputes regarding cost sharing between and benefits for manufacturers, logistics service providers, distributors and retailers [VIS 07]. Nonetheless, IT strategy, business infrastructure and IT infrastructure need to be coordinated if full benefits are to be derived from IT investments. This is the essence of the concept of strategic alignment [HUA 07].

4.5. Case study methodology

In this section we present the methodology that we used in our case study.

4.5.1. *Methodology overview*

The need for empirical analysis in the context of alignment research has been outlined by Chan and Reich [CHA 07], who found that "research on strategic alignment is too mechanistic and fails to capture real life". For this reason, extensive empirical research has recently been undertaken on strategic alignment. Most of this research has focused on quantitative methodologies and very few case studies focus on a description of the complexity of RFID implementation projects in a supply chain. Exceptions are Loebbecke's case studies [LOE 07a, LOE 07b].

We conducted a single case study to reach an in-depth and insightful understanding of this contemporary phenomenon [YIN 03]. By taking into account the RFID pilot project, the case study method addresses strategic and operational aspects. The retail sector is a pioneer in the implementation of RFID technology and although research has been conducted in this sector (by Kaufhof in Germany and Wal-Mart in the US), none of it has been in France. We chose one of the main French retailers for our cast study because:

– the company is a forerunner in RFID technology projects;

– the jewelry supply chain with RFID has never been studied before;

– moreover, the project studied has completed its pilot phases and is now starting its implementation stage at more than 80 jewelry stores.

Data were collected at the corporate level and in the retailing centers. Qualitative data were obtained, using interviewing techniques. We held five semi-structured interviews with people involved in the pilot project.

4.5.2. *Description of the case study*

4.5.2.1. *The company*

Founded in 1898, the Casino Group is a leading medium-sized food retailer, with products in more than 10,000 stores with multiple retail formats (hypermarkets, supermarkets, urban markets and discount markets). Its operating performance, which has grown steadily in past years, now exceeds the industry average with nearly 25 billion Euros in revenue in 2007. This is the result of the Group's unique position in the market and its ability to anticipate changing lifestyles and consumer practices. The company offers a different approach to retailing, one tailored to meet each consumer's specific expectations. Moreover, it has sought to behave in a responsible manner not only towards its customers, but also towards its social and economic stakeholders. In order to practice these values, the group has been a forerunner and innovative player in several domains (for example, for its urban network the company uses river transportation). The RFID technology project is one of the new challenges that the company has tackled.

4.5.2.2. *The RFID project*

The RFID pilot project was launched in 2006. The objectives were both to improve the productivity of sales in Boutique Or stores, and to ensure the reliability of supply processes.

4.5.2.2.1. The chronology of the project

The project was launched in June 2006 and the implementation phase, introducing RFID tags in all 80 Boutique Or stores, ended in June 2009 (see Figure 4.5).

TIME	06/2006	11/2006	01/2007	01/2008	04/2009	06/2009
STRATEGY	Casino's CIO department starts a study on RFiD technology with an IT service provider company		Casino's CIO department launches the RFiD project.		Agreement of Casino's Headquarters to deploy RFiD tags in the 80 Boutique Or stores	
PROJECT			Pilot project 1: Start of the RFiD study on sustainable smart chips	Pilot project 2: implementation in a pilot store with throw away smart chips	RFiD tags are implemented in all 80 Boutique Or stores	

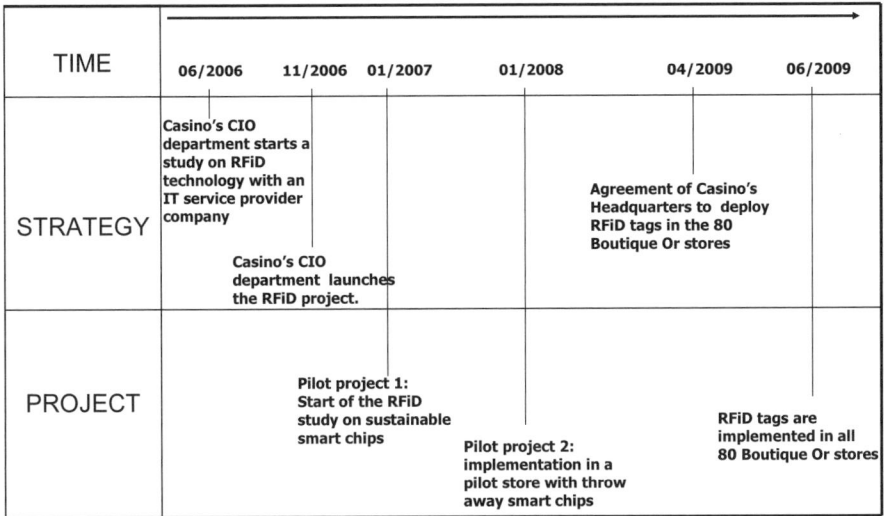

Figure 4.5. *Chronology of the RFID project*

During that period, the Casino Group hesitated between two orientations of the project. A first pilot phase (Pilot project N°1 in Figure 4.5) was aimed at implementing sustainable and HF (High frequency) tags. Casino Group finally decided not to pursue this for two reasons: first, the cost of each tag (although this dropped from €0.60 in 2005 to €0.15 in 2009) and the implementation of sustainable tags would have meant investing in specific and costly hardware and processes in order to recycle the tags. In addition, the high frequency tag was only readable at a short distance of up to 1.5 meters, and the Casino Group preferred to invest in ultra-high frequency (UHF) tags, readable at up to eight meters. In January 2008, Casino Group started its Pilot project No.2 (Figure 4.5) based on UHF technology and throw-away tag.

4.5.2.2.2. Participants in the RFID project

Casino Group's jewelry supply chain is described in Figure 4.6. Not all of the participants in this supply chain are involved in the RFID project. Some supporting participants, like the tag producer and the wafer-thin paper tag producer, however, have directly participated in the project. In the next section, we focus only on the jewelry supply chain (see Figure 4.6).

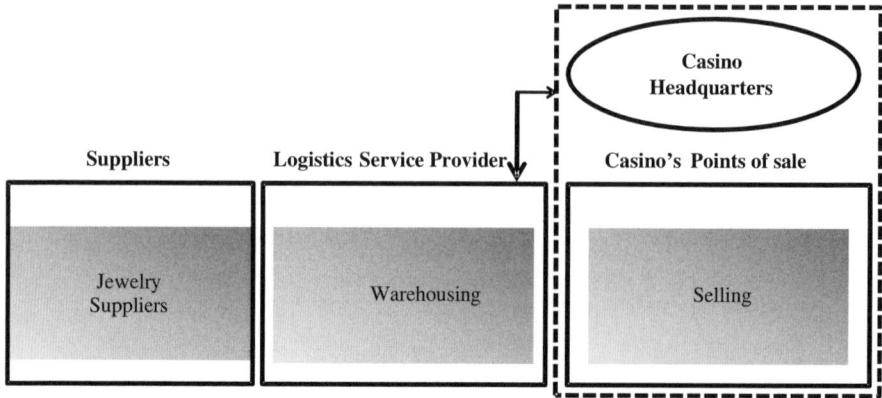

Figure 4.6. *Main participants of Casino Group's jewelry supply chain*

The RFID project is characterized by the large number of participants involved:

– *Jewelry suppliers*: there are more than 60 jewelry suppliers worldwide dealing with Casino Group, which then distributes the products.

– *Casino Group*: there are different departments involved in the retailer's project. At Casino Group's headquarters there are four departments involved:

- *the IS department (called CIT)*: this department initiated the RFID project in the jewelry supply chain and is in charge of implementing the IT infrastructure,

- *purchasing*: this department negotiates the prices of the jewelry that will be sold in the Boutique Or stores,

- *supply*: this department overviews all supply chain issues, such as the traceability of the products and respect for quality, price and delivery times,

- *hypermarkets department (textile business unit)*: this department holds both textile and jewelry products. It is responsible for quality, innovation, and sales results.

– *Casino's 80 Boutique Or stores*: in 2009, the company operated 80 stores, mainly in France, inside Casino Group's hypermarkets. They sell jewelry such as watches, rings, earrings and bracelets directly to customers, like any other jewelry store. These department stores are completely independent from hypermarkets in terms of sales policy.

– *Logistics service provider (LSP) warehouse*: this is a LSF that receives the jewelry from suppliers, stores the products, prepares orders, prints RFID tags according to the type of product, and delivers them to the Boutique Or stores. Once a year, Casino Group and the LSF jointly participate in the warehouse inventory. The LSF is in charge of these services for Casino Group as well as another jewelry store. In order to avoid problems between the two retailing companies, the LSF has physically divided the warehouse into two distinctive areas to which the products are allocated.

– *Printer*: this company is equipped to produce labels from paper rolls. It inserts RFID tags inside the paper rolls, then cuts them up, making specific paper tags that are attached to the jewelry to describe each piece (weight, number of carats etc.).

– *Tag producer*: this company develops the UHF tags for the Casino Group that are used to manage their supply chain. It also participated in creating specific RFID readers for paper tags, as these materials did not initially exist in their offer. These readers can be considered to be the "hardware" material of the RFID project.

4.5.2.2.3. The physical process and information flow

The processes and information flow in the integrated supply chain are summarized in Figure 4.7.

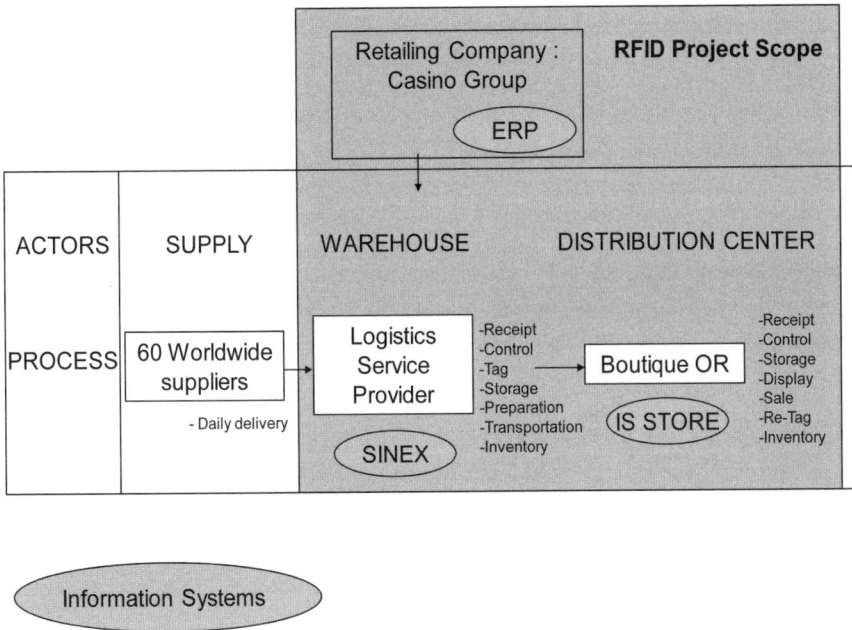

Figure 4.7. *Key processes and information flow along the supply chain*

The LSF receives products daily from the suppliers and manages them for the Casino Group. Once the products have been controlled, they are tagged by the LSF and stored for a next delivery. Deliveries to the Boutique Or stores are made once a week. After the delivery, Boutique Or's sales personnel check the products using the RFID reader and store or display them according to the status of the product (on stock or on order).

There are three main processes in this supply chain, going from the jewelry suppliers to the LSF warehouse, and then from the warehouse to the Boutique Or stores:

  * Process 1: day-to-day receipts

Daily, 60 jewelry suppliers worldwide deliver their products to the LSP. There is no international standard identification number for jewelry; each supplier has its own identification numbers.

  * Process 2: weekly receipts

Once a week, the LSP delivers products to each Boutique Or store according to the inventory levels sent by each Boutique Or store. Each store then has to record receipt of the products inside their local IS before displaying the jewelry. This process needs to be as fast as possible because an item of jewelry that has not been recorded cannot be sold.

  * Process 3: annual inventories

Once a year, both the LSP warehouse and each Boutique Or store have to inventory the products. This process is particularly difficult and time-consuming as pieces of jewelry are small and need to be manipulated manually. It includes a change of the sales presentation in the shop window of each Boutique Or store.

4.5.2.2.4. The IT infrastructure

The IT infrastructure of Casino Group's jewelry supply chain is independent of the retailer's main ERP GOLD system. Actually, an IT infrastructure has been developed specifically for the RFID project.

There are three main IS that support the RFID project:

– *ERP GOLD*: this is the main ERP of the Casino Group, which centralizes all key data. It is not currently integrated with SINEX.

– *SINEX*: this is the IS that has been developed for the LSP. SINEX is in charge of dealing with both inventories and day-to-day reception of jewelry from suppliers.

The LSP also physically holds the hardware equipment, such as the tag printers and RFID readers. Both types of equipment belong to Casino.

– *IS in Boutique Or stores*: is composed of different systems that are not integrated with one another. Each IS is dedicated to a specific task: collection, receipts, inventories, and editing tags when necessary (such as when a paper tag has broken or prices are changed through promotions).

4.5.3. *The case study analysis*

In order to analyze the RFID implementation, we used Fosso-Wamba *et al.*'s framework [FOS 07], which we adapted and completed to illustrate our case study (see Table 4.1). Their framework, specifically developed for RFID projects, is composed of a sequence of three main phases that describe a RFID project implementation: seeking opportunities, pilot project and validation, and RFID project deployment.

4.5.3.1. *Phase 1: opportunity seeking*

This initial phase deals with the opportunities to implement the RFID project in a specific value chain. It is composed of six steps, described below.

4.5.3.1.1. Step 1: primary motivation (why?)

Step 1 describes the primary motivation behind the RFID project. In Casino Group's case, the opportunity stemmed not from a strategic decision to test a new technology, but from an external IT vendor who proposed to run a preliminary study on RFID implementation for Casino Group's IT department.

4.5.3.1.2. Step 2: analysis of the product value chain (what and why?)

Step 2 selects the product value chain that has the required characteristics to test such a technology.

At Casino Group, the IT department decided to experiment with RFID technology implementation on jewelry-related activities, which depend on the textile business unit, first. These activities are characterized by:

– small products handled manually;

– low level of demand;

– high-value units;

– items made with metal components (gold, silver, etc.) that are not always readable by RFID tags.

The choice of this product value chain was motivated by the following:

– the jewelry business has its own value chain, independent of the food supply chain, from suppliers down to the points of sale;

– in terms of ISs, this jewelry supply chain also has its own ISs that are not integrated with the main ERP of the Group;

– it has only has one LSP;

– it has its own independent IT system.

4.5.3.1.3. Step 3: identification of the critical activities (which?)

The aim of this step is to identify the relevant activities that could be affected by the project for all partners involved in the value chain. At Casino Group, the activities involved in the project are:

– reception of the jewelry at the warehouse;

– picking at the warehouse;

– inventories at the warehouse;

– reception of jewelry at the points of sale;

– inventories of jewelry at the points of sale.

4.5.3.1.4. Step 4: mapping the network of firms supporting the product value chain (who and with whom?)

This step identifies the partners involved in the project and the relevant links with the network. At Casino Group the partners are:

– Casino Group (Casino headquarters and 80 points of sale);

– a single LSP.

To reduce the complexity and scope of the project at this stage of its implementation, jewelry suppliers were not yet involved in the project (see section 4.4.2.2.2).

4.5.3.1.5. Step 5: mapping of intra-organizational processes for the opportunities identified (how within the organization?)

This step deals with the main processes in the organization that are concerned with the product value chain identified in step 2. At Casino Group, six internal processes are identified for the product value chain concerned:

– purchasing;

– replenishment at the point of sale;

– demand management (warehouse replenishment);

– IT integration;

– selling;

– invoicing.

4.5.3.1.6. Step 6: mapping of inter-organizational processes for the opportunities identified (how between organizations?)

This step involves:

– *Delivery (from suppliers to the warehouse)*: the LSP warehouse regularly sends orders to jewelry suppliers located worldwide. Suppliers then deliver the orders to LSP's warehouse. This process is not equipped with RFID tags.

– *Ordering (from points of sale to warehouse)*: based on the sales in Boutique Or shops, each shop sends its order to the LSP's warehouse via the Casino Group's ERP.

– *Delivery (from warehouse to points of sale)*: based on the order list of each Boutique Or, the LSP prepares the jewelry and sends it to the stores, which are informed of the delivery via SINEX.

4.5.3.2. *Phase 2: pilot project and validation*

The objective of the second phase is to develop a pilot project for validating the feasibility of RFID implementation. With respect to the inter-organizational alignment problem, the goal is to identify the business opportunities that could be derived from this new technology, and to propose process and IT reconfiguration to fit with RFID. It consists of four steps, explained below.

4.5.3.2.1. Step 7: evaluation of RFID network opportunities

This step evaluates network opportunities in the product value chain with respect to the product (level of granularity), the firms involved in the network, and the specific activities in the product value chain.

In this step, the improvement in performance of the main activities due to RFID implementation is identified:

– increasing productivity at the point of sale by time savings and reducing human errors during reception and inventory control;

– improving inventory control at the warehouse;

– traceability of jewelry all along the supply chain;

– value-added services at the points of sale: jewelry engraving.

4.5.3.2.2. Step 8: evaluation of potential RFID network applications

This step evaluates potential network applications, including scenario-building and process-optimization ("as could be"), i.e. the HOW within and between organizations.

In this step, an initial scenario of RFID application is proposed. The objective is to define the possible ways of using RFID within and between organizations. At Casino Group and its partners, the following applications were found:

– tag editing:

  - labeling the products with RFID tags at the warehouse,

  - labeling the products with RFID tags at the points of sale;

– tag reading:

  - using RFID for reception of the products at the points of sale,

  - using RFID for inventory control.

4.5.3.2.3. Step 9: mapping of intra- and inter-organizational processes using RFID technology

This step consists of defining the intra- and inter-organizational processes to be integrated in the new RFID technology.

In January 2008, the Casino Group pilot project was developed at only one point of sale for testing different kinds of tags. The pilot process mainly concerned the automatic reception of orders.

For the LSP, the pilot process consisted of re-labeling all the products delivered to this specific point of sale.

4.5.3.2.4. Step 10: validating business and technological processes integrating RFID technology with key respondents

Feasibility analysis and evaluation of the challenges, including ERP and middleware integration and process automation, was carried out here. All of the business processes, applications and technological developments that were needed for the RFID project were validated in this step.

At Casino Group, this step included the development of some specific RFID readers that were adapted to very small products, such as jewelry, along with software modifications to imbed the RFID application in legacy systems:

– developing wireless middleware to compare delivery orders with the items received;

– developing a specific RFID reader for jewelry;

– developing a specific software for writing the RFID tags and printing them on the labels.

4.5.3.3. *Phase 3: RFID project deployment*

The last phase concerns the validation of the pilot project and the deployment of the technology on the entire supply chain.

4.5.3.3.1. Step 11: proof of concept with the pilot project

Here proof of concept is carried out through evaluation including ERP, middleware integration and process automation at the level of all the supply chain members, and the decision to go for the beta test replicating proof of concept scenarios in a real-life setting.

The objective of this step is to validate the development, alterations and observations in the pilot project, in order to propose the final plan.

At Casino Group, this step included:

– updating software; and

– the design of a new reader better suited to the case.

At the LSP, this step included:

– a re-engineering of the sourcing business process so that the tag could be attached when the product was received, instead of when it was delivered, as in the pilot project;

– the development of an integrated software able to define the tag directly from Casino Group's IS.

4.5.3.3.2. Step 12: pilot replication and evaluation of the anticipated benefits and impacts of RFID

This is the final step of implementation, consisting in the deployment of the solution for all members of the project. It involves appropriation of the system by the various organizations involved and their staff members.

In this step, Casino Group deployed the designed solution at its 80 points of sale in April 2009. This involved implementing the RFID technology and relevant software, training the users, etc.

The LSPs now attach a RFID tag to all products received from the suppliers, which means that all the products in the warehouse have a tag.

Figure 4.8 shows the supply chain with all of the organizations affected by the project, and the main processes that have been aligned for this IT implementation.

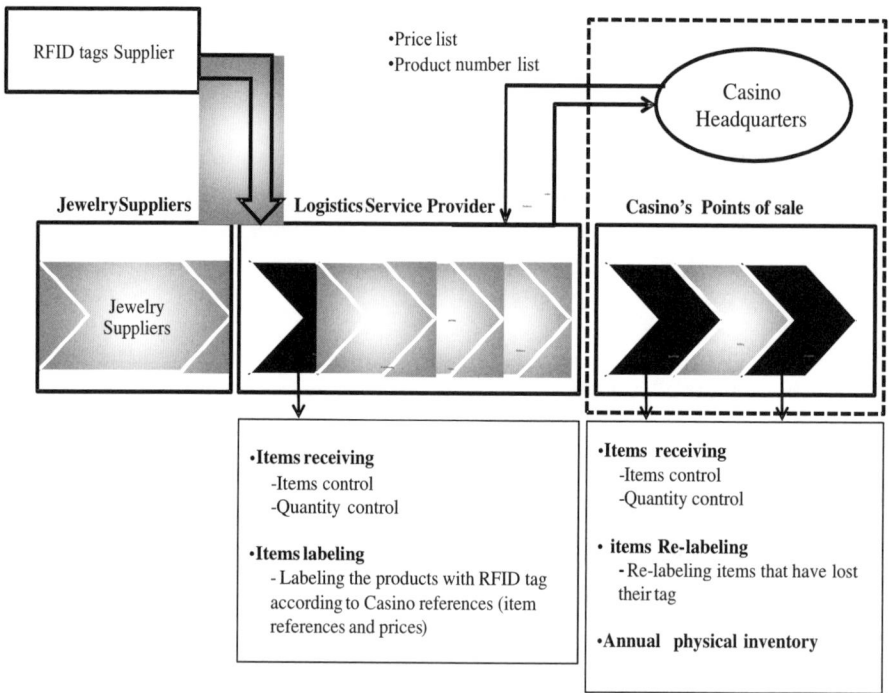

Figure 4.8. *Final supply chain, including intra- and inter-organizational processes*

4.5.3.4. *Summary of the project phases*

Phase 1: Seeking opportunities	
Step 1	Determination of the primary motivation to adopt RFID: understanding the primary motivation for considering the use of RFID technologies (WHY?)
Step 2	Analysis of the product value chain (PVC): understanding the activities specific to a given product (WHAT?)
Step 3	Identification of critical activities in the PVC: identification of critical PVC activities (WHICH activities to select and WHY?)
Step 4	Mapping of the network of firms supporting the PVC: mapping the supply chain network to understand the links within the network of firms supporting the product (WHO and WITH WHOM?)
Step 5	Mapping of intra-organizational processes for the opportunities identified as they are carried out now ("as is") (HOW within the organization?)
Step 6	Mapping of inter-organizational processes for the opportunities identified as they are carried out now ("as is") (HOW between organizations?)
Phase 2: Pilot project and validation	
Step 7	Evaluation of RFID network opportunities in the PVC with respect to the product (level of granularity), firms involved in the network and specific activities in the PVC
Step 8	Evaluation of potential RFID network applications including scenario building and process optimization ("as could be") (HOW within and between organizations?)
Step 9	Mapping of intra- and inter-organizational processes integrating RFID technology
Step 10	Validating business and technological processes integrating RFID technology with key respondents. Feasibility analysis and evaluation of the challenges, including ERP and middleware integration and process automation
Phase 3: RFID project deployment	
Step 11	Proof of concept with the pilot project: evaluation including ERP, middleware integration and process automation at all supply chain member levels, and decision to go for the beta test replicating proof of concept scenarios in a real-life setting
Step 12	Pilot replication and evaluation of anticipated benefits and impacts of RFID. Appropriation by the different organizations involved and their staff members

Table 4.1. *Steps undertaken in the field study, adapted from [FOS 07]*

4.6. Intra- and inter-organizational strategic alignment routes

Figure 4.9 describes the different levels of intra- and inter-organizational alignments between the main participants of the supply chain: Casino Group, the LSP, the tag producer, and the label producer.

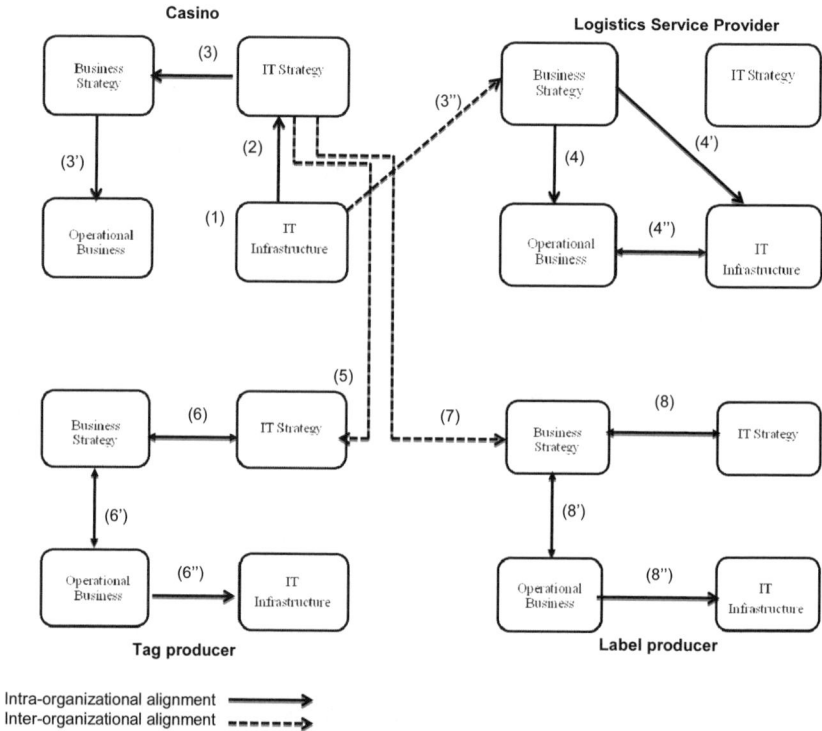

Figure 4.9. *Intra- and inter-organizational strategic alignments of Casino Group's RFID project*

The arrows in the figure describe the different fits over time in both intra- and inter-organizational alignments in Casino Group's RFID project.

The project was launched with the idea of inserting an innovative IT, i.e. RFID tags, into one of Casino Group's supply chains. This idea was pushed by a manager, based at the IT department (1), who became responsible for the project. He lobbied for it first at the IT department (IT strategy) (2) and then at the hypermarket department (textile business unit) directly linked with the Casino Group's corporate department (3). The group officially agreed to start the RFID project in January

2007. The hypermarket department (business strategy) asked the 80 Boutique Or stores to adapt their processes for the day-to-day receipts and then for the annual inventory (3′).

Casino Group chose a supply chain with few impacts in the main food and textile chains, with a reduced number of products, and that was not in any way integrated with their main ERP system: jewelry. They contacted the LSP's corporate department (3″) and asked them to agree to collaborate on a RFID project in their jewelry supply chain. The LSP agreed and altered both its operational processes to fit with Casino Group's requirements (reception, warehouse, order picking and delivery). It also altered its IT infrastructure (investing in a smart RFID printer and in RFID readers, and developing the IS SINEX) (Steps 4, 4′, 4″).

The following step was to involve both the tag producer and then the label producer. Casino Group first contacted the tag producer (5) to test the physical properties of the tags for managing jewelry. In the scenario phase, they initially opted for a high frequency tag before considering UHF tags in the pilot project (6, 6′). The tag producer also participated as a pioneer by building specific RFID readers especially for managing jewelry (6″). The corporate department of the tag producer finally decided to register a patent with a view to extending its RFID hardware offer to other customers who had supply chains with similar characteristics, i.e. small, metallic, high-value products.

Casino Group's IT department then negotiated with the label producer and asked it to adapt the size/format of its label according to the type of jewelry, and then to include tags (7). As the label producer was not equipped to insert the tags into the labels, Casino Group asked the tag producer to do so. The tag producer finally agreed (8) and the labels were sent back to the label producer to be cut to the right format (8′, 8″).

4.7. Conclusion

Gunasekaran *et al.* [GUN 04a] have suggested that "the alignment between information model and supply chain models or objectives needs further investigation". These new research challenges call for:

– an identification of critical IT success factors for an integrated and aligned supply chain;

– attainment of alignment between the IT and business model in the supply chain context;

– an empirical test of the SAM model in the context of inter-organizational relationships.

In order to meet this challenge, we conducted research on a jewelry supply chain. The case study provides answers to the dynamics of alignment in such a supply chain. The main conclusions that can be drawn are the following:

– There is not only one strategic alignment that works but multiple alignments. Indeed, our case study shows several alignments progressively taking place throughout the two-year course of the project.

– These alignments are particularly complex as they include a large number of partners. This is because the supply chain includes not only the horizontal supply chain of the core product (jewelry), but also the vertical supply chain of RFID tags. RFID projects actually need a matrix supply chain, both horizontal and vertical, to manage a product consisting of a piece of jewelry plus a tag.

– These alignments are incremental and are the result of the interactions between different types of alignment in the supply chain. Each intra-organizational alignment has an impact on the other intra-organizational alignments of the partners in the same supply chain. Finally, the extended inter-organizational alignment model can be compared to an ecosystem with continuous micro intra-organizational alignments that lead to a global and incremental inter-organizational alignment.

Our research nevertheless shows some limits concerning the methodology. As we focus on a single case study, our findings are contextual and cannot be generalized. Moreover, the RFID project was complex as it was emerging and included many different participants located in different companies or in different services. Goals and objectives were therefore multiple. The second limit concerns the data collection. We collected only primary data and have not triangulated these with secondary data.

4.8. Bibliography

[ANG 05] ANGELES R., "RFID technologies: Supply chain applications and implementation issues", *Information Systems Management*, vol. 22, no. 1, 2005, pp. 51-65.

[ARS 08] ARSHINDER A.K., DESHMUKH S.G., "Supply chain coordination: Perspectives, empirical studies and research directions", *International Journal of Production Economics*, vol. 115, no. 2, 2008, pp. 316-335.

[AVI 04] AVISON D., JONES J., POWELL P., WILSON D., "Using and validating the strategic alignment model", *Journal of Strategic Information Systems*, vol. 13, no. 3, 2004, pp 223-246.

[BOW 00] BOWERSOX D.J., CLOSS D.J., STANK T.P., KELLER S.B., 2000, "Integrated supply chain logistics makes a difference", *Supply Chain Management Review*, vol. 4, no. 4, 2000, pp. 70-78.

[BYR 03] BYRD T.A., DAVIDSON N.W., "Examining possible antecedents of IT impacts on supply chain and its effects on firm performance", *Information & Management*, vol. 41, no. 2, 2003, pp. 243-255.

[CHA 07] CHAN Y.E., REICH B.H., "IT alignment: What have we learned", *Journal of Information Technology*, vol. 22, no. 4, 2007, pp. 297-315.

[CIB 97] CIBORRA C.U., "De Profundis? Deconstructing the concept of strategic alignment", *IRIS*, no. 20, 1997, 13 pages.

[COL 07] COLTMAN T., DEVINNEY T. and MIDGLEY D., "E-business strategy and firm performance: a latent class assessment of the drivers and impediments to success", *Journal of Information Technology*, vol. 22, no. 2, 2007, pp. 87-101.

[FIM 07] FIMBEL E., *Alignement Stratégique. Synchroniser les Systèmes d'information avec les Trajectoires et Manœuvres des Entreprises*, Village Mondial, Pearson Education France, 2007.

[FOS 07] FOSSO-WAMBA S., LEFEBVRE L.A., LEFEBVRE E., "Integrating RFID technology and EPC network into a B2B retail supply chain: a step toward intelligent business processes", *Journal of Technology Management and Innovation*, vol. 2, no. 2, 2007, pp. 114-124.

[GAL 91] GALLIERS R., "Strategic information systems planning: myths, reality and guidelines for successful implementation", *European Journal of Information Systems*, vol. 1, no. 1, 1991, pp. 55-64.

[GAL 04] GALLIEN R.D., "Reflections on information system strategizing", in AVGEROU, CIBORRA C., LAND F., *The Social Study of Information and Communication Technology,* 1st edition, Oxford University Press, 2004, pp. 262-331.

[GIL 98] GILMOUR P., "Benchmarking supply chain operations", *Benchmarking: An International Journal*, vol. 5, no. 4, 1998, pp. 283-290.

[GUN 01] GUNASEKARAN A., PATEL C., TIRTIROGLU E., "Performance measure and metrics in a supply chain environment", *International Journal of Operations & Production Management*, vol. 21, no. 1/2, 2001, pp. 71-87.

[GUN 04a] GUNASEKARAN A., PATEL C., MCGAUGHEY R.E., "A framework for supply chain performance measurement", *International Journal of Production Economics*, vol. 87, no. 3, 2004, pp. 333-347.

[GUN 04b] GUNASEKARAN A., NGAI E.W.T., "Information systems in supply chain integration and management", *European Journal of Operational Research*, vol. 159, no. 2, 2004, pp. 269-295.

[HAN 97] HANMAN, S., "Benchmarking your firm's performance with best practice", *International Journal of Logistics Management*, vol. 8 no. 2, 1997, pp. 1-17.

[HEN 93] HENDERSON J.C., VENKATRAMAN N., "Strategic alignment: leveraging information technology for transforming organizations", *IBM Systems Journal*, vol. 38, no. 2/3, 1993, pp. 472-484.

[KAP 06] KAPLAN R.S., NORTON D.P., *Alignment using the Balanced Scorecard to Create Corporate Strategy*, Harvard Business School Press, 2006.

[KOH 06] KOH, S.C.L., SAAD S.M., "Managing uncertainty in ERP-controlled manufacturing environments in SMEs", *International Journal of Production Economics*, vol. 101, no. 1, 2006, pp. 109-127.

[HUA 07] HUA G.B., "Applying the strategic alignment model to business and ICT strategies of Singapore's small and medium-sized architecture, engineering and construction enterprises", *Construction Management & Economics*, vol. 25, no. 2, 2007, pp. 157-169.

[LAM 98] LAMBERT D.M., COOPER M.C., PAGH J.D., "Supply chain management: implementation, issues and research opportunities", *International Journal of Logistics Management*, vol. 9, no. 2, 1998, pp. 1-19.

[LAS 98] LASETER T., *Balanced Sourcing: Cooperation and Competition in Supplier Relationships*, San Francisco Press, California, 1998.

[LED 89] LEDERER A.L., MENDELOW A.L., "Co-ordination of information systems plans with business plans", *Journal of Management Information Systems*, vol. 6, no. 2, 1989, pp. 5-19.

[LEE 97] LEE H.L., PADMANABHAN V., WHANG S., "Information distortion in a supply chain: The bullwhip effect", *Sloan Management Review*, vol. 43, no. 4, 1997, pp. 546-558.

[LI 09] LI G., YANG H., SUN L., SOHAL A.L., "The impact of IT implementation on SC integration and performance" *International Journal of Production Economics*, vol. 120, no. 1, 2009, pp. 125-138.

[LOE 07a] LOEBBECKE, C., "Piloting RFID along the supply chain: a case analysis", *Electronic Markets*, vol. 17, no. 1, 2007, pp. 29-37.

[LOE 07b] LOEBBECKE, C., "Use of innovative content integration information technology at the point of sale", *European Journal of Information Systems*, vol. 16, no. 3, 2007, pp. 228-236.

[MAC 91] MACDONALD H., "The strategic alignment process", in MORTON S., *The Corporation of the 1990's: Information Technology and Organizational Transformation*, Oxford University Press, 1991.

[MIL 78] MILES R.E., SNOW C.C., "Organizational strategy, structure and process", *Academy of Management Review*, vol. 3, no. 3, pp. 546-562.

[MOM 02] MOMME J., "Framework for outsourcing manufacturing: strategic and operational applications", *Computers in Industry*, vol. 49, no. 1, 2002, pp. 59-75.

[NEU 04] NEUBERT G, OUZROUT Y and BOURAS A., "Collaboration and integration through information technology in supply chains", *International Journal of Technology Management*, vol. 28, no. 2, 2004, pp. 259-273.

[NIE 07] NIEDERMANN F., MATHIEU R.G., MORLEY R., KWON I.W., "Examining RFID in supply chain management", *Communications of the ACM*, vol. 50, no. 7, 2007, pp. 92-101.

[PAL 00] PALMER J.W., MARKUS M.L., "The performance impacts of quick response and strategic alignment in specialty retailing", *Information Systems Research*, vol. 11, no. 3, 2000, pp. 241-259.

[REY 08] REY M., NEELY A., "Beyond words: testing alignment among inter-organizational performance measures", *Measuring Business Excellence*, vol. 14, no 1, 2010, pp. 19-27.

[ROM 03] ROMANO P., "Co-ordination and integration mechanisms to manage logistics processes across supply networks", *Journal of Purchasing and Supply Management*, vol. 9, no. 3, 2003, pp. 119-134.

[SIM 05] SIMATUPANG T.M., SRIDHARAN R., "An integrative framework for supply chain collaboration", *International Journal of Logistics Management*, vol. 16, no. 2, 2005, pp. 257-274.

[SLE 05] SLEDGIANOSWKI D., LUFTMAN J., "IT business strategic alignment maturity: A case study", *Journal on Cases on Information Technology*, vol. 7, no. 2, 2005, pp. 102-120.

[SMA 01] SMACZNY T., "Is an alignment between business and information technology the appropriate paradigm to manage IT in today's organizations?", *Management Decision*, vol. 39, no. 10, 2001, pp. 797-802.

[VIS 07] VISICH, J.K., LI S., KHUMAWALA B.M., "Enhancing product recovery value in closed-loop supply chains with RFID", *Journal of Managerial Issues*, vol. 19, no. 3, 2007, pp. 436-452.

[VOO 06] VOORDIJK H., MEIJBOOM B., DE HAAN J., "Modularity in supply chains: a multiple case study in the construction industry", *International Journal of Operations and Production Management*, vol. 26, no. 6, 2006, pp. 600-618.

[YEU 06] YEUNG J.H.Y, SELEN W., SUM C., HOU B., "Linking financial performance to strategic orientation and operational priorities", *International Journal of Physical Distribution & Logistics Management*, vol. 36, no. 3, 2006, pp. 210-221.

[YIN 03] YIN R.K., *Case Study Research: Design and Method*, Sage Publication, 2003.

Chapter 5

Ontology of SCOR for the Strategic Alignment of Organizations and Information Systems

5.1. Introduction

Inter-organizational alignment between business and information systems (IS) at strategic and operational level is a key performance factor of supply chains (SCs). Although the technological and business issues are known, the main difficulty remains in the ability of methodologies and tools to address the semantic dimension of alignment when confronted with the scientific challenge of providing a consistently heterogenous trade expertise.

Nowadays, internet technologies (e.g. XML-based file formats, such as RDF, OWL, etc.) are increasingly used in IS, especially in IS for organizations such as companies. The diffusion of these technologies to IS seems to result mainly from the economies of scale induced by the many applications (RSS streams for blogs, XML tags of all documents, etc.) of the internet. These economies of scale then reduce the costs of the conception, development, installation and maintenance of inter-organizational IS. Applying Internet-based technologies impacts on the structure of IS themselves, however, since they have traditionally been tightly coupled, while internet technologies implement loosely coupled systems.

Chapter written by Pierre-Alain MILLET, Lorraine TRILLING, Thierry MOYAUX and Omar SAKKA.

The first impact of internet technologies on IS is due to the concept of service-oriented architecture (e.g., Web services), but these technologies also propose the concept of ontologies (e.g., semantic Web) to model knowledge. According to Gruber [GRU 93] "an ontology is a formal explicit specification of a shared conceptualization". In short, ontologies may be defined as formal models of some knowledge about the world. The purpose of this chapter is to study the impact of ontologies on the alignment between inter-organizational IS and business practices, i.e., how the transmission of information in ontologies facilitates collaboration in an SC. This is a key challenge for knowledge interoperability [YE 08]. We use the Web ontology language (OWL) proposed by the semantic Web community[1] to study how ontologies may support inter-organizational collaboration. In this context, this chapter proposes to create an OWL ontology of the supply chain operations reference (SCOR) model delivered by the SC Council[2]. We thus explore the advantages of ontologies in inter-organizational IS. Such a model in OWL requires the formalizing of SCOR, since the past and current versions of this model have been presented as texts. It is interesting to note, however, that the SC Council also tries to formalize some parts of the SCOR (see the good practices in SCOR v. 9, for example).

Achieving this goal incurs many benefits for inter-organizational collaboration in an SC. First of all, we think the OWL language improves the interoperability of IS. In fact, OWL has been developed with heterogeneity in mind and is hence able to tackle the different "languages" used in an SC, e.g. a seller and a buyer may use "ship" and "boat" to designate the same equipment, and an ontology should carry out the translation between these two vocabularies. Therefore, OWL ontologies should help every business partner to interpret, and thus to understand, an OWL model in the same way by improving the quality of information exchange between two partners. In this way, these organizations could keep their points of view on common business matters consistent by more tightly connecting their respective IS. Besides interoperability, we also hope that OWL ontologies can help highlight ambiguities between business partners, thus improving inter-organizational collaboration. For instance, we hope that two partners using "ship" can detect that this word refers to different concepts for them. Note here that model consistency is required by model-driven engineering. Thus, the consistency of the business models of two partners is also required to align their respective processes. The third reason for an OWL ontology of SCOR is that ontologies may be used partially. For instance, it is not critical that all of the knowledge of an organization be formally represented in an ontology – and we even believe that some parts should be kept informal because they are unclear, or even inherently fuzzy. Another example deals with the fact that a part of an ontology may not need to be translated into the

1 www.w3.org/2004/OWL/, accessed 4.28.10.
2 www.supply-chain.org, accessed 4.28.10.

language of another organization, or even to have a counterpart in that language. Consequently, two partners may not need to resolve the ambiguity between "ship" and "boat" if they only use "truck" as means of transport. This shows that the partial translation of knowledge is sometimes sufficient for two partners to collaborate, and OWL ontologies allow this.

Building an OWL-based ontology of SCOR is not an end in itself but constitutes the starting point of several analyses, studies and developments. An OWL-based model of SCOR presents the advantage of expressing the knowledge of the SCOR model as a set of inter-related concepts that can be analyzed by means of ontological principles. This representation as an ontology enables us, for example, to study the completeness and consistency of the SCOR model without scrolling the hundreds of pages of its text description. Using the strength of OWL-enabled software, such as reasoners, would suffice. This helps us to understand the relations between some concepts included in the SCOR model, such as processes, best practices and performance attributes, and to verify that there are no contradictions or missing links.

As noted above, the OWL language may constitute knowledge support in IS for increasing their interoperability. This formalization should also help in studying the consistency of the SCOR model with existing models previously transformed into an ontology. In the context of inter-organizational collaboration, ontologies may also help in studying the alignment between the SCOR model and exchange norms (such as OAGIS 9.0 of the Open Applications Group[3]). From a more operational point of view, a SCOR ontology is a good starting point for SC simulation that relies on a famous model built by and for the industry. Finally, and we draw the reader's attention to this point, if we consider the SCOR model of a representation of SC processes, associated with best practices and attributes of economic performance, it is interesting to complete the SCOR model with other considerations – for example oriented toward sustainable development, such as Green SCOR – and to assess the consistency of the OWL-based models of some SC thus obtained.

This chapter is organized as follows. The next section outlines the background of this work. Section 5.3 details how we have obtained an OWL ontology of SCOR. In section 5.4 we then discuss the impact of our approach on the strategic alignment of organizations. Finally, section 5.5 concludes and proposes some future research tracks.

---

3 www.oagi.org/, accessed 4.28.10.

5.2. Background

Our approach to building an ontology from a reference model consists in successively studying state of the art in the formalization of knowledge in enterprise modeling (EM) and in ontologies for semantic alignment, the existing EM languages and, finally, the SCOR reference model that will be our case study.

5.2.1. *Enterprise modeling and ontology*

EM enables the externalizing, making and sharing of enterprise knowledge [CHE 03]. It is a tool used every time knowledge workers wish to formalize, share or validate their knowledge. EM models may be simple drawings but are often formalized using modeling languages, produced using modeling tools such as ARIS, and managed in the context of a modeling framework. Tools can either be used as stand-alone enterprise knowledge model views, integrated as front-ends to other systems, used as ERP packages, or be part of a contextual user environment. EM is a particular kind of modeling technique, as compared to IT architecture models or data models. Business models describe business knowledge, including the software applications used by a business from an external point of view termed "usage view", but not from an internal, computational point of view.

EM is a key factor for enterprise engineering and re-engineering activities, especially in the context of collaborative enterprises and inter-organizational IS, because of the need for enterprises to adapt their business to new collaborative requirements. It can deliver models that are understandable by all participants and formalized enough to map the enterprise engineering and re-engineering activities directly onto the execution of the business process.

In order to provide the required inter-operability, the models have to adhere to a common representation for both model enactment and human understanding. International standardization is a means to provide the necessary model commonality [KOS 99]. Much academic work on EM has converged towards international norms that represent the state of the art of EM:

– a modeling framework defining viewpoints, phases and genericity as three axes of model management (ISO 19439) [ISO 06a];

– modeling constructs and their relations, representing the meta-model of a business modeling language (ISO 19440) [ISO 06b].

Models need terms (names, verbs, etc.), however in order to identify and describe the constructs modeled in the EM language used. These terms relate to their own knowledge about the enterprise. They introduce an inherently non-formal characteristic of any EM. To share business knowledge, a common modeling language is not sufficient. A common business language is required, at a semantic level, to share the understanding of any constructs used in the modeling language. This is a condition in order to practice interoperability in inter-organizational systems. Project Athena [CHE 03] proposes an interoperability framework that distinguishes three levels of interoperability: business, knowledge and ICT[4] systems. Business interoperability is the organizational and operational ability of an enterprise to cooperate with other external organizations.

Knowledge interoperability is the compatibility of the skills, competencies and knowledge assets of an enterprise with those of other, external organizations. Interoperability at ICT-system level is the ability of an enterprise's ICT systems to cooperate with those of external organizations. For the Athena project, the *semantic dimension* cuts across these three levels. Each participant elaborates different interpretations of syntactic description. To ensure consistency between different semantic interpretations, a precise and computer-processable meaning must be associated with each concept. This can be achieved using an ontology in order to formally annotate meaning.

Shared business knowledge exists in any trade formalized by practitioners skilled in the arts of training, assessing and auditing their trade. This business knowledge is often formalized as a "reference model" used in a "standard-based" EM for a common acceptance of models. They are defined in modeling frameworks as "generic enterprise models". We will present one such well-known reference model called SCOR in section 5.3, as a case study of our research project on semantic alignment.

The ability to use such a reference model in engineering projects is an example of semantic alignment. Thus, ontologies become a main issue in business modeling, especially for the use of reference models in engineering projects. Ontologies can help to build specific models from some generic models to fit the requirements of a specific business.

Ontology for business engineering was proposed by the University of Edinburgh to improve tools for EM [USC 98]. Their EM relies on two descriptions, i.e. one textual and the other one in a semi-formal language called Ontolingua. To support model-driven engineering, an ontology of activity was introduced by the University of Toronto [THA 94]. Based on a comparison of these proposals, a comprehensive ontology for the company was designed in a hierarchical approach as a "core ontology enterprise" [BER 01b]. Completing these ontologies focused on enterprise

---

4 Information and communication technology.

structure, another business ontology proposes a classification of businesses in which a distinction is made between business and enterprise models [OST 04].

In fact, ontologies may be seen as complementary to meta-models. Although work on ontologies serves to enrich the meta-models used in EM – as for example in the field of libraries [LAG 01] – the large size of a modern IS and the multidisciplinarity of the underlying business knowledge make it impossible to produce a single ontology for the multiplicity of areas. A hierarchical approach is possible with a global meta-model that links business models using various business ontologies. Approaches using three and four levels were compared by Naumenko and Wegman [NAU 03]. The semantic consistency between models is, however, an open issue related to the general problematic of alignment.

A mapping approach based on a concept that combines physical with information objects has been proposed as part of a model-driven architecture [BAI 06], and a framework for positioning ontologies or thesauri in a meta-model of an IS support has been introduced for engineering IS [TER 06]. Similarly, ontologies are used to assist the alignment of business processes with e-commerce standards [SEN 07]. We can therefore consider a hierarchical approach to reference models and business ontologies. A reference model is described using a modeling language and a meta-model to ensure global and structural consistency. It relies on ontologies to enable the exchange and sharing of knowledge, thus guaranteeing semantic consistency in all usages and interpretations of the model.

5.2.2. *Ontology and alignment*

The strategic alignment model (SAM) was introduced by Henderson and Venkatraman [HEN 93]. This model aims to support the integration of IT into business strategy. As shown in the four corner boxes in Figure 5.1, SAM is based on the alignment of four domains: IT strategy, IT infrastructure and processes, business strategy, and business infrastructure and processes. In order to support this alignment, Gudas and Brundzaite [GUD 06] extended SAM by adding a knowledge-management level represented by the two boxes in the middle of Figure 5.1, i.e. business and IT knowledge management.

These authors propose that the company rely on its central knowledge base, shared by the four original domains represented in the four corners. They think that, for strategic alignment, the alignment of knowledge should become a central focus.

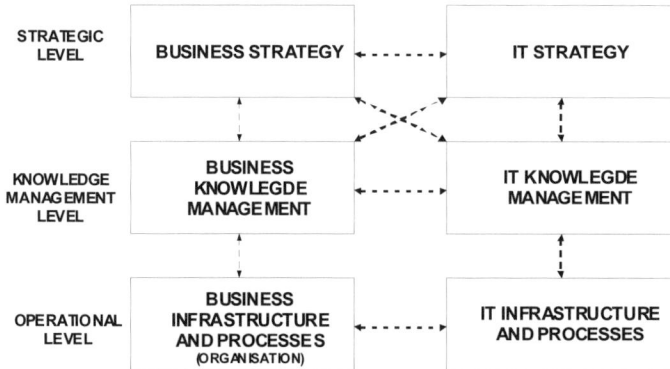

Figure 5.1. *The SAM [HEN 93] in Figure 4.3 complemented with knowledge-management components [GUD 06]*

As seen in the previous section, knowledge in IS is represented in a variety of ways. For instance, databases or collections of documents, emails and XML schemas exist in large numbers. In addition, computational resources and flows of information are constantly increasing. People are consequently faced with a high level of heterogeneity. One aspect of the growing heterogeneity in IS is the desire to combine existing representations together and to work on a transparent level with them [EHR 07]. Information integration has always been a challenge. It makes it possible to work more easily with knowledge from different sources.

Multiple conflicts of a semantic nature may, however, exist. These semantic problems must be solved in order to ensure a good integration between industrial IS. Semantic integration consists of making systems interoperate and cooperate at an abstract level by providing mechanisms allowing us to compare and recognize the resemblances and differences between the various concepts examined [IZZ 09]. Izza analyses the main techniques used to integrate heterogenous industrial applications semantically. In particular, we are interested in the semantic techniques based on ontologies.

We therefore believe that it is necessary to define "semantics" and "ontology" in detail.

Semantics is the study of meaning. The word is derived from the Greek word "semantikos" ("significant") [LID 40]. In linguistics, it is the study of the interpretation of signs or symbols used by agents or communities within particular circumstances and contexts. More recently, semantics has been developed in the IT domain with the evolution of the Web to the semantic Web [BER 01a], where it is "a formal form of representation of human knowledge" [WOO 75]. Semantics is a fundamental aspect of application integration. To correctly ensure this integration, it is necessary for the various applications used to be able to interpret the information exchanged in the same way. One of the most effective means for the formal representation of semantics is in an ontology.

Artificial intelligence and Web researchers have adopted the term "ontology" for their own needs. The first definition of ontology in the field of computing is proposed in [NEC 91]. These authors define ontology as "the basic terms and relations comprising the vocabulary of a topic area as well as the rules for combining terms and relations to define extensions to the vocabulary". Gruber [GRU 95] proposed the most prominent definition of ontology as "an explicit specification of a conceptualization". A conceptualization refers to an abstract model of some phenomenon in the world by identifying the relevant concept of that phenomenon [STU 98]. Here, "explicit" means that the types of concepts used and the constraints on their use are explicitly defined [HER 07]. The benefits of using ontologies include reuse, sharing and portability of knowledge across platforms, and improved documentation, maintenance and reliability [USC 98]. Ontologies lead to a better understanding of a field and to more effective and efficient handling of information in that field.

Knowledge may have different representations, so we now find several ontologies in an area for the same field of application. Furthermore, applications may need to use ontologies from various areas or from different views of one area. On the other hand, ontology builders may want to use existing ontologies as a basis for the creation of new ontologies, by either extending these existing ontologies or combining knowledge from different smaller ontologies. In each of these cases it is important to know the relationships between the terms in the different ontologies. It is then necessary to have tools allowing builders to make the link between the knowledge expressed in each ontology. Thus, ontology alignment makes it possible to reconcile the opinions of several experts [BAC 04] from a semantic point of view. Currently, a certain number of ontology alignment approaches exist to help the user to achieve interoperability between ontologies.

Aligning something means "bringing into line" [MER 97]. This very brief definition emphasizes the fact that aligning is an activity that causes the objects involved to be in some sort of mutual relationship. In the literature, several definitions and methods of ontology alignment have been proposed.

Euzenat and colleagues [EUZ 07] define ontology matching as the process of finding the relations between ontologies, and ontology alignment as the result of the process in which these relations are declaratively expressed.

Klein [KLE 01] and Ehrig [EHR 07] define the term "ontology alignment" as: "Given two ontologies, aligning one ontology with another means that for each entity (concept, relation or instance) in the first ontology, we try to find a corresponding entity, which has the same intended meaning, in the second ontology." Formally, alignment is defined by the *map* function as follows:

$$sim(e_1, e_2) > t \Rightarrow map(e_1) = e_2$$
$$map : O \rightarrow O'$$

In this definition, O and O' are two ontologies to be aligned, and t indicates a minimal threshold of similarity *sim* belonging to the interval $[0, 1]$, so that two entities $e_1 \in O$ and $e_2 \in O'$ may be assumed to be similar. For instance, Noy [NOY 04], Shvaiko and Euzenat [SHC 05], and Bach [BAC 06] use the measures of similarity between strings and composite structures for *sim*. Similarity may be hard to assess since the ontologies to be aligned may be represented in different languages.

Lambrix and Tan [LAM 06] propose a framework for ontology alignment. This framework is shown in Figure 5.2. It consists of two parts. The first part (I in this figure) calculates alignment suggestions. The second part (II) interacts with the user to decide on the final alignments. Some systems may not have the second part.

An alignment algorithm receives two source ontologies as input. The algorithm may include several matchers. The matchers may implement strategies based on linguistic matching, structure-based strategies, constraint-based approaches, instance-based strategies, strategies that use auxiliary information, or a combination of these. Each matcher utilizes knowledge from one or multiple sources. The matchers calculate similarities between the terms from the different source ontologies.

Alignment suggestions are then determined by combining and filtering the results generated by one or more matchers. By using different matchers, and combining and filtering the results in different ways, we obtain different alignment strategies. The suggestions are then presented to the user who accepts or rejects them. The acceptance and rejection of a suggestion may influence further suggestions. Next, a conflict checker is used to avoid conflicts introduced by the alignment relationships. The output of the alignment algorithm is a set of relationships between terms from the source ontologies.

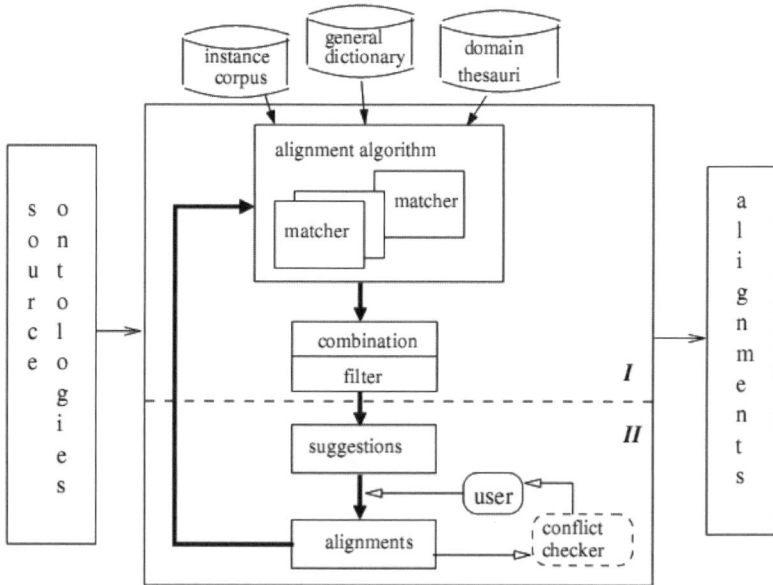

Figure 5.2. *Alignment framework [LAM 06]*

These different approaches to ontology-matching or -alignment are currently used to solve the "semantic challenge". Compared to language translation, ontology-mapping is still an open issue. Language translation exists even if it is not a fully automated process, especially for complex and semantically rich sentences. Regarding knowledge, some tools are being developed and some specific problems can be solved but, generally speaking, knowledge-mapping is a complex and unsolved problem. Our aim is to build a specific case using normalized knowledge on SCs drawn from existing business models and to study how knowledge-mapping can help strategic alignment.

5.2.3. *Business modeling languages and business models*

There are a great number of EM methodologies, techniques and languages, such as GRAI-GIM, CIM-OSA, GERAM, IDEF and ARIS, which provide a theoretical framework to describe the relations between processes, functions, objects and information. After a short presentation on GRAI, CIMOSA and GERAM, which are historically the three main contributions toward the standardization of EM with the ISO 19439 and 19440 norms, we will illustrate the enrichment of EM from a modeling language, which can be very simple, such as IDEF. This enrichment is achieved by adding a meta-model defining a business language syntax, which can be as rich as ARIS, and then building the model on extensive business knowledge as the SCOR reference model for SC.

GIM: The GRAI Laboratory of the University of Bordeaux has developed the GRAI integrated methodology (GIM) within the framework of the ESPRIT projects Open CAM and IMPACS [DOU 95]. GIM is a product of the complementarity of the GRAI, IDEF0 and MERISE methods used to analyze and design production systems. GIM contains user-oriented and a technically oriented methods. The former transforms user requirements into user specifications in terms of functions, information, decisions and resources. The latter transforms the user specification into technical specifications in terms of information and manufacturing the technology components required to implement the system.

CIM-OSA: The European ESPRIT Consortium AMICE has developed a CIM open system architecture (CIM-OSA) as a pre-normative modeling language for EM [ZEL 95]. The main goal of CIM-OSA is to support the process-oriented modeling of manufacturing enterprises and to provide execution support for the operation of enterprise systems based on those models. Its process-oriented modeling approach describes all enterprise activities in a common way. Such activities include manufacturing processes on the shop floor as well as management and administrative processes. It also provides a modular approach (domain process) for EM by identifying three modeling levels (requirement definition, design specification and implementation) and four views (function, information, resource and organization) as part of an open set. CIM-OSA is intended to provide a descriptive, rather than prescriptive, methodology supporting enterprise lifecycle modeling. It attempts to provide a reference architecture from which a particular architecture can be derived to fulfill the needs of a particular enterprise. Applying CIM-OSA will result in complete descriptions of enterprise domains and of their contained business processes, including their relationships with external agencies.

GERAM: The generalized enterprise reference architecture and methodology (GERAM) has been developed in the framework of the IFAC/IFIP task force on EM. It is based on the findings that existing enterprise architecture, and its associated methodologies, had to be extended to become a complete architecture and methodology for guiding enterprise integration programs from their initial conception to their actual construction and use. Therefore, GERAM is not intended as a new proposal for enterprise reference architecture. It is a framework that organizes existing enterprise integration knowledge and provides an overall structure to use those existing methods and modeling techniques [BER 96]. It is the result of generalization, based on the three most complete enterprise reference architectures: CIM-OSA, GIM and PERA. GERAM looks at the life history of an enterprise (or any business entity) in terms of tasks carried out on that enterprise.

The *IDEF* suite (ICAM definition) was developed in the 1970s by the US Air Force in a project called ICAM (integrated computer aided manufacturing). It contains the following views [NIS 93]:

– IDEF0: Functional point of view. This is the structured representation of the functions, activities or process-modeled system. More commonly known as SADT (structured analysis design technique), it represents a flow of processing "activities" transforming "inputs" into "outputs" under the constraints of "controls" and by means of "mechanisms".

– IDEF1: Informational point of view. Relying on a dictionary containing an explicit definition of each element of the model, this view offers diagrams containing the rules and procedures for defining and building the corresponding database.

– IDEF2 and IDEF3: A dynamic point of view that represents the temporal behavior of the system modeled. IDEF2 relies on the principle of queues. IDEF3 introduces logical connectors to explain situation synchronization, sequence and parallel activities.

An IDEF0 model is composed of a hierarchical series of diagrams that gradually display increasing levels of detail describing functions and their interfaces within the context of a system. The components of the IDEF0 syntax are boxes and arrows, rules and diagrams. Boxes represent functions, defined as activities, processes or transformations. Arrows represent data or objects related to functions. Rules define how the components are used, and the diagrams provide a format for depicting models both verbally and graphically. The format also provides the basis for model configuration management.

According to the IDEF0 standard, a process can be represented as in Figure 5.3. An IDEF0 model diagram is then composed of several activity boxes and relationships that capture the overall activity [NIS 93]. IDEF0 is defined only as a grammar providing syntax in order to describe these relations, without any indication of business knowledge structure in any domain.

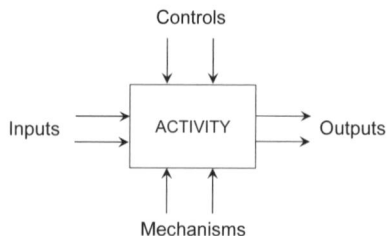

Figure 5.3. *IDEF0 syntax*

ARIS is a framework designed by [SCH 98] that aims to represent a system according to five complementary views: functional, data, product/service, organizational and process views. ARIS uses a modeling language with various kinds of models. The model for business processes is known as event-driven process chains, which is the centre of the "ARIS House". It connects all other views and describes the dynamics of the business processes. The "ARIS House" represents a concept for comprehensive computer-aided business process management. Furthermore, ARIS House was developed to implement business models in IS. As ARIS connects applications with functionalities, tasks and organizational units, it represents an approach that is closer to the requirement of alignment (see Figure 5.4). There are links between the different viewpoints at an operational level. The value chain representation supports a top-down approach from strategic to operational alignment.

The ARIS language proposes a large number of constructs for different points of view. Therefore, ARIS is not only a modeling language; it contains a high-level meta-model of business constructs required by EM. These constructs are close to the ISO 19439 norm, but present some particularities and are more varied. For example, from the organizational view the ARIS language proposes constructs such as "work station", "organizational unit", "type of person", "internal person", "external person", etc.

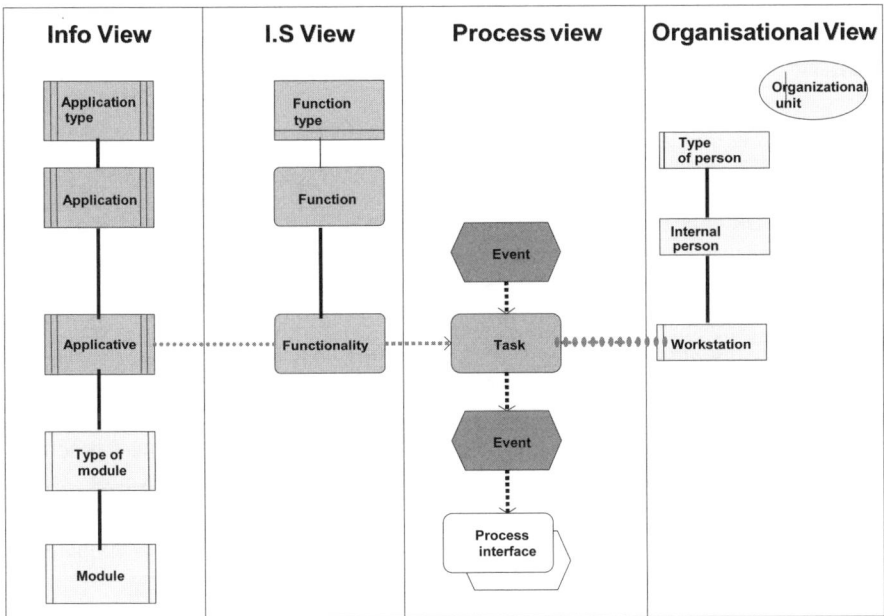

Figure 5.4. *Existing ARIS approach*

5.2.4. SCOR reference model

The SCOR model is a tool for analysis, diagnosis, design and implementation of SC management. It is one of the well-known business reference models [HUA 05, ROD 06, STA 00] and is used to help analyze, evaluate and improve global SC. For that purpose, SCOR proposes a vision throughout the SC to facilitate the representation of its various flows (material, financial, etc.). It also provides a terminology and standardized processes enabling a general description of SCs and their translation into process maps.

The SCOR model (see Figure 5.5) is based on the identification of five management processes: plan, source, make, deliver and return.

The process begins with "business process re-engineering" to represent a situation from the basic elements proposed by SCOR. It continues with a "benchmarking" step in a partnership approach based on assessment tables. The process ends by analyzing the "best practices" and defining the reference model of the target company.

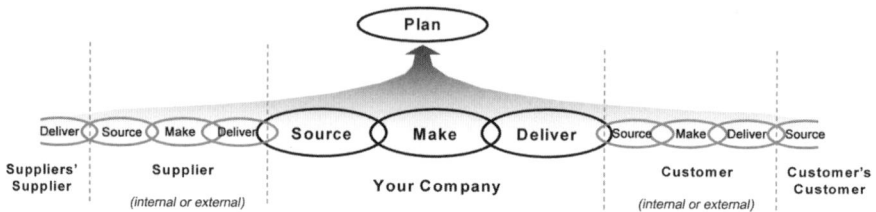

Figure 5.5. *SCOR model [SCC 08]*

The SCOR model is organized hierarchically at four levels. Level 1 (strategic) uses five process types: plan, make, source, deliver and return. This is the highest and most aggregated level. Level 2 (tactical) is the configuration level using process categories (make to stock, make to order, etc.) that takes into account SC typologies. In line with the company's strategy, this intermediate level makes it possible to (re)configure the SC from 30 sub-processes. Level 3 (operational) is the main modeling level using process elements linked by information flow and physical flows. Companies can specify the activities of the sub-processes, best practices, breaches of flux, the functionalities of software and tools. Level 4 is the implementation level and has to be defined specifically for each SC. This lower level, which is not included in the reference model, is suitable for each company to define the basic tasks involved in activities.

The original SCOR model in version 9.0 is a textual bookmarked 650-page file. It contains: 27 main processes (level 2) detailed in 171 elements of process (level 3);

274 information elements defined as input or output of process elements (level 3); 489 best practices identified at process levels 2 and 3, with 350 texts describing features of the information system required for each best practice; and 498 metrics used at levels 1, 2 and 3, classified in five performance categories (cost, assets, reliability, agility and responsiveness).

The SCOR model spans all customer interactions, all physical material transactions and all market interactions. However, it does not attempt to describe every business process or activity. Specifically, the model does not address sales and marketing, product development, research and development, human resources, and some elements of post-delivery customer support. These processes are the subject of ongoing parallel research projects developing the DCOR model for design activities and the CCOR model for customer relations.

Using the SCOR model, a specific SC representation links all geographical or organizational business entities that have to be modeled. Each business entity – like production facilities, distribution activities or sourcing activities – is represented by its appropriate process. Material flows are represented point-to-point by solid-line arrows at a process level. A SC ties together the set of source-make-deliver SC processes through which a given product family flows. The appropriate planning-process categories are then situated, using dashed lines to show the links to the execution processes. Finally, the global plan process, which aggregates the outputs of operational plan processes, is given. An illustration is shown in Figure 5.6.

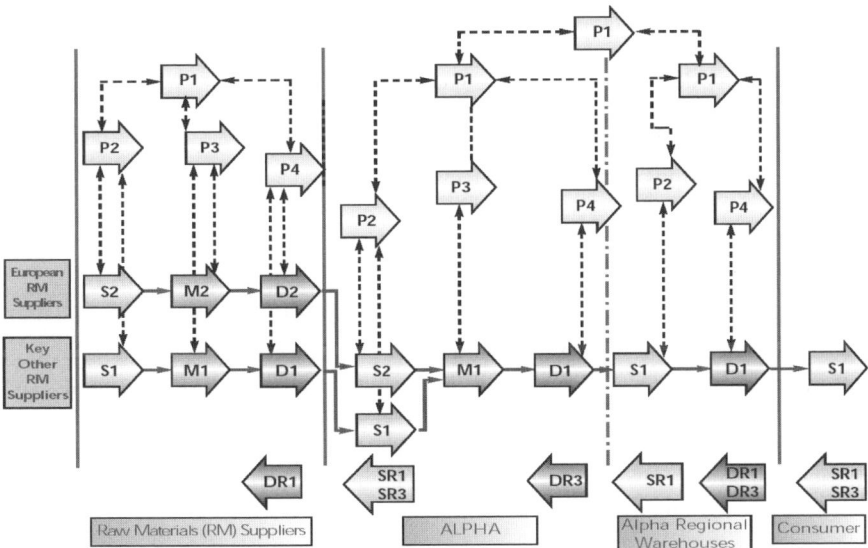

Figure 5.6. *SCOR process map [SCC 08]*

Configuring these processes, different entities of a SC can be depicted and thus compared. Furthermore, by using common performance attributes called "metrics", SC structures are analyzed relative to their performance. The "best practices" provided allow performance improvements to single entities or to the SC as a whole. Best practices are also linked to "features" describing how to functionally support the realization of the best practices. Even though the features are not fully standardized and are described only textually, they can be seen as a link between processes and the IS, since those features are integrated parts of IT applications. Each process is detailed in process elements, providing descriptions of required information in- and outputs. This builds the information flow through the SC.

5.3. SCOR model and its representations in XML (ARIS and OWL)

A business model aims to formalize all or part of the company in order to understand or explain an existing situation. This model is always associated with a purpose. It needs (depending on requirements) to be able to take account of the structural, functional and behavioral aspects and also to understand the viewpoint of a participant.

These models are mainly presented in the syntactic components, however, and the guarantee of a semantic model is based on the analyst's expertise. It is thus necessary to transmit all or part of the semantics by a language such as OWL. This is only possible by means of its semantic enrichment, which can lead to the creation of new concepts represented in an ontology.

An ontology describes the following concepts:

– the classes of the objects to be organized;

– the relationships between the objects;

– the properties or attributes of the objects.

In order to enrich the representation of enterprise models, the solution proposed in this paragraph is to transform the textual model of SCOR into an ontology and then to enrich it by adding semantic annotations, rules, restrictions, etc. In other words, transforming SCOR into a set of classes, relationships and properties will simplify it, and information regarding informal or implicit knowledge embedded in the reference model will thus be lost. Adding semantic annotations, rules and restrictions, however, will reduce this information loss, while the ontology of SCOR will be usable by computers.

We first introduce the SCOR model as a business reference model and then explain how transformation of a business model ontology can be done, what advantages an ontology can provide compared to other kinds of models (e.g. the textual description of SCOR), and the prospect of obtaining a broader and semantically richer ontology of a business model.

5.3.1. *SCOR meta-model*

The SCOR model is composed of the following constructs:

– *process* and *process elements*: standard descriptions of the individual elements that make up the SC processes;

– *metrics*: standard definitions of key performance measurements;

– *best practices*: descriptions of best practices associated with each of the process elements;

– *features*: identification of software functionality (features) that enables best practices;

– *input/output*: identification of information exchanged between processes.

These elements represent a SCOR meta-model (see Figure 5.7) that can be mapped to the 19440 modeling constructs [MIL 08]. Some SCOR constructs, such as "practices" and "features", play a key role in the interaction between 19440 viewpoints, practices as organizational and resource viewpoints, and features as functional and resource viewpoints. This reinforces the importance of SCOR study as an alignment tool.

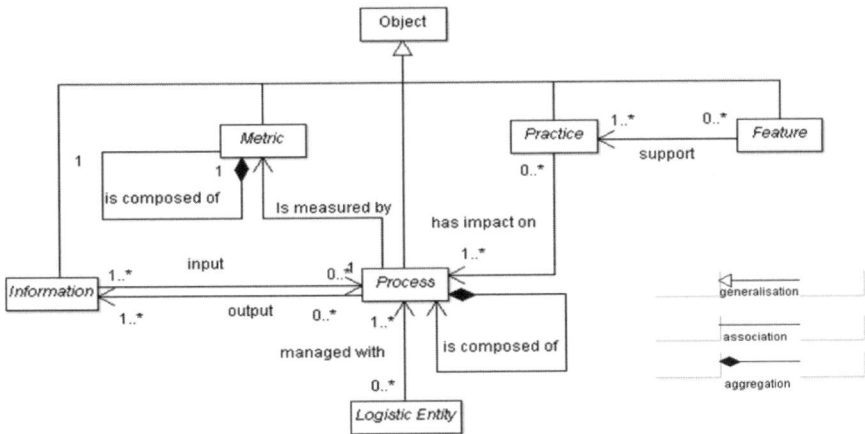

Figure 5.7. *SCOR meta-model*

With all these business concepts, SCOR organizes domain-specific business knowledge, defined in a modeling language that is easily mapped to ARIS language. Using only five modeling constructs, SCOR represents an extensive formalization of this knowledge in a business language that well-known and recognized by SC experts. In the following sub-sections we consider the advantage of a SCOR ontology for making this knowledge more consistent and processable.

5.3.2. SCOR/ARIS

The ARIS framework is generally used to design and manage business processes. To support this method, IDS Scheer has developed a design platform allowing the creation of models that represent different aspects of the system in the same database. Each model is made out of a set of inter-related objects. Hence, the database includes the models, objects, and relations between the objects. Associations between an object and a model giving a detailed description of the object can be created. These associations between objects and models allow us to explore the whole database by travelling from one model to another. This gives some consistency to the representation.

The SCOR reference model can be expressed thanks to the ARIS formalism and included in a database, as explained above. There is no one way to create a SCOR/ARIS model, since this transformation requires a certain interpretation of the original SCOR models and several choices have to be made. In the following we describe the structure of a SCOR/ARIS model provided by the Supply Chain Council.

The SCOR/ARIS model is structured in six main directories, plus one dedicated to the legend that defines the objects selected to model SCOR with ARIS (see Figure 5.8). The first three directories are dedicated to the description of the strategic level (top level), tactical level (configuration level) and operational level (process category level). The fourth directory comprises the performance attributes classified in five performance categories (cost, assets, reliability, agility and responsiveness). The fifth directory includes all the inputs and outputs of the processes recorded in a SCOR data overview model. Finally, the sixth directory groups together all of the practices.

The links between the constructs of the SCOR meta-model, i.e. process, metric, best practice, input and output, are expressed in the SCOR/ARIS model by means of function allocation diagrams, as shown in Figure 5.9. Those links described in the diagrams are all included in the database and allow us to test the model with requests such as: what are the processes that require such best practices to reach high performance attributes?

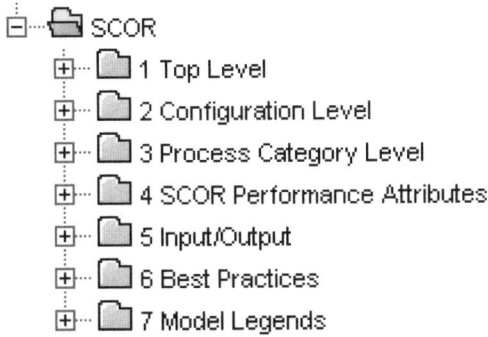

Figure 5.8. *Tree of the SCOR/ARIS model*

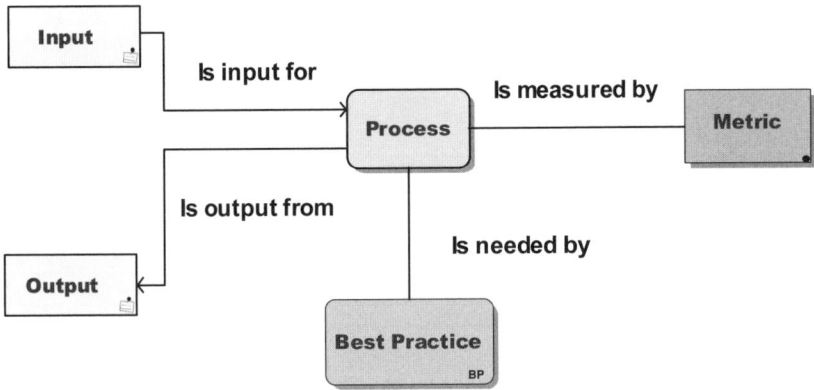

Figure 5.9. *ARIS concepts supporting SCOR/ARIS*

To build the SCOR/ARIS model, several choices have been made. The model is structured in tree directories that give a classification of the different elements. This organization is in itself an interpretation of the original textual SCOR model. The features are not part of the SCOR/ARIS model, whereas they are included in the original version. As introduced in section 5.2.4, since version 8.0 of SCOR, the features that used to be linked with processes are now included as attributes of good practice. Hence, they are not formalized enough to be included in the SCOR/ARIS model.

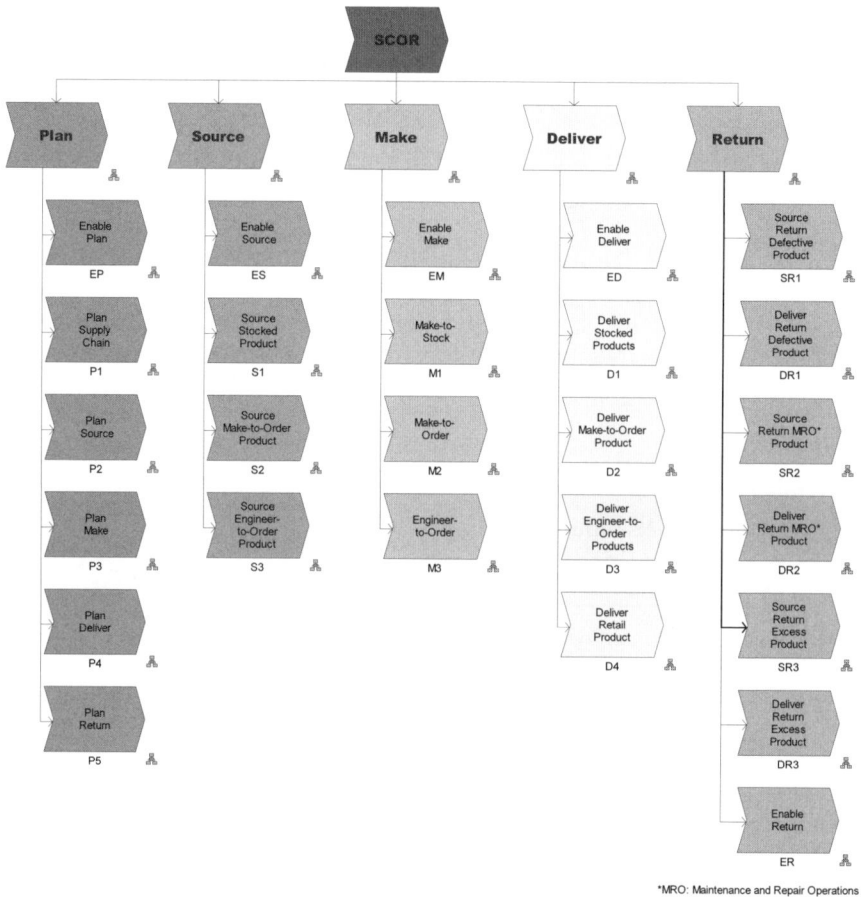

Figure 5.10. *Overview of SCOR level 1 and 2 processes*

Figure 5.10 gives an overview of the SCOR level 1 and level 2 processes, represented in the ARIS formalism thanks to a value-added chain. The little sign in the bottom right corner of each box indicates that the object (i.e. the process) is described in more detail, using one or several models, and allows easy navigation throughout the database. Hence, we can open two models from the "Make-to-Stock" process box: a value-added chain and a function-allocation diagram.

In the function-allocation diagram (see Figure 5.11), we can see the best practices that are recommended when setting up the make-to-stock process, as well as the metrics that are associated with the process.

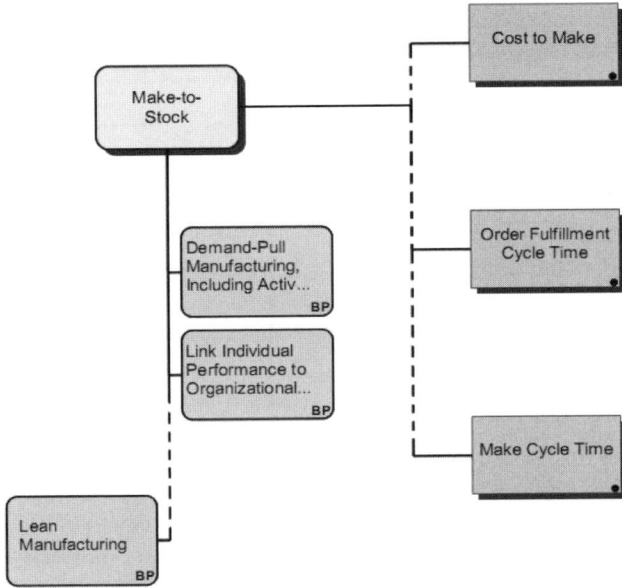

Figure 5.11. *Function allocation diagram of the make-to-stock process (level 2)*

The value-added chain (see Figure 5.12) describes the level 3 processes contributing to the make-to-stock process. Each level 3 process is detailed in a function allocation diagram, as shown in Figure 5.13.

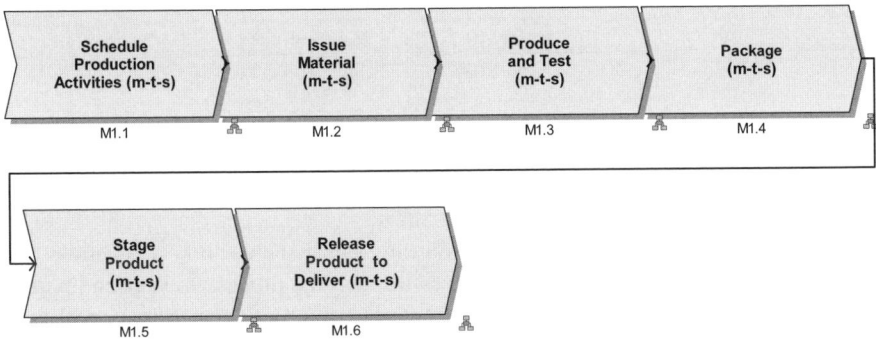

Figure 5.12. *Value-added chain of the make-to-stock process (level 2)*

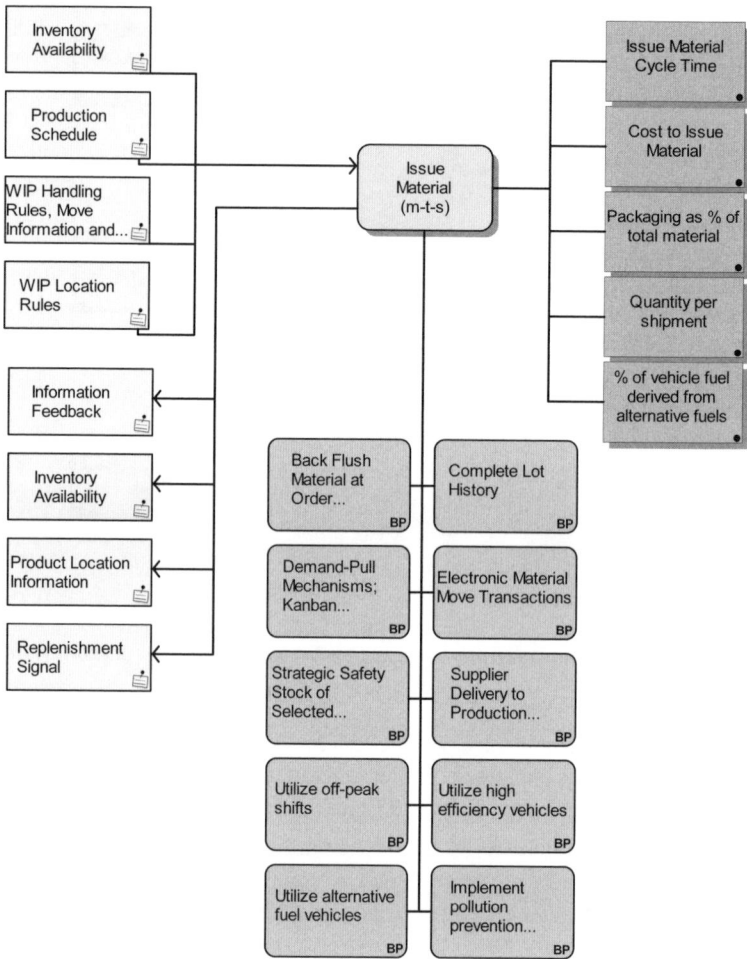

Figure 5.13. *Function-allocation diagram of the issue material process (level 3)*

In the SCOR/ARIS model there are no direct links between best practices and metrics. Best practices are related to metrics through the processes. We can imagine that the adoption of one or several best practices for a particular process will have an influence on one or several metrics related to that process, but this influence is not obvious and has not been formalized in the original SCOR model. Nevertheless, in the original paper version of SCOR an effort has been made to improve the description of some of the best practices and to formalize how best practices have an impact on metrics. As an example, in the original SCOR model the impact of the best practice "lean methodology" on the global performance attributes such as reliability, responsiveness, agility, cost and assets is analyzed. For the impact on costs, it says that "Cost reduction is a typical impact of lean as non-value-added processes are removed and efficiency increases. Response times are also reduced, which results in faster cash flow cycles." [SCC 08] From this sentence we can deduce that there is a link between "lean methodology" best practice and "cost to make", "make cycle time", and "order fulfillment cycle time" metrics. Those attributes will be improved if this recommended best practice is applied to the "make-to-stock" process (see Figure 5.11). However, this knowledge textually described in the original SCOR model is not included in the SCOR/ARIS model, since it has to be interpreted from the original model.

5.3.3. SCOR/OWL

OWL is an ontology language for the semantic Web developed by the W3C organization. It has three increasingly expressive sublanguages – OWL Lite, OWL DL and OWL Full [HOR 03]. OWL is intended to be used when the information contained in documents needs to be processed by applications, as opposed to situations where the content only needs to be presented to humans. OWL can be used to explicitly represent the meaning of terms in vocabularies and the relationships between those terms; in other words, OWL can represent ontologies. Therefore, using OWL ontologies to share knowledge between business partners should help them to better interpret, understand and benefit from that knowledge.

Business modeling and ontology are two existing approaches by which to formalize enterprise knowledge. The SCOR model, like many business reference models, was first described textually, with some illustrative diagrams. It was then represented using a business modeling language. We have used the ARIS representation of the SCOR model as a computable existing representation of SCOR. In this section we will first show how we transform SCOR/ARIS into SCOR/OWL. The SCOR/OWL version will therefore only contain some of knowledge of the SCOR/ARIS version. Finally, we will compare these two versions and see the differences in knowledge management allowed by OWL in comparison with ARIS.

The transformation of SCOR/ARIS into SCOR/OWL can be summarized in the following steps:

– export SCOR/ARIS from ARIS into an ARIS XML file;

– parse this ARIS XML file in OWL to obtain an OWL XML file;

– import this OWL XML file in Protégé to obtain the SCOR/OWL model. (Protégé is a free, open-source platform with a set of tools to construct domain models and knowledge-based applications with ontologies[5]).

Our contribution is the parser in the second step. To express SCOR/ARIS knowledge in an OWL XML file, we have to decide for each ARIS XML tag, depending on an ARIS modeling object, how to represent it as an OWL XML tag. The result is a transformation rule of each ARIS XML element into OWL XML elements. Despite the apparent simplicity of this transformation, the following critical issues must be addressed:

– The document type definition of an ARIS XML file defines a rich structure, including graphical characteristics such as colors, positions, etc., and authorization information including owners, rights, etc. The aim of our transformation is to capture the knowledge contained in the SCOR model. Should all this information be considered as semantic content? That is obviously not the case for font or character set, for example. However, the position of an object in a model, above or below another one, may contain some assessment by the model designer on the relations between these objects. In our work we consider neither the graphical information of models, nor model management information such as authorizations, creation/update dates, etc.

– Since ARIS is a business modeling language, it uses a meta-model containing several types of constructs (components, functions, interfaces process, module processes, organizational units, entities, etc.). The issues are how we can present this diversity of types in an ontology using only the notion of concept, and what class hierarchy we can build from the ARIS meta-model.

– ARIS organizes knowledge using models that are partial "views" on the knowledge, and groups that are a hierarchical structure of knowledge. These concepts do not exist in OWL. We therefore have to decide whether to consider ARIS models as knowledge elements or not. Taking them into account means that we consider that the decision of a designer to create an ARIS model contains a semantic signification. The "point of view" makes sense by itself. If we do not take models into account we consider that, irrespective of the models used to present the knowledge, all of the semantic content is included in the objects and relations presented in the models.

– ARIS uses a hierarchical structure using the "association" between an object and some models. An object may be described through an association with a model containing other objects. However, it can also be a contextual model that does not represent a hierarchical structure. In our case, these associations may be

---

5 Available at: http://protege.stanford.edu/, accessed 28.4.10.

implemented as a hierarchy of concepts in OWL. This implementation is specific to the SCOR model, but is not necessarily valid in other cases.

– Once the transformation rules to create OWL concepts and relations are clear we have to decide how we will choose the types of relations (transitive, functional or symmetrical) to represent them in OWL. Moreover, some restrictions can be defined through concepts in OWL; for example, two concepts may be mutually exclusive. Unfortunately, this notion is not represented in ARIS. Of course, plan process is a very different concept to metric cycle time. On the other hand, the concepts make-to-stock and make-to-order cannot be considered to be exclusive. They may both be used in a middle-sized company where the production process is often heterogenous and variable and is thus both a make-to-stock and a make-to-order concept.

To address these issues, we propose a meta-model of both ARIS and OWL implementations to clearly explain the transformation rules. We thus ensure that there is some genericity and extensibility in the designed transformation rules, even if they are partially SCOR model dependent. The ARIS meta-model presented in Figure 5.14 contains "elements" that have many attributes.

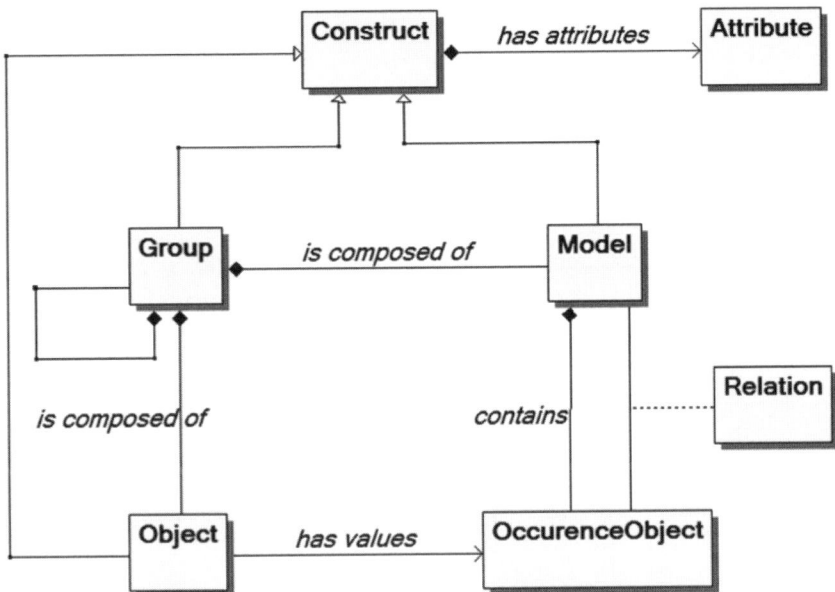

Figure 5.14. *ARIS meta-model export*

As explained above, we will not take attributes regarding graphical format or model management into account. Figure 5.14 shows that elements are groups (used for the organization of objects in the ARIS application), models (used as groups of objects presented from a certain view), objects (which support the main semantic content), and object occurrences called "ObjectOcc" (which are the occurrence of an object in a model). Groups are composed of (sub)-groups, objects and models. Models are composed of object occurrences. An object can be associated with a model (which is a particular description of the content or context of this object). An object occurrence is linked to the reference object. For a better understanding of this meta-model, we add a rule contained in the ARIS application, and not in the XML export, but which is essential to the model's consistency: for each kind of model, some objects are allowed. We then add an association class linking models and object occurrence. In a conceptual meta-model, we would have to explain the roles of relations between objects, but in the ARIS XML file these relations are implemented as attributes of objects. We will only consider these kinds of attributes containing relations or associations of the ARIS object.

The OWL meta-model described in Figure 5.15 is made of OWL classes and properties[6]. Classes may be of different kinds (union, intersection, complement and enumeration). Properties may be data properties or object properties.

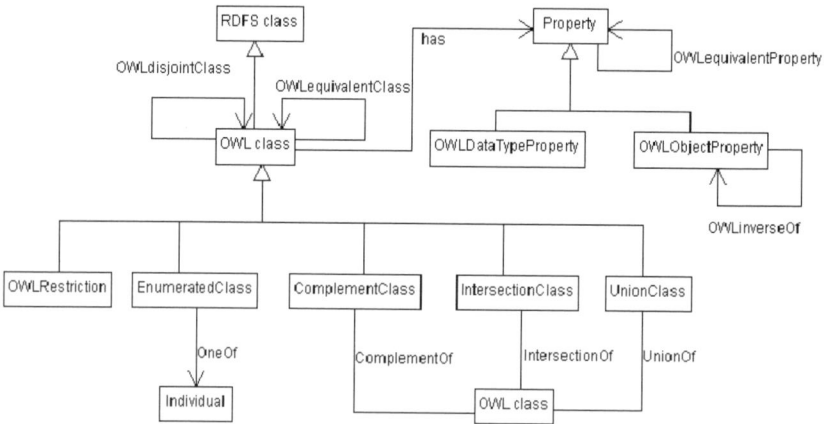

Figure 5.15. *OWL meta-model*

Comparing the meta-models in Figures 5.14 and 5.15, some answers to our queries may be proposed:

6 www.w3.org/TR/owl-features/, accessed 28.4.10.

– ARIS objects and groups are defined as concepts in OWL. Considering groups as a concept can be considered as information regarding the management of formalized knowledge, and not the knowledge itself. In the case of the SCOR model, we consider groups as a concept in order to be sure to capture all semantic knowledge regarding the grouping of objects, for example when grouping all metrics by categories of costs, assets, reliability, etc.

– ARIS associations are defined as a hierarchy of classes in OWL. Considering the SCOR model, these associations are clearly used as a hierarchical description. Each process on level 2 has, for example, a "function allocation diagram" model that describes the content of this process in terms of level 3 process elements.

– ARIS models will not be considered as concepts, but only as an OWL datatype property in the OWL class related to each ARIS object used in this ARIS model. Therefore, models are not considered to be an element of knowledge but only as a viewpoint on the knowledge.

– All ARIS relationships between ARIS objects will be represented as OWL object properties.

Other ARIS object attributes are transformed into OWL data properties.

5.4. Use of business models and ontology for strategic alignment

5.4.1. *Comparison of three representations of SCOR*

We may distinguish three forms of representation of SCOR, as summarized in Table 5.1.

Name of the representation	Form	Advantages	Source
Original SCOR	Text	Complete	SCC[7]
SCOR/ARIS	XML	Computable	SCC and IDS Scheer[8]
SCOR/OWL	OWL	Computable	Our contribution

Table 5.1. *Overview of the three representations of SCOR*

– *Original SCOR (SCOR/text)*: The textual model of SCOR proposed by the Supply Chain Council is the reference for our work. We consider this model as the

---

7 www.supply-chain.org, accessed 4.28.10.
8 www.ids-scheer.com, accessed 4.28.10.

complete knowledge standardized by business practitioners. We investigate the advantages and drawbacks that other kinds of representations may have in comparison with this text model.

– *SCOR/ARIS*: We call SCOR/ARIS the representation of SCOR using the ARIS language; a representation provided by the Supply Chain Council. This language uses a proprietary meta-model described in Figure 5.14. This representation provided by ARIS is not the only one of its kind. Some efforts have also been made to normalize knowledge embedded in the SCOR/txt using only a spreadsheet to manage lists of concepts. Other representations using modeling tools exist. In all cases, the transformation is an interpretation of the knowledge. The ability of ARIS to express various viewpoints is key when making a computable representation of SCOR, especially with the objective of alignment between different points of view.

– *SCOR/OWL*: We call SCOR/OWL our version of SCOR/ARIS transformed into an OWL representation. This transformation is discussed in section 4.3. Consequently, the semantics included in the SCOR/OWL version is a subset of the semantics in SCOR/ARIS.

We illustrate the example used to compare the SCOR/ARIS model with its SCOR/OWL representation. Relations between "cost-to-make", "make-cycle-time", "order fulfillment cycle time" metrics and the "make-to-stock" process shown in Figure 5.11 (see section 5.3.2) with the SCOR/ARIS representation are presented as a concept diagram in Figure 5.16 and as an OWL file generated by our parser in Figure 5.17.

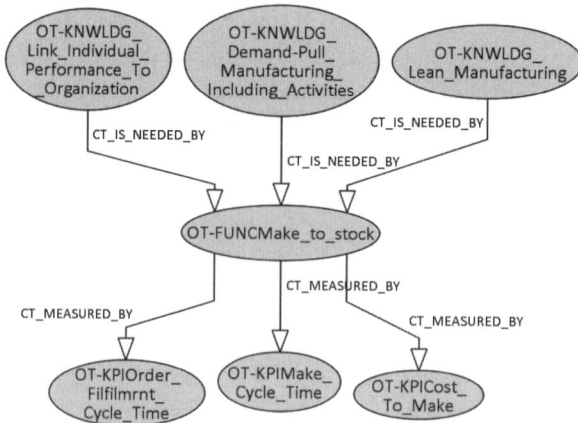

Figure 5.16. *An example of SCOR/OWL graph*

```
<owl:ObjectProperty rdf:ID="CT_MEASURED_BY2613">
   <rdfs:range rdf:resource="#OT_KPIMake_Cycle_Time"/>
   <rdfs:domain rdf:resource="#OT_FUNCMake_to__Stock"/>
</owl:ObjectProperty>

<owl:ObjectProperty rdf:ID="CT_IS_NEEDED_BY2986">
   <rdfs:domain rdf:resource="#OT_KNWLDG_Lean_Manufacturing"/>
   <rdfs:range rdf:resource="#OT_FUNCMake_to__Stock"/>
</owl:ObjectProperty>
```

Figure 5.17. *An example of the SCOR/OWL code*

We now compare each of the representations of SCOR considered side by side.

SCOR/text versus XML-based SCOR: We may refer to SCOR/ARIS and SCOR/OWL together as XML-based SCOR. In short, this comparison emphasizes the advantages and drawbacks of knowledge that computers can understand. The advantages stem from the automation of knowledge management with XML-based SCOR, while the drawbacks come from their incomplete representation of knowledge. This is the consequence of the XML modeling process, which has to decide from a textual description to exclude imprecise content of the SCOR/text. For example, formalizing some SCOR/text description requires external tacit knowledge, for example that "time-to-market" is a key metric in to-order typology and technological SCs.

It is an advantage that a great deal of = knowledge is already informally managed by computers (e.g. e-mails) but cannot be used by them. In particular, computers may store and manipulate (copy/paste, search for strings, etc.) versions of SCOR in some electronic format, but cannot manipulate the knowledge. XML-based SCOR, on the other hand, allows computers to claim they understand the representation of the model of a SC. For this purpose, XML proposes tags, which are used by computers to infer new knowledge. With these tags computers can check the consistency of certain SC models represented with OWL, or the consistency of SCOR with exchange standards such as Electronic Data Interchange (EDI) or Open Applications Group Integration Specification (OAGIS).

On the other hand, representing SCOR in XML also has a few drawbacks, which all seem to come from the poorer information represented. In fact, formalizing everything forces us to make everything explicit, since unlike humans, computers cannot handle implicit knowledge. Making knowledge explicit requires a filter, which reduces the knowledge spectrum as the filter removes some knowledge from the text because it cannot represent the total meaning in textual SCOR. In addition, interpretation may be required to transform the original SCOR into some XML-based SCOR. In fact, formalizing SCOR requires the removal of ambiguities. These are made obvious among people in different parts of a SC who have their own interpretation of the original SCOR.

In summary, XML-based SCOR allows computers to carry out much more reasoning than humans could do with the original SCOR, but on poorer information.

SCOR/ARIS versus SCOR/OWL: As noted above, each of these two representations of SCOR is consistent with the other. More precisely, SCOR/OWL, generated through an automatic XML transformation, is a subset of SCOR/ARIS, but with the ability to add semantic knowledge using the benefits of ontologies, specifically knowledge reasoning, taking into account trade rules that are often implicit in reference models. This main difference will be studied in section 5.4.2.

Regarding the usage of both approaches, the main difference is that SCOR/OWL is described by means of a more generic meta-model and is used to build domain-specific knowledge. In contrast, SCOR/ARIS is described by means of a specific meta-model dedicated to business models and, in the SCOR/ARIS case, is used to model standard business knowledge. The OWL meta-model is domain-independent while the ARIS meta-model is domain-dependant. In addition, SCOR/ARIS is used mainly in enterprise engineering projects to support decision-making, change management, and communication. SCOR/OWL, on the other hand, is used in enterprise knowledge-management projects to support knowledge-mapping and alignment. The SCOR/ARIS model is "user oriented" while SCOR/OWL is mainly "expert oriented". SCOR/ARIS helps to make decisions on organizations, processes, and roles, while SCOR/OWL helps to decide about concepts, glossaries, and classifications. Even if these two representations are computable, we use SCOR/ARIS to simulate and evaluate metrics, and we use SCOR/OWL to define and validate semantic rules by reasoners. In fact, both SCOR/OWL and SCOR/ARIS can use XML-based tools (XSLT transformations, etc.), but only SCOR/OWL can use OWL-specific knowledge tools (reasoner Racer, Protégé plug-ins such as the inference engine Jesstab, etc.).

Using one or two representations depends on user needs. Enhancement of SCOR knowledge is always informal, using mainly text to identify and describe concepts and relations. A computable version is required for engineering projects, however. Knowledge engineering is best supported by SCOR/OWL, while organizational engineering requires SCOR/ARIS. Business models and ontologies are complementary for enterprise engineering. Alignment is a semantic issue requiring ontologies, and an informational issue requiring business models.

5.4.2. *Knowledge-adding and -reasoning with SCOR ontology*

To make the SCOR ontology usable for reasoning, we need to complete the SCOR/ARIS with constraints that are not formalized in SCOR/ARIS but are described, even implicitly, in SCOR documentation. For example, the S3 process (source engineer-to-order) must supply an M3 process (engineer-to-order) and cannot supply an M1 process (make-to-stock). These configuration rules have been added to SCOR/ARIS using the following model updated from previous work focused on the use of the SCOR model for strategic alignment [MIL 09].

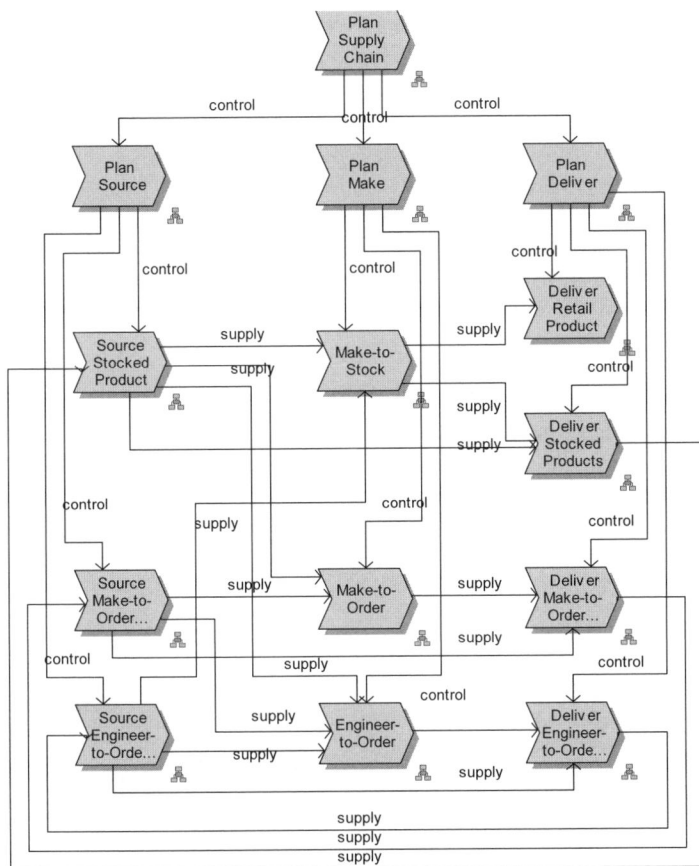

Figure 5.18. *SCOR configuration rules*

The consequence is that, from a semantic point of view, some SCOR/ARIS relations are restrictions to be defined in OWL as properties. In the previous example, a restriction can be expressed as follows: "a to-order process has to supply a to-order and not a to-stock process" or "a to-order process has as its source a to-order or a to-stock process". However, because this type of constraint is not formalized in the ARIS meta-model we have to manually add it in SCOR/OWL, or define some specific transformation rules to create OWL restrictions, depending on ARIS relations. This is a clear example that a generic transformation of an ARIS model into an OWL model is not sufficient. For each ARIS model an expert has to define the restrictions that can be added, at the meta-model level, and even sometimes at the detailed model level.

As an example we can consider the role of SCOR/OWL in Figure 5.19, in which a reasoner is able to detect inconsistencies. SCOR/ARIS provides the tree of processes of levels 1, 2 and 3 in Figure 5.19a (e.g., deliver, make, make-to-stock, etc.). One instance (case) of a SC has been created as "individuals". This case includes one make-to-order process (called CM for "case make"), which is linked to two source processes by a **hasSource** relationship (inverse of supply): one make-to-order source (called CS for "case source") and one engineering-to-order source (called CCS for "second case source"). In order to allow reasoning, this ontology was enriched with restrictions. These restrictions were manually added in the ontology, using two inverse OWL properties – **hasSource** and **supplies:**

– a make-to-order process (M2 in SCOR) "**hasSource**" only a source stoked product (S1) or a source make-to-order process (S2);

– a make-to-order process (M2 in SCOR) "**supplies**" only the deliver make-to-order (D2) or deliver engineering-to-order process (D3).

The top of Figure 5.19b shows the input and output of **hasSource** properties and the lower picture in Figure 5.19b illustrates the rule that gives a restriction between M2 (thus, its individual CM) and S1 or S2 by a **hasSource** property.

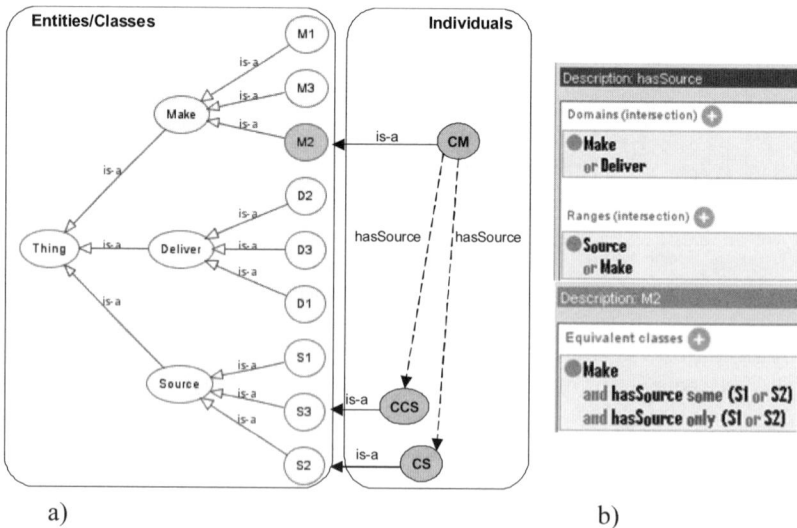

a)   b)

Figure 5.19. *Example of incoherency detectable in SCOR/OWL: a) classes, individuals and properties in our sample, b) hasSource description and restriction on class M2 in our sample*

Reasoner Fact++ available in Protégé exploits this ontology to detect the inconsistency between S3 and **hasSource**. In fact, Figure 5.19b shows that CM (i.e., the individual instance of M2, thus of Make) is related by **hasSource** to "some (S1 or S2)" and to "only (S1 or S2)". Therefore, CCS (which is an S3) cannot be related by **hasSource** to M2, which is pointed out by Fact++.

Even if the reasoner is able to detect inconsistencies, as explained above, the SCOR/OWL model does not include enough conditions necessary and sufficient to allow classification. The restriction on M2 regarding **hasSource** property is sufficient do detect whether the rule is complied with or not, but cannot help to infer individual classes from the relations between them. The classification requires us to exploit more knowledge supported by SCOR, and especially to analyze the dependencies between processes, via information inputs and outputs.

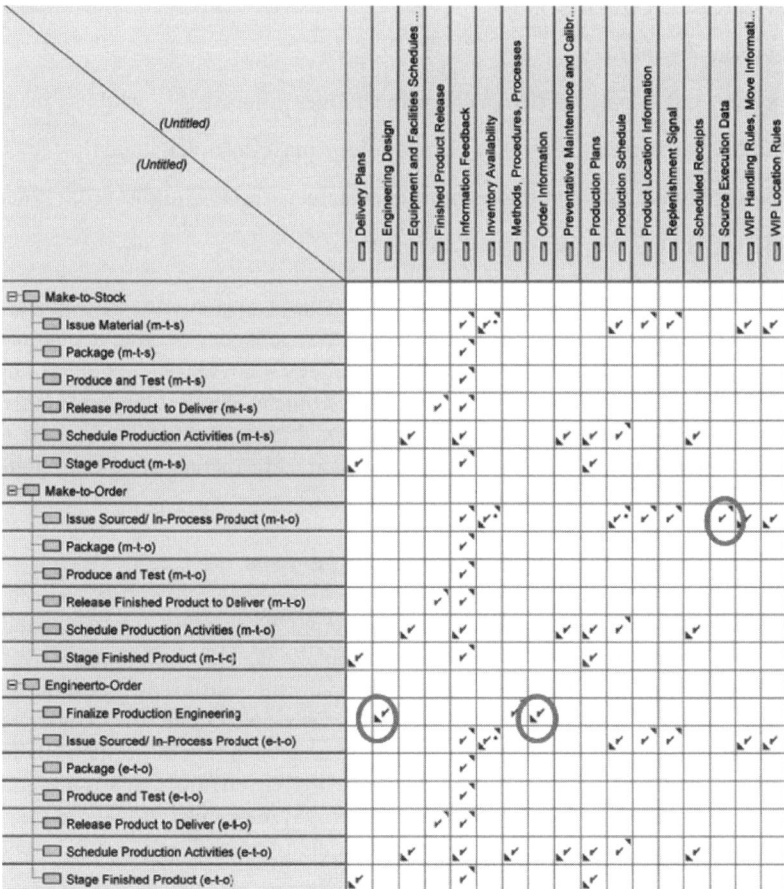

(Untitled) / (Untitled)	Delivery Plans	Engineering Design	Equipment and Facilities Schedules…	Finished Product Release	Information Feedback	Inventory Availability	Methods, Procedures, Processes	Order Information	Preventative Maintenance and Calibr…	Production Plans	Production Schedule	Product Location Information	Replenishment Signal	Scheduled Receipts	Source Execution Data	WIP Handling Rules, Move Informati…	WIP Location Rules
Make-to-Stock																	
Issue Material (m-t-s)					✓	✓					✓	✓	✓			✓	✓
Package (m-t-s)						✓											
Produce and Test (m-t-s)						✓											
Release Product to Deliver (m-t-s)				✓		✓											
Schedule Production Activities (m-t-s)		✓				✓			✓	✓	✓			✓			
Stage Product (m-t-s)	✓					✓					✓						
Make-to-Order																	
Issue Sourced/ In-Process Product (m-t-o)					✓	✓					✓	✓	✓		⊙		✓
Package (m-t-o)						✓											
Produce and Test (m-t-o)						✓											
Release Finished Product to Deliver (m-t-o)				✓		✓											
Schedule Production Activities (m-t-o)		✓				✓			✓	✓	✓			✓			
Stage Finished Product (m-t-c)	✓					✓					✓						
Engineer-to-Order																	
Finalize Production Engineering		⊙					⊙										
Issue Sourced/ In-Process Product (e-t-o)					✓	✓					✓	✓	✓			✓	✓
Package (e-t-o)						✓											
Produce and Test (e-t-o)						✓											
Release Product to Deliver (e-t-o)				✓		✓											
Schedule Production Activities (e-t-o)		✓				✓		✓	✓	✓	✓			✓			
Stage Finished Product (e-t-o)	✓					✓					✓						

Figure 5.20. *Dependences between processes M1, M2, M3 and information*

The matrix in Figure 5.20 represents all dependencies described in SCOR between the information input and output flow of processes and the process elements of the three make typologies (to-stock M1, to-order M2 and engineer-to-order M3). Comparing the three situations, it is clear that the M1 informational description is fully included in the M2 and M3 ones. The differences between M1 and M2 are limited to the "Source Execution Data" information. This information concept includes "data which will provide measurement of actual supplier performance against internal and/or external standards to provide feedback to achieve and maintain the performance required to meet the customer's needs". The SC experts validating SCOR consider this information to be specific to make-to-order typology. The consequence is that we can define an OWL restriction enabling us to define the make-to-order process (M2) as a defined class that respects all of these conditions. Thus, any "make" process can be classified as make-to-order by the OWL reasoner if it is:

– a make process;

– it has some supply processes and some deliver processes;

– it only has source make-to-stock and source make-to-order sourcing,

– only delivering deliver make-to-order or deliver engineering-to-order process;

– it uses "source execution data" as input.

Clearly, the SCOR reference model has not been designed to help in defining this kind of classification rule. SCOR experts are supposed to be able to characterize a make process, depending on the SC typology. To externalize this implicit knowledge embedded in SCOR we have to complete SCOR with business rules, expressed in a logical manner that can be designed using Protégé. With these rules, a complete SCOR/OWL ontology is more than a transformation of SCOR/ARIS.

5.4.3. Consequences for inter-organizational alignment

The approach presented in the previous section makes it possible to consider the alignment challenge using both representations: the "business model" representation, using SCOR/ARIS to model the different views of the interdependence between organizations, for example; and the "ontological" representation, using SCOR/OWL to model the understanding of participants facing these interdependencies, for example. These two representations support alignment in the different scenarios of the SAM [HEN 93] described in Figure 5.1. We consider alignment as a mapping between models used to describe each level and domain of SAM. For example, the business strategy can be defined in a SCOR approach using metrics, practices and a level 2 process, while the operational level can be described using process elements. For IT domains, the SCOR model does not describe IT strategy but the informational dimension, using features and information input/output (level 3). Each participant can nevertheless have its own interpretation of knowledge embedded in the different models used to describe each SAM view. Semantic gaps or mismatches therefore have to be detected and solved using an explicit representation of that knowledge. This can be integrated at the knowledge level added to the SAM (see section 5.2.2). We propose to enrich this extended SAM, as shown in Figure 5.21, using ontological constructs: concepts, properties and restrictions.

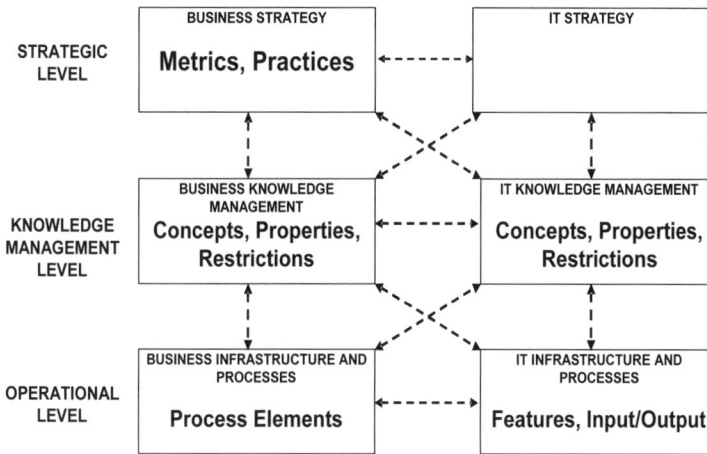

Figure 5.21. *Knowledge-extended SAM with SCOR/OWL constructs*

Aligning business strategy with the IT strategy, from a business modeling point of view, requires us to link metrics and practices with process elements. The SCOR reference model contains a standard linkage but the business engineer working on a specific SC also has to make his or her specific knowledge on the SC case compliant with the standard SCOR reference. To do so, SCOR ontology will allow the engineer reasoning by which to check the consistency of the specific model with the SCOR reference. For example, if the engineer considers the specific make process as a "make-to-stock" process using information classified as "source execution data" or linking a source process classified as "source-to-order", the reasoner could detect a semantic error regarding the SCOR reference. In some situations, but not all, the reasoner can propose a classification of a specific process in the SCOR taxonomy, proposing for example some "asserted classes" to the business engineer or classifying a specific individual in a SCOR class.

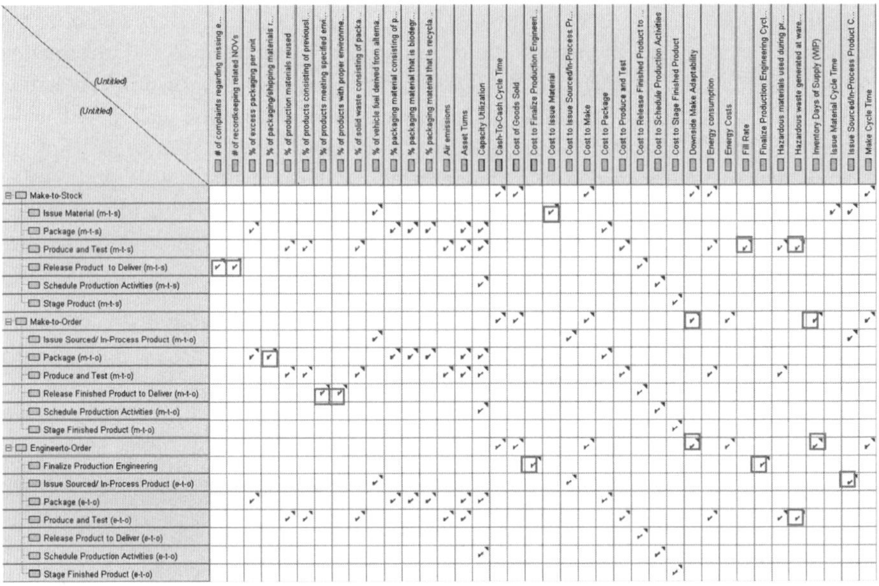

Columns (metrics):

- # of compliants regarding missing e...
- # of recordkeeping related NOV's
- % of excess packaging per unit
- % of packaging/shipping materials r...
- % of production materials reused
- % of products consisting of previous...
- % of products meeting specified emi...
- % of products with proper environm...
- % of solid waste consisting of packa...
- % of vehicle fuel derived from altern...
- % packaging material consisting of p...
- % packaging material that is biodegr...
- % packaging material that is recycla...
- Air emissions
- Asset Turns
- Capacity Utilization
- Cash-To-Cash Cycle Time
- Cost of Goods Sold
- Cost to Finalize Production Engineeri...
- Cost to Issue Material
- Cost to Issue Sourced/In-Process Pr...
- Cost to Make
- Cost to Package
- Cost to Produce and Test
- Cost to Release Finished Product to ...
- Cost to Schedule Production Activities
- Cost to Stage Finished Product
- Downside Make Adaptability
- Energy consumption
- Energy Costs
- Fill Rate
- Finalize Production Engineering Cycl...
- Hazardous materials used during pr...
- Hazardous waste generated at ware...
- Inventory Days of Supply (WIP)
- Issue Material Cycle Time
- Issue Sourced/In-Process Product C...
- Make Cycle Time

Rows (processes):

Make-to-Stock
- Issue Material (m-t-s)
- Package (m-t-s)
- Produce and Test (m-t-s)
- Release Product to Deliver (m-t-s)
- Schedule Production Activities (m-t-s)
- Stage Product (m-t-s)

Make-to-Order
- Issue Sourced/In-Process Product (m-t-o)
- Package (m-t-o)
- Produce and Test (m-t-o)
- Release Finished Product to Deliver (m-t-o)
- Schedule Production Activities (m-t-o)
- Stage Finished Product (m-t-o)

Engineer-to-Order
- Finalize Production Engineering
- Issue Sourced/In-Process Product (e-t-o)
- Package (e-t-o)
- Produce and Test (e-t-o)
- Release Product to Deliver (e-t-o)
- Schedule Production Activities (e-t-o)
- Stage Finished Product (e-t-o)

Figure 5.22. *SCOR dependences between processes and metrics*

When the engineer has a SCOR-compliant model for business operations, he or she can use SCOR/OWL to check the alignment with the business strategy level. For instance, he or she can use the representation of metrics (or practices) in the business model to check certain restrictions on relations between these metrics and processes (or between these practices and processes).

Figure 5.22 presents an example of possible restrictions between processes and metrics. Each line is a process element of a make process, grouped by typologies (make-to-stock, make-to-order and engineer-to-order processes). Each column represents a metric defined in the SCOR reference model, and the matrix shows the relations between metrics and those processes that are "SCOR compliant". Relations circled in the matrix are specific to a process typology and can be used to define OWL restrictions on the "evaluated by" relation. Reasoning on the SC ontology can check the SCOR consistency of the model and can even help to identify forgotten metrics or practices required.

5.5. Conclusion

Effective and efficient SC management needs to integrate heterogenous applications in SCs, based on common representations and exchange of information semantics. The body of current related research does not adequately address the problem because it fails to deal with knowledge interoperability. A key contribution of this research is that it transforms the SCOR model into an ontology. We use OWL to benefit from the advantages of ontologies that can make collaboration in an SC easier through transmission of information, and that can be used to assist the alignment of business processes with business standards concerning processes, exchanges, products, etc. This type of modeling in OWL requires a formalized SCOR built from the original text version using a modeling tool, and has to be enriched using rules and semantic restrictions applying to concepts used in the SCOR model.

The ontology of SCOR presented in this chapter is the first step in work on the use of ontologies in SC and on strategic alignment. We have described how we created our ontology and have compared it to two other representations of SCOR. This work is a base for semantic alignment studies using ontology-mapping or ontology-merging approaches. This formalization should also be of help to anyone studying the consistency of the SCOR model with other models previously transformed into ontologies. Moreover, from an operational point of view, the SCOR ontology is a good starting point for SC simulation that relies on a famous model built by and for the industry. Finally – and we draw the reader's attention to the following point – if we consider the SCOR model as a representation of SC processes, associated with best practices and attributes reflecting economic performance, then it is interesting to add other considerations. Such considerations can, for instance, be oriented towards sustainable development (e.g. green SCOR), and used to assess the consistency of the completed OWL-based model.

5.6. Bibliography

[BAC 04] BACH T.L., DIENG-KUNTZ R., "On ontology matching problems (for building a corporate semantic Web in a multi-communities organization)". *ICEIS 2004: Software Agents and Internet Computing*, 2004, pp. 236-243.

[BAC 06] BACH T.L., Construction d'un web sémantique multi-points de vue, PhD thesis, École de Mines, Sophia Antipolis, 2006.

[BAI 06] BAÏNA S., PANETTO H., BENALI K., "Apport de l'approche MDA pour une interopérabilité sémantique : Interopérabilité des systèmes d'information d'entreprise", *Ingénierie des Systèmes d'Information (ISI)*, vol. 11, no. 13, 2006, pp.11-29.

[BER 96] BERNUS P., NEMES L., "A framework to define a generic enterprise reference architecture and methodology", *Computer Integrated Manufacturing Systems*, vol. 9, no.3, 1996, pp. 179-191.

[BER 01a] BERNERS-LEE T., HENDLER J., LASSILA O., "The semantic web", *Scientific American*, vol. 284, no. 5, 2001, pp. 28–37.

[BER 01b] BERTOLAZZI P., KRUSICH C., MISSIKOFF M., "An approach to the definition of a core enterprise ontology: CEO", *OES-SEO 2001, International Workshop on Open Enterprise Solutions: Systems, Experiences, and Organizations*, 2001, p. 14-15.

[CHE 03] CHEN D., DOUMEINGTS G., "European initiatives to develop interoperability of enterprise applications–basic concepts, framework and roadmap", *Annual Reviews in Control*, vol. 27, no.2, 2003, pp 153-162.

[DOU 84] DOUMEINGTS G., Méthode GRAI: méthode de conception des systèmes en productique, PhD thesis, University of Bordeaux, Bordeaux, 1984.

[EHR 06] EHRIG, M., *Ontology Alignment: Bridging the Semantic Gap*, Springer, 2006.

[EUZ 07] EUZENAT J., MOCAN A., SCHARFFE F., "Ontology alignments: an ontology management perspective", in: *Ontology Management*, vol. 7, 2007, pp. 177-206.

[GRU 95] GRUBER T.R., "Toward principles for the design of ontologies used for knowledge sharing", *International Journal of Human Computer Studies*, vol. 43 no. 5, 1995, p. 907-928.

[GUD 06] GUDAS S., BRUNDZAITE R., "Knowledge-based enterprise modelling framework", *Advances in Information Systems*, 2006, pp. 334-343.

[HEN 93] HENDERSON J.C., VENKATRAMAN N., "Strategic alignment: leveraging information technology for transforming organizations", *IBM Systems Journal*, vol. 38, no. 2-3, 1993, pp. 472-484.

[HOR 03] HORROCKS I., PATEL-SCHNEIDER P-F., VAN HARMELEN F., "From SHIQ and RDF to OWL: the making of a Web Ontology Language", *Web Semantics: Science, Services and Agents on the World Wide Web,* vol. 1, no. 1, 2003, pp 7-26.

[HUA 05] HUANG S.H., SHEORAN S.K., KESKAR H., "Computer-assisted supply chain configuration based on supply chain operations reference (SCOR) model", *Computers & Industrial Engineering*, vol. 48, no. 2, 2005, pp. 377-394.

[ISO 06a] ISO 19439, *Enterprise Integration: Framework for Enterprise Modelling*, International Standards for Business, Government and Society, 2006, www.iso.org.

[ISO 06b] ISO 19440, *Enterprise Integration: Constructs for Enterprise Modelling*, International Standards for Business, Government and Society, 2006, www.iso.org

[IZZ 09] IZZA S., "Integration of industrial information systems: from syntactic to semantic integration approaches", *Enterprise Information Systems*, vol. 3, no. 1, 2009, pp. 1-57.

[KLE 01] KLEIN M., "Combining and relating ontologies: an analysis of problems and solutions", *Ontologies and Information Sharing*, vol. 47, 2001, pp 53-62

[KOS 99] KOSANKE K., NELL J.G., "Standardisation in ISO for enterprise engineering and integration", *Computers in Industry*, vol. 40, no.2-3, 1999, pp. 311-319.

[LAG 01] LAGOZE C., HUNTER J., *The ABC Ontology and Model*, National Institute of Informatics, Tokyo, Japan, 2001

[LAM 06] LAMBRIX P., TAN H., "SAMBO–a system for aligning and merging biomedical ontologies", *Web Semantics: Science, Services and Agents on the World Wide Web*, vol. 4, no. 3, 2006, pp. 196-206.

[LID 40] LIDDELL H.G., SCOTT R., *A Greek-English Lexicon*, Clarendon Press, Oxford, 1940.

[MER 97] MERRIAM-WEBSTER I., *The Merriam-Webster Dictionary*, Merriam-Webster Inc., 1997.

[MIL 08] MILLET, P-A., Une analyse de l'intégration organisationnelle et informationnelle. Application aux systèmes d'information de type ERP, thesis, National Institute of Applied Sciences of Lyon, 2008.

[MIL 09] MILLET P-A. SCHMITT P., BOTTA-GENOULAZ V., "The SCOR-model for the alignment of business processes and information systems", *Enterprise Information Systems*, vol. 3, no. 4, 2009, pp. 393.

[NAU 03] NAUMENKO A., WEGMANN A., "Two approaches in system modeling and their illustrations with MDA and RM-ODP", *ICEIS'03, 5th International Conference on Enterprise Information Systems*, 2003.

[NEC 91] NECHES R., FIKES R., FININ T., GRUBER, T., PATIL R., SENATOR T., SWARTOUT W.R., "Enabling technology for knowledge sharing", *AI Magazine*, vol. 12, no. 3, 1991, pp. 36-56.

[NIS 93] National Institute of Standards and Technology, *Integration Definition of Function Modeling (IDEF0), Federal Information Processing Standards Publication 183*, FIPSP, 1993.

[NOY 04] NOY N.F., "Semantic integration: a survey of ontology-based approaches", *ACM Sigmod Record*, vol. 33, no. 4, 2004, pp. 65-70.

[OST 04] OSTERWALDER A., The Business Model Ontology: A Proposition in a Design Science Approach, PhD thesis, École des Hautes Études Commerciales, University of Lausanne, 2004.

[PRO 00] PROTHMAN B., "Meta data: Managing needles in the proverbial haystacks", *Potentials, IEEE*, vol. 19, no. 1, 2000, pp. 20-23.

[ROD 06] RODER A.,TIBKEN B., "A methodology for modeling inter-company supply chains and for evaluating a method of integrated product and process documentation", *European Journal of Operational Research*, vol. 169, no. 3, 2006, pp. 1010-1029.

[SCC 08] SUPPLY-CHAIN COUNCIL, *SCOR Supply Chain Operations Reference Model, Version 9.0*, SCC, 2009, available at: http://www.supply-chain.org/, accessed 4.28.10.

[SCH 98] SCHEER, A-W., SCHNEIDER K., "ARIS-architecture of integrated information systems", in: *Handbook on Architectures of Information Systems,* Springer Berlin Heidelberg, 1998, pp. 605-623.

[SEN 07] SENG J., LIN W., "An ontology-assisted analysis in aligning business process with e-commerce standards", *Industrial Management & Data Systems*, vol. 107, no.3, 2007, pp. 415-437.

[SHV 05] SHVAIKO P., EUZENAT J., "A survey of schema-based matching approaches", *Lecture Notes in Computer Science*, vol. 3730, 2005, pp. 146-171.

[STA 00] STADLER H., KILGER C., *Supply Chain Management and Advanced Planning; Concepts, Models, Software and Case Studies*, Springer-Verlag, Berlin, 2000.

[STU 98] STUDER R., BENJAMINS V.R., FENSEL D., "Knowledge engineering: principles and methods", *Data & Knowledge Engineering*, vol. 25, no.1-2, 1998, pp. 161-197.

[TER 06] TERRASSE M.N., SAVONNET M., LECLERC E., GRISON E., BECKER G., "Do we need metamodels AND ontologies for engineering platforms?", *International workshop on Global Integrated Model Management*, Shanghai, 2006, pp. 21-28

[THA 94] THAM K., FOX M., GRUNINGER M., "A cost ontology for enterprise modeling", *Third Workshop of Enabling Technologies: Infrastructure for Collaborative Enterprises*, 1994, pp. 197-210.

[USC 98] USCHOLD M., KING M., MORALEE S., ZORGIOS Y., "The enterprise ontology", *The Knowledge Engineering Review*, vol. 13, no. 1, 1998, pp. 31-89.

[YE 08] YE, Y. YANG D., JIANG Z., TONG L., "Ontology-based semantic models for supply chain management", *The International Journal of Advanced Manufacturing Technology*, vol. 37, no. 11, 2008, pp 1250-1260.

[WOO 75] WOODS, W.A., "What's in a link: Foundations for semantic networks", in *Representation and Understanding*, D.G. Bobrow and A.Collins (eds.), Academic Press, 1975

[ZEL 95] ZELM M., VERNADAT F.B., KOSANKE K., "The CIMOSA business modelling process", *Computers in Industry*, vol. 27, no. 2, 1995, pp. 123-142.

PART III

Focus on Coordination Mechanisms

Chapter 6

Analysis of Strategic Behaviors within Supply Chains: Complementarity between Modeling and Experimentation Methodologies

6.1. Introduction

When using a modeling approach to study supply chain performance it is often considered easier to represent and formalize the economic and technological parameters of the logistics system rather than focusing on more human-oriented factors. The fact that human behavior can have a strong impact on overall performance, however, tends to limit purely techno-economic models. With this in mind, the objective of this chapter is to analyze decision-making behaviors of supply-chain managers in order to assess their potential impact on the local performance of each node of the logistic system, as well as on the overall performance of the supply chain. Our research is based on a modeling approach and thus, necessarily, on restrictive hypotheses, notably concerning the way to represent decision behaviors.

The second objective of this chapter lies in its highlighting the strong complementarity between two distinct scientific approaches applied to analyze the performance of identical systems. The first approach can be used to study strategic decision-making behaviors using a mathematically-formalized modeling method.

Chapter written by Xavier BOUCHER, Patrick BURLAT, Alexis GARAPIN, Daniel LLERENA and Natallia TARATYNAVA.

Here, game theory makes it possible to formalize cooperative and non-cooperative decision strategies, whose effect on economic performance can be objectively evaluated [TAR 09a]. Game theory models, however, rely on restrictive behavioral assumptions on the necessity to develop complementary experiments to provide theoretical results with more realistic human behaviors. Recently, the complementarity between analytical and experimental game theory led to what Colin Camerer [CAM 03] called a "behavioral game theory", that is to say a theory of strategic interactions that is rooted in real human behaviors. The behavioral game theory proposes a frame for modeling human behaviors in strategic interactions in a general, predictive and realistic way. It aims to renew the classic game theory without rejecting its basic concepts and its formal frame.

With the same objective of studying more realistic human behaviors, the current research proposes the use of the experimental economics methodology. This methodology aims at going beyond theoretical conclusions by experimentally studying the real behaviors of strategic interactions among individuals. The scientific challenge consists: (i) in testing and assessing a model in a controlled environment; but also (ii) in identifying typical patterns of human behavior in a given context, which could bring some innovations into the theoretical models in use. Thus, game theory and experimental economics appear to be complementary in terms of objectives and scientific protocol. In this chapter we demonstrate this complementarity.

To study strategic decisions, a well-defined decision context is required. The application case reported here consisted of studying a situation of inventory management within a supply chain to analyze the economic impact of replenishment decisions distributed among various decision makers. It is considered that a supply chain can be split into a network of basic and interconnected "supplier/distributor" nodes. This chapter focuses on such a node: a two-echelon supply chain, consisting of a supplier and retailer facing a competitive but uncertain final demand, and a decision situation characterized by asymmetric information between them.

Section 6.2 introduces the two scientific approaches used: game theory and experimental economics methodology. Section 6.3 first precisely defines the decision situation of the inventory management considered in this research, before developing the results of the game theory and application of the experimental economics protocol. Finally, the conclusion summarizes the added value of the method and introduces further perspectives.

6.2. Methodological approaches

The objective of this section is to provide a basic and easily understandable introduction to both game theory and the experimental economics methodology. Supply chain literature in these two domains is vast. We highlight some key references, but our aim is not to provide an exhaustive review of the state of the art.

6.2.1. *Modeling methodology based on the use of game theory*

6.2.1.1. *The use of game theory for logistic systems*

Game theory is used to analyze situations where the decision of one of the participants has some impact on the output of others. Within supply chains, game theory offers insights enabling us to anticipate the behaviors of rational participants when confronted with conflicting situations, or with cooperative or power relationships, in a context of complete or incomplete information. As supply chains are distributed decision systems where local decision-making often leads to sub-optimal performance for the overall chain, game theory is a way to detect loss of efficiency within such decentralized organizations, and to propose coordination mechanisms to improve performance [TAR 09b].

Game theory is frequently used in logistic systems to model inventory management and capacity allocation. The benefits of the chain for each participant are modeled by means of utility functions and expressed in a mathematical form. Each rational player in the game then aims to optimize his or her utility, knowing that every other player will have the same incentive. This can lead to traps, known as Nash equilibrium (NEQ), from which nobody has any intention of unilaterally deviating. In other words, a NEQ is a position where every player is happy with the decision he or she has just made when seeing the decision of the other players. Solving a game analytically means identifying such positions and computing whether or not they are optimal for the players and/or for the whole chain. However, analytical resolution turns out to be quite complicated when the number of partners is high or when the dynamic behaviors of players are taken into account. In such cases, game theory is associated with other methods, such as simulation [DEL 99, REN 06]. In this chapter, experimental economics is mobilized to enhance the analytical resolution of models.

6.2.1.2. *Local and global performances of supply chains*

Decisional situations are classified into cooperative and non-cooperative strategic games. Non-cooperative games formalize interactions where the decisional agents are free to select their actions and where these agents are considered as rational agents, i.e. endeavoring to maximize their advantages (advantages are measured by a so-called utility function: profits in the case of supply chains). The cooperative games represent situations where the players can create collaborative coalitions, and where decisions have to be taken jointly in order to achieve some collective aim. An analysis of supply chains based on cooperative games is given by [LIN 07].

This chapter concentrates on non-cooperative situations, where each participant individually makes decisions. This approach more closely represents typical situations in logistic management. A common consequence of the lack of cooperation, however, is a loss of efficiency: the performance achieved with a local optimum is often lower than the overall optimum. Such performance losses have been underlined by [CAC 99]. These authors use a non-cooperative game model to study stock management decisions for a supply chain. They analyze the supply chain with a retailer with a stationary stochastic demand on one side and its supplier on the other. The supply company manages its inventories according to a base stock policy, where an order is made in each period of time to obtain a pre-determined reorder level. Each participant follows its interests to find the best replenishment level and thus to minimize the mean cost. In such a situation, when calculating an overall optimum, all the stocks in the system can be considered. With local optimization, on the other hand, only the local stock of each company is taken into account. Cachon and Zipkin [CAC 99] show that the one-shot game that is local optimization of stock levels converges towards a suboptimal NEQ. The results of the overall optimization provide the upper limit for the decentralized chain. To counter-balance such losses, distinct coordination mechanisms can be used to promote an overall optimum that differs from the coalitions of cooperative games. Several types of coordination mechanism have been studied in the literature, including contracts, vendor manager inventor and information sharing, which is discussed below.

Contracting concerns both mono- and multi-period situations. With a mono-period, several different types of contract have been shown to coordinate supply chains with inventory-dispatching and profit-sharing. For instance, buy-back contracts [CAC 02] and revenue-sharing contracts [GIA 04] lead to optimal inventory levels, maximizing the expectation of profits for both the supplier and retailer. These authors have demonstrated that those two types of contract coordinate a supply chain efficiently by appropriately dividing profits between the firms. [CAC 99] and [CAC 01] have proposed a linear transfer payment contract based on the retailer's inventory and backorders, and established that this contract is able to increase the efficiency of a decentralized supply chain so it approaches the optimal profit of a centralized chain. Multi-period contracts are different from mono-period contracts since inventory is left over at the end of each period. With multi-period contracts, a supply chain will be coordinated effectively if a reorder point exists that simultaneously maximizes the expected profits for both the supplier and the retailer. Two main contracts have been shown to efficiently coordinate such chains: quantity flexibility (see [TSA 99] for example) and buy-back contracts [CAC 02].

Contracts are, of course, only one of several alternative solutions for improving decentralized supply chain performance. Game theory is well-suited to studying conflicting situations linked to asymmetric, imperfect or incomplete information among decision makers. Information sharing between a retailer and a supplier makes it possible to better forecast production requirements, although this has a well-known risk of a bullwhip effect, studied by [LEE 97]. The interested reader is referred to an overview of information sharing and the consequences to supply chain coordination in [CHE 03]. Corbett and Tang analyze a supply chain with a manufacturer and a supplier in two different modes: complete and incomplete information games [COR 02]. The production cost per unit to the manufacturer is not known by the supplier (this cost appears as a random variable to the supplier). The authors have shown that the chain can be coordinated by just exchanging information about this cost. Other studies have focused on sharing market-forecasting information. Cachon and Larivière have modeled a supply chain with a leader (the manufacturer) facing a random market demand, and imposing a system of maximum and minimum orders on their supplier [CAC 01]. In the complete information game mode, these authors have demonstrated that the manufacturer will obtain a total profit equivalent to that of the centralized supply chain, leaving a null gain (break-even) to its supplier. Moreover, in the case of information asymmetry, when the manufacturer has a better idea of market conditions, there is a tendency to transmit exaggerated forecasts to the supplier to avoid back-order costs and increase its profits.

Thus, game theory provides appropriate theoretical tools for studying some of the numerous decision parameters found in supply chain management. Experimental economics methodology affords a complementary point of view.

6.2.2. *Experimental economics methodology*

Experimental economics is the application of experimental methods to the study of economic questions. It creates environments in the laboratory that make it possible to study a particular aspect of individual decision making by controlling its effects. It is often difficult to distinguish in the "real" data that which concerns particular characteristics of the economic agents from that which concerns the particular circumstances in which the decision was made (information available to make the decision, relevant elements in determining the consequences of this decision, etc.). Experimental economics allows all the parameters in question to be controlled.

Conducting an experiment in economics requires three conditions: an environment, an institution and behaviors. The environment encompasses all the characteristics of the experiment, i.e. the number of agents and the number and type of goods under consideration. Environment also defines the particular characteristics of each player, such as their utility functions, initial endowments, and production and cost functions. The institution consists of all the means of communication between players in the experiment. It describes the rules of decision making and organizes the individual choices and possible interactions between the players within a definite environmental framework. Concretely, the institution is the experimental protocol. Finally, the behaviors are all of the choices of players can make according to the characteristics defined in the environment and the institutional rules.

Experimental economists generally hold to some methodological guidelines, first defined by Nobel laureate Vernon Smith in his seminal article "Induced value theory" [SMI 76]. Induced value theory is based on the idea that the proper use of a reward medium allows an experimenter to induce pre-specified characteristics in the subjects so that their innate characteristics are less relevant. The first principle is non-satiation: the agent (player) always prefers to lay out more remuneration than it already holds, which means that the utility of each player is an increasing function of its payoffs. The second principle is salience, which means that for each player the reward corresponds to a clear outcome function, for example profit or utility, and the player understands this. The third principle is dominance: the rewards in the experiment are supposed to explain the acts of the players better than any other factor, which means that any influence other than the player's payoffs is negligible in the agent's decision making in the experiment. These main principles are widely applied in the laboratory by incentivizing subjects with real monetary payoffs. Additional guidelines for experimental economists are: anonymity in the experiment (blind or double-blind procedures), publishing full experimental instructions, not using deception, and avoiding introduction of a specific, concrete context [FRI 04].

Experiments are used to test the validity of economic theories and new market mechanisms. Using cash-motivated subjects, experiments may be conducted in laboratory settings or in the field. They create real-world incentives to better understand many concepts in economics. Experimental economics aims in particular to test, and possibly amend, the traditional postulates in microeconomics. This assumes that individuals are purely selfish beings with perfect rationality and self-control. More particularly, individual decision-making in risky contexts is analyzed in order to improve the classical expected utility theory and/or develop new decision theories. Experimental methods are also applied to the design of new market institutions, for instance in the context of liberalizing network industries. The majority of the bidding procedures used by various governments to sell mobile telephony licenses, for example, were tested in laboratory settings. More generally, economic engineering (consisting of proposing mechanisms of exchange, intermediation, etc., appropriate to various situations) has largely benefited from this new tool.

Experimental economics also sheds new light on subjects' decision making in strategic interaction settings, thus mobilizing game theory. Game theory has become an essential tool in the analysis of supply chains with multiple agents, often with conflicting objectives, so this field of experimental economics is the most relevant to our analysis of strategic behaviors. Note that experimental studies have focused on individual decision making in the supply chain context. This approach is natural, according to the history of experimental economics that was initially focused on individual behaviors. A large proportion of these studies concerns inventory decision making in simple contexts, such as the newsvendor problem.

Schweitzer and Cachon, for instance, analyze retailers' behaviors in relation to inventory orders [SCH 00]. In two different profit conditions (one with high-profit products and one with low-profit conditions) these authors show that choices systematically deviate from those that maximize expected profits: subjects order too few high-profit products and too many low-profit products. Choices of inventory orders are consistent with a preference to reduce ex-post inventory error (i.e. the absolute deviation between the amounts ordered and the actual demand). This preference causes subjects to choose order quantities that are too close to the mean demand. In fact, the main objective of this work is to compare experimental data with theoretical models of individual decision making, such as the prospect theory or expected utility theory.

Another related study by [KES 04], in contrast with the work of [SCH 00], introduces the analysis of direct interactions between two subjects in a newsvendor context into the experimental design. The main objective of this work is related to the relative efficiency of wholesale price contracts and, more particularly, to the influence of the supplier's pricing decision on the retailer's quantity decision. Based on a game-theory model, these authors find that observed behaviors of suppliers and retailers are very different from the equilibrium solution. Suppliers charge lower wholesale prices than predicted, which implies an equal split of the net profit if the retailer can sell all of the units to the consumers. Moreover, the retailers order less than they could in response to these lower wholesale prices. These behaviors could be explained by their risk-averse preferences.

Note that these experimental studies are conducted in supply chain contexts in order to analyze subjects' behaviors in relation to risk and demand uncertainty. However, an analysis of supply chains also entails the study of interactions between economic participants from a dynamic point of view. Economic and industrial relationships in such contexts are rarely occasional or one-off interactions: they are frequently long-term relationships with repeated interactions between the same participants. Individual decisions therefore change in light of the experience of past interactions and increased knowledge about the supply chain partners. These important aspects of supply chain context are integrated into our analysis in the following section, in terms of modeling and experimental methodologies.

6.3. Scientific protocol and a specific case study

The overall objective of the scientific protocol presented below is to study the impact of managers' decision behaviors on supply chain performances, in a decentralization context. In the current chapter, the study is limited to a two-echelon supply chain (supplier and retailer, with an external demand), which delimit the frontiers of a basic model. This basic model could be used further to analyze the behavior of a larger supply chain. By applying the two approaches introduced above, the scientific protocol can be split into two main steps:

– use of game theory to demonstrate theoretical results concerning the managers' potential decision behaviors;

– introduction of more realistic behaviors of living "decision-makers" by applying the experimental economy approach.

Of course, the second step could help us to validate the added value of the theoretical analysis but it also highlights its limits. In section 6.3.1 we start by explaining the decision situation under study, before applying game theory and then experimental economy methodology in the following two sections.

6.3.1. *The basic model under study*

In this section we formalize a basic node of a logistic chain composed of a retailer working on an order (MTO policy) to meet a stochastic demand, and a supplier who makes to stock (MTS policy). The two participants are linked by a linear wholesale price contract. We study this decision situation over a temporal period that covers the decisions of both participants, as well as one effective occurrence of the demand (in game theory, such a model is said to be a mono-period).

The supplier's production depends on its forecasts. During each decision period, it replenishes its inventory according to a base stock policy. The supplier is the only one who incurs inventory costs for any unsold or surplus products; however, the retailer has better knowledge of the final demand and should pass along this information in the form of demand forecasts to the supplier. The supplier must decide whether to trust or to ignore these estimates, and this decision will influence its choice of replenishment level.

The goals of both the supplier and retailer consist of determining the quantity to be produced to be offered for sale at the beginning of each period. In the logistic system studied in this chapter, the provider does not manage any stock consisting of unsold products, which are considered as lost. Since this cost is assigned to the supplier alone, at the order time the retailer does not take any risk of over-production.

Thus, the supply chain analyzed has only one stocking point (by the supplier). The supplier's base stock policy means its crucial decision variable is the reorder level (N), which maximizes its expected profit. The supplier pays the unsold product costs (h_S) per unit of product. This cost represents the elimination of overproduction during a given period. The production costs per unit of product are noted c_s and c_R respectively for the supplier and the retailer. The back-order costs of the market are distributed between the supplier and the retailer where b_S and b_R are the respective unit back-order costs. They include potential revenue loss, loss of goodwill, or any additional cost that may be incurred finding alternative providers. The retailer sells products on the market at the unit price p and pays the supplier for intermediate products at the unit price r. The supplier has a non-limited output inventory, and the delivery time and order time are set to zero. All of the cost parameters are public knowledge.

The retailer sends the forecast to the supplier in time t_1 before real-time demand occurs (see Figure 6.1). We assume that the market demand is a scaled random variable $\theta \cdot X$, where X is a non-negative random variable. $\theta \in R^+$ is defined as the demand size parameter. To capture the essence of uncertain market conditions, we assume that θ is a random variable with two possible values – "high" and "low": θ_i, $i = \{H, L\}$. The probability of each event is $P(\theta_L) = \alpha$, $P(\theta_H) = 1-\alpha$, $\alpha \in]0,1[$. The high and low market-demand random variables are therefore $D_H = \theta_H \cdot X$ and $D_L = \theta_L \cdot X$, respectively. The distributions of both θ and X are common knowledge.

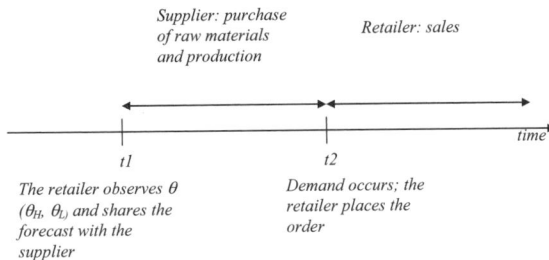

Figure 6.1. *Timescale for supply chain events*

Figure 6.2 shows various information flows in the supply chain. Note that the retailer knows, with certainty, the level of future demand, noted (θ_H, θ_L for a high or low demand) at time t_1 when he sends forecasts to the supplier. The supplier is further away from the source of the market demand, and thus faces more random noise. The supplier does not have the same level of market expertise and intelligence. This additional level of uncertainty is modeled by a white noise e with mean 0 and standard deviation σ. In other words, the supplier's demand random variable is, $D_i' = \theta_i \cdot X + e$, with $i = H, L$. It follows that $Var(D_i') > Var(D_i)$, with $i = H, L$.

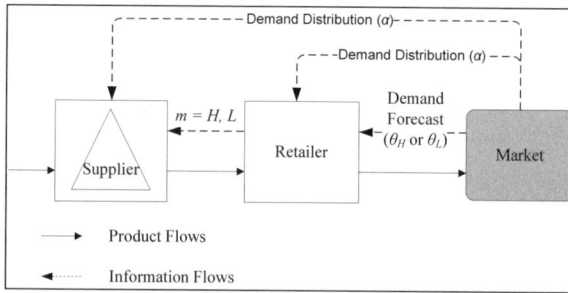

Figure 6.2. *Information flows in the MTS/MTO supply chain*

6.3.2. *Application of game theory*

6.3.2.1. *Description of the game*

The decision process involving the retailer and the supplier can be described by a so-called "game-tree" (the notion of "game" refers to "strategic game" here). This decision tree (see Figure 6.3) shows the sequence of decisions of the two decision makers, with the possible alternatives. The whole decision process leads to economic profits, noted Π_R and Π_S for the retailer and the supplier respectively. Each terminal node in the tree can bring distinct profits, induced by the sequence of decisions.

The game begins with a random draw of θ. That means, the retailer observes θ (either θ_H or θ_L), but the supplier does not. The retailer then sends a non-binding forecast m to the supplier (Figure 6.3): $m = H$ signifies that the future demand is going to be high, and $m = L$ signifies that it is going to be low.

Thus, the retailer's strategy consists in sending a forecast $m = H$ or $m = L$, but considering that the message it sends to the supplier does not necessarily correspond to the exact demand θ_i that has been observed. If the high-demand retailer sends $m = H$ (or $m = L$ for a low-demand retailer) we call this truthful forecast sharing.

Conversely, if the high-demand retailer sends $m = L$, we call this non-truthful forecast sharing. As a consequence, two strategies are defined for the retailer: a cooperative (C) strategy consisting in sending a truthful forecast, and a non-cooperative one (NC), when a non-truthful forecast is sent. The supplier's strategy is also two-fold: to trust (C) or not to trust (NC) the retailer's forecast. The fact that the supplier has imperfect information is shown by the ellipse in Figure 6.3, which delineates the supplier's information set.

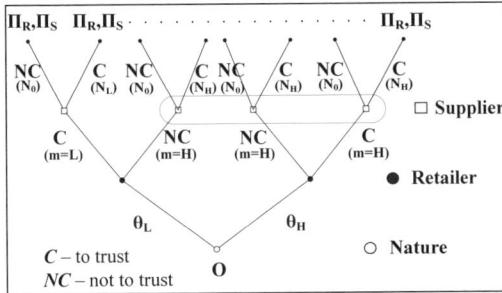

Figure 6.3. *Game tree – whether or not to trust a retailer's forecast*

After the market demand is confirmed, the retailer places an order with the supplier equal to the real market demand. The resulting function measured for the decision makers is given by their profits: Π_R for the retailer and Π_S for the supplier. These profits can be mathematically expressed, and thus calculated, depending on the cost parameters expressed in the previous section. The profit of each company is evaluated as the difference between the total incomes and the total costs. For the retailer, the incomes are generated by the market sales, and several costs are considered: purchase of an intermediary supplier's product, production and back-order costs. For the supplier, the revenue is the retailer's financial transfer and expenses are: production, unsold products and back-order costs.

The game and its description are common knowledge to both players. This is a non-cooperative, one-shot, cheap-talk game with imperfect and asymmetrical information. Cheap-talk games differ from signaling games in that the signals sent in a cheap-talk game are costless, whereas the signals sent in signaling games have cost implications.

6.3.2.2. *Main results*

Game theory aims to anticipate the alternative outcomes of decision situations by analyzing result functions of the decision makers (profits in this case). More particularly, we intend to demonstrate decision equilibriums, i.e. decisions representing a convergence point for all the decision makers, when the initial hypothesis of rational behaviors of the parties is respected. For instance, the well-known NEQ is a key concept of game theory. A NEQ is a result that none of the decision makers intends to change when considering the alternative strategies of the other parties. Thus, such equilibrium corresponds to a stable outcome of the strategic game.

The objective of this publication is not to mathematically demonstrate all the results obtained. Any interested reader will find such justifications in [TAR 08] and [TAR 09a]. Instead, we explain the methodological approach and provide a synthesis of the results, notably concerning the NEQ.

The game outcomes are analyzed in respect of the profits Π_R and Π_S. These profits depend first and foremost on the final demand D (which takes the high values D_H or the low ones D_L). They are estimated by a mathematical expectation of D. Second, these profits also depend on the replenishment level decided by the supplier. Three distinct replenishment levels are considered: N_H and N_L that maximize the expected profit with either a high or a low demand from the market, then N_0 which maximizes the supplier's profit when it does not take the forecast transmitted by the retailer into consideration (i.e. when it estimates its profit based on its own knowledge of the market, represented by the probability a). Finally, the profits can only be determined by considering a full sequence of decisions, represented by one of the branches of the game tree (see Figure 6.3), i.e. when decision behaviors (to cooperate or not to cooperate) have been selected by both parties. This is expressed by the game matrix presented in Figure 6.4.

In this matrix, each decision maker can follow a cooperative or a non-cooperative decision. The resulting profits in each matrix element are distinct. The analytical method that we apply consists of mathematically determining the utility functions of the decision makers and then studying order relationships among the profits characterizing each strategy. The goal is to identify and demonstrate potential decision equilibriums.

Retailer

		C	NC
Supplier	C	$\Pi_R{}^*, \Pi_S{}^*$	$\Pi_R{}^\circ, \Pi_R{}^\circ$
	NC	$\Pi_R(NC_R, C_S),$ $\Pi_S(NC_R, C_S)$	$\Pi_R{}^\circ, \Pi_S{}^\circ$

~Nash equilibrium

Figure 6.4. *Game theory matrix for the mono-period game MTS/MTO*

As an example, we denote the game outcome when the retailer provides truthful forecasts and the provider trusts the retailer, as "mutual cooperation". The profit expectations in mutual cooperation for the retailer ($\Pi_R *$) and for the supplier ($\Pi_S *$), respectively, are calculated by the following two formulae:

$$\Pi_R * = (1-\alpha)\mathrm{E}\left[(p-r-c_R)\min\left(N_H, D_H\right) - b_r\left(D_H - N_H\right)^+\right] +$$
$$\alpha\mathrm{E}\left[(p-r-c_R)\min\left(N_L, D_L\right) - b_r\left(D_L - N_L\right)^+\right],$$

$$\Pi_S * = (1-\alpha)\mathrm{E}\left[r\min\left(N_H, D_H'\right) - c_S N_H - h_S (N_H - D_H')^+ - b_S (D_H' - N_H)^+\right] +$$
$$\alpha\mathrm{E}\left[r\min\left(N_L, D_L'\right) - c_S N_L - h_S (N_L - D_L')^+ - b_S (D_L' - N_L)^+\right].$$

The comparative study of the profits identified in the matrix in Figure 6.4 demonstrates the existence of a single NEQ corresponding to a mutual non-cooperative strategy by the decision makers. In such a situation, the retailer transmits unreliable forecasts and the provider's strategy consists of not trusting such forecasts. As a consequence it is in the retailer's interests to always communicate a high market demand in order to get the supplier to generate a higher inventory level, since the retailer does not pay for this stock. When anticipating such behavior by the retailer, the supplier considers that it is no longer able to distinguish between truthful and untruthful forecasts. The best supplier strategy then consists of completely ignoring the retailer's forecasts.

The analytical study demonstrates that the NEQ constitutes a stable solution, but not the best outcome of the game when both decision makers' profits are considered. The retailer's strategy, which involves lying to obtain a supplementary inventory reserve by the provider, leads both parties of the supply chain to take decisions leading to a loss of performance with regard to a mutual cooperation strategy. However, since they rationally consider that the NEQ is a stable solution, the decision makers cannot reject this non-cooperative solution (when considering a "one-shot" game).

This result is also linked to the fact that, until now, when using the game theory we have studied a non-iterated one-shot decision situation, where the parties are not concerned about their reputation nor long-term interests. The analysis of a similar strategic game repeated over several time periods could change the NEQ: notions of trust or reputation (if you succeeded in modeling them) could lead to the decision to converge towards the optimum profit. A theoretical study of the repeated game would require complementary methods to go beyond the limits of the analytical approach developed here. We would like to point out, however, that general theoretical results for repeated cheap-talk games show the possibility of NEQ corresponding to the mutual-cooperation outcome. For instance, such repeated games have been studied by [REN 06]. With a decision that is similar to the game described in the current chapter, Ren proposes two potential strategies (trigger strategy and review strategy) that, under given conditions, can lead to mutual cooperation in the context of a repeated game. In the research presented hereafter, the experimental economy methodology is used to analyze realistic behaviors of supply-chain decision makers in a context of repeated games. The objective is notably to analyze potential change concerning the theoretical NEQ. We will try to show whether there is a clear equilibrium appearing in the repeated decision situation or not.

6.3.3. *Application of experimental economics methodology*

In this section we present our application of experimental methodology to the game theory model described above. After a short explanation of the practical conditions of our experiments, the general organization of our protocol is presented, followed by an analysis of the results.

When arriving in the room, subjects receive a personal code both to preserve their anonymity and to log onto the software dedicated to the experiment. The experiment is divided into two phases, which are entirely independent of each other. The subjects have been warned that two phases will occur, without knowing before the end of the first phase what the content of the second phase will be. Instructions are distributed at the beginning of each phase and read aloud to ensure that everyone has the same information. The subjects' understanding of the instructions is checked by means of a simple questionnaire corrected collectively after the reading. Subjects are told that they will be paid in cash at the end of the experiment. Their payoffs are in Euros in the first phase and in Yen in the second phase. The Yen are converted into Euros at a public exchange rate (¥2,000 = €1) that is common information to all subjects. An experimental session lasts about two hours. Subjects can individually earn an average of about €20. Below we describe the general organization of the experiment before detailing our results.

6.3.3.1. *General organization of the scientific protocol*

Phase 1. A risk-aversion test

In the first phase of the experiment, we conduct a standard experimental test [HOL 02] consisting of a menu of 10 lottery choices designed to make inferences about risk aversion under various payment conditions. Each of the 10 lotteries presents two options (A and B) to the subjects. The options differ in their probability of getting a high or low payoff. The subjects have to choose one option, A or B, for each of the 10 lotteries. They are told that only one lottery will be drawn for their actual payoff, and that this payoff will cumulate to increase their earnings in the second phase of the experiment. To obtain their payoff, subjects throw a 10-sided dice twice: the first time to determine the relevant lottery, and the second time to determine the payoff for the chosen option. This procedure is executed at the end of the experiment, after the second phase, so that the subjects' behaviors in the second phase are not influenced by their earning in the first phase.

Phase 2. A computer-assisted game theory experiment

6.3.3.1.1. Overview

The second phase begins after all of the subjects' decision sheets for the lotteries have been collected. Subjects are assigned individually and randomly to two groups: a group of retailers and a group of suppliers. The suppliers make goods in quantities ordered by the retailers, and the retailers sell the goods in a final market with a random demand. The random final demand can take two forms of distribution: "high" (that is a continuous and uniform distribution in the interval [100, 200]) and "low" (continuous, uniform distribution in the interval [50, 150]). The demand can be "high" with a 0.5 probability and "low" with a 0.5 probability. Subjects are told that the game will be played over many periods with the same partner, but they are not told the exact number of periods in order to prevent end-game strategic behaviors. In the experiment, subjects actually played 30 periods.

6.3.3.1.2. The decision process

The decision process is now explained. First, the retailer receives an exact forecast of the final demand (a simple message displaying whether the demand in the next period is "high" or "low"). He/she then sends a "cheap talk" message to the supplier, in which he/she is totally free to announce the form of the final demand, either "high" or "low". The supplier then decides on his/her production level for the period, namely: $N_L = 100$, which is an optimal level corresponding to a random demand distributed uniformly between the bounds [50, 150]; $N_H = 150$. This is an optimal level of production corresponding to a random demand distributed uniformly between the bounds [100, 200]; $N_0 = 125$. This, in turn, is an optimal level of production for a random demand that is "low" with a 0.5 probability and "high" with a 0.5 probability. N_0 is a production level that does not take into account the message sent by the retailer.

The production times are considered to be null so that the quantities produced are immediately available. In the case of overproduction – the supplier produces quantities in excess of the retailer's order – the supplier cannot store the quantities for the next period and incurs a loss. Once the supplier's production decision is made, the exact value of the final demand of the period in progress is communicated to the retailer. The retailer then orders the quantity of products from the supplier and this order corresponds exactly to the value of the final demand. According to the quantities ordered, the supplier delivers the quantities available to the retailer. The times of order and delivery are regarded as null, so the quantities delivered to the retailer are immediately sold on the final market.

6.3.3.1.3. Payoffs

The retailer's payoff function for a period is:

$$\Pi_R = \left(p - r - c_R\right)\min\left(N, d\right) - b_R\left(d - N\right)^+$$

with:

p: the price of the final good (p = ¥35);

d: the exact value of the final demand, $d \in$ [50, 200];

r: the unit price paid by the retailer to the supplier (r = ¥20);

c_R: the unit cost of retail (c_R = ¥5);

bR: the unit cost of stock shortage (bR = ¥10); and

N: the quantity produced by the supplier.

The supplier's payoff function for a period is:

$$\Pi_S = r\min\left(N, d\right) - c_S N - h_S\left(N - d\right)^+ - b_S\left(d - N\right)^+$$

with:

c_S: the unit cost of production (c_S = ¥10);

h_S: the unit cost of the unsold goods (h_S = ¥5); and

b_S: the unit cost of stock shortage (b_S = ¥5).

The payoff functions are made known to both types of players. At the end of each period, each subject can see on his/her computer screen the detailed computation of his/her payoff for the period. The individual payoff cumulates from period to period. Subjects begin the second phase with a ¥1,000 individual endowment. This endowment is not updated at each new period.

6.3.3.1.4. End of the experiment

At the end of the experiment, subjects fill in a debriefing form in which they can write any comments they may have, and answer short questions about their strategic behavior during the experiment. Once they have completed this form, they draw their lottery (see phase 1). They are then called individually into a separate room where they privately receive their payoff in cash before leaving the experimental laboratory.

6.3.3.2. *Experimental results*

We conducted two sessions of the first phase: one with engineering students from the Ecole des Mines de Saint-Etienne and one with engineering students from the Institut Polytechnique de Grenoble. The data on sessions and the number of observations are given in Table 6.1[1].

University	St-Etienne	Grenoble
Nb of sessions	1	1
Nb of observations	9	8
Total	10	9

Table 6.1. *Number of sessions and experimental observations*

We analyze the behaviors of subjects with two indicators:

– for the retailer, the rate of false messages (R_{FM}), measured by the ratio between the number of false messages M_H sent to the supplier (i.e. when the forecast was in fact D_L) and the number of low forecasts received by the retailer;

– for the supplier, the rate of trust (R_T), measured by the ratio between the number N_H decisions (high production levels) and the number of high messages M_H received from the retailer.

The first indicator measures whether retailers use the cheap-talk mechanism in order to induce suppliers to produce more than the optimum according to the true level of market demand. The second indicator expresses the supplier's trust in the messages transmitted by the retailer. In other words, suppliers with a low rate of trust do not care about the forecast transmitted when they make their production decisions.

According the number of periods played in a session, and in order to analyze the evolution of the different indicators over time, we break down the 30 periods into three separate sequences of 10 periods.

Our experimental observations are summarized in Tables 6.2 and 6.3.

---

1 By observation we mean a pair of subjects who interact during all the periods.

Groups	Loc.	Rate of false message (Mh/DI)			
		Periods 1 to 10	Periods 11 to 20	Periods 21 to 30	30 periods
Group 1	St-Et.	0.3333	0.0000	0.0000	0.0714
Group 2	St-Et.	0.1429	0.2000	0.2500	0.1875
Group 3	St-Et.	0.0000	0.1429	0.2000	0.1176
Group 4	St-Et.	0.2500	0.2857	1.0000	0.3846
Group 5	St-Et.	1.0000	1.0000	0.8000	0.9286
Group 6	St-Et.	0.5000	0.0000	0.3333	0.3125
Group 7	St-Et.	0.2857	0.0000	0.1667	0.1579
Group 8	St-Et.	0.0000	0.0000	0.0000	0.0000
Group 9	St-Et.	0.2500	0.1429	0.0000	0.1333
Group 10	Gre.	0.0000	0.0000	0.0000	0.0000
Group 11	Gre.	0.5714	0.4000	0.2500	0.4375
Group 12	Gre.	0.4000	0.7143	0.4000	0.5294
Group 13	Gre.	0.7500	0.8571	1.0000	0.8462
Group 14	Gre.	0.3333	0.1667	0.0000	0.1429
Group 15	Gre.	0.1667	0.0000	0.0000	0.0625
Group 16	Gre.	0.0000	0.0000	0.0000	0.0000
Group 17	Gre.	0.5000	0.5000	0.1111	0.3158
		0.3225	**0.2594**	**0.2654**	**0.2722**

Table 6.2. *Rates of false messages according to groups and place (St-Et. = École des Mines de Saint-Etienne; Gre. = Institut Polytechnique de Grenoble)*

Groups	Loc.	Rate of trust (Nh/Mh)			
		Periods 1 to 10	Periods 11 to 20	Periods 21 to 30	30 periods
Group 1	St-Et.	0.5000	0.7500	1.0000	0.7059
Group 2	St-Et.	0.5000	1.0000	0.7143	0.7647
Group 3	St-Et.	0.8000	0.7500	0.8333	0.8000
Group 4	St-Et.	0.8571	0.6000	0.6000	0.6818
Group 5	St-Et.	0.7000	0.1000	0.0000	0.2759
Group 6	St-Et.	0.8571	1.0000	1.0000	0.9474
Group 7	St-Et.	1.0000	1.0000	0.6000	0.8571
Group 8	St-Et.	0.1667	0.0000	0.0000	0.0909
Group 9	St-Et.	0.2857	0.0000	0.0000	0.1176
Group 10	Gre.	1.0000	1.0000	1.0000	1.0000
Group 11	Gre.	0.4286	0.1429	0.2000	0.2632
Group 12	Gre.	1.0000	0.5000	0.5556	0.6667
Group 13	Gre.	0.6667	0.3333	0.1000	0.3571
Group 14	Gre.	0.5000	0.6000	0.8000	0.6111
Group 15	Gre.	0.4000	0.5000	1.0000	0.6000
Group 16	Gre.	0.6667	0.7500	1.0000	0.8182
Group 17	Gre.	0.8750	0.2857	1.0000	0.6471
		0.6590	**0.5478**	**0.6120**	**0.6003**

Table 6.3. *Rates of trust according to groups and place (St-Et. = Ecole des Mines de Saint-Etienne; Gre. = Institut Polytechnique de Grenoble)*

The first objective of this work was to establish whether training engineering students in economics, particularly in game theory, could influence behaviors when these students are asked to make decisions in an experimental supply chain setting. The two samples that the Mann Whitney test applied to the rate of false messages (calculated over the 30 periods) confirm the hypothesis that there is no difference between the two populations of students (p $value$ = 1.0000). This is also the case with rate of trust (p $value$ = 0.7728). Tests applied to the three separate sequences of periods (from period 1 to 10, from period 11 to 20, and from period 21 to 30) lead to the same results in terms of there being no significant differences between the two populations.

These tests show that training in economics, particularly in game theory, has no effect on students' behaviors. For the analysis below, we can consider our data as experimental observations from a single population.

We first analyze the *retailers' behaviors*. First of all, we observe that the rate of false messages is relatively high. According to game theory applied to a cheap-talk context, theoretical results in an infinitely repeated game are truth messages from the retailers and, consequently, imply perfect trust. In our experiment, the average rate of false messages is 32.25% in the first 10 periods, 25.94% in the next 10 periods, and 27.22% in the last 10 periods. These relatively high rates reveal that subjects did not follow the theoretical predictions. Retailers try to induce suppliers to produce more than the optimal level corresponding to a low demand on the final market. In other words, retailers induce the suppliers to support any unsold costs in order to decrease shortage costs of the supply chain as much as possible.

We can observe that, in the first 10 periods, four retailers out of 17 (i.e. nearly 24%) never send false messages to their suppliers, and that this number of retailers increases to seven in the next 10 periods and the last 10 periods (i.e. 41%). Globally, only three subjects are characterized by a null rate of false messages. Conversely, the number of retailers characterized by a rate of false messages of at least 50% is relatively high: five subjects in the first 10 periods, four in the next 10 periods (i.e. nearly 24%) and three in the last periods (17%).

The rates of false messages differed from one subject to the next. First, as noted above, we find that three retailers (R8, R10 and R16) never send false messages during the experiment. On the other hand, only one retailer almost always sends false messages (R5). Other retailers can be gathered into three sample groups:

– a group with six retailers characterized by a decreasing rate of false messages (R1, R9, R11, R14, R15, R17);

– a group with four retailers characterized by increasing rates of false messages (R2, R3, R4, R13);

– a group with three subjects characterized by more unstable changes in their rates of false messages (R6, R7, R12).

Figure 6.5 shows the evolution of the average rates of false messages for each of these three sample groups.

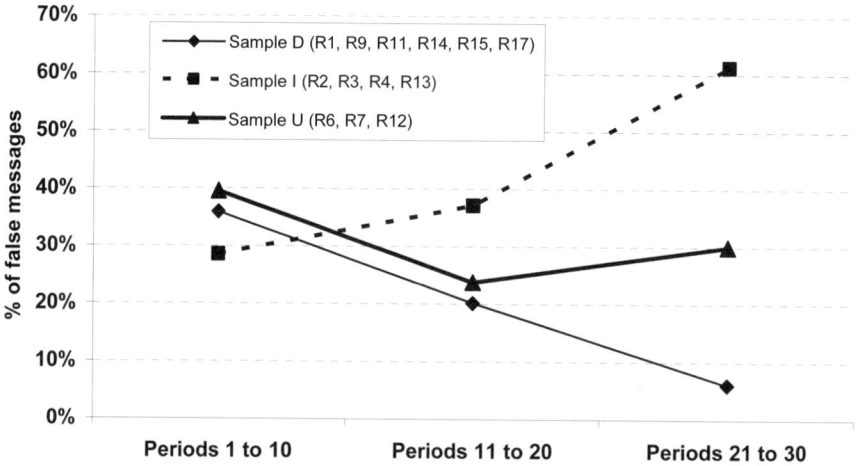

Figure 6.5. *Evolution of the rates of false messages*

The evolution indicates that, for some retailers, repeated interactions with their supplier decreases opportunistic behaviors. This is clearly the case for retailers in sample *D*, with an average rate of periods equal to 1.85% in the last sequence. With the retailers who never send a false message during the experiment, we find that eight retailers end the last sequence of periods without sending any false messages[2] (i.e. 47%). Nevertheless, for the retailers in sample *I* we observe that the rates of false messages increase, especially in the last 10 periods. This is due to retailers 4 and 13 who always send a false message at the end of the experiment.

With *suppliers' behaviors*, the average rates of trust must be compared with our theoretical expectation. Recall that in our context theoretical results in an infinitely repeated game are truth messages from the retailers. With this expectation in mind, the suppliers should always trust the forecasts transmitted by their retailer.

We find that the average rate of trust is 60.00%. Only one supplier (S10) is characterized by a rate of trust equal to 100%, which means that he always trusts his

---

2 Retailer 17 is not included here but he only sends one false message (in period 30).

retailer's forecasts. While this average rate is higher in the first 10 periods (65.90%), it decreases in the next sequence of periods (54.78%), and gets closer to 60% at the end of the experiment. As for the rates of false messages, the suppliers' behaviors differ from one subject to another. Our observations can also be gathered into three sample groups according the level and evolution of the individual supplier's rates of trust:

– a group with five suppliers characterized by increasing rates of trust (S1, S6, S14, S15, S16);

– a group with seven suppliers characterized by decreasing rates of trust (S4, S5, S7, S8, S9, S12, S13);

– a sample with four suppliers characterized by more unstable changes in their rates of trust (S2, S3, S11, S17).

Figure 6.6 shows the evolution of average rates of trust for each of these three sample groups.

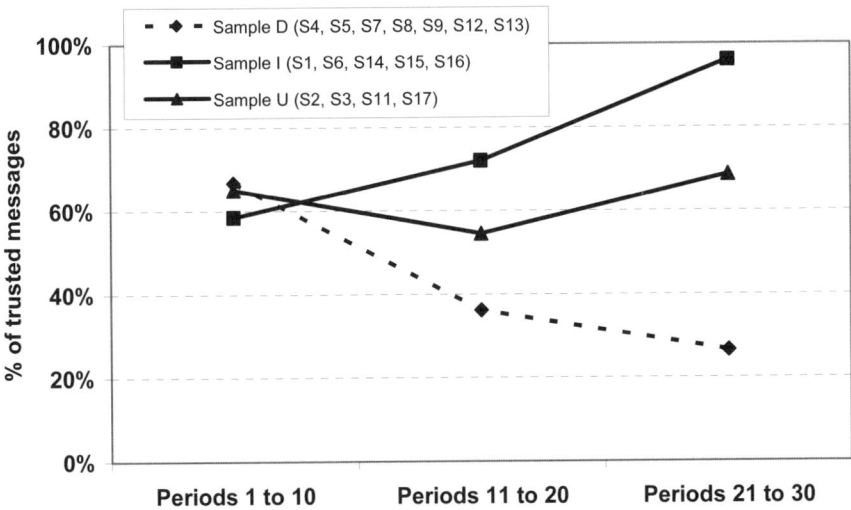

Figure 6.6. *Evolution of the rates of trust*

For some suppliers, the rates of trust increase with repeated interactions and are close to full trust at the end of the experiment (sample *I*). With supplier S10 (who always trusts the retailer), there are six subjects characterized by full confidence in their retailers: their average rate of trust is 97%. On the other hand, in the last 10 periods sample *D* ends up with an average rate of trust equal to 26.51%. In this sample, four suppliers conclude the experiment without trusting their retailers.

After the analysis of individual retailers' and suppliers' behaviors, we propose to examine the *dynamics of each group*. The 17 groups of paired individuals (a retailer with their respective supplier) can be gathered into four samples according their dynamics.

The first sample concerns five groups (G1, G5, G8, G10 and G16) that are characterized by a *relatively stable and clear dynamic*. In groups G10 and G16, the retailers adopt a clear strategy that consists of always sending true forecasts to their suppliers, who in return choose to produce to the corresponding level. This behavior is also observed in group G1, after only one or two false messages at the beginning of the experiment. Note that in G1, the retailer stops his initial strategy according the production decisions of the supplier, who chooses the median level (i.e. N_0) when the message is "high demand". The last two groups are also characterized by a relatively stable dynamic, even if the behaviors are not well coordinated. In G8, the retailer always sends the true forecasts to his supplier. But the supplier has decided to produce the median level, regardless of the message (low or high demand).

The second sample concerns four groups (G9, G11, G12 and G13) that are characterized by a *climate of conflict between the two parties*. In the three last groups, the retailers frequently send false messages to their suppliers. Their behavior is, however, revealed by low demand levels and the suppliers adopt retaliatory decisions. These decisions consist of producing low levels of products in the following periods when high forecast messages are sent (instead of a median level). Note that these behaviors persist until the last periods of the experiment.

The third sample concerns three groups (G14, G15 and G17) that are characterized by *difficulties in the relationships* between the two parties. Contrary to the preceding sample, however, the climate of conflict seems to disappear with repeated interactions. Moreover, the suppliers' reactions to false messages are less radical: they just choose the median level of production in the following periods. Finally, these groups converge to produce a relatively stable trend of cooperative behavior.

The last sample, which concerns four groups (G2, G3, G4, G6 and G7), is also characterized by *persistent difficulties in the relationships*. As in the third sample, the suppliers' reactions to false messages are less radical but the retailers continue to occasionally send false messages until the end of the experiment. It seems that if the climate in these groups has not deteriorated, it is thanks to the passive suppliers' reactions.

6.4. Conclusion

The objective of this chapter was to analyze decision-making behaviors of supply chain managers in order to assess their potential impacts on the local performance of each node of the logistic system, as well as on the overall performance of the supply chain. Starting with a modeling approach with restrictive hypotheses concerning the way to represent decentralized decisions, this work also applies experimental economics in order to capture the real nature of subjects' behaviors. The strong complementarities between these two distinct scientific approaches allows us to test the validity of our theoretical results but also to go beyond the analytical approach when the decision context is more complex – as in infinitely repeated games. It is characterized by some heterogenity in individual behaviors.

Apart from our specific results, we can conclude this chapter with general comments and perspectives from this cross-methodologies approach. From the viewpoint of the modeling approach, the combination of analytical demonstrations (i.e. game theory) and an experimental methodology provides a substantial added value. As noted above, the first goal of the experiment was to compare theoretical results with experimental ones. The above conclusion has proved, in a sense, that the theoretical model was insufficient to fully represent the behaviors being studied. The experiment does not highlight a clear game equilibrium on either a fully cooperative behavior or a fully non-cooperative one. On the contrary, because of other behavioral characteristics of the decision makers we observe distinct dynamics in the development of the retailer/supplier relationship. In fact, experimentation can help game theory modeling in several ways. First, as the theoretical analysis of the current game in a repeated situation presents mathematical difficulties that are not easy to overcome, experimentation can help to identify potential equilibriums of repeated strategic games when they appear clearly. When such equilibriums do not appear clearly, the results remain very positive from a scientific point of view: they highlight the need to change the hypotheses used in the models and can reveal a new pertinent orientation towards redefining models. In the current study, experimental conclusions open new perspectives on modeling dynamic strategies that evolve over time. They also highlight the need to represent in the trust/confidence mechanisms among participants in greater detail, so that potential behaviors can be differentiated by considering relationship factors.

With experimental economics, the complementarities approach is very helpful to researchers. Applying experimental tools to supply chain contexts allows us to analyze subjects' behaviors in depth when these subjects are interacting in a specific context. In other words, this approach constitutes a step towards "field experiments" where, contrary to traditional economic experiments, the subjects face real and contextualized problems. [HAR 04] propose six factors that can be used to determine the field context of an experiment: "the nature of the subject pool, the nature of the information that the subjects bring to the task, the nature of the commodity, the nature of the task or trading rules applied, the nature of the stakes, and the environment that subjects operate in".

To obtain greater relevance, experimental economists are recruiting subjects in the field rather than in the classroom, and are using the field context rather than abstract terminology in instructions. In our work, the subjects are still recruited in classrooms, but they are engineering students from two leading schools and are characterized by some experience in industrial problem solving. Our experimental design is however mainly in the field, according to the nature of the tasks and information given to the subjects. We "submerge" our subjects in a real supply chain context, with complex and uncertain decisions about levels of production, information sharing, etc.

Admittedly, when running field experiments we may lose some of the control exerted in traditional laboratory experiments. Some unexpected behaviors may therefore occur, but they may often be indicators of key features of real-world settings that may have been neglected in the laboratory. As our empirical results show, trust and/or conflicts between subjects are important factors in the dynamics of the relationship. Such factors, and their evolution in a repeated game would certainly not have the same outcome and impact in a pure and abstract laboratory experiment.

6.5. Bibliography

[CAC 99] CACHON G.P., ZIPKIN P.H., "Competitive and cooperative inventory policies in a two-stage supply chain", *Management Science*, vol. 45, no.7, 1999, pp. 936-953.

[CAC 01] CACHON G.P., LARIVIERE M.A., "Contracting to assure supply: how to share demand forecasts in a supply chain", *Management Science*, vol. 47, no.5, 2001, pp. 629-646.

[CAC 02] CACHON G.P., "Supply chain coordination with contracts", in: S. GRAVES and T. de KOK (eds.), *Handbooks in Operations Research and Management Science: Supply Chain Management*, Elsevier, Netherlands, 2002.

[CAM 03] CAMERER C.F., *Behavioral Game Theory*, Princeton University Press, 2003.

[CHE 03] CHEN F., "Information sharing and supply chain coordination", in: GRAVES S., and de KOK, T. (eds.), *Handbooks in Operations Research and Management Science: Supply Chain Management*, Elsevier, Netherlands, 2003.

[COR 02] CORBETT C.J., TANG C.S., *Designing Supply Contracts: Contract Type and Information Asymmetry. Quantitative Models for Supply Chain Management*, Kluwer, 2002.

[DEL 99] DELAHAYE, J.P., MATHIEU, P., "Des surprises dans le monde de la coopération", in: *Les Mathématiques Sociales, Pour la Science*, Belin, Paris, 1999, pp.58-66.

[FRI 04] FRIEDMAN D., CASSAR A., *Economics Lab. An Intensive Course in Experimental Economics*, Routledge, 2004.

[GIA 04] GIANNOCCARO, I., PONTRANDOLFO, P., "Supply chain coordination by revenue sharing contracts", *International Journal of Production Economics*, vol. 89, 2004, pp. 131-139.

[HAR 04] HARRISON G.W., LIST J.A., "Field experiments", *Journal of Economic Literature*, vol. XLII, 2004, pp. 1009-1055.

[HOL 02] HOLT C.A., LAURY S.K., "Risk aversion and incentive effects", *American Economic Review*, vol. 92, no.5, 2002, pp. 1644-1655.

[KES 04] KESER C., PALEOLOGI G.A., Experimental investigation of supplier-retailer contracts: The wholesale price contract, CIRANO working paper no.2004-s57, 2004.

[LEE 97] LEE H. L., PADMANABHAN P., WHANG S., "Information distortion in a supply chain: the bullwhip effect", *Management Science*, vol. 43, no.4, 1997, pp. 546-558.

[LIN 07] LING L., FEIQI D., "Equilibrium solution of two enterprises cooperative game", *Journal of Systems Engineering and Electronics*, vol. 18, no.2, 2007, pp. 270-274.

[REN 06] REN, Z.J., COHEN M.A, HO T.H., TERWIESCH C., *Sharing Forecast Information in a Long-term Supply Chain Relationship*, Berkeley, 2006, available at: http://faculty.haas.berkeley.edu/hoteck/PAPERS/Ren.pdf, accessed 4.29.10.

[SCH 00] SCHWEITZER M., CACHON G.P., "Decision bias in the newsvendor problem: experimental evidence", *Management Science*, vol. 46, no.3, 2000, pp. 404-420.

[SMI 76] SMITH V.L, "Experimental economics: Induced value theory", *American Economic Review*, vol. 66, no. 2, 1976, pp. 274-279.

[TAR 08] TARATYNAVA, N., BURLAT, P. AND BOUCHER, X., "Partage des prévisions dans une chaîne logistique à deux niveaux", *7ième Conférence Internationale de Modélisation et Simulation*, MOSIM'08, France, 2008.

[TAR 09a] TARATYNAVA, N., BURLAT, P., BOUCHER., X., "Forecast sharing, within a two echelon supply chain", *13th IFAC International Symposium on Information Control Problems in Manufacturing (INCOM'09)*, Moscow, Russia, June 3-5, 2009.

[TAR 09b] TARATYNAVA N., Modélisation de la coopération dans les réseaux d'entreprises par la théorie des jeux, doctoral thesis, Ecole Nationale Supérieure des Mines de Saint Etienne, November 2009.

[TSA 99] TSAY A.A., LOVEJOY W.S., "Quantity flexibility contracts and supply chain performance", *Manufacturing & Service Operations Management*, vol. 1, no.2, 1999, pp. 89-111.

Chapter 7

Coordination Mechanism as a Mitigation Action to Manage Supply Chain Risks

7.1. Risk management in supply chains

In modern supply chain (SC) networks, firms seek to increase their competitive edge by employing new strategies, such as re-centering some of their activities by outsourcing, proposing an increased diversity of products to capture a market share, and so on. Even though efficient in a stable environment, these strategies augment the vulnerabilities of firms in an uncertain environment, thus resulting in operational risks that need to be taken into account.

In this chapter we first present a literature review on risk management, focusing in particular on risk management in SCs. Second, we present a global model of a SC with several suppliers, a manufacturer, a retailer and customers. This model is subject to some common SC risks, for instance in transportation and in product and process quality. We then introduce coordination among SC partners as a risk-mitigation action in SCs. To this end, we zoom in on a sub-network of the SC: the coordination between suppliers and the manufacturer. A supplier selection mechanism to enhance the purchasing policy of the manufacturer is described. The whole system under study and the supplier selection mechanism are then modeled using petri nets (PNs) and object oriented design (OOD) techniques. Finally, some numerical results are presented, followed by concluding remarks.

Chapter written by Gülgün ALPAN, Van-Dat CUNG, Fabien MANGIONE and Gonca TUNCEL.

In the literature we find various definitions of "risk". In this chapter, we take the definition given by the Association for Project Management (APM) as a basis since it highlights several notions, namely, objectives, occurrences and impacts. According to the APM: "Risk is defined as an uncertain event or a set of circumstances which, should it occur, would have an effect on the achievement of one or more objectives" [APM 04]. We revisit these notions throughout this chapter.

A typical process of risk management contains four basic steps [HAL 04]. This procedure seems to receive consensus in the literature and is applicable to risk management in SC processes as well:

– *Risk identification*: this first step helps in developing a common understanding of the future uncertainties surrounding the SC, thus recognizing potential risks in order to manage these scenarios effectively.

– *Risk assessment*: refers to the assignment of probabilities to risk-bearing events in the system defined in the first step. The consequences of these risk events are also identified in this step. Associating probabilities to risks is not an easy task and requires tedious work. A company's own experiences, benchmarking on other companies' performance results, or forecasting analysis can be used to this end.

– *Risk-management actions*: in [MUS 06], risk-management actions are classified as risk taking, risk mitigation, risk avoidance and risk transfer. We can also classify them as reactive or proactive actions. For instance, the integration of back-up scenarios should a pre-identified risk actually occur is considered to be a "reactive action", while risk mitigation actions that act directly on the pre-identified risks in order to reduce either the probability of occurrence or the degree of severity of its consequences are typically proactive.

– *Risk monitoring*: is the final step of a classical risk-management process where the system is supervised in order to detect the risks when they occur.

Even though there is a consensus on the above procedure, a wide range of risk analysis methodologies exist for implementing the above steps in an industrial environment [TIX 02].

Risk management in SCs is a relatively new topic. In the literature, SC management, performance analysis and risk management have generally been considered separately. Risks are mostly addressed from the financial or economic perspective [WIN 06]. Although some recent literature tackles risk management from the logistics point of view, these studies often look at a single organization's vulnerabilities [JUT 05] and tend to focus on a single point of view, such as supply, demand, product or information management [TAN 06]. This chapter is not intended to be a list of all these earlier works on risk management. The interested reader can refer to [TAN 06], where extensive bibliographical research on risk management in SCs is presented.

7.2. A SC model

In this chapter we consider the classical SC network, shown in Figure 7.1, as a base SC configuration. For illustration purposes, the number of suppliers is limited to two. Similarly, only immediate suppliers and customers are considered. We note that the model can easily be extended to more suppliers and higher levels of complexity by including the suppliers of suppliers and the customers of customers, etc. We will first present the relationships between SC partners, as well as possible operational risks inherent in this system.

The relationship between the manufacturer and the retailer is considered to be a pull policy with some safety stock. The process starts when the customer order arrives at the manufacturer. Each order has an arrival time, due date, and a customer tolerance for tardy jobs. If the inventory level at the manufacturer is enough to fulfill the order, the final products are sent directly from the manufacturer to the customers through the retailer. If this is not the case, an assembly operation is started at the manufacturer, and a purchase order for raw materials is sent to the corresponding supplier.

Components A and B are provided by suppliers S1 and S2, respectively. When the components are processed by the suppliers, they go through a quality check. If there is a problem with quality that can be solved, the component is reworked; otherwise it is rejected. After the quality-control process, parts are delivered to the manufacturer by the corresponding transporters (T1 and T2). Upon reception they are assembled by the manufacturer to obtain a final product. At the end of the assembly process, the products are inspected and, if necessary, reworked. Finally, the finished products are transferred by a transporter (T3) to the retailer, where the customers can collect their products.

The status of the customer orders waiting to be fulfilled is updated according to the following rules: (i) if an order is delayed, contact the customer and take the due time tolerance for the delayed order; (ii) if the current time is already out of the tolerance range, cancel the order with a lost sales cost; and (iii) if the delayed order is within the due time tolerance, then assign a higher priority so that the order can be handled as soon as possible.

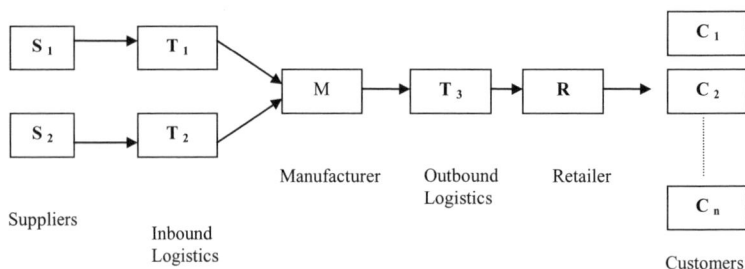

Figure 7.1. *A classical SC network*

At least one classical operational risk is considered per SC partner:

– quality problems arising from the processed products at *suppliers* and/or *manufacturer*;

– technical problems and breakdown of the machinery at the *manufacturer*;

– uncertainty in *customer* demand;

– disruptions in the *inbound/outbound* logistics, such as damages or loss of a shipment due to accidents, or delayed arrival of a vehicle because of heavy traffic, etc.

These operational risks can be integrated into the model separately, as follows. First, if any failure is observed, an attempt is made to solve the resulting problem. This adds additional time to the normal transfer time. If the problem is not solved and the freight is lost, the transportation order is renewed. Quality failures may be handled in a similar manner. On the other hand, when there is a technical problem/breakdown of the machinery, or a shortage of operators, the manufacturing process is put on hold until the source of disruption is solved. The uncertainty in customer demand is modeled as random order arrivals.

7.3. Using a coordination mechanism as a risk mitigation action

In previous research [TUN 07] we modeled the operational risks described in section 7.2. This model was then tested in an industrial case study [TUN 09] in which the operational risks inherent in the company were first identified and the occurrences assessed via an Failure Modes and Effects Analysis (FMEA) table. These risks were then incorporated into the model. The model was used to simulate different risk scenarios, to capture the riskiest activity in the SC in terms of impacts that the risks will generate on the overall cost of the SC network. Risk mitigation actions are then proposed to minimize the impact of the company's operational risks.

The case study highlighted several advantages of the model originally given in [TUN 07]. One of the major advantages is that a combination of risk-bearing factors (from different partners) can easily be tested simultaneously. Hence, a global insight on the performance of the SC network can be obtained. Furthermore, if needed, the model can also be used to test the sensitivity of the system to variations in an individual parameter, such as demand or lead time variations.

In the earlier studies the objective was to minimize overall cost incurred in the SC, including all SC partners. The proposed mitigation actions were local, i.e. actions were only taken for each SC partner, however. For instance, if the manufacturer encountered quality problems, we assumed that a mitigation action could be the organization of educational programs for the employees or the implementation of Kaizen groups to reduce such problems locally.

In this section, with the same objective in view, we show how coordination among SC partners can be used as a global mitigation action to reduce a set of SC risks, such as demand fluctuations and uncertainties in the supplier's production capacities impacting inventory levels, back-order costs and demand fill rate as quality of service.

7.3.1. *Coordination in SCs*

Malone [MAL 97] defines SC coordination as a "pattern of decision-making and communication among a set of actors who perform tasks to achieve a goal". The usual goal for coordination is to reduce overall SC costs and to share the savings or individual participants' benefits [SIM 00]. Furthermore, coordination can balance risk sharing among the SC partners [ROM 03].

Coordination along the SC is usually separated into two levels [THO 96]:

– *strategic level/long-term decisions*: plant or distribution center (DC) opening, make or buy, etc.;

– *operational level/short-term decisions*: where to produce this command, which tools to use, etc.

[THO 96] also define three categories of operational coordination: buyer-vendor coordination, production-distribution coordination and inventory-distribution coordination. In this section, buyer-vendor coordination is presented to illustrate a coordination mechanism as a risk mitigation action.

7.3.2. A buyer-vendor coordination mechanism based on historical risk data

The coordination mechanism presented in this section is based on a model proposed by Chan and Chan [CHA 06]. This buyer-vendor coordination is a two-stage mechanism with one manufacturer (buyer) and n suppliers (vendors). The manufacturer's periodic decisions that have to be made include the quantity, the date of order and the choice of supplier for each purchase.

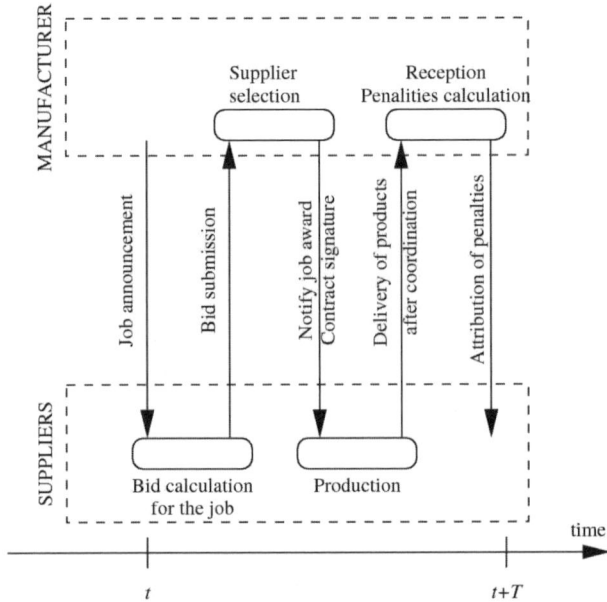

Figure 7.2. *Buyer-vendor coordination mechanism*

Figure 7.2 illustrates the coordination mechanism and what is done in each period. A period T starts at the date of the manufacturer's job announcement and ends at the date when the penalties are assigned to the suppliers. Given the demands following a normal distribution $N(\mu, \sigma)$, period T can be defined by the economic order quantity (EOQ) model with $T = \sqrt{\dfrac{2.C_c}{C_s.\mu}}$, where C_c is the ordering cost and C_s the inventory holding cost of the manufacturer.

When a job is announced, the manufacturer indicates a range of quantities that are needed $[Q_{low}, Q_{high}]$. This range is computed from the fixed order quantity $Q = \mu.(T + L)$, where L is the order lead time, moderated with the safety stock $S_s = \rho.\sigma.\sqrt{T + L}$, where ρ is the service level. Thus, we have $Q_{low} = Q - S_s$ and $Q_{high} = Q + S_s$.

Each supplier submits a bid considering its own production capacity reservation for this demand and the possible start time. The bid consists of a delivery due date in response to the manufacturer's request. This expected delivery due date for supplier i at period t is defined as $EDDD_i = D_{it} + Q/C_i$ where D_{it} is the longest due date of the supplier and C_i its production capacity for achieving the order if supplier i is selected.

The manufacturer selects the supplier from whom it will purchase its raw materials. Chan and Chan propose to use the earliest delivery due date as the criterion for supplier selection, i.e. the supplier with $EDDD = \min_{i}(EDDD_i)$ is selected. Note that only one supplier is selected in this process.

The contract between the manufacturer and the selected supplier is then signed. In the contract, the quantity is not fixed; a range of quantities is proposed. The maximum quantity of the range is the quantity announced during the bid plus the manufacturer's safety stock, while the minimum quantity of the range is the difference between the two amounts.

Consequently, a range of delivery due dates $[D_{low}, D_{high}]$ is also defined. The manufacturer will be authorized to request its purchase from the beginning of this date range (expected delivery due date proposed by the selected supplier minus the safety stock divided by the supplier capacity, $D_{low} = EDDD - S_s/\mu$). However, the manufacturer must get its purchase back when the end of the date range is reached (expected delivery due date plus the safety stock divided by the supplier capacity, $D_{high} = EDDD + S_s/\mu$). This leads to the following model:

– the production process starts for the manufacturer (consuming its own inventory, which decreases) and for the suppliers (their inventory levels increase);

– when the lower bound of the range of delivery due dates is reached and the manufacturer needs its products or when the upper bound of the range is reached and the shipment has to be made, two possibilities can occur:

- the selected supplier can ship what has been contracted so that the delivery is made and the coordination is completed, or

- the selected supplier cannot deliver the requested quantity, and a first delivery of what has been produced is made. A second delivery will be made when the complementary quantity has been produced;

– if the shipment is not made on time the supplier is penalized, depending on quantity and/or delay, as defined in the contract.

In this model, as the goal is to minimize the overall SC cost, the penalty is converted into a cost. The total cost includes the inventory costs (manufacturer's and suppliers'), the back-order costs and penalty costs.

Although Chan and Chan have considered historical penalties in their study, these have not been introduced in the iterative supplier-selection process over several periods. Yet these penalties based on historical information could reduce the risks that the manufacturer takes when selecting a supplier. Moreover, the delivery due date is in practice not the only criterion used in supplier selection. In the next section we therefore present a multi-criteria method with historical penalties that improves this model by minimizing the risks for the manufacturer.

7.3.3. A multi-criteria analysis for the definition of an ordering policy

The literature contains many studies on supplier selection, including a fairly large number of reviews:

– Weber, Current and Benton [WEB 91] studied the criteria and the analytical methods for supplier selection;

– Holt [HOL 98] reviewed the different methods for contractor evaluation and selection modeling methodology;

– Degraeve, Labro and Roodhooft [DEG 00] classified the vendor selection model; and

– De Boer, Labro and Morlacchi [BOE 01] positioned the literature review in a supplier selection framework.

One of the main decisions a purchasing and/or manufacturing manager has to make is to select the best supplier for each period. This decision is impacted by several factors. Roa and Kiser [ROA 80] identified up to 60 criteria for supplier selection. Hence, it is a multi-criteria decision problem and a trade-off has to be made between conflicting tangible and intangible factors to find the best suppliers. Scoring methods can solve this multi-criteria decision problem. The analytic hierarchy process (AHP) developed by Saaty in 1980 [SAA 80] is one of the most popular multi-criteria decision-making methods. It is widely adapted in many applications [VAI 06]. AHP was used by Narasimhan [NAR 83] for the first time in the supplier selection process. Then [GHO 98] confirmed that the method is performs well and is commonly used [BAR 97, NYD 92, PAL 06, TAM 01] in the supplier selection process.

The AHP method is based on the four steps described below [SAA 80]:

1. Define the problem and determine the kind of knowledge sought.

2. Structure the decision hierarchy from the top. Start with the goal of the decision, then the objectives from a broad perspective, through the intermediate levels (criteria on which subsequent elements depend), to the lowest level (which usually is a set of alternatives).

3. Construct a set of pair-wise comparison matrices. Each element in an upper level is used to compare the elements in the level immediately below with respect to it.

4. Use the priorities obtained from the comparisons to weigh the priorities in the level immediately below. Do this for every element. Then for each element in the level below, add its weighed values and obtain its overall or global priority. Continue this weighing and adding process until the final priorities of the alternatives at the lowest level are obtained.

One of the main advantages of the AHP method is the creation of a hierarchical structure that urges the managers to define their needs. Moreover, the definition of the objectives and criteria includes compromises that clarify the situation from a management point of view [HAN 02]. Many other benefits are presented in the literature [DAV 06, HAN 02, VAI 06].

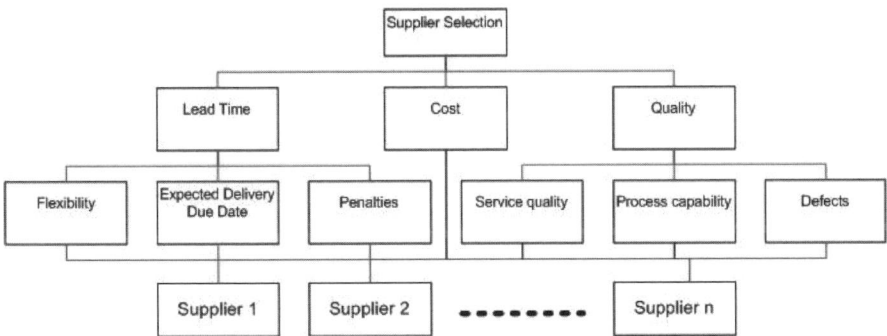

Figure 7.3. *Hierarchy structure*

The main drawback of the coordination model presented in [CHA 06] is the mono-criterion in supplier selection (expected delivery due date), when in reality managers make their decisions based on three main criteria: quality, price and lead time. We have solved this problem by integrating the AHP for supplier selection in the model. Figure 7.3 illustrates the structure proposed for the second step of the AHP. Of course, many other criteria can be used, but for the sake of clarity we will use three criteria and six sub-criteria.

In the case of qualitative data that cannot always be measured, we use a discrete scale ranging from one (equally important) to nine (much more important) to quantify, for instance, flexibility and quality of service. These comparisons are given by the managers, depending on their wishes. In the case of quantitative data, we use real values: expected delivery due date, penalties, cost, and process capability.

For example, the penalty pairwise comparison between supplier i and supplier j can be calculated as follows: $P(Si)$ is the difference between the quantity ordered and the quantity delivered on time for the supplier i. This use of penalties can manage historical information and thus achieve a wiser choice at each period.

Most of the studies use the multi-criteria method for a single selection that is mostly related to supplier pre-qualification [ELS 07]. The pre-qualification is a decision made at the tactical level, as defined by [THO 96]. Here, we use the multi-criteria method in every production period and for every bid with dynamic updated data. Hence the decisions taken are related to the operational level. In Figure 7.2, AHP is used in the supplier selection process (in operational level) and its data are updated with the penalty calculations.

7.4. A PN model of SC networks subject to operational risks

In this section we present a PN model of the SC network illustrated in Figure 7.1. OOD methodologies will also be used to incorporate the coordination mechanism explained in section 7.3.

The reasons for choosing PNs as a base model are numerous:

(i) PNs are well-defined graphical techniques for the specification and design of discrete-event dynamic systems [DES 95, DIC 93, MOO 96, MUR 89, ZHO 93, ZUR 94]. SC networks are mostly represented as discrete-event dynamic systems.

(ii) Some typical behaviors of SC networks, such as concurrent and asynchronous activities, multilayer resource-sharing, routing flexibility, limited buffers and precedence constraints, can be explicitly and concisely modeled by PNs.

(iii) Several extensions of the basic PN formalisms allow for the modeling of various notions: time (e.g. time PNs), stochastic behavior of the system (e.g. stochastic PNs), complex structured data, and algebraic expressions to annotate net elements (e.g. high-level PNs, such as colored PNs or CPNs).

(iv) PNs very easily support modular modeling techniques and are therefore handy in extending simple models into generic ones.

(v) The PN models can be computerized using existing PN modeling tools and hence enable simulation for decision making.

(vi) Finally, unlike earlier work reported on risk management [TAN 06], the PN models permit an easy interface by which to model and analyze several disruptions (in demand, transportation, quality, etc.) at the same time and on the same model.

7.4.1. *PNs in SC management*

PNs are typically used in the modeling, analysis and control of computer systems, communication protocols, and production systems. There are some recent applications in SC management as well. One of the earliest works is [VIS 00]. This study is focused on the comparison of two different production-control policies on the inventory holding and order delay costs.

Similarly, in [VAN 00], PNs are used to model and compare different network design scenarios in the food industry. PNs are used not only to simulate system behavior; they can also serve to verify various desired system properties, such as deadlock freeness (e.g. all merchandise reaches its destination) or boundedness (e.g. no overflows in the inventory) [CHE 05, DON 01].

Since PN modeling is often modular, SC objects are easily modeled [LIU 07] and the exchange of intra- and inter-organizational data are handled in a hierarchical structure [MEV 04]. There are also some studies that investigate the well-known notion of SC management, such as the bullwhip effect [MAK 04]. More recently, in [TUN 07] and [TUN 09], the PN modeling is used to integrate risk-management issues into the SC network modeling.

7.4.2. *The model*

A SC can be viewed as a collection of objects with rules governing their dynamics and interactions to generate desired objects (products). PNs and OOD concepts are complementary to achieve the goal of system development at the incremental stage, and enable us to model the complex system structures in detail, so that the strategies to operate these systems can be applied effectively in a more realistic environment.

The properties and behavior of the objects are modeled by the data/attribute and methods/operations of the corresponding system object. Note that real-world objects include not only physical objects, such as supplier, manufacturer, transporter and so on, but also logical objects, such as supplier selection process, part routing process, and so on [VEN 98].

OOD methodology, used for the development of the decision-support system of the SC under study, is summarized as follows [CHE 03, TUN 05, VEN 98]:

– OOD concepts are applied to find objects in the SC and to model the static relations among them by developing an object modeling technique (OMT) diagram. The OMT diagram is then used to explicitly represent different kinds of static relations, such as generalization, aggregation and association among the objects in the SC network.

– PNs are used to model the dynamic behavior of the SC, based on the static relations of the OMT diagram. We use the CPNs here, since these modeling tools can handle product process variability while remaining compact. The SC objects are hence modeled as CPN classes. Job announcements, bid submissions and part/product flows in the OMT diagram are transformed into token color classes in the CPN model.

– A centralized supplier-selection mechanism is proposed to evaluate the possible suppliers by using AHP to identify the most appropriate out sources.

– The system parameters of each object that is a member of a given class are then assigned. For instance, if there are n suppliers within the supplier class, internal parameters (e.g. n, production lead times of each supplier, type of products they can produce, etc.) are assigned at this step.

– All CPN classes are then integrated into a single system model by linking the input and output places of each CPN object. Deadlock prevention can be provided by bidding communication protocols between the system objects.

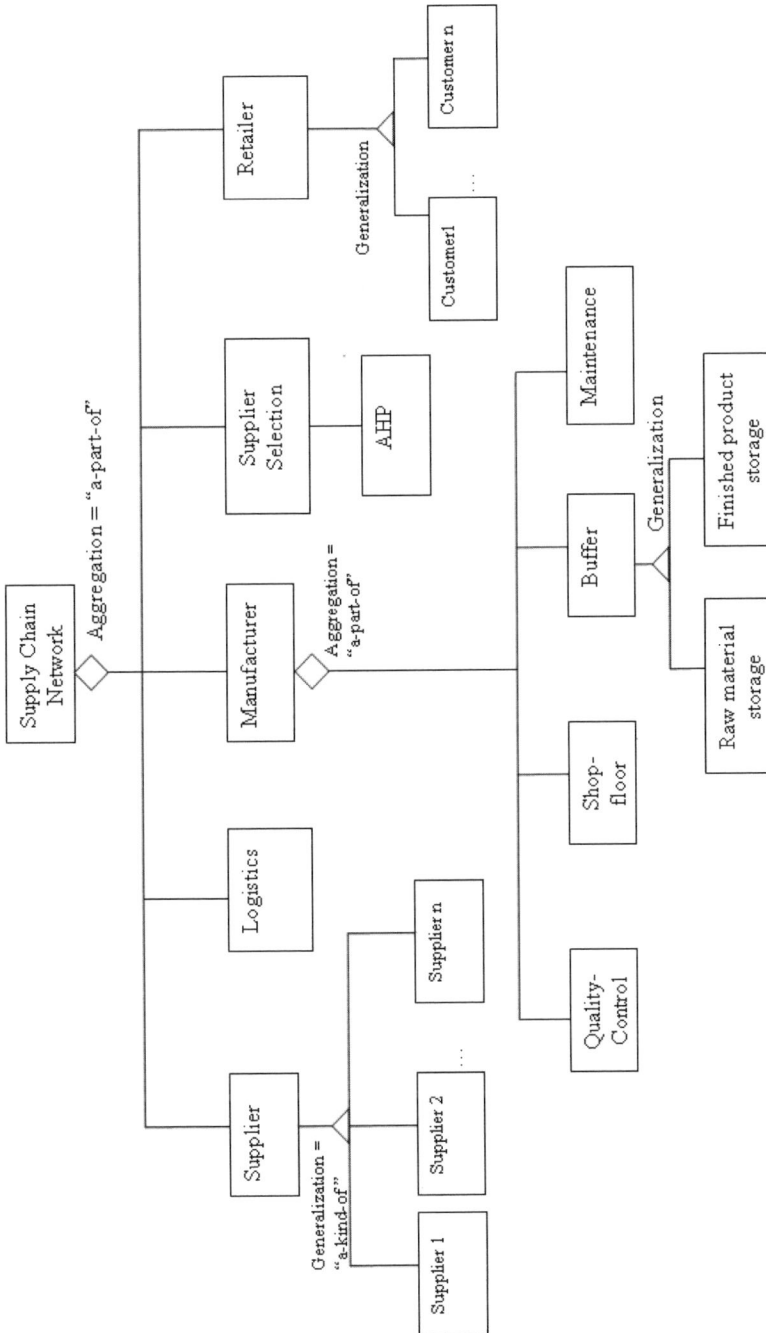

Figure 7.4. *Aggregation and generalization of the SC network*

In Figure 7.4, the OMT model of the SC under study is presented. Aggregation can be described as a "part-whole" or "a-part-of" relationship in which objects representing the components of a structure are associated with an object representing the entire assembly [BOO 98]. Generalization or inheritance describes the relationship between a class and its refined version, and is used to share the similarities among classes while preserving their diversities [KUO 98]. Aggregation is drawn with a small diamond indicating the assembly end of the relationship. The notation for inheritance is a triangle connecting a super class to its subclasses. Individual classes of SC objects are defined as follows:

– manufacturer class;

– supplier class;

– logistics (transportation) class;

– retailer class; and

– supplier selection class.

For each object identified in Figure 7.4 we generated a CPN class. These classes are illustrated in Figures 7.5 through 7.7.

The supplier selection object is not generated as a CPN class, since this module already exists as a Visual Basic program, as described above. The final PN model will communicate with this program only for the purpose of reading and writing data in this separate module. Similarly, the logistics object is not generated for the logistics class, since in the following sections the main focus is on the risks generated by relations between the supplier, retailer and manufacturer.

Transportation operations are hence directly included in the other objects. Nevertheless, we note that it is possible to generate the supplier selection object as well as the transportation object among the CPN classes.

The properties and behavior of SC objects are modeled by internal and external data/attributes and operations/methods of their deriving classes. Internal places and transitions are used to model the operations and dynamic behaviors inside the object class. As shown in the figures, there are three types of transition:

– Transitions illustrated by empty rectangles function in the same way as classical PN transitions. They receive tokens from their upstream places and once the firing time is over they deposit tokens into their downstream places.

– Transitions with a thick line on the side are called action transitions. These can change the data/attributes attached to a token. For instance, the due date tolerance can be calculated within an action transition and a new due date can be assigned to a component (modeled by a token).

– Transitions with a black diamond are predicate transitions. They can be only triggered if certain conditions are satisfied. Hence, they include some "if-then" rules. For instance, if there are no system failures, then the manufacturer can continue to produce (if P8=0, then M1 fires).

Note that a transition may be an action transition and a predicate transition at the same time.

Input places (illustrated by a double circle) and output places (illustrated by a triangle inside a circle) are used to model the external data/attributes that will serve as an interface to parts flow and information, and control the flow between SC objects. All the related PN class models are then connected through the input and output places to obtain the complete model and control logic of the system. The black diamonds on the corners of each CPN class are called the port sets (see Table 7.8). Each of these port sets is an ordered set of input/output places and is used to match the input and output places of different classes.

Compared to the PN models given in [TUN 07] and [TUN 09], the following model incorporates not only the OOD techniques – so that the size of the model can easily be augmented – but also a global mitigation action, which in this chapter is defined as coordination between the manufacturer and the supplier. More precisely, a supplier-selection mechanism is embedded in the model as a coordination strategy of the SC management.

This mechanism functions as follows: customer orders are generated with attributes such as their arrival time in the system, due date and tardiness tolerance, by transition D1 at retailer class. The manufacturer is informed by sending a token through the output place R_ORDERS, which is the input place of the manufacturer class. When a new order arrives at the manufacturer from the retailer (i.e. the transition M_INFORM fires), the manufacturer sends a job announcement to all suppliers via a token sent through output place J_ANNC, which is the input place of the supplier class (the range of quantities required is defined in section 7.3.2). The suppliers reply to the manufacturer, submitting the bidding statements through transition S_INFORM (e.g. the expected delivery due dates). Transition S_SELECT receives bid data from the suppliers and uses this information for supplier selection by integrated AHP module coded in Visual Basic. After the selection of a supplier, the manufacturer sends a purchasing order to the selected supplier by releasing a token into the output place M_ORDERS. A token here is sent to the input place of the destination object (i.e. selected supplier), which is connected by a link. This is made possible by having a single address associated with any object of the model, and a token routing mechanism. When a new purchase order arrives at the chosen supplier (i.e. a new token in input place M_ORDERS), the operational process can start by firing transition S1.

A token in internal place P9 guarantees that each component of a given order is processed at a particular time. Once operations of parts are completed at the supplier, parts that have no quality problems are transferred to the packing area by firing transition SQ. On the other hand, transition SQ_R1 sorts defective parts. If the defect on the part can be solved, it is reworked (i.e. firing of transition S_RW); otherwise transition SQ_R2 fires and inserts a token in place M_ORDERS, so that another processing operation can start for this purchase order. Ready parts are transferred to the manufacturer by firing transition ST. If a transportation failure occurs, then transition ST_R fires and the transportation is either delayed (transition ST_RS) or freight is damaged/lost (transition ST_D). For the damaged/lost freight, a new processing order is sent by inserting a token in place M_ORDERS.

Ready parts from the supplier are received at the manufacturer by input place S_PARTS. If the operational system is available (i.e. a token in place P1) and there is no system failure (i.e. a token in place P7), production can start by firing transition M1. A quality control process monitors the production operation. Parts that have no quality problem are moved to storage areas for finished products by transition PQ. Defective products are reworked by firing transition P_RW. For the other parts that have unsolvable quality problems, a new production operation is demanded by insertion of a token in place P6. Finished products are transferred to the retailer by either transition PT (normal transportation) or PT_RS (delayed transportation because of any disruption factor). For freight damaged or lost due to accidents or other unusual failures, a new production operation is also demanded by adding a token in place P6. When a system failure risk occurs, transition M_F fires, and takes a token from place P7, then releases a token in P8, which blocks the firing of transition M1 (operations at manufacturer). System disruption is solved by transition PF_R, which transfers the token from place P8 to P7 again. Customer orders waiting to be executed are represented by tokens in internal place P19 at the retailer class. The orders that have already exceeded the due date tolerance are systematically checked and cancelled by transition O_CANCEL, and system performance measures are updated. When a finished product arrives from the manufacturer by the incoming token through the input place P_ARRIVE, which is the manufacturer's output place, the orders that are not out of the due date tolerance are delivered to the customer, and necessary performance measures are updated.

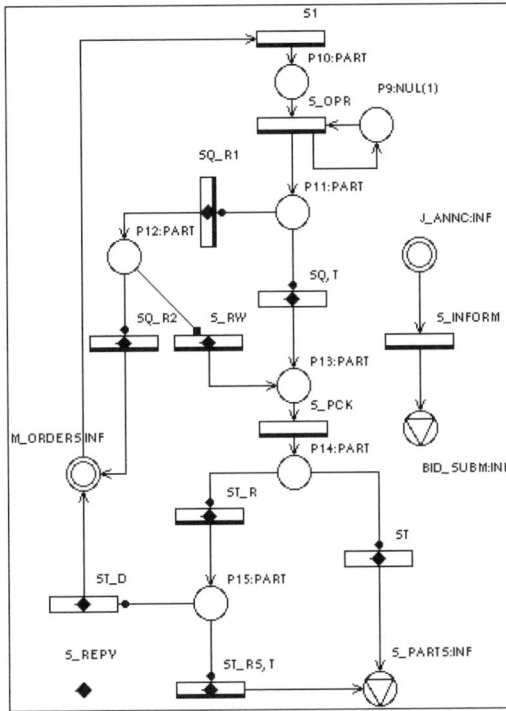

Figure 7.5. *CPN model of the supplier class*

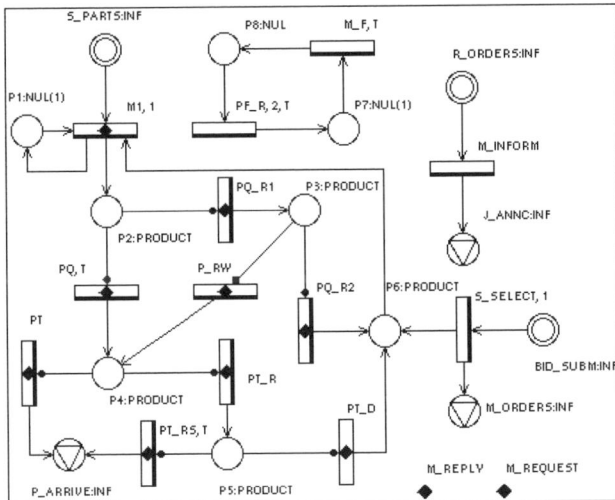

Figure 7.6. *CPN model of the manufacturer class*

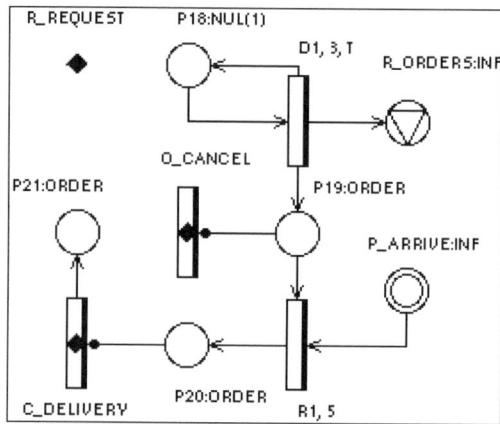

Figure 7.7. *CPN model of the retailer class*

Tables 7.1 to 7.3 give the interpretation for each transition, while Tables 7.4 through 7.8 give the interpretation for each place of the CPN models. We note that the transition names, which are in bold italics, identify the operational risks inherent to the system.

Transition name	Description
S1	Starting of inventory replenishment at the supplier
S_OPR	Processing by the supplier
SQ	Receiving parts that have no quality problems
SQ_R1	Receiving parts that have quality problems
S_RW	Reworking parts
SQ_R2	Rejecting the parts that have unsolvable quality failure
S_PCK	Pick/packaging the ready parts
ST	Transportation of the parts from the supplier to the manufacturer
ST_R	Transportation risk between the supplier and the manufacturer
ST_RS	Resolving/backing up the transportation failure
ST_D	Damage/loss of freight
S_INFORM	Receiving the job announcement from the manufacturer and submitting the bidding statement

Table 7.1. *Description of the transitions at supplier class*

Transition name	Description
M1	Processing by the manufacturer
PQ	Receiving the products that have no quality problem
PQ_R1	Receiving the products that have a quality problem
P_RW	Reworking the products
PQ_R2	Rejecting the products that have unsolvable quality failure
M_F	System failure risk (machine breakdowns)
PF_R	Resolving the system disruptions
PT	Transportation from manufacturer to retailer
PT_R	Transportation failure risk between manufacturer and retailer
PT_RS	Resolving/backing up the transportation failure
PT_D	Damage/loss of freight
M_INFORM	Receiving the sales order from the retailer and sending the job announcement to potential suppliers
S_SELECT	Receiving the bids from suppliers and selecting the best supplier according to AHP, then sending the purchasing order

Table 7.2. *Description of the transitions at manufacturer class*

Transition name	Description
D1	Arrival of customer orders and assigning due date tolerance to the corresponding tardy order
R1	Comparing existing customer orders with the manufacturer's responses
C_DELIVERY	Checking due date status of the order. If it does not exceed the due date tolerance, deliver it to the customer with a notification about the order delay if it is a tardy job
O_CANCEL	Cancellation of the orders that already exceed the due date tolerance

Table 7.3. *Description of the transitions at retailer class*

Place name	Description
P9	Availability of the supplier operational system
P10	Raw parts waiting in the input buffer of the supplier
P11	Parts processed by the supplier
P12	Defective parts
P13	Parts that have no quality failure
P14	Ready parts (packed) for transportation
P15	Delayed or damaged freight because of the transportation failure

Table 7.4. *Description of the internal places at supplier class*

Place name	Description
P1	Availability of the manufacturing process
P2	Products processed by the manufacturer
P3	Defective products
P4	Products that have no quality failure and are ready for transportation
P5	Delayed or damaged freight because of transportation failure
P6	Current (active) working orders at the manufacturer
P7	System is working without any failure
P8	System is blocked because of machinery breakdowns or operator failures

Table 7.5. *Description of the internal places at manufacturer class*

Place name	Description
P18	Availability of the order processing system
P19	Customer orders with the related information
P20	Customer orders evaluated for their due date status
P21	Delivered orders

Table 7.6. *Interpretations of the internal places at retailer class*

Place name	Description
J_ANNC	Job announcements sent from manufacturer to potential supplier *(input place of supplier class; output place of manufacturer class)*
M_ORDERS	Purchasing orders sent from manufacturer to selected supplier *(input place of supplier class; output place of manufacturer class)*
BID_SUBM	The bidding statement submitted by the supplier *(input place of manufacturer class; output place of supplier class)*
S_PARTS	The parts transferred from supplier to manufacturer *(input place of manufacturer class; output place of supplier class)*
R_ORDERS	Customer orders arrive from retailer *(input place of manufacturer class; output place of retailer class)*
P_ARRIVE	Finished products transferred from manufacturer to retailer *(input place of retailer class; output place of manufacturer class)*

Table 7.7. *Description of the interface (input/output) places*

Place name	Description
R_REQUEST	Information flow from retailer to manufacturer
M_REPLY	Information flow from manufacturer to retailer
M_REQUEST	Information flow from manufacturer to supplier
S_REPLY	Information flow from supplier to manufacturer

Table 7.8. *Description of the port sets (ordered sets of input/output places from the interfaces between classes)*

The CPN models in the above figures are then integrated into a complete model of the system by linking the corresponding input and output places of each object, as described above. Figure 7.8 shows the integrated model of the complete SC network. Each line represents the link set between the SC objects.

Since the structure of the proposed model is highly modular, miscellaneous control strategies and rules can easily be embedded, and the system can be tested with respect to various performance measures under assorted experimental conditions. Furthermore, we can change different input parameters, such as the number of suppliers, transporters, risk arrival rates, demand distribution, and so on. This flexibility of the model facilitates the study of the effects of different parameters on the system, as well as the evaluation of the supplier selection mechanism's performance on the risk-bearing events.

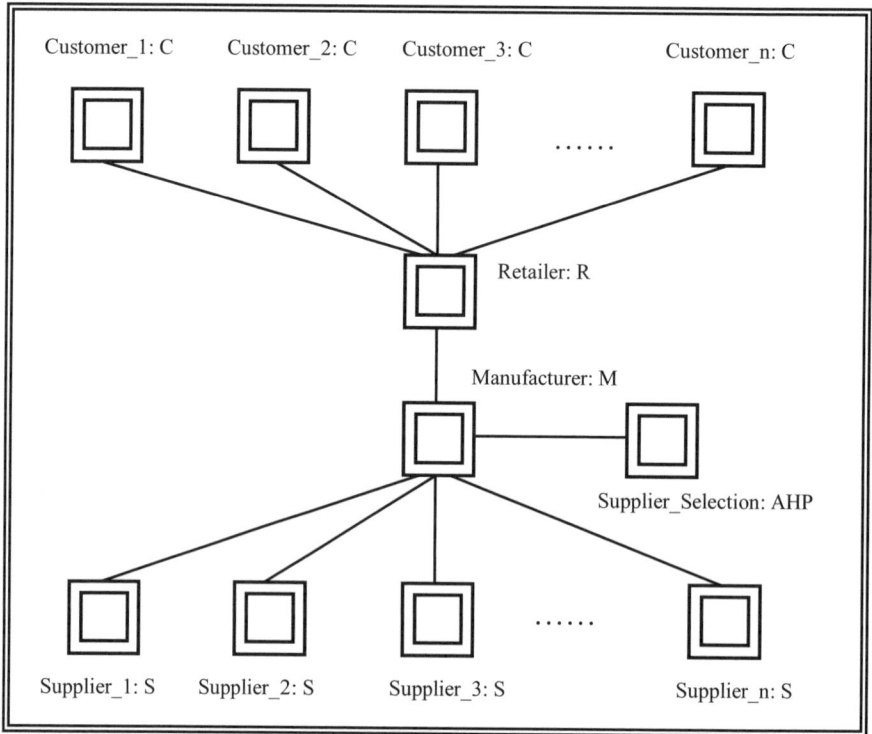

Figure 7.8. *Global model of the overall SC network*

7.5. Numerical results on the buyer-vendor coordination

We have generated several data sets of demand ranked from low uncertain demand (1) to high uncertain demand (4). We varied the production capacities of the suppliers as well, from 1 (low variation) to 4 (high variation). The simulations performed with this coordination model show that it is able to keep the total cost of the system and the back-order cost of the manufacturer low even when the uncertainties increase (see Figures 7.9 and 7.10). The demand fill rate is calculated as the fraction of demand immediately filled from the inventory on hand. This is one of the performance metrics that can reflect customer satisfaction. As we can observe in Figure 7.11, the coordination mechanism is able to reach high fill rates of over 90%, even for the high uncertainties. Moreover, the use of the coordination mechanism can improve the fill-rate by more than 5% when compared to a model without a coordination mechanism (fixed quantities and delivery due dates).

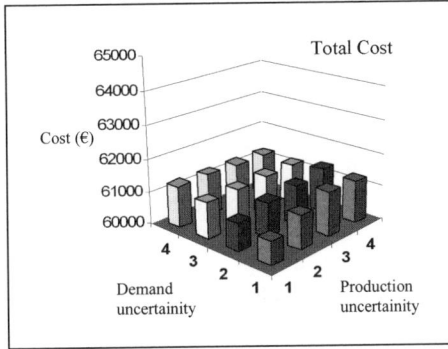

Figure 7.9. *Total cost of the system*

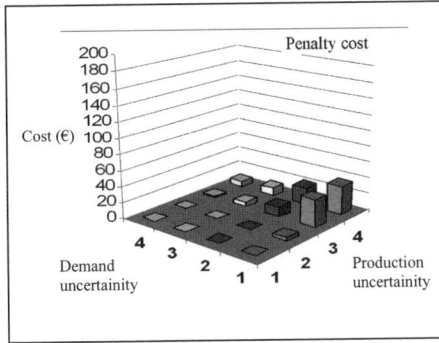

Figure 7.10. *Back-order cost incurred by the manufacturer*

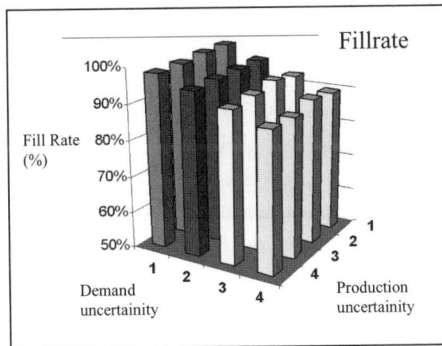

Figure 7.11. *Customer order fill rate*

7.6. Conclusion

In this chapter we have presented a SC model and a buyer-vendor coordination mechanism. This mechanism is based on an iterative procedure for supplier selection. The AHP method is used to take into account several criteria (costs, quality and lead time) inside the supplier selection mechanism. We have illustrated how this coordination mechanism can be used as a mitigation action to reduce operational risks of the SC partners.

For modeling and simulation purposes, we have used the PN and OOD framework. This framework is generic enough to easily integrate intra- or inter-partner mitigation actions, as well as the individual behavior of each SC partner.

Now that the framework is set, other criteria and coordination mechanisms can be implemented and tested to measure how these mechanisms contribute to reducing the level of risks in SCs.

7.7. Bibliography

[APM 04] ASSOCIATION FOR PROJECT MANAGEMENT, *Project Risk Analysis & Management (PRAM) Guide*, 2nd edn., APM Publishing, High Wycombe, Bucks, UK, 2004.

[BAR 97] BARBAROSOGLU G., YAZGAC T., "An application of the analytic hierarchy process to the supplier selection problem", *Production and Inventory Management Journal*, vol. 38, no. 1, 1997, pp. 14-21.

[BOO 98] BOOTH A.W., "Object-oriented modeling for flexible manufacturing systems", *International Journal of Flexible Manufacturing Systems*, vol. 10, 1998, pp. 301-314.

[CAC 04] CACHON G.P., "The allocation of inventory risk in a supply chain: push, pull, and advance-purchase discount contracts", *Management Science*, vol. 50, no. 2, 2004, pp. 222-238.

[CHA 06] CHAN F.T.S., CHAN H.K., "A simulation study with quantity flexibility in a supply chain subjected to uncertainties", *International Journal of Computer Integrated Manufacturing*, vol. 19, no. 2, 2006, pp. 148-160.

[CHE 05] CHEN H., AMODEO L., CHU F., LABADI K., "Modeling and performance evaluation of supply chains using batch deterministic and stochastic petri nets", *IEEE Transactions on Automation, Science, and Engineering*, vol. 2, 2005, pp. 132-144.

[CHE 03] CHEN J., CHEN, F.F., "Performance modelling and evaluation of dynamic tool allocation in flexible manufacturing systems using coloured Petri nets: An object-oriented approach", *International Journal of Advanced Manufacturing Technology*, vol. 21, no. 2, 2003, pp. 98-109.

[CHO 01] CHOPRA S., MEINDL P., *Supply Chain Management: Strategy, Planning and Operation*, Prentice Hall, Upper Saddle River, NJ, 2001.

[DAV 06] DAVIDSSON P., JOHANSSON S., SVAHNBERG M., "Using the analytic hierarchy process for evaluating multi-agent system architecture candidates", *Agent-Oriented Software Engineering VI – Lecture Notes in Computer Science*, vol.3950, Springer-Berlin Heidelberg, 2006, pp. 205-217.

[DEB 01] DE BOER L., LABRO E. MORLACCHI P., "A review of methods supporting supplier selection", *European Journal of Purchasing and Supply Management*, vol. 7, no. 2, 2001, pp. 75-89.

[DEG 00] DEGRAEVE Z., LABRO E., ROODHOOFT F., "An evaluation of vendor selection models from a total cost of ownership perspective", *European Journal of Operational Research*, vol. 125, no 1, 2000, pp 34-58.

[DES 95] DESROCHERS A.A., AL-JAAR R.Y., *Applications of Petri Nets in Manufacturing Systems*, Institute of Electrical and Electronics Engineers Press, New York, 1995.

[DIC 93] DICESARE F., HARHALAKIS G., PROTH J.M., SILVA M., VERNADAT F.B., *Practice of Petri Nets in Manufacturing*, Chapman & Hall, London, 1993.

[DON 01] DONG M., CHEN F.F., "Process modelling and analysis of manufacturing Supply chain networks using object-oriented petri nets", *Robotics and Computer Integrated Manufacturing*, vol. 17, 2001, pp. 121-129.

[ELS 07] EL-SAWALHI N., EATON D., RUSTOM R., "Contractor pre-qualification model: State-of-the-art", *International Journal of Project Management*, vol. 25, no. 5, 2007, pp. 465-474.

[GHO 98] GHODSYPOUR H., O'BRIEN C., "A decision support system for supplier selection using an integrated analytic hierarchy process and linear programming", *International Journal of Production Economics*, vol. 56-57, 1998, pp. 199-212.

[HAL 02] HALLIKAS J., VIROLAINEN V.M., TUOMINEN M., "Risk analysis and assessment in network environments: A dyadic case study." *International Journal of Production Economics*, vol. 78, 2002, pp. 42-55.

[HAN 02] HANDFIELD R., WALTON S.V., SROUFE R., MELNYK S.A., "Applying environmental criteria to supplier assessment: A study in the application of the analytical hierarchy process", *European Journal of Operational Research*, vol. 141, 2002, pp. 70-87.

[HOL 98] HOLT G.D., "Which contractor selection methodology?", *International Journal of Project Management*, vol. 16, no. 3, 1998, pp. 153-164.

[JUT 05] JÜTTNER U., "Supply Chain Risk Management", *International Journal of Logistics Management*, vol. 16, no. 1, 2005, pp. 120-141

[KER 06] KERSTEN W., BÖGER M., HOHRATH P., SPATH H., "Supply chain risk management: Development of a theoretical and empirical framework", *Managing Risk in Supply Chains*, vol. 1, 2006, pp. 3-17.

[KUO 98] KUO C.H., HUANG H.P., YEH M.C., "Object-oriented approach of MCTPN for modeling flexible manufacturing system", *International Journal of Advanced Manufacturing Technology*, vol. 14, 1998, pp. 737-749.

[LIU 07] LIU R., KUMAR A., VAN DER AALST W., "A formal modeling approach for supply chain event management", *Decision Support Systems*, vol. 43, no. 3, 2007, pp. 761-778.

[MAK 04] MAKAJIC-NIKOLIC D., PANIC B., VUJOSEVIC M., "Bullwhip effect and supply chain modelling and analysis using CPN tools", *Proc. of the Fifth Workshop and Tutorial on Practical Use of Coloured PNs and the CPN tools*, Aarhus, Denmark, October 8-11, 2004, DAIMI PB-570, pp. 219-234.

[MAL 87] MALONE T.W., "Modeling coordination in organizations and markets", *Management Science*, vol. 33, no. 10, 1987, pp. 1317-1332.

[VON 04] VON MEVIUS M., PIBERNIK R., "Process management in supply chains – a new petri net based approach", *In Proceedings of the 37th Hawaii International Conference on System Sciences*, IEEE, 2004.

[MOO 96] MOORE K.E., GUPTA S.M., "Petri net models of flexible and automated manufacturing systems: a survey", *International Journal of Production Research*, vol. 34, no. 11, 1996, pp. 3001-3035.

[MUR 89] MURATA T., "Petri nets: Properties, analysis and applications", In *Proceedings of IEEE*, vol. 77, no. 4, 1989, pp. 541-580.

[MUS 06] MUSSIGMANN N., "Mitigating risk during strategic supply network modelling", *Managing Risk in Supply Chains*, vol. 1, 2006, pp. 213-226.

[NAR 83] NARASIMHAN R., "An analytical approach to supplier selection", *Journal of Purchasing and Materials Management*, 1983, pp. 27-32.

[NED 06] NEDEB C., FRIEDEWALD A., WAGNER L., NEUMANN L., "Risk management in maritime transportation networks", *Managing Risk in Supply Chains*, vol. 1, 2006, pp. 239-252.

[NYD 92] NYDICK R.L., HILL R., "Using the analytic hierarchy process to structure the vendor selection process", *International Journal of Purchasing and Materials Management*, vol. 28, no 2, 1992, pp 31-6.

[PAL 06] PALANEESWARAN E., NG S.T., KUMARASWAMY M., CHAN W.H.K., "Analytic hierarchy process based supplier selection framework for construction contractors", *The Construction and Building Research Conference of the Royal Institution of Chartered Surveyors*, September 2006.

[ROA 80] ROA C.P., KISER G.E., "Educational buyers' perceptions of vendor attributes", *International Journal of Purchasing and Materials Management*, vol. 16, 1980, pp. 25-30.

[ROM 03] ROMANO P., "Co-ordination and integration mechanisms to manage logistics processes across supply networks", *Journal of Purchasing and Supply Management*, vol. 9, no. 3, 2003, pp. 119-134.

[SAA 80] SAATY, T.L., *The Analytic Hierarchy Process*, McGraw-Hill, New York, 1980.

[SIM 00] SIMCHI-LEVI D., KAMINSKY P. SIMCHI-LEVI E., *Designing and Managing the Supply Chain*. Book & CD-ROM edition, McGraw-Hill/Irwin, 2000.

[TAM 01] TAM M.C.Y., TUMMALA V.M.R. "An application of the AHP in vendor selection of a telecommunications system", *Omega*, vol. 29, no. 2, 2001, pp. 171-182.

[TAN 06] TANG C.S., "Perspectives in supply chain risk management", *International Journal of Production Economics*, vol. 103, 2006, pp. 451-488.

[TIX 02] TIXIER J., DUSSERRE G., SALVI O. GASTON D., "Review of 62 risk analysis methodologies of industrial plants", *Journal of Loss Prevention in the Process Industries*, vol. 15, 2002, pp. 291-303.

[THO 96] THOMAS D.J., GRIFFIN P.M., "Coordinated supply chain management", *European Journal of Operational Research*, vol. 94, no. 1, 1996, pp. 1-15.

[TUN 05] TUNCEL G., BAYHAN G.M., "A high-level petri net based decision support system for real-time scheduling and control of flexible manufacturing systems: an object-oriented approach", in: Sunderam, V., van Albada, G.D., Sloot, P.M.A., Dongarra, J.J. (eds.), *Lecture Notes in Computer Science*, Springer-Verlag, Berlin, 2005, pp. 843-851.

[TUN 07] TUNCEL G., ALPAN G., "A high level petri net based modeling approach for risk management in supply chain networks", *Proceedings of the 21st European Simulation and Modeling Conference – ESM 2007*, pp. 178-185, Malta, 2007.

[TUN 09] TUNCEL G., ALPAN G., "Risk assessment and management for supply chain networks: A case study", *Computers in Industry*, vol. 61, no. 3, 2010, pp. 250-259.

[VIS 00] VISWANADHAM N., RAGHAVAN N.R.S., "Performance analysis and design of supply chains: A petri net approach", *Journal of Operations Research Society*, vol. 51, no. 10, 2000, pp. 1158-1169.

[VAN 00] VAN DER VORST J.G.A.J., BEULENS A.J.M., VAN BEEK P., "Modelling and simulating multi-echelon food systems", *European Journal of Operational Research*, vol. 22, 2000, pp. 354-366.

[VAI 06] OMKARPRASAD V.S., KUMAR S. "Analytic hierarchy process: An overview of applications", *European Journal of Operational Research,* vol. 169, no. 1, 2006, pp. 1-29.

[WEB 91] WEBER C., CURRENT J.R., BENTON W.C., "Vendor selection criteria and methods", *European Journal of Operational Research*, vol. 50, no. 1, 1991, pp. 2-18.

[WIN 06] WINKLER H., KALUZA B., "Integrated performance – and risk management in supply chains – basics and methods" *Managing Risk in Supply Chains*, vol. 1, 2006, pp. 19-36.

[ZHO 93] ZHOU M.C., DICESARE F., *Petri Net Synthesis for Discrete Event Control of Manufacturing Systems*, Kluwer Academic Publishers, Norwell, Massachusetts, 1993.

[ZUR 94] ZURAWSKI R., ZHOU M.C., "Petri nets and industrial applications: A tutorial" *IEEE Transactions on Industrial Electronics*, vol. 41, no. 6, 1994, pp. 567-582.

[VEN 98] VENKATESH K., ZHOU M.C., "Object-oriented design of FMS control software based on object modeling techniques diagrams and Petri nets" *Journal of Manufacturing Systems*, vol. 17, no. 2, 1998, pp. 118-136.

Chapter 8

Simulation of Trust in Supply Chains

8.1. Introduction

Trust is difficult to define, even informally. Some social scientists define it along several dimensions that can be quantified, but how to put all of these separate measures together is still an open question. The concept of trust is ever more present in computer systems today.

This chapter is a joint effort by social and computer scientists towards the understanding of trust in supply chains (SCs). We explore the loop between (the strengthening or weakening of) trust and the effect of this trust on the performance of SCs. This raises two main questions: how does trust impact on the level of information (granularity, quality, diversity of information types, etc.) shared in SC? And does trust always increase the performance of SC?

To investigate these questions we have adopted a multi-agent simulation approach. This has enabled us to define a simulation model of an SC in which we vary the level of trust in order to study either: (i) the impact of trust on the performance of the SC; or (ii) the impact of SC dynamics on the evolution of trust.

The outline of this chapter is as follows. Sections 8.2 through 8.5 review the literature on trust in the social sciences. Section 8.6 reviews the point of view of computer science. The contribution of this chapter, to a multi-agent model of an SC in which performance impacts and is impacted by trust, is introduced in section 8.7.

Chapter written by Yacine OUZROUT, Ludivine CHAZE, Olivier LAVASTRE, Carine DOMINGUEZ and Syed Hossain AKHTER.

An instance of this model is presented in section 8.8 along with some experimental results.

8.2. Literature review: the impact of trust on information-sharing and collaboration

To trust is to believe strongly in someone or something, to have a sense of security in a relationship, to approve the overall behavior of another entity. Thus, trust is commonly regarded as a spontaneous or acquired belief in the moral, emotional or professional behavior of another person, implying that we are unable to imagine that person's deceit, treachery or incompetence.

Trust has largely inspired researchers in sociology [GRA 85], economics [WIL 91] and management [GUL 95, RIN 94]. It has also been studied in relationship marketing, where it appears to be a central variable of dyadic exchange [AND 90] and a factor explaining the direction of long-term inter-firm relationships [GAN 94]. The method used in this chapter can be summed up in the following steps.

8.2.1. *Evolution of trust in the human sciences*

Many of the famous ancient Greek philosophers, including Socrates, Plato and Aristotle, focused on the concept of trust. They saw it as an elusive phenomenon that nevertheless played an important role in the daily organization of society. Within trust, they distinguished between two different kinds of virtue: intellectual virtues (e.g. reason) and moral virtues (e.g. honesty) that inspires citizens' trust in their rulers [NEV 04].

For several centuries after that, rationalism and uncertainty caused the very principle of trust to be rejected. According to Descartes, all certain knowledge and rationale is usable and provides access to knowledge. Kant [KAN 87] studies the relationship between trust and knowledge. He concludes that reason (which is, by definition, rational, objective and unbiased) cannot be the only element for creating knowledge; there are other factors (trust is one of these). He thus explored the idea of several degrees of trust. This principle was later developed with calculated probability [BAY 63]. Contemporary philosophers seem to settle for the coexistence between trust and rationality. In this sense, Gurviez [GUR 98] argues that trust is a belief potentially dissociated from knowledge, which authorizes action and helps to build a social bond. In fact, trust is a feeling underlying any form of calculation.

Trust can take different forms. McAllister [MCA 95], studying relations of trust among executives, shows that all forms of trust are factors influencing development, behavior and performance in inter-organizational relationships. Based on the psychosocial literature and the work of Lewis and Weigert [LEW 85], McAllister [MCA 95] argues that:

– Cognition-based trust is based on individual information on others' reliability and dependability. It requires information that can oscillate between total control and total ignorance. In the former, it is not necessary to have trust; in the latter, there is no rational basis for trust.

– Affect-based trust is based on emotions and on the interpersonal attention and bonds between individuals. McAllister contends that trust is an informal form of coordination to reduce certain administrative costs.

Servet [SER 97] argues that there are also two other forms of trust:

– Vertical trust is present in relationships between superiors and subordinates. The nature of this relationship is inherently asymmetrical and it is therefore necessary to distinguish between ascending and descending trust. These relationships do not reflect perfectly the unequal power and the different commitments.

– Horizontal trust operates between individuals performing similar functions.

Trust has long been neglected in economics. Microeconomics excludes even the notion of trust in people's behavior, seen as *a priori* rational and as seeking optimal personal gain. Williamson [WIL 85] highlights the opportunistic aspect of the individual who readily uses trickery or deception to maximize his or her own gains. In introducing the concept of trust, microeconomists even consider opportunism as useless, and always refer to the trade-off between risk and opportunity. However, Boissin [BOI 99] highlights an evolution in thinking, recognizing trust as a requirement in industrial relations to achieve the respective interests of each partner.

Exploring the notion of trust further, several studies have focused on thematic conventions [BAU 99, HAR 99, SAL 89]. These conventions represent a set of formal rules, or the absence thereof, among several people, thus allowing for optimal coordination. According to Orlean [ORL 94], in a particular situation conventions smooth the behavior of partners, who then adhere to the expectations of their counterpart. Thus, behavioral regularity creates trust and reduces uncertainty.

In Arrow [ARR 74], "trust is an important lubricant of the social system" and its study is fully meaningful in the context of social relations. In 1986, Zucker [ZUC 86] described three forms of trust:

– trust based on the process (process-based trust or personal experience);

– trust based on cultural norms (characteristic-based trust);

– trust associated with a formal structure, whether individual or organizational (institution-based trust).

The definition adopted here is that of Giddens [GID 90], who states that the notion of trust is based on a belief in the reliability of a person or system, that is to say faith in the probity, the love for each other, and faith in the correctness of abstract principles (noted by [NEV 04]). According to Neveu [NEV 04], trust serves to simplify the complexity of modern society and needs to be understood according to definitions in the philosophy of social science.

8.2.2. *Objects of trust*

Trust is considered as an alternative mechanism of control in international relations between firms. It can replace or supplement the mechanisms of the market (price) or hierarchy (authority) [BRA 89]. Once established, this trust stabilizes relationships, which in turn increases the chances of its development [RIN 92, RIN 94]. Trust is then supposed to make inter-firms' relations more efficient by reducing opportunism and strengthening cooperation in a way that does not exist in formal contracts [MOR 94, OUC 80, RIN 92]. It is therefore regarded as an essential component of inter-firm relations [ALT 93]. Hardy and Philips [HAR 98] argue that inter-firm trust is built through a process of communication, and that shared values provide a basis for non-opportunistic behavior. In the same vein, Reve and Stern [REV 86] suggest that trust between members of a channel can be strengthened through shared values and communication. Culture and shared values, the communicative skills of those involved in the inter-organizational relationships, integrity, sincerity, honesty, transparency, good will, predictability, competence and expertise of partners, along with respect for confidentiality of the information exchanged, are all aspects of trust [HAN 02, LEF 06, MOO 93].

8.2.2.1. *Trust as an entity*

Hosmer [HOS 95] discusses the possibility of breaking trust down into four levels:

– *Individual*: trust is individual attention, optimistic about the outcome of an event.

– *Interpersonal*: trust relates to the notions of dependency and vulnerability. Its interpersonal nature may be a condition of cooperation, particularly in the context of unequal relationships between the parties. This type of trust has several determinants. The most important are often regarded as competence and reputation.

– *Economic transactions*: the economic exchange could be considered as a form of interpersonal behavior.

– *Social structures*: one of the missions of the law is to guarantee or secure lines of trust. The process of economic development tends to shift the trust of individuals socially.

Organizational (or institutional) trust occurs between an individual and the organization as a corporation. It can be critical, involving: past and present reputation, power, performance, size and culture of the organization.

8.2.2.2. *Inter-organizational trust*

Lorenz [LOR 01] contends that inter-organizational trust is based on interpersonal trust, since its emergence depends on the relations of trust between participants.

Shapiro *et al.* [SHA 92] were among the first to propose a typology distinguishing three kinds of trust. This typology, widespread in management science, was adopted by Lewicki and Bunker [LEW 96], Sheppard and Tuchinsky [SHE 96] and later by Rousseau *et al.* [ROU 98], in particular. It is thus possible to distinguish:

– *Deterrence-based trust* [SHA 92], also known as calculus-based trust [LEW 96]. As the name suggests, this type of trust appears when one party has trust in others because the cost of sanctions for breaches of trust exceed the potential gains in the case of opportunistic behavior. Trust is thus constrained by fear of "punishment".

– *Trust-based computing* [ROU 98] or knowledge-based trust [LEW 96, SHA 92]. Trust is the result of a rational choice: one party will trust the other because it intends to take action that will be favorable. This decision will stem from an interpretation of information deemed credible about expected behaviors and the presumed intentions of others [BAR 83]. To be unambiguous, this information must be exchanged regularly: the more one party has regular information exchanges with the other, the more familiar it will be with the party, and the more easily and accurately it will be able to anticipate its behavior. Reputation can be an additional factor of influence in establishing trust. The research results in the short term may also be a way to test the other party [ROU 98].

– Finally, *relationship trust*, also called affective trust [COL 90, MCA 95] or identity-based trust [LEW 96]. This trust is based on the past and the memory of former relationships with the other party, when it was serious and reliable. It is thus possible to be confident and to have positive expectations. Social psychologists have shown that the fact of belonging to the same social network leads to more honest (trustworthy) behavior and to the development of this type of trust within and outside an individual's own group.

The advantages of trust are clear, because its presence can make incompleteness in contracts acceptable. Generally, not all of the elements and possible consequences of the relationship have to be specified because, as Jarillo [JAR 98] explains, the partners' decision criteria and motivations are the same. When trust is established, the nature of the relationship will be influenced in three main respects. First, the magnitude of risk associated with opportunistic behavior decreases, as does its perception by the partners. Thus, the costs generated by having to counteract opportunistic behavior and to establish mechanisms to monitor each other (in the case of mistrust) disappear. Second, as Williamson argues [WIL 94], the congruence of goals means that, through common objectives, problems and inequities will tend to disappear in the short to long term. Finally, trust can be mutually beneficial, allowing for some degree of incompleteness of contracts and *ad hoc* adjustments [GAN 94, MOH 94].

The congruence of goals is made possible by establishing trust between two parties. Trust allows both parties to improve the quality of the exchange relationship and the of goal congruence, as risks can be shared and possibly reduced [MAC 74]. Risk reduction is due to the long-term nature of relational exchange that reduces the opportunistic temptations of both parties. This reduction will also lower the costs of bureaucratic management because the parties will use relational means to achieve the goals of joint production. In short, goal incongruence is high in situations where the content and rarity of information, and asymmetric dependence on it, encourage opportunistic rather than cooperative behavior. Conversely, the congruence of purpose will be predominant when the parties, *ex ante* and naturally, have the same interests, and when they believe that their gains in the case of cooperative behavior will be higher than in the case of opportunism.

8.2.3. *Conclusion*

Trust can be approached differently. First, in classical economics, parties are seen as individuals whose social context does not influence their behavior. However, in sociology and socioeconomics, trust emerges as a complex system that should not only be considered in legal terms. Trust explains certain behaviors inherent in inter-organizational relationships. This complexity begs the question of whether trust stems from calculations made by the stakeholders in their own interests, or whether it describes a specific type of interaction directly linking people together irrespective of their interests [ORL 94].

8.3. Literature review: from trust in the organization to trust in inter-organizational relationships

"Our implication of the boundedness of capabilities is that no firm – even the most integrated – has the capabilities necessary for all activities in the chain of production. The result is that firms must link up with other firms" [LAN 92]. Every organization must establish exchange relationships with other industrial firms, whether they are subcontractors or suppliers selling goods and/or services. Companies buy from their partners upstream in order to meet their own requirements and those of their customers in terms of production, quality, price, quantity, delivery time, and so on. They must build relationships with relevant partners upstream to satisfy their different needs.

8.3.1. *Is trust useful for business?*

8.3.1.1. *Trust, opportunism and bounded rationality*

In neoclassical economics, efficiency is maximized and bounded rationality is the assumption that learning is based on the economics of transaction costs. Influenced by Simon, of whom he was a student, Williamson dropped out the traditional concept of substantive rationality. This type of rationality (from Chicago school) is based on a clear understanding of the transaction conditions, where as the transaction conditions are unknown (or even unrecognized) by the individuals and the firm in the transaction.

The concept of bounded rationality was developed by Simon [SIM 61], based on the finding that individuals have limited cognitive capacities: economic agents are supposed to be "intentionally rational, but only to a limited extent" [WIL 94]. According to Kreps [KRE 90], bounded rationality has two major consequences: an increase in both pre-transaction costs and contracting costs incurred. Bounded rationality implies that economic agents cannot foresee all of the contingencies of future situations. As Radner proposed it, contracts are therefore necessarily incomplete [RAD 68]. Williamson showed that complete contracting is no longer a realistic organizational alternative when the assumption of bounded rationality is taken into account [WIL 94]. This feature of incompleteness broadens the scope of transaction costs along four axes [TIR 98]:

– first, not all of the contingencies with which the parties will be confronted are predictable or imaginable at the time of signing the contract;

– second, even if everything could be planned and imagined, there would be too many contingencies and comments for inclusion in the contract;

– third, checking the contract (to verify in detail that all partners can meet all of the conditions) has a high cost;

– finally, provision for legal constraints, to ensure that the contract is not breached, entails high legal costs.

If rationality is not bounded, the terms of the trade are negotiated in a planned manner. If there is no opportunism, but rationality is bounded (missing information), it is not possible to rely purely on trust and the promise of future conduct. When there is bounded rationality and opportunism, it is necessary to manage and control the transaction by the "rule". The cost of this control will be much higher if the investment is specific (idiosyncratic) and the transaction casual. In this case, an arbitrator will be required to resolve potential conflicts [MAR 91]. According to Williamson [WIL 94] there are two ways to economize on bounded rationality: the first concerns the decision making and the second the structures of governance. Thus, organizations are one way to "save the bounded rationality". Bounded rationality is then nothing but a complicated way to say that information is costly [WIL 94].

8.3.1.2. *Opportunism*

This is the second behavioral factor influencing trust into inter-organizational relations. Williamson [WIL 85] defines opportunism as seeking self-interest with guile [WIL 91]. This includes the most obvious forms, such as lying, stealing and cheating, including both active and passive forms, *ex ante* and *ex post* [WIL 94]. Three levels can be distinguished in the pursuit of personal interest:

– the highest level dealing with the economics of transaction costs is opportunism;

– the intermediate stage is merely the pursuit of an interest;

– the lowest level (which is practically zero) consists of obedience.

Ex ante and *ex post* opportunism are known in the insurance literature under the respective terms adverse selection and moral hazard [GIL 90]. Adverse selection (or *ex ante* opportunism) is a consequence of the difficulty (or inability) of insurers to distinguish between clients' risk levels. Moral hazard (or *ex post* opportunism) is the accentuation of negligent conduct by the insured when they know they are covered by an insurance contract. More generally, opportunism refers to the disclosure of incomplete or misleading information, especially calculated efforts to mislead, distort, disguise, confuse or cause confusion. It is responsible for real or artificial asymmetric information, which greatly complicates problems of economic organization [WIL 94]. Thus "transactions subject to *ex post* opportunism will be profitable if safeguards can be devised *ex ante*" [WIL 94]. This refers to the simple contracting schema (see Figure 8.1).

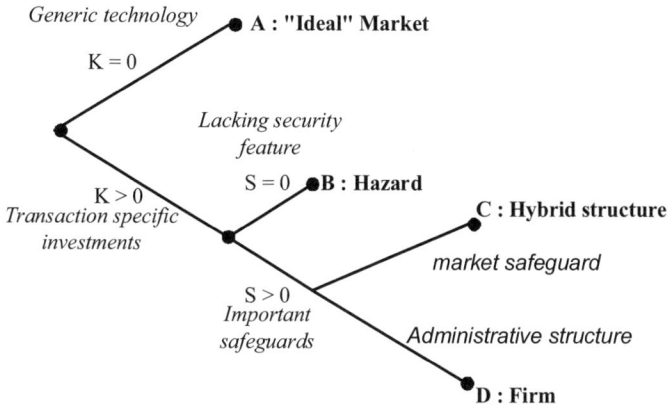

Figure 8.1. *Simple contracting scheme (adapted from [WIL 85, WIL 93, WIL 94])*

Brousseau [BRO 89] argues that opportunism has two sources. First is the costly nature of information. Here the necessary trade-off is between deciding to make a decision now, with the information available (but such information is fragmented), or choosing to seek additional information before deciding (thus incurring higher investigation costs but in the hope of obtaining more comprehensive and relevant information [REI 95]). The second is the complementarities of assets.

To this analysis of opportunism we can add a reference to the incongruity of purpose (one of two sources of transaction costs), because opportunism is a particular form of the inconsistency of purpose. If the participants' bounded rationality and opportunism were eliminated, then complete contracts could be written and governance structures would be unnecessary.

8.3.1.3. *Trust and commitment*

In the literature on trust in marketing, the role of commitment is crucial and is an essential ingredient in building inter-organizational relationships in the long term [AND 92, MOR 94]. Moorman *et al.* [MOO 93] and Gundlach *et al.* [GUN 95] define commitment as the participants' desire to maintain a relationship that adds value, and to make a sustained effort to protect themselves and anticipate potential problems. Dwyer *et al.* [DWY 87] define it as an implicit or explicit guarantee of the continuity of the relationship, and maintain that commitment is the highest level of relational links.

In the context of inter-organizational exchange, commitment is characteristic of a stage of development of the relationship. The commitment phase in development models of inter-organizational relationships [DWY 87, FOR 84, HIL 72, ROB 67, WEB 72] is the fact that, once interdependencies are established, true loyalty exists. The partners have no real inclination to change because trust and its benefits are apparent in the relationship. Three elements characterize engagement [SCA 79] and thus the development of the industrial trade relationship:

– the inputs (resources, information, emotional factors, social ties, etc.) provided by each partner are necessary to the others and constitute an important element of the relationship [BLA 64];

– the sustainability of the exchange: both partners should recoup their investment and their resources if they are to maintain a lasting relationship. In case of failure of the exchange at this stage, a net loss of investments will occur;

– the stability of the contributions is essential to prevent entropy of the physical exchange that would cause disintegration of the relationship between the two partners. In other words, the parties must continue to "feed" the trade.

The following diagram affords a better understanding of the various alternatives for the development of industrial exchange, depending on the investments made by both partners.

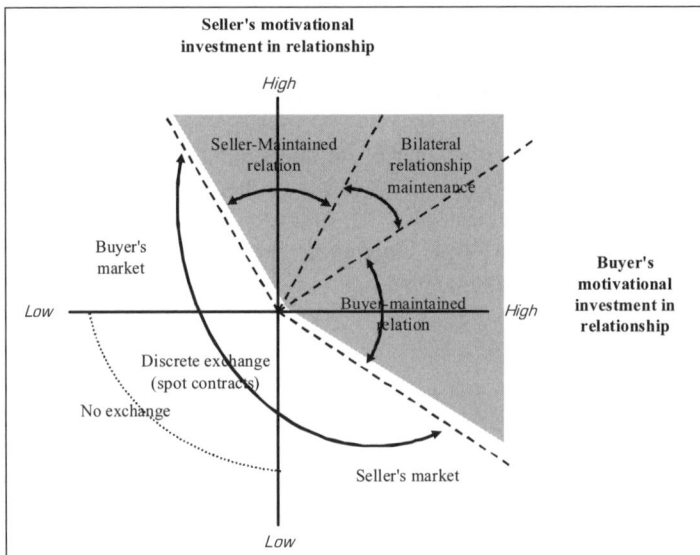

Figure 8.2. *The hypothesized realm of the buyer-seller relationship (adapted from [DWY 87])*

As part of the industrial exchange in four stages (search for information on potential sources of supply; establishment of the relationship; development of trade; and breach of the exchange relationship), the relationship must be located in the shaded part of the scheme. Consequently, a relationship, entered in the unshaded, will be an *ad hoc* relationship, without any development phase of the exchange and for which costs will be minimal disruption. The axes define the investment incentive of each party in the relationship, especially in the expected net benefits of the relationship.

Both schemes have the terms and conditions of developing an industrial exchange relationship given in Figure 8.3.

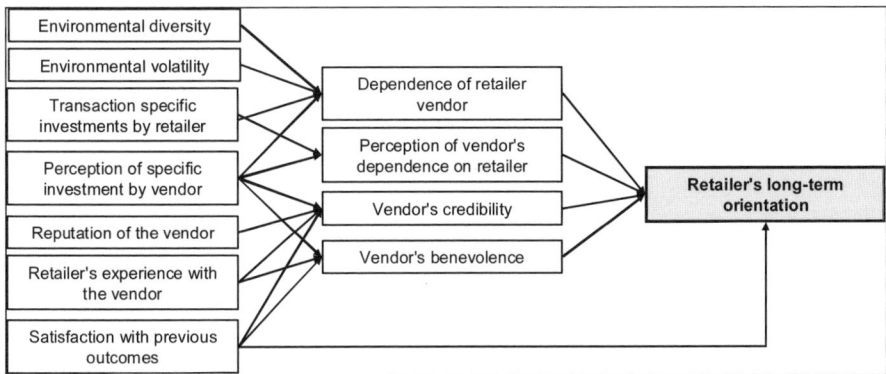

Figure 8.3. *Model of retailer's and vendor's long-term orientation (adapted from [GAN 94])*

8.3.1.4. *Conclusion: towards a calculated trust?*

Williamson asserts that, in market relations, "trust is irrelevant to commercial exchange and reference to trust in this connection promotes confusion". As Granovetter [GRA 00] has pointed out, for Williamson the firm is a "functional alternative" to the trust, whose authority is substituted for bargaining and allows parties to settle disputes constructively. Even if trust negated opportunistic behavior, the establishment of an authority as a control mechanism represents a significant cost for those concerned. According to Williamson, even in trust, man is a self-interested and scheming person. Rationality inevitably pushes the parties to maximize their well-being and to act individualistically in their own environment. Orlean [ORL 94] and Karpik [KAR 98], on the other hand, highlight the limits of Williamsonian theories and develop the concept of trust and its use in the field of management science research.

8.3.2. *Trust in inter-organizational settings*

In 1998, Karpic [KAR 98] argued that Williamson's work [WIL 94] is not representative of them and underline that Williamson needs to exclude a concept that seems to threaten the unity of the neo-classic model. Moreover, since trust was considered secondary to a mechanism of coordination of economic activities reduced to the market and the organization, it also threatened the coherence of the transaction cost theory. This theory, despite the proliferation of variations and hybrids, was fundamentally dualistic. For Williamson, the trust calculated would appear to be useless. In fact, calculation does not require trust; only common interests push for cooperation. Yet the basic concept of trust excludes any form of calculation. While Coleman considers trust to be a series of unselfish acts, Williamson posits a world of computing and common observation in which each individual has the same vision of his or her social life. In this world, social exchange is also regulated by calculation. This is different to the work of Karpik and Lahiri [LAH 98], who observed a plurality of knowledge mobilized in social action. Thus, since each situation can be associated with an action inherent to each individual, and therefore not resulting from a calculation, it offers a unique solution. As each individual has their own free will, their decisions depend on multiple frames of interpretation and discussion processes. Hence, they depend on personal opinion processes that are more complex than the calculation to which Williamson refers.

Karpik [KAR 98] then aims to deconstruct Williamson's arguments explaining an economic perspective and the calculated behavior of social trust. Williamson seeks to demonstrate the behavioral assumption of an opportunism-based world of computing and common observation. The eco-sociological approach contrasts with that type of socioeconomic approach. Trust has its place in both the social and economic worlds. Karpik therefore calls for an analysis of the process of trust and its role in economic regulation.

Like the trial developed by Karpik, the concept of trust has been the subject of many studies, such as Salais and Storper [SAL 93] and Orlean [ORL 94]. The latter also reverts to Williamson's vision of trust. In line with the work of Douglas [DOU 89], he shows that trust can be an independent mode of interaction between people, over and above their individual interests and calculations. For these authors, social relations are not reducible to simple formatting games of interest. It is therefore important to examine both the interests and trust in order to better understand social and economic relations. Orlean [ORL 94], by inverting the way of Williamson's reasoning based on economic relations, proposes a model of universal behavior based on a calculation where the relationship between humans cannot be found in a permanent social shape. In this case, trust will depend on the specific relationship between the various stakeholders and include a large variety of factors. The author also endeavors to show that trust between partners plays a part in consolidating and stabilizing relations. We can, moreover, consider that there are moral ties in any cooperation between two individuals.

By incorporating the work of Kreps, Orlean [ORL 94] demonstrates what he calls the incompleteness of the market logic. This he defines as a configuration where the strict horizontality of the relationship – in the sense that individuals share nothing except their desire to maximize their personal utility – leads to a dead end [ORL 94]. For both authors, mutual trust must use one of the following: the contract (judiciary), the oath (or deity belief), or reputation in a society. This is desecrated in the case of interactions when the duration is unknown by the parties. Orlean [ORL 94] argues that the introduction of an external load or lack of interest in the game creates a social space beyond all logic and market, making trust possible. Thus, for X to trust Y, both must belong to the same community or religious law (contract and oath). The issue of trust in others becomes a question of belief in each other as reliable members of the community. Therefore, X and Y are not abstract individuals charged by the sole desire to increase their well-being in all circumstances. Orlean [ORL 94] maintains that partners are caught in some non-economic social relationships that define them by giving them an identity. So, the economic theories disregarding subjective aspects of membership by substituting them with the universality of interest need to be amended. The importance of trust in inter-organizational relationships, for example, can be approached as a form of belonging to a community of faith. Social mediation in the institutional environment is therefore essential to trust. This concept can enter the new logic, whose characteristic is to give rise to modes of behavior representation for other agents radically distinct from traditional strategic forms [ORL 94], and thus understand the basis of the trust.

It is also interesting to compare the work of Boltanski and Thevenot [BOL 91], cited and expanded on by Salais and Storper [SAL 93]. This perspective highlights the existence of different forms of trust in relational environments, and particularly in inter-organizational relationships. Generally, trust is regarded as having a positive impact on the Inter-Organisational Relationship (RIO) by eliminating, or at least limiting, opportunistic behavior [DWY 87, RIN 94, UZZ 97]. Trust, it is argued, ensures the adequacy of ethical values among partners and facilitates the establishment of a virtuous circle of successful relationships [LOR 96]. These studies highlight not only the subjectivity present in any cooperation, but also the influence of time, learning mechanisms and interconnections in the evolution of inter-organizational relationships. A limited partnership is not a simple organizational link. It continues through relationships and is influenced by the personality of the protagonists and their interpersonal conventions [BRU 05, DET 98, FRO 98]. It leads to the belief in partnerships as facilitators of exchange in a social network [GRA 00]. In one of his studies, Brulhart [BRU 05] concludes that the experience of working together with partners to generate routines and reflexes facilitates the functioning of cooperation and coordination because everyone can gain a mutual understanding of others and their idiosyncrasies. It is then possible to discuss how to build this "mutual understanding".

Building trust in relationships may require the presence of institutions. Pavlou [PAV 02] distinguishes inter-organizational trust from institutional trust. Institutional trust is in fact considered as an antecedent of trust. Inter-organizational trust is defined as "the subjective belief with which organizational members collectively assess that a population of organizations will perform potential transactions according to their confident expectations, irrespective of their ability to fully monitor them" [PAV 02, p. 218]. Thus defined, it consists of two dimensions. First, credibility, which relates to "a party's predictability, reliability, honesty, expertise, and competence" or "the extent to which a buyer organization believes that seller firms have the intention to perform the transaction effectively and reliably because of fears of imposing costs on opportunism" [PAV 02, p. 219]. The second dimension is benevolence. This refers to "the expectation that a party will act fairly and will not take unfair advantage of the trustor, even given the chance" or the "extent to which buyer organizations believe that seller organizations have intentions and motives beneficial to them, even when new conditions without prior commitment arise" [PAV 02, p. 219]. The level of trust in inter-organizational relationships and exchanges has direct consequences on the level of information-sharing between partners.

8.3.3. *Trust and inter-organizational information-sharing in a SC*

Trust is considered to be a necessary antecedent of information sharing in a SC [GAL 03, MAD 09]. Information sharing has always been considered to be beneficial in a SC. Lee and colleagues [LEE 97] were the first to identify information asymmetry as the main reason for the amplification of the demand signal and the fluctuation of the inventory level along a SC. This phenomenon, called the "bullwhip effect", has been extensively analyzed [CAC 00, COH 04]. Information sharing can also yield other advantages, such as reducing costs, improving service levels, and reducing lead times and stock-outs [ANG 04]. It not the quantity of data exchanged in the SC that is most important, however, but its quality and ability to generate the highest benefits and performance [BAL 98, GOS 04, PRE 00] . Gosain *et al.* [GOS 04] recommend that organizations prioritize their investments towards improving the quality of information shared with their business partners rather than sharing low-quality information in a broad variety of areas.

The notion of an information supply chain (ISC) has only recently been introduced. It aims to create and unify concepts, methods, theories and technologies for information-sharing problems [LEG 08]. According to Sun and Yen [SUN 05], "an ISC fulfils users' information requirements by a network of Information-Sharing Agents (ISA) that gather, interpret, and satisfy the requirements with proper information".

Inter-organizational information systems (IOIS) support information-sharing in a SC, Electronic Data Interchange (EDI) being the most well-known IOIS. The higher the level of integration between IOIS, the more efficient the information-sharing in a SC will be [SAE 05].

Another key point is the type of information that is shared along the SC [LEE 00]. Seidmann and Sundararajan [SEI 98] distinguish four levels of information-sharing. First, the order is the simplest form and, strictly speaking, is not considered as information sharing. Second, operational information-sharing includes the transmission of information on an operative level exceeding order information, such as inventory levels. Third, the sharing of strategic information requires long-term contractual agreements. Finally, strategic and competition information-sharing includes, for example, the sharing of market information between competing firms. According to Lee and Whang [LEE 00], information sharing on the inventory level can contribute to decreases in necessary safety stock levels and is the basis of many collaboration models. Other types of data shared lead to different benefits in the SC. We will now look at factors that promote trust and mutual understanding.

8.4. The trust model: criteria and variables to define trust

Our literature review, the first part of our research shows that no real consensus exists on the subject of trust. Consequently, some qualifiers or distinctions are recurrent: trust may be weak or strong, tenuous or robust, personal or institutional, etc.

8.4.1. *The measurement scale*

The concept of trust is very large; too large to be measured directly.

If we consider all this includes, without going into details of the criteria/variables characterizing trust, the notion of trust cannot be measured by one scale alone. We therefore need to use several indirect variables (such as honesty, cooperation or communication) to measure trust. We are, however, going to detail the variables/criteria. In our fieldwork, we are interested in the perception and representation of managers. With closed questions, we asked respondents for their level of agreement or disagreement with a statement.

The measurement scale used was a Liker scale of seven items:

1. Strongly agree;

2. Agree;

3. Agree somewhat;

4. Undecided;

5. Disagree somewhat;

6. Disagree;

7. Strongly disagree.

Neutrality (i.e. the average) is 4. This statistical methodology follows the recommendations of classical science management, including of Evrard, Pras and Roux [EVR 93]. A scale with seven categories instead of five is preferred. Many of these are commonly implemented in research using this measurement tool. As shown by Churchill and Peter [CHU 84, PET 86], scores revealing the highest reliability are found in studies where there are a large number of items constituting the scale, with many points in each item. Evrard, Pras and Roux [EVR 93] argued that the optimal number of items is seven (with a margin of two or more categories). To simplify the modeling and simulation, groups of items were made. Thus, the terms "strongly disagree", "disagree" and "disagree somewhat" were grouped under the heading "disagree"; and "strongly agree", "agree" and "agree somewhat" were grouped under the heading "agree". These groupings are possible and do not call into question the robustness of statistic treatments.

8.4.2. *The criteria for measuring trust*

Many scales for measuring trust exist in the management literature. Morgan and Hunt [MOR 94], for example, use the Larzerele and Huston [LAR 80] dyadic scale which includes the major facets of trust (reliability, integrity and strong belief). [SWA 85, SWA 88], and [SCH 85] also established scales, designed primarily to measure the purchasing manager's trust in the seller. These scales are mainly found in the English-speaking world, where a difference is made between "trust" and "confidence". We can say that "trust" refers to the reliability and belief in something and that "trust" means the trustworthiness and honesty of an individual. Guibert [GUI 96] adapts this precise scale to the French context and obtains the following items:

In your relationship with your supplier:

1. He is perfectly honest and loyal;

2.   You can count on him;

3.   I have great trust in him.

With trust, as indicated by the following diagram from Morgan and Hunt [MOR 94], involvement in the relationship can be established.

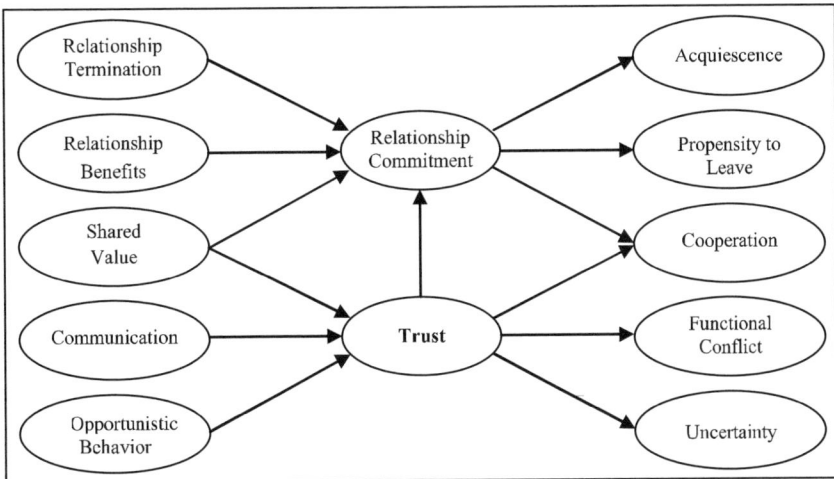

Figure 8.4. *The Key Mediating Variable (KMV) model of relationship marketing [MOR 94]*

Personal relationships can also serve as a basis for establishing trust, especially in small to medium enterprises where the heads of the two companies are very close (few intermediaries – such as a buying center – between the two partners) in the phases of negotiation and in course of the relationship. These interpersonal relationships play a role in choosing a new supplier: the more the client company has personal relationships with its suppliers, the less it will need to seek information about them and the lower the costs of information searches will be. Zaheer and Venkatraman [ZAH 94] operationalized inter-firm trust in the insurance sector by using three items on a Likert scale of seven points (ranging from strongly agree to don't agree at all). They thus obtained a Cronbach's alpha of 0.81:

– the main company and our agency have a high degree of mutual trust;

– the company is primarily known for its fair trade (fair dealing);

– the main company is delivering.

Bensaou and Venkatraman [BEN 95] measured mutual trust between manufacturers and suppliers in terms of the following two criteria (alpha 0.77):

– degree of mutual trust between partners (seven-point Likert ranging from "extremely low" to "extremely strong");

– degree of comfort in sharing information with critical and sensitive partner (seven-point Likert ranging from "very uncomfortable" to "very comfortable").

Inter-organizational trust was measured by Hart and Sounders [HAR 98b] in the context of EDI on a five-point scale ranging from "extremely unimportant" to "important" to "critical" through the following items (they obtained an alpha of 0.95):

– honesty and accuracy of time (deadline) established by partners;

– monitoring partners' promises;

– partners' honesty in business negotiations.

There is also more or less direct trust, proposed by Guibert [GUI 96] from the Morgan and Hunt scale [MOR 94], on three items that have obtained an alpha of 0.88 in the relationship with a supplier (five-point Likert scale):

– he is perfectly fair and honest;

– you can count on him;

– we have great trust in him.

Sohier [SOH 97] measures trust between customers and suppliers based on the work of Ganesan [GAN 94], who assesses the credibility and goodwill of partner exchange in three respects:

– *credibility*: this supplier always keeps its commitments;

– *benevolence*: the supplier is prepared to take extraordinary measures to respond appropriately to our needs;

– *opportunism*: in some cases the supplier uses its position to impose its conditions of sale and delivery.

Sako [SAK 98] explored the relationship between trust and inter-organizational performance in a sample of 1,415 automotive suppliers in Japan, the US and Europe. The author conceptualizes the three aspects: contractual trust, competence and benevolence. The list of items used is as follows (on a Likert scale of five points ranging from "strongly agree" to "totally disagree"):

– *trust contract*: we prefer to have everything written in detail in our contract (inverted scale);

– *jurisdiction*: the advice we give our customers is often not useful (inverted scale);

– *honesty (fairness)*: we depend on our client, whom we have often treated in an honest way.

8.4.3. *The criteria*

All criteria are derived from a critical review of the literature and, to a lesser extent, from a qualitative survey of supply chain management. We consider that the different variables (or criteria) of trust are:

– honesty (e.g. the supplier's compliance with the contract);

– credibility (e.g. the supplier always keeps its commitments);

– experience (e.g. the supplier is aware of good practices and has the knowledge necessary to meet my needs);

– jurisdiction (e.g. the advice we give our partners is useful);

– sincerity (e.g. the supplier is frank and honest);

– predictability (e.g. the supplier has no opportunistic behavior);

– transparency (e.g. this supplier shares complete information on the processes);

– goodwill (e.g. the supplier is prepared to take extraordinary measures to respond appropriately to our needs);

– commitment (e.g. the supplier invests in the relationship);

– respect for the confidentiality of information exchanged (e.g. the provider respects the confidentiality of information that I provide);

– communication skills (e.g. the supplier meets our needs through effective communication);

– shared values (e.g. suppliers share the same moral values as us);

– similarity (e.g. the supplier belongs to the same network as we do);

– sharing working methods (e.g. the supplier agreed with us on all processes that are common or individual);

– influence in the network (e.g. the supplier is recognized in the professional network);

– sharing information, type of information shared.

8.5. The trust model: the proposed trust model

The literature on trust mobilizes the human and social sciences, thus reflecting a great wealth of variables to characterize and define the concept, as evidenced by the 15 variables identified in the literature review (above). This suggests that trust is a weighted average of all the defining criteria:

$$Cc = (\alpha.Ho + \beta.Cr + \gamma.Ex + \delta.Co + \varepsilon.S + \zeta.Pr + \eta.T + \theta.Bv + \iota.En + \kappa.Rp + \lambda.Ha + \mu.Pv + \nu.Rs + \xi.Pt + o.I) / (\alpha + \beta + \gamma + \delta + \varepsilon + \zeta + \eta + \theta + \iota + \kappa + \lambda + \mu + \nu + \xi + o)$$

However, the literature does not attempt to precisely define the weight of each criterion. Each individual or entity is expected to have its own scale of values against the various criteria of the components of trust, i.e. the weight of each set of weights for each criterion. In this research we consider that, overall, a criterion is *a priori* identical and equal to 1. In our present research, behavior representing trust would be expressed as follows:

$$Cc = (Ho + Cr + Ex + Co + S + Pr + T + Bv + En + Rp + Ha + Pv + Rs + Pt + I) / 15$$

where:

Cc = behavior of trust;

Ho = honesty;

Cr = credibility;

Ex = experiment;

Co = competence;

S = sincerity;

Pr = predictability;

T = transparency;

Bv = goodwill;

In = commitment;

Rs = respect the confidentiality of information exchanged;

Ha = communication skills;

Pv = shared values;

Rs = resemblance;

Pt = sharing working methods; and

I = Influence in the network.

8.5.1. *Behavior as regards trust and information exchange*

To classify behaviors and relate them to a phenomenon of information-sharing, we propose the following scale:

– 0 <CC <0.5: behavior of mistrust;

– 0.5 ≤ Cc <1.5: behavior of moderate trust;

– 1.5 ≤ Cc <2: behavior of trust.

0<Cc<0.5	0,5 → 1.5	1.5 → 2
		Trust

```
├────────────┼──────────────────────────┼────────────────┤
```

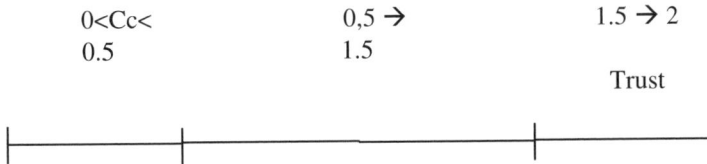

We believe that there is a strong positive correlation between the amount of information exchanged and the level of confidence. We will now analyze the relationship between trust and the following elements:

– The quality of the relationship (performance, stability):

- *the more I trust, the better the overall performance of the relationship will be.*

- information sharing,

- investments to implement and support the information system between partners,

- short-term information (operational/execution),

- medium-term information (tactical),

- long-term information (strategic);

- *the more I trust, the more we share and exchange long-term information (strategic information).*

- *the more I trust, the more I invest in advanced IT systems.*

– Relationship policies:

- *the more I trust, the less I control the activity of my partner.*

– Decision-making:

- the more I trust, the more the decisions are taken collectively.

– Dependency:

- the more I trust, the more the decisions are taken collectively, and the more dependent I am on my partner.

Based on these elements, we also have to define the type of information that will be shared at the different levels of the SC. We distinguish the sharing of operational information (called operational and tactical level here) from the sharing of strategic information [SEI 98]:

– at the strategic level (long term: several months/years), for example production planning, distribution management and policies, transportation optimization strategies, forecasting, etc.;

– at the tactical level (medium term: several days/weeks), for example purchasing, inventory management, transportation management, production management, etc.;

– at the operational level (short term: one or several days), for example delivery system, ordering process, billing process, etc.

Depending on the level of trust, the following information is available to the partner:

– visibility of the customer orders;

– visibility of the supplier stock level;

– visibility of the final customer demand;

– visibility of the customer forecast.

We analyze the impact of trust on information-sharing and on the global performance of the relationship. The quality of the information will differ, depending on the level of trust:

– information transmitted with various levels of comprehensiveness, for example when we send the order history, we send the full history or only that of the last x periods;

– information not transmitted;

– information deliberately truncated.

In a SC, the more we trust, the more we exchange information on the demand as well as on the forecast of the last consumer. *In a SC*, the more we trust, the more we exchange information on the level of stocks as well as on the forecast of the suppliers.

Different levels of trust imply various types of shared information. Very simply, we can propose:

– *level 1 of trust*: sharing operational information;

– *level 2 of trust*: sharing tactical/strategic information.

Data shared in a SC	Example of data shared in SC	References
Operational	– Product (identification, classification, description)	[LEG 08]
	– Customer demand: place order with sales data (prices, sales category, brand, currency, tax rate)	
	– Order status (incoming order, deliver goods, shipping delay, production delay)	[LEE 00; LEG 08]
	– Outgoing delivery	
	– Incoming delivery	[MOB 02; TAN 01]
	– Advanced shipping notice	[PAT 07]
	– Sales forecast	
	– Promotional plans	[MAD 09]
Tactical – strategic	– Supplier costs	
	– Overall costs	
	– Lead time	
	– Supplier inventory level	[COH 04; LEE 00]
	– Final customer sales (at the point of sales)	[MOB 02]
	– Supply capacity	[PAT 07]
	– Promotional strategies	
	– Pricing strategies	
	– Targeted supplier relationship	
	– Forecasting data	
	– Market research data	[FEL 03]
	– Consumer needs	[COH 04]

Table 8.1. *Type of information shared in a SC*

There are various levels of visibility in a supply chain (see Figure 8.5):

– *minimum visibility*: company A is only able to see the demand of company B;

– *medium visibility*: company A is only able to see the demand of the levels N+2 (companies B and C in the diagram);

– *maximum visibility*: company A is only able to see the demand of the first level of the SC (company D in the diagram), including the demand of all the participants in the chain.

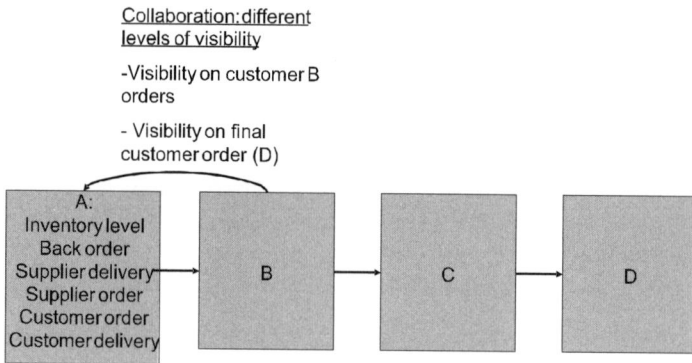

Figure 8.5. *Types of trust behavior generate different types of shared information*

The literature distinguishes the antecedents of trust (what explains trust in a SC) from the determinants of trust (the elements or criteria that characterize trust) [PAV 02]. In our case, we combine the antecedents and criteria of trust to speak about "behavior of trust in the SC".

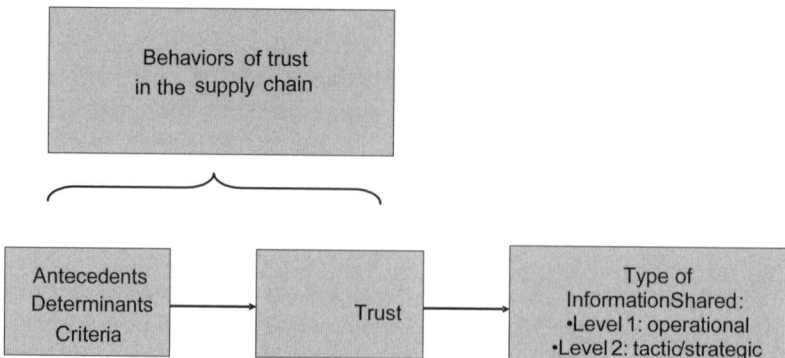

Figure 8.6. *Types of trust behavior generate different types of information-sharing*

The final step in the model defines global levels of performance for the supply chain. The simulation model will illustrate different scenarios:

– *For the company that receives the information*, depending on the behavior of trust, the company will:

- not take into account the information;

- check the received information before using it, to ensure that it is relevant;

- consider the information received is totally relevant (and therefore not verify it).

– *For the company that sends the information*, depending on the behavior of trust (level of trust and criteria), the company will:

- send the real and relevant information;

- send the real and relevant operational information;

- send the real and relevant tactic/strategic information;

- send relevant but incomplete information;

- send false information;

- not send information.

8.6. Literature review: trust as seen by computer scientists

We now turn our attention to the engineering sciences, especially computer science. We focus more particularly on multi-agent systems, since this field seems to be the area most closely related to trust in SCs. Other fields of computer science may also use the word "trust" but in different contexts. For instance, network security also involves trust, but in the sense that a resource may be used by an agent only if this agent is trusted by a recognized authority, and this trust is proven by the possession of a certificate digitally signed by the authority. In other words, this authority has provided a piece of authentic, unforgeable and non-repudiable information testifying that the considered agent is allowed to use the resource. Of course, the point of view of security is not completely disconnected from that of multi-agent systems, since security concerns lead to the development of the tools necessary to establish trust in a multi-agent system. This can be seen in the famous figure of the semantic Web architecture (see Figure 8.7) in which trust is at the top. This trust is enabled by digital signature (developed by the security community) in order to contribute to the semantic Web, which is a community closely related to that of multi-agent systems.

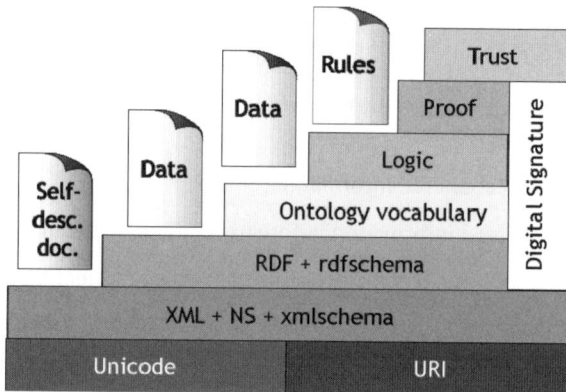

Figure 8.7. *Trust in the semantic Web architecture*
(www.w3.org/2000/Talks/1206-xml2k-tbl/slide10-0.html)

Next, multi-agent systems naturally model decision-making when several decision-makers interact. In fact, an agent may be defined as an autonomous program that is reactive, proactive and has social abilities [WOO 02]. The important feature in this definition is the social abilities of the agents that provide them with beliefs about other agents, and thus trust. Consequently, trust is important for multi-agent systems. For instance, Ramchurn and colleagues [RAM 04] review the literature on trust in multi-agent systems and show that the purpose of trust is to minimize the uncertainty in interactions. They also summarize the research on trust in multi-agent systems, as shown in Figure 8.8. The reader is referred to this review for details.

Despite all the attention paid by the multi-agent community to SC [CHA 06], we found little research on trust in SC. We actually only found one model by Meijer [MEI 06, TYK 08]. He worked on a game and its associated simulation called the "trust and tracing game". This game models a three-level SC in which players trade products of hidden quality where the quality of the traded items is either "high" (e.g. fresh food) or "low". This information is obtained from the suppliers, but they may lie. When a firm does not trust its supplier, it asks the tracing agency (i.e. the game leader) for the true value of the information. If the tracing agency confirms what the supplier announced, then the firm has to pay a tracing fee. Otherwise, the tracing agency fines the cheater. Hence, the supplier has incentives to reveal the real quality of the products, in order to not be detected and fined.

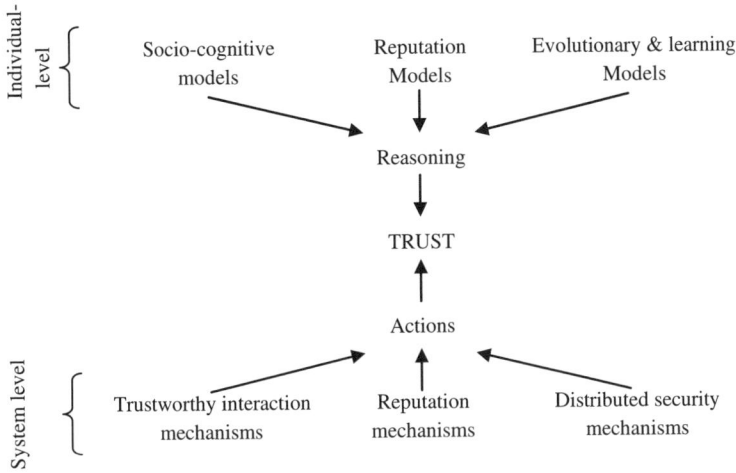

Figure 8.8. *A classification of approaches to trust in multi-agent systems [RAM 04]*

8.7. The simulation model

Based on the model of trust described above, we propose a simulation model to implement the different criteria and behaviors of trust, using some intelligent agents. The aim of this simulation model is to evaluate the performance of a SC, taking into account the level of trust between the partners in the chain. We will make the connection between level of trust and level of performance by analyzing information sharing between the companies. As we saw in the previous section, the type of information shared depends on the level of trust and the behavior of trust between the partners.

In the first part of this section we describe the simulation model and the design of the different agents, including the trust behaviors, and then present a case study, some experiments and results.

This section presents architecture for modeling the dynamic behavior of the proposed SC trust model. Our aim is to design an efficient simulation tool that can be applied to evaluate the global performance of the chain, based on the trust behaviors of its participants. The link between trust and performance will be obtained via the level and the quality of information sharing. For that purpose, we first implement the trust variables and behaviors inside the agents, and then define some strategic policies to simulate different relationships between participants in the SC.

8.7.1. *Background on multi-agent simulations of SCs*

A SC is defined as a network of suppliers, factories, warehouses, distribution centers, and retailers through which raw materials are acquired, processed, and delivered to customers [FOX 00]. In order to make SC decisions, it is necessary to identify the entities and flows within the chain. Finally, the identified and monitored elements need to be managed to improve the overall working of the SC and possibly to optimize it. Here, we identify the elements in a SC, their features and the challenges associated with SC management. We classify [NFA 08] the elements in a supply chain as entities and flows. Entities include all manufacturers, logistics providers, electronic exchanges and internal departments that participate in the business process. These entities have three common features:

– *Dynamic*: SCs are more flexible now. In today's business environment, there are no obligations for companies to be part of a SC for a certain time period; they may join or leave, depending on their own interests. This changes the structure and flows in the SC. Information in the chain, e.g. on prices, demands, technologies, etc., is also changing continuously.

– *Distributed*: the elements are distributed across various geographical locations. The planning and operating systems used by an entity may also be geographically distributed, for example there may be a dedicated inventory database residing at each warehouse of a manufacturer. The SC management information might even reside as rules-of-thumb with the people responsible for performing the various tasks in the business process.

– *Disparate*: the entities in a SC use different systems built on different platforms for the planning and management of their business. Information pertaining to the various elements is also disparate. For example, chemical shipments can be tracked through emails, faxes, telephone calls or online reports.

In Ferber [FER 99], a multi-agent system is a collection of possibly heterogeneous computational entities with their own goals and problem-solving capabilities. Dong *et al.* [DON 02] suggest a set of interactive agents for a harbor SC network. They present a multi-agent architecture to model and simulate a SC information system, and propose a shared environment based on agents simulating ordering processes. Research on agent-based SC management can be divided into three types: (1) agent-based architecture for coordination; (2) agent-based simulation of SCs; and (3) the dynamic design of SCs by agents. Our current work is a combination between the first two types of research. It proposes an agent-based architecture with decision-making agents to ensure collaboration and information sharing between SC participants.

Software agents can be defined in different ways, depending on the way they are implemented and the tasks they perform. Wooldridge and Jennings [WOO 95] suggest that any computer system (software or hardware) should have the following properties to be qualified as an agent:

– *autonomy*: it should have some control over its actions and should work without human intervention;

– *social skills*: it should be able to communicate with other agents and/or with human operators;

– *reactivity*: it should be able to react to changes in its environment;

– *pro-activeness*: it should also be able to take initiatives based on pre-specified goals.

The above-mentioned properties are generic for an agent. An agent may exhibit more of one property than another, depending on its architecture and embedded intelligence. This architecture enables agents to perform parallel tasks just as a human or organization would do. The addition of more activities or threads to a particular activity will also add new functionalities to an agent. Furthermore, the same agent class may be used within different applications. Tasks performed at each step may be as simple as querying a database or as complex as collaborating with other agents to jointly solve an optimization problem. Agents have been used to accomplish a variety of tasks. They have been used to assist process and equipment design, perform enterprise integration studies, and take care of decision-making processes in a business.

8.7.2. *The trust simulation model*

We now show how we use such multi-agent systems to model a SC, in which trust impacts and is impacted by the companies' performance. To shift from the proposed generic model to an agent-based model, let us start with the modeling of each participant in the SC (central company, customers and suppliers). To represent the three main functions of the company (source, make and deliver), and to consider the control processes in the SC and its environment, each participant is modeled by different agents, in line with the trust model. As outlined in section 8.5, the trust simulation model in the SC is composed of five agents: the *client-agent*, which simulates the processes related to the customer; the *retailer-agent*, which manages the demand-generation and orders in line with the client-agent; *wholesaler-agent*, which simulates the source of the supplies for the retailer-agent; the *factory-agent*, which simulates the production process, i.e. production decision and thereafter the supply of the product; and the *trust-model-agent*, which determines the level of trust during demand generation and information sharing within the SC.

The agents' behaviors are determined by the message protocols required for their interactions in the trust model in the SC, and behaviors are classified based on message types. Every agent other than the trust-model-agent is required to demonstrate one-shot behavior for loading the coefficient and initializing the agent's shared memory data for inventory, backlog, received order, and stock levels. In the trust simulation model, every agent requires cyclic behaviors for concurrent messages between agents in the SC. The different cyclic behaviors are required for receiving demand messages, updating virtual stocks, updating inventory and supply status, generating demand, and calculating trust level to determine the performance of the SC.

The trust-model-agent implements the trust criteria defined in section 8.5 with all the trust parameters. Cyclic behavior transmits the message from other agents to this agent in order to calculate the level of the trust behavior. All these agents are implemented using a Java Agent Development Environment (JADE) framework.

An agent modeling language (AML) class diagram is used to represent the relationships between these agents and to define attributes, operations, roles, protocols, etc., for the simulation of the SC, as shown in Figure 8.9. AML abstraction allows us to represent different levels of abstraction when designing class diagrams. Figure 8.9 shows the conceptual level of the class diagram of a participant. It illustrates, as an example, the implementation level for the agent *Retailer* along with the different behavior and trust model.

In the decision-making process, the agent uses the trust criteria and level of trust behavior to make decisions during the generation of demand. The most important part of decision making is the demand-generation strategy that allows the agent to choose the most appropriate demand based on the level of trust. FIPA-ACL communication language [FIP 08] is used by the agents in this application to exchange their knowledge and information during negotiations. Consequently, the agents in our system must use protocols respecting the above criteria, which mainly depend on three parameters:

– the trust behavior of each participant in the chain;

– SC management methods and behaviors to manage their decision making;

– information to be shared: orders, demand, forecast, stock levels, etc.

The agents pass from one given state to another, depending on the actions occurring in the environment or the received messages. The AML "state chart" diagrams seem to be an interesting approach by which to represent agents' behaviors. The essential factor considered when state diagrams are drawn up is the parallel (competitive) aspect of a participant's activities. The following state diagram describes the main behaviors of the "retailer" agent:

AML Model for the agent RETAILER

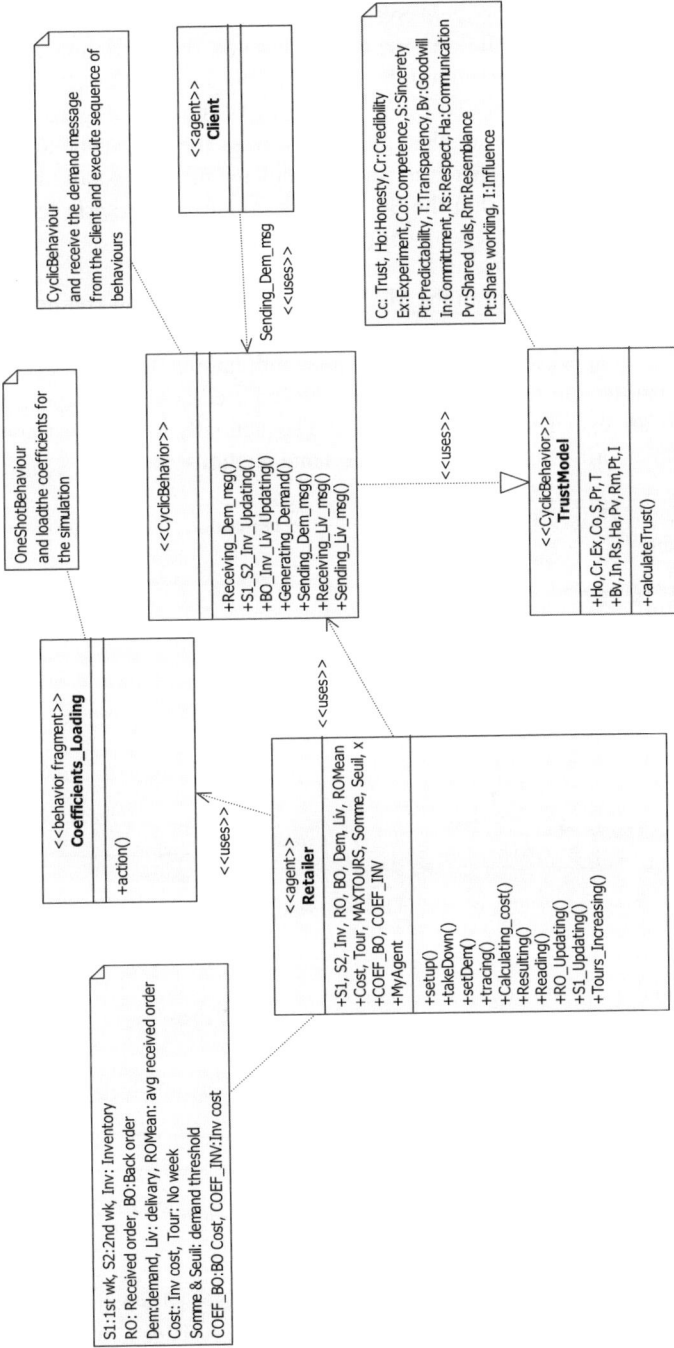

Figure 8.9. *The AML state diagram of the "retailer" agent*

The beer game Multi-Agent System (MAS) model employs four specific agents of the SC to represent: the retailer, the wholesaler, the distributor and factory, and another client agent along with this SC. One of the agents of this "retailer" model, in association with one-shot and cyclic behaviors, is shown in Figure 8.10. The AML model also incorporates another important "trust model" agent to associate trust behavior with the SC. This trust model implements the proposed formulation of human trust behavior within the SC network, along with criteria for the trust level and calculation of the trust behavior (see section 8.5).

Typically, every agent in the MAS model of the proposed architecture, as shown in Figure 8.9, has properties to manage virtual store, inventory, demand, orders received, tour-specific costs, and other relevant features. In the lifecycle of an agent, a single call to one-shot behavior loads the required coefficients, and all the cyclic behaviors are executed in parallel with and sequentially to the registration within the agent framework. Other agents have the same relationships.

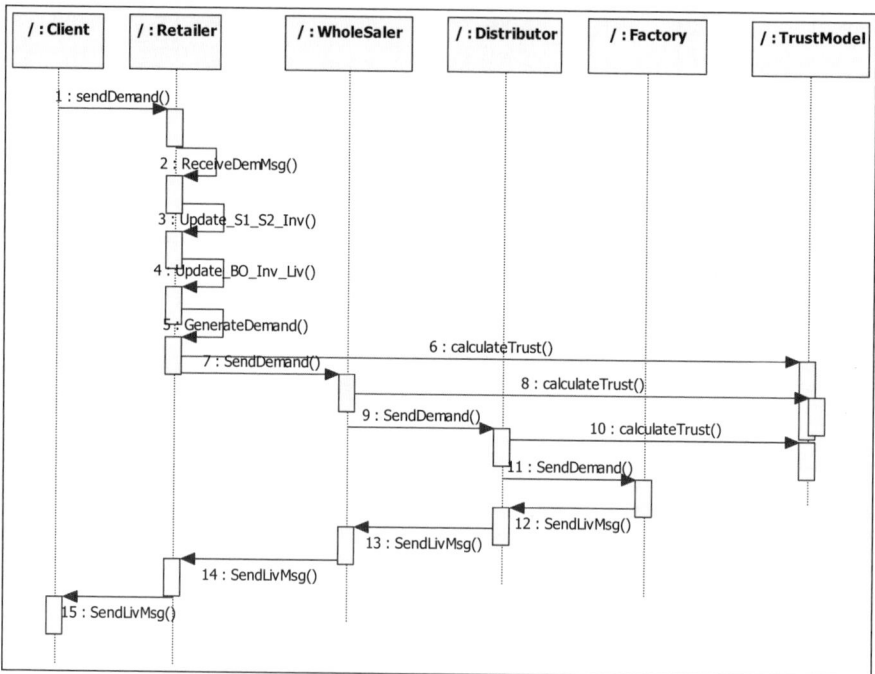

Figure 8.10. *Dynamic model of agents' collaboration when the level of trust is moderate*

The agent interaction model is shown in Figure 8.10 when the level of trust is moderate and the information based on the inventory it generates. In this case, the corresponding demand is generated by the agent. At every demand-generation step of the different agents, a cyclic call to calculate Trust() behavior of the trust-model agent is made to ensure the level of trust and information sharing.

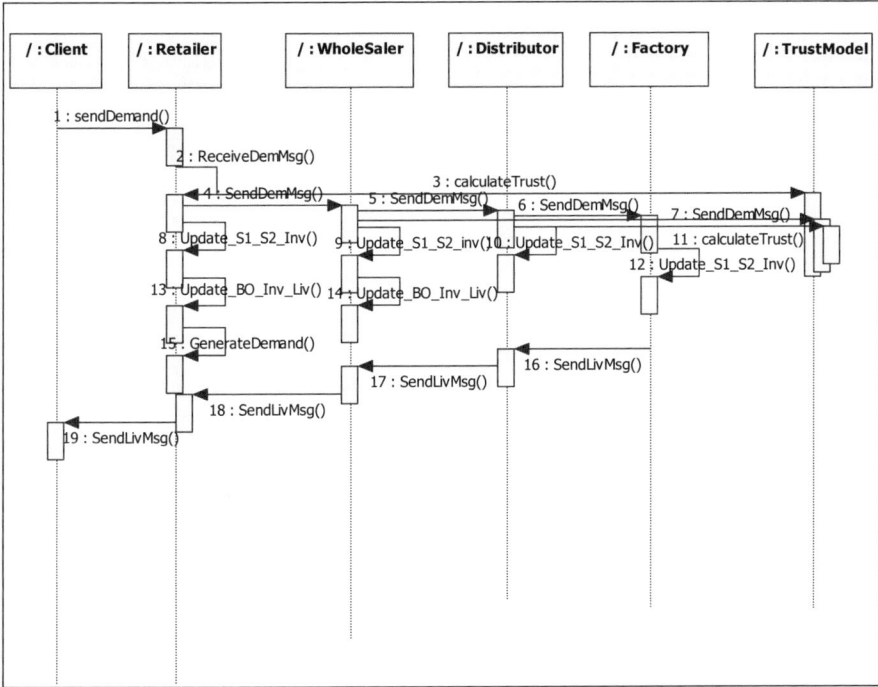

Figure 8.11. *Dynamic model of agents' collaboration when the level of trust is high*

In Figure 8.11, different message interactions are shown among the agents. Here, another agent interaction model is shown in when the level of trust is high and the information flows from different agents are on a real-time basis. This means that the SC is connected through information systems and, due to the level of the trust, the demand information flows in real time across the SC. As shown in Figure 8.11, the demand messages are sent across different agents, based on the validation of the trust model in real time.

In the simulation of trust in SCs through MAS, different agents interact through cyclic behaviors with the trust-model agent to evaluate the behavior of trust. The SC performance is then tested against different scenarios. The following sections present the case study of all of these scenarios.

8.8. Simulation model: the case study

To validate the proposed multi-agent simulation model, we propose the MIT beer game as an example of SC management. This example has attracted much attention from both SC management practitioners and academic researchers. There are four types of agent in this chain (see Figure 8.12), sequentially arranged: retailer, wholesaler, distributor and manufacturer. In the MIT beer game, as played with human subjects, each self-interested agent tries to achieve his/her own goal of minimizing his/her inventory costs when ordering from his/her supplier. Each agent makes his/her own prediction of his/her customers' future demand, based on his/her own observations.

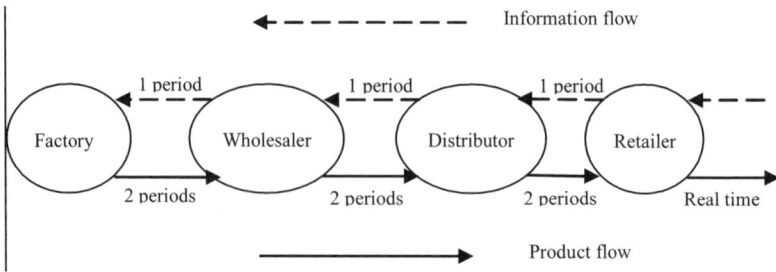

Figure 8.12. *The beer game SC flows*

The main idea of this case study is to make the link between the level of trust between companies in the SC, and the global performance of this chain. For this purpose we simulate different scenarios with different levels of information sharing (delay, quality, etc.) based on the participants' trust behavior. The observed performance of human beings managing SCs is usually far from optimal, from a system-wide point of view (see Figure 8.13). This may be due to a lack of incentives for information sharing, bounded rationality, or possibly the consequence of individual rational behavior that works against the interests of the group.

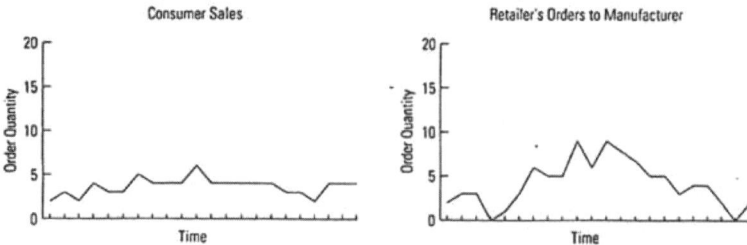

Figure 8.13. *The bullwhip effect*

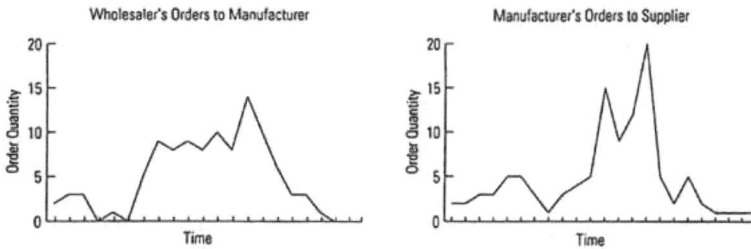

Figure 8.13. (Continued) *The bullwhip effect*

The basic setup and temporal ordering of events in the MIT beer game are as follows:

– new shipments arrive from the upstream player (or, in the case of the manufacturer, from the factory floor);

– orders are received from the downstream player (or, for the retailer, exogenously from the end customer);

– the orders just received plus any backlog orders are filled;

– the agent decides how much to order to replenish stock;

– inventory costs and backlog costs are calculated.

In the beer game, each player in the SC decides on the generation of demand based on inventory, virtual stock, backlog and the demand during the period. We first calculate the demand level based on a period or week. Initially, the demand level is the inventory of the week. In week one, the demand level is the sum of the virtual stock, inventory and the backlog of this week. For effective demand-level calculation, we compared the backlog of the week with the previous week. In case of greater backlog of the week, the demand level is the sum of the virtual stock, the demand of the previous week, inventory, and the difference of the backlogs between this week and the week before. Otherwise, the demand level is the sum of the previous week's demand, the virtual stock, the inventory and this week's backlog.

We begin by calculating the threshold of the demand, based on the week. Initially the threshold is the average of the order received. In the first week, the threshold of the demand is calculated as the sum of the average orders received in the previous two weeks. In other cases, the threshold is the sum of the three average orders received in the current week and two previous weeks. If the threshold is less than the demand level, then the week's demand is set at zero. If the threshold is equal to the demand level, the week's demand is set at the order received that week or the previous week, based on information sharing. Otherwise, the week's demand is the difference between the threshold and the demand level. In the beer game simulation, we calculated the total inventory cost as well as the penalty cost for the backlog items, based on the backlog and inventory levels of each agent per week.

In this section we report on multiple rounds of experiments conducted using our simulation model. In all of the rounds, we tested SC performance under deterministic demand, as set up in the MIT beer game (the final customer demands four cases of beer in the first four weeks and then demands eight cases of beer per week starting from week five and continuing until the end of the 35-week game). In the first round, we have *a behavior of non-trust* between the companies, so that there is no communication or information sharing between them, except for the customers' orders to their supplier. In the second round, the "behavior of trust" is moderate ($0.5 \leq Cc < 1.5$), which means that the companies share not only the orders, but also information about their stocks (levels of stock are sent by the suppliers to their customers). In the third and fourth scenarios, we have a "behavior of trust" between the participants ($1.5 \leq Cc < 2$). In this case, the companies share the orders and levels of stocks, and reduce the delay in information sharing (from one week to real time) by using integrated information systems (we simulate the fact that the companies connect their ERPs, for example). They have information in real time on the orders sent by their customer. The following table shows the configuration of the four scenarios.

	Information shared	Information flow	Physical flow
Scenario 1	Orders	Delay: 1 week	Delay: 2 weeks
Scenario 2	Orders + stock level	Delay: 1 week	Delay: 2 weeks
Scenario 3	Orders	Delay: real time	Delay: 2 weeks
Scenario 4	Orders + stock level	Delay: real time	Delay: 2 weeks

Table 8.2. *Overview of the main parameters of the three experiments*

We now briefly describe each round of experiments and our findings.

8.8.1. *Scenario 1*

The goal of the first scenario is to test the SC performance in the worst collaborative case. After calculation by the agents, the behavior of trust in this case is "no-trust" between the companies involved in the SC. This behavior corresponds to the classical beer game in which the players do not communicate with the others and make their decisions with no information other than the orders received from their customers. The delays of the different flows, information and products are equal to two weeks for each. The results (see Figure 8.14) show that the demand generated increases from the first agent to the last one (the bullwhip effect), even if the final customer's demand does not change. This scenario validates our multi-agent simulation model because, based on non-trust behavior, the global performance of the SC – inventory levels and backlog levels – corresponds to what we have in the real beer game.

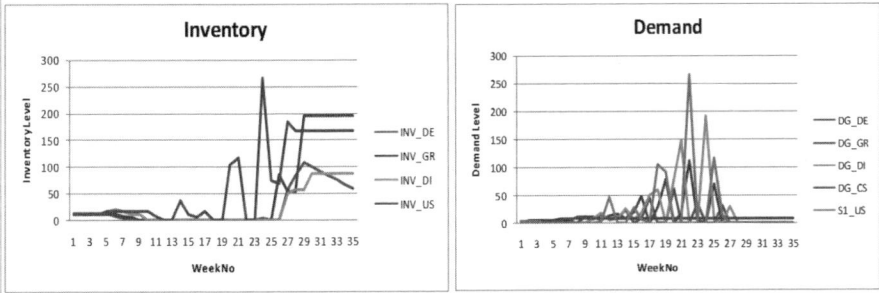

Figure 8.14. *Scenario 1: the demand generated (bullwhip effect) and inventory level*

The demand of the first agent "retailer" is provided by the market (this demand is equal to four for the first four weeks, and afterwards to eight until the end of the 35 weeks). For the wholesaler (GR), distributor (DI) and manufacturer (US), their current demand will be the order from their downstream partners, which are the retailer (DE), wholesaler and distributor. For the 35 weeks a cost is calculated for each agent separately. For the first scenario, we find that the maximum demand generated is equal to 266 for the last agent in the SC, the factory. In terms of backlogs, the maximum is 184 for the distributor agent.

8.8.2. *Scenario 2*

In the second round of experiments, we tested the case of moderate "behavior of trust". The *trust-model agent* calculates the behaviors of trust based on the trust criteria. The results for the agents of the SC are in the interval: $0.5 \leq Cc < 1.5$. In this case, we simulate a low level of information sharing: the companies share not only the orders, but also information about their stocks. Each agent will use the *SendMessage()* behavior to send information about the level of their stocks to their customer. We used a special parameter to represent this information about stock (variable $S2_i[Tour]$ in which i is the agent number in the SC and *Tour* is the week number). The agents use this new information to generate the week's demand knowing the exact level of their supplier's stock. In this way they can optimize the value of the demand generated.

The results (see Figure 8.15) show that the demand generated is still increasing between the first agent and the last one, but we find that the performance is better than in the first scenario. Here, the maximum level for stocks is equal to 168 (the level was 266 in the first scenario), and the maximum level of backlog is 154 (backlog was 184 in the first scenario). The quantities are decreasing in this scenario because of information sharing between the agents in the SC.

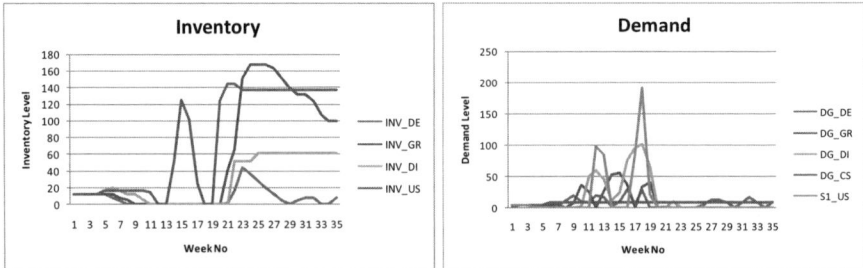

Figure 8.15. *Scenario 2: the demand generated and inventory level*

8.8.3. *Scenario 3*

In the third round of experiments there is a trust behavior that allows the partners of the SC to collaborate. In this case, the companies share the orders and reduce the delay in information sharing (from one week to real time) by using integrated information systems. They have information in real time on the orders sent by their customers. As in the first scenario, the only information shared between the agents is the demand generated (order).

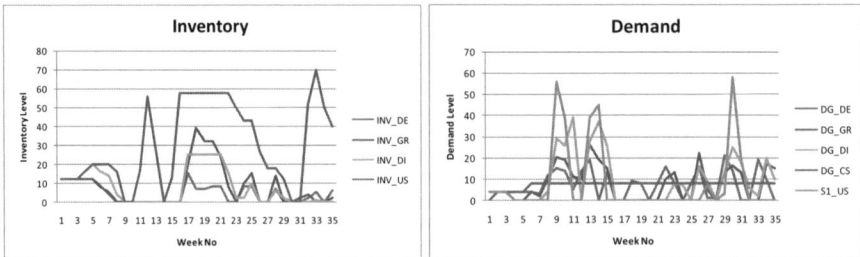

Figure 8.16. *Scenario 3: the demand generated and inventory level*

Reducing the delay in information flow enables the agents to better react to the variation in SC demand. The results show a real decrease in average level of backlogs and inventory (see Figure 8.16 and Table 8.3 below): from 40 (average inventory) in the two first scenarios, to 13 in this one; and from about 15 (average backlog), to five in the collaborative scenario. In terms of inventory, the maximum level is equal to 65 (where it was 168 in the previous scenario). For the backlog, the maximum level is divided by three, compared to the last scenario (40 *versus* 154). These results illustrate the trust behavior between the partners.

8.8.4. *Scenario 4*

The final experiment corresponds to the "best" collaborative scenario between the agents. Their behavior of trust (Cc) calculated by the agent is between 1.5 and 2. As the agents trust each other, they share not only orders but also information about stock levels, and integrate their information systems to reduce the information-flow delay. They are involved in a real collaborative process. The different indicators of the simulation show an improvement in the global performance of the supply chain (see Figure 8.17 and Table 8.3 below).

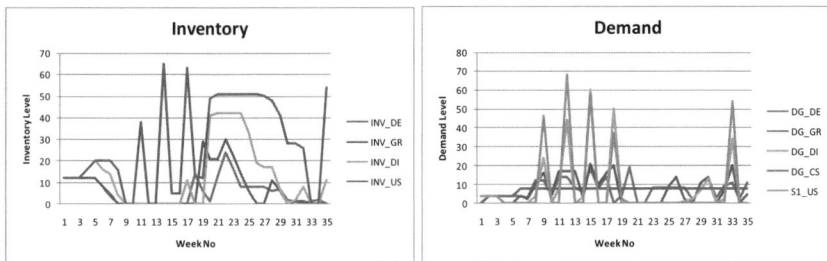

Figure 8.17. *Scenario 4: the demand generated and inventory level*

	Inventory		Backlog		Total coast (€)
	Avg.	*Max.*	*Avg.*	*Max.*	
Scenario 1	42	263	18	184	2,710
Scenario 2	40	168	13	154	2,150
Scenario 3	13	65	5	40	1,649
Scenario 4	13	58	4	34	1,545

Table 8.3. *Overview of the main results of the four experiments*

The first analysis of these results is that, in the beer game case study, the different delays (information and physical flows) do not allow the partners of the supply chain to be reactive. In fact, even if they try to anticipate their ordering process, they cannot really change the performance of their company because of the delay. We find that a reduction in delay of information flow (from one week to real time) increases the global performance of the chain. The level of trust directly impacts on the level and quality of information sharing, which in turn improves the performance of the companies by reducing the delay and enabling them to anticipate the variation in market demand.

8.9. Conclusion and perspectives

In this chapter we have carried out an exhaustive literature review on trust in organizational and inter-organizational relationships. From computer scientists' point of view, we have furthered the understanding of trust and correlated the trust model with SC collaboration through several experimental simulations using multi-agent systems.

Trust is considered as a necessary antecedent of information sharing in SCs, where information sharing has always been seen as beneficial. Information asymmetry is the main reason for the amplification of the demand signal and fluctuation of the inventory level along a supply chain. Information sharing can also yield other advantages, such as reducing costs, improving service levels, and reducing lead times and stock-outs.

After the literature review, we described the proposed trust model based on 15 criteria, measurement scales, and the concept of "trust behavior", which represent an aggregation of the evaluation of the trust criteria in a relationship. From these behaviors, we analyzed the links between trust criteria, collaboration, and information sharing. We then looked at questions like:

– What information is shared?

– At which level of the organization is information shared?

– What is the link between trust and information sharing?

– What is the impact of information sharing on the performance of the SC?

– Etc.

To answer these questions, we defined the type of information that will be shared at the different levels of the SC, and the corresponding trust model with all its variables. From these specifications, we proposed a simulation model based on a multi-agent architecture and designed the different agents needed to model the trust behaviors, the collaboration and the information sharing in a SC context.

We validated the trust simulation model on a case study – the MIT beer game – which is an example of SC management that has attracted much attention from both SC management practitioners and academic researchers. We then reported multiple rounds of experiments conducted using this simulation model. Finally, we tested different scenarios focusing on the "trust behaviors" of the agents in the SC. Our main finding is that, in a SC, the level of trust directly impacts on the level and quality of information sharing, which improve performance by reducing lead time and enabling companies to anticipate variations in market demand.

8.10. Bibliography

[ALT 93] ALTER C. HAGE J., *Organizations working together*, Sage Publications, Newbury Park, London, 1993.

[AND 90] ANDERSON J., NARUS J., "A model of distributor firm and manufacturer firm working partnerships", *Journal of Marketing*, vol. 54, no. 1, 1990, pp. 42-58.

[AND 92] ANDERSON E., WEITZ B., "The use of pledges to build and sustain commitment in distribution channels", *Journal of Marketing Research*, vol. 29, 1992, pp.18-34.

[ANG 04] ANGULO A., NACHTMANN H., WALLER M.A., "Supply chain information sharing in a vendor managed inventory partnership", *Journal of Business Logistics*, vol. 25, no. 1, 2004, pp. 101-120.

[ARR 74] ARROW K.J., *Les Limites de l'Organisation*, PUF, 1974.

[BAL 98] BALLOU D., WANG R., PAZER H., KUMAR-TAYI G., "Modeling information manufacturing systems to determine information product quality", *Management Science*, vol. 44, no. 4, 1998, pp. 462-484.

[BAR 83] BARBER B., *The Logic and the Limits of Trust*, Rutgers University Press, New Brunswick, 1983.

[BAU 99] BAUDRY B., "Incertitude et confiance: une réflexion sur les logiques de coordination dans la relation d'emploi", in: Thuderoz C., Mangematin V., Harrisson D., (eds), *La Confiance: Approches Économiques et Sociologiques*, Gaëtan Morin Europe, Paris, 1999, pp. 237-260.

[BAY 63] BAYES T., "An essay towards solving a problem in the doctrine of chances", *Philosophical Transactions of the Royal Society,* no. LIII, 1763 pp. 376-418.

[BEN 95] BENSAOU M., VENKATRAMAN N., "Configurations of interorganizational relationships: A comparison between U.S. and Japanese automakers", *Management Science*, vol. 41, 1995, pp. 1471-1492.

[BLA 64] BLAU P. M., *Exchange and Power in Social Life*, John Wiley & Sons, New York,1964.

[BOI 99] BOISSIN J.P., "Opportunisme, confiance et théorie néoinstitutionnaliste de l'organisation industrielle", in: THUDEROZ C., MANGEMATIN V., HARRISSON D. (eds), *La confiance: Approches Économiques et Sociologiques*, Gaëtan Morin Europe, Paris, 1999, pp. 99-126.

[BOL 91] BOLTANSKI L., THEVENOT L., *De la Justification, Les Économies de la Grandeur*, Nrf Essais, Gallimard, 1991.

[BRA 89] BRADACH J.L., ECCLES R.G., "Price, authority and trust: From ideal form to plural forms", *Annual Review of Sociology*, vol. 15, 1989, pp. 97-118.

[BRO 89] BROUSSEAU E., "L'approche néo-institutionnelle de l'économie des coûts de transaction", *Revue Française d'Economie*, vol. IV, no. 4, 1989, pp. 125-166.

[BRU 05] BRULHART F., "Expérience du partenariat, expérience du partenaire, connivence interpersonnelle: quel impact sur la réussite du partenariat vertical?", *M@n@gement*, Vol. 8, no. 2, 2005, pp. 167-191.

[CAC 00] CACHON G.P., FISHER M., "Supply chain inventory management and the value of shared information", *Management Science*, vol. 46, no. 5, 2000, pp. 1032-1048.

[CAC 04] CACHON G. P., NETESSINE S., "Game theory in supply chain analysis", in: D. SIMCHI-LEVI S.D., WU Z. SHEN (eds), *Handbook of Quantitative Supply Chain Analysis: Modeling in the E-Business Era*, Kluwer, Boston, 2004, pp. 13-66.

[CHA 06] CHAIB-DRAA B., MÜLLER J., "Multi-agent-based supply chain management", *Studies in Computational Intelligence*, vol. 28, Springer, 2006.

[CHU 84] CHURCHILL G.A. Jr., Peter J.P., "Research design effects on the reliability of rating scales: A meta-analysis", *Journal of Marketing Research*, vol. 21, no. 4, 1984, pp. 360-375.

[COH 04] COHEN KULP S., LEE H.L., OFEK E., "Manufacturer benefits from information integration with retail customers", *Management Science*, vol. 50, no. 4, 2004, pp. 431-444.

[COL 90] COLEMAN J.S., *Foundations of Social Theory*, Belknap Press of Harvard University, Cambridge, 1990.

[DET 98] DETCHESSAHAR M., "L'homologie des trajectoires socioprofessionnelles des acteurs de la coopération inter-entreprises: un vecteur de confiance et de stabilité", *Revue Finance, Contrôle, Stratégie*, vol. 1, no. 1, 1998.

[DON 02] DONG W.Y., SOUNG H.K., NAK H.K, "Combined modeling with multi-agent systems and simulation: its application to harbor supply chain management", *Proceedings of the 35th International Conference on System Sciences*, Hawaii, 2002.

[DOU 89] DOUGLAS M., *Comment Pensent les Institutions*, La Découverte, Paris, 1989.

[DUR 93] DURKHEIM E., *De la Division du Travail Social*, Quadridge/Presses Universitaires de France, 1993.

[DWY 87] DWYER F.R., SCHURR P.H., OH S., "Developing buyer-seller relationships", *Journal of Marketing*, vol. 51, no. 2, 1987, pp. 11-27.

[EVR 93] EVRARD Y., PRAS B., ROUX E., *Etudes et Recherches en Marketing*, 2nd edition, Nathan, 1993.

[FEL 03] FELDBERG F., VAN DER HEIJDEN, "Inter-organisational information sharing and the use of decision aids in category management", In: WIGAND R.T., TAN Y., GRICAR J., PUCIHAR A., LUNAR T., *Proceedings of the 16th Bled eCommerce Conference*, Bled, Slovenia, CIP-Katalozni Zapis o Publikaciji, 2003, pp. 583-593.

[FER 99] FERBER J., *Multi-agent System: An Introduction to Distributed Artificial Intelligence*, Addison Wesley Longman, Harlow, 1999.

[FIP 08] FIPA, "FIPA specification. Part 2, agent communication language", *Foundation for Intelligent Physical Agents*, FIPA, 2008, available at: http://www.fipa.org, accessed 4.29.10.

[FOR 84] FORD D., "Buyer/seller relationships in international industrial markets", *Industrial Marketing Management*, vol. 13, no. 2, 1984, pp. 101-112.

[FOX 00] FOX M. S., BARBUCEANU M., TEIGEN R. "Agent-oriented supply chain management", *The International Journal of Flexible Manufacturing Systems*, vol. 12, 2000, pp. 165-188.

[FRO 98] FROEHLICHER T., "Les liens sociaux entre dirigeants et le déclenchement de la coopération interentreprises", *Finance, Contrôle, Stratégie*, vol. 1, no. 1, 1998, pp. 99-124.

[GAL 03] GALLIVAN M.J., DEPLEDGE G., "Trust, control and the role of interorganizational systems in electronic partnerships", *Information Systems Journal*, vol. 13, 2003, pp. 159-190.

[GAN 94] GANESAN S., "Determinants of long term orientation in buyer–seller relationships", *Journal of Marketing*, vol. 58, no. 2, 1994, pp. 1-19.

[GID 90] GIDDENS A., *The Consequences of Modernity*, Stanford University Press, Stanford, 1990.

[GIL 90] GILSON R.J., MNOOKIN R.H., "The implicit contract for corporate law firm associates: ex post opportunism and ex ante bonding", in: AOKI, GORDON C. (ed), *New Deals. Business, Labor, and Politics in America*, 1920-1935, Cambridge University Press, Cambridge (Ma.), 1990.

[GOS 04] GOSAIN S., MALHOTRA A., EL SAWY O.A., "Coordinating for flexibility in e-business supply chains", *Journal of Management Information Systems*, vol. 21, no. 3, 2004, pp. 7-45.

[GRA 85] GRANOVETTER M., "Economic action and social structure: The concept of embeddedness", *American Journal of Sociology*, vol. 91, no. 3, 1985, pp. 481-510.

[GRA 00] GRANOVETTER M., *Le Marché Autrement*, Desclée de Brouwer, Paris, 2000.

[GUI 96] GUIBERT N., "L'effet structurant des nouvelles technologies de l'information et de la communication sur la relation client–fournisseur", *Systèmes d'Information et Management*, vol. 1, no. 4, 1996, pp. 29-48.

[GUL 95] GULATI R., "Social structure and alliance formation patterns: A longitudinal analysis", *Administrative Science Quarterly*, vol. 40, no. 4, 1995.

[GUN 95] GUNDLACH G.T., ACHROL R.S., MENTZER J.T., "The structure of commitment in exchange", *Journal of Marketing*, vol. 59, 1995, pp. 78-92.

[GUR 98] GURVIEZ P., Le rôle central de la confiance dans la relation consommateur-marque, doctoral science thesis from Gestion, Aix Marseille University 3, 1998.

[HAN 02] HANDFIELD R.B., BECHTEL C., "The role of trust and relationship structure in improving supply chain responsiveness", *Industrial Marketing Management*, vol. 31, 2002, pp.367-82.

[HAR 98a] HARDY C., PHILLIPS N., "Strategies of engagement: lessons from the critical examination of collaboration and conflict in an interorganizational domain", *Organization Science*, vol. 9, 1998.

[HAR 98b] HART P., SAUNDERS C., "Emerging electronic partnerships: antecedents and dimensions of EDI use from the supplier's perspective", *Journal of Management Information Systems*, vol. 14, no. 4, 1998, pp 87-111.

[HAR 99] HARRISSON D., "Confiance identitaire, confiance cognitive et processus d'innovation", in: THUDEROZ C., MANGEMATIN V., HARRISSON D. (eds), *La Confiance: Approches Économiques et Sociologiques*, Gaëtan Morin Europe, Paris, 1999, pp. 209-236

[HEI 90] HEIDE J., JOHN G., "Alliances in industrial purchasing, the determinants of joint action in buyer – supplier relationships", *Journal of Marketing Research*, vol. 27, 1990, pp 24-36.

[HIL 72] HILL R.W., "The nature of industrial buying decisions", *Industrial Marketing Management*, vol. 2, no. 1, 1972, pp. 45-55.

[HOS 95] HOSMER L.T., "Trust: the connecting link between organizational theory and philosophical ethics", *Academy of Management Review*, vol. 20, 1995, pp 379-403.

[JAR 98] JARILLO J.C., "On strategic networks", *Strategic Management Journal*, vol. 9, 1998, pp. 31-41.

[JOR 06] JORION P., *Value at Risk: The New Benchmark for Managing Financial Risk*, 3rd edition, McGraw-Hill, 2006.

[KAN 87] KANT E., *Critique de la Raison Pure*, Gallimard, Paris, 1987.

[KAR 98] KARPIK L., "La confiance: réalité ou illusion ? Examen critique d'une thèse de Williamson", *Revue Economique*, vol. 49, no. 4, 1998, pp. 1043-1056.

[KRE 90] KREPS D.M., "Corporate culture and economic theory", in: ALT J.E., SHEPSLE, K.A. (eds), *Perspectives on positive Political Economy*, Cambridge University Press, MA, 1990, pp. 90-142.

[LAH 98] LAHIRE B., *L'Homme Pluriel*, Les ressorts de l'action, Nathan, Paris, 1998.

[LAN 92] LANGLOIS R.N., "Transaction-cost economics in real time", *Industrial and Corporate Change*, vol. 1, no. 1, 1992, pp. 99-127.

[LAR 80] LARZELERE R., HUSTON T.L., "The dyadic trust scale: towards understanding interpersonal trust in close relationships", *Journal of Marriage and the Family*, August 1980, pp. 595-604.

[LEE 97] LEE H.L., PADMANABHAN B., WHANG S., "Information distortion in a supply chain: the bullwhip effect", *Management Science*, vol. 4, 1997, pp. 546–558.

[LEE 00] LEE H.L., Whang S., "Information sharing in a supply chain," *International Journal of Manufacturing Technology and Management*, vol. 1, no. 1, 2000, pp. 79-93.

[LEF 06] LEFAIX-DURAND A., POULIN D., BEAUREGARD R., KOZAK R., "Relations interorganisationnelles et création de valeur, synthèse et perspectives", *Revue Française de Gestion*, vol. 32, no. 164, 2006, pp. 205-228.

[LEG 08] LEGNER C., SCHEMM J., "Toward the inter-organizational product information supply chain. Evidence from the retail and consumer goods industries", *Journal of the Association for Information Systems*, vol. 9, no. 3/4, 2008, pp. 19-150.

[LEN 05] LENG M., PARLAR M., "Game theoretic applications in supply chain management: A review", *INFOR*, Vol. 43, no. 3, 2005, pp 187-220.

[LEW 85] LEWIS D.J., WEIGERT A., "Trust as a social reality", *Social Forces*, vol. 63, 1985, pp 967-985.

[LEW 96] LEWICKI R.J., BUNKER B.B., "Developing and maintaining trust in work relationships", in: KRAMER R.M., TYLER T.R., *Trust in Organizations: Frontiers of Theory and Research*, Sage, Thousand Oaks, 1996.

[LOR 96] LORENZ E., "Confiance, contrats et coopération économique", *Sociologie du Travail*, vol. 96, no. 4, 1996, pp. 487-508.

[LOR 01] LORENZ E., "Models of cognition, the contextualisation of knowledge and organisational theory", forthcoming, *Journal of Management and Governance*, 2001.

[MAC 74] MACNEIL I.R., "The many futures of contract", *Southern California Law Review*, no. 47, May 1974, pp. 691-748.

[MAD 09] MADLBERGER M, "What drives firms to engage in interoganizational information sharing in supply chain management?", *International Journal of e-Collaboration*, vol. 5, no. 2, 2009, pp 18-42.

[MAR 91] MARCHESNAY M., "De l'hypofirme à l'hypogroupe – Naissance, connaissance, reconnaissance", *Les Cahiers du L.E.R.A.S.S.*, no.23, May 1991.

[MCA 95] McALLISTER D.J., "Affect- and cognition-based trust as foundations for interpersonal cooperation in organizations", *Academy of Management Journal*, vol. 38, 1995, pp. 24-59.

[MCN 05] McNEIL A., FREY R., EMBRECHTS P., *Quantitative Risk Management: Concepts Techniques and Tools*, Princeton University Press, 2005.

[MEI 06] MEIJER S., HOFSTEDE G.J., BEERS G, OMTA S.W.F., "Trust and tracing game: Learning about transactions and embeddedness in a trade network", *Production Planning & Control*, vol. 17, no. 6, 2006, pp. 569-583.

[MOB 02] MOBERG C.R., CUTLER B.D., GROSS A., SPEH T.W., "Identifying antecedents of information exchange within supply chains", *International Journal of Physical Distribution and Logistics Management*, vol. 32 no. 9/10, 2002, pp. 755-770.

[MOH 94] MOHR J., SPEKMAN R., "Characteristics of partnership success: Partnership attributes, communication behavior, and conflict resolution techniques", *Strategic Management Journal*, vol. 15, no. 2, 1994, pp. 135-152.

[MOO 92] MOORMAN C., ZALTMAN G., DESHPANDE R., "Relationships between providers and users of market research: The dynamics of trust within and between organizations", *Journal Of Marketing Research*, vol. 24, 1992, pp.314-328.

[MOO 93] MOORMAN C., DESHPANDE R., ZALTMAN G., "Factors affecting trust in market research relationships", *Journal of Marketing*, vol. 57, 1993, pp. 81-101.

[MOR 94] MORGAN R.M., HUNT S.D., "The commitment trust theory of relationship Marketing", *Journal of Marketing*, vol. 58, 1994, pp. 20-38.

[MOY 09] MOYAUX T., LLERENA D., BABOLI A., "Choice of an ordering strategy taking account of risks about customer service levels and on-hand inventories", *Proceedings of the International Conference on Industrial Engineering and Systems Management*, (IESM), Montreal, PQ, Canada, 2009.

[NEV 04] NEVEU V., "La confiance organisationnelle: définition et mesure", *Actes du 15è Congrès de l'AGRH*, vol. 2, 2004, pp. 1071-1110.

[NFA 08] NFAOUI E., El BEQQALI O., OUZROUT Y., BOURAS A., "An approach of decision-making support based on collaborative agents for a large distribution sector", *International Journal of Information Systems and Supply Chain Management*, vol. 2, no. 2, 2008, pp. 16-35.

[ORL 94] ORLÉAN A., "Sur le rôle respectif de la confiance et de l'intérêt dans la constitution de l'ordre marchand", *Revue du Mauss*, no. 4, 1994, pp. 17-35.

[OUC 80] OUCHI W., "Market, bureaucracies and clans", *Administrative Science Quarterly*, vol. 25, 1980, pp. 129-141.

[PAP 01] PAPILLON J.C., "Une synthèse de quelques critiques récentes de l'économie des coûts de transaction", In: JOFFRE P., GERMAIN O. et WILLIAMSON E.O. (eds), *La Théorie de Coûts de Transaction. Regard et Analyse du Management Stratégique*, Paris, Vuibert, 2001, pp. 75-88.

[PAT 07] PATNAYAKUNI R., RAI A., SETH N., "Relational antecedents of information flow integration for supply chain coordination", *Journal of Management Information Systems*, vol. 23, no. 1, 2007, pp. 13-49.

[PAV 02] PAVLOU P., "Institution-based trust in inter-organizational exchange relationships: the role of online B2B marketplaces on trust formation", *Journal of Strategic Information Systems*, 2002, vol. 11, pp. 215-243.

[PET 86] PETER J.P., CHURCHILL G.A., "Relationships among research design choices and psychometric properties of rating scales: A meta-analysis", *Journal of Marketing Research*, 1986, no. 33, pp. 1-10.

[PRE 00] PREMKUMAR G.R., "Interorganizational systems and supply chain management: an information processing perspective", *Information Systems Management*, vol. 17, no. 3, 2000, pp. 56-69.

[RAD 68] RADNER, R., "Competitive equilibrium under uncertainty", *Econometrica*, vol. 36, 1968, pp. 31-58.

[RAM 04] RAMCHURN S., HUYNH D, JENNINGS N., "Trust in multi-agent systems", *The Knowledge Engineering Review*, vol. 19, no. 1, 2004, pp. 1-25.

[REI 95] REIX R., *Systèmes d'Information et Management des Organisations*, Vuibert, 1995.

[REV 86] REVE T., STERN L.W., "The relationship between inter organizational form, transaction climate and economic performance in vertical inter firm dyads", in: *Marketing Channels: Relationships and Performance*, Lexington, 1996, pp. 75-102.

[RIN 92] RING P.S., VAN DE VEN A.H., "Structuring cooperative relationships between organizations", *Strategic Management Journal*, vol. 13, 1992, pp. 483-498.

[RIN 94] RING P.S., VAN DE VEN A.H., "Developmental processes of cooperative Interorganisational relationships", *Academy of Management Review*, vol. 19, 1994, pp 90-118.

[ROB 67] ROBINSON P.J., FARIS C.N., WIND Y., *Industrial Buying and Creative Marketing*, Alleyn and Bacon Inc, 1967.

[ROU 98] ROUSSEAU D.M., SITKIN S.B., BURT R.S., CAMERER C., "Not so different after all: a cross-discipline view of trust", *Academy of Management Review*, vol. 23, 1998, pp. 393-404.

[SAE 05] SAEED K, MALHOTRA M, GROVER V, "Examining the impact of interorganizational systems on process efficiency and sourcing leverage in buyer-supplier dyads", *Decision Sciences*, vol. 36, no. 3, 2005, pp. 365-396.

[SAI 08] SÁIZ M.E., HENDRIX E.M.T., "Methods for computing Nash equilibria of a location–quantity game", *Computers & Operations Research*, vol. 35, no. 10, 2008, pp. 3311-3330.

[SAK 98] SAKO M., "Does Trust improve business performance?" *Trust Within and between Organizations*, Lane & Bachmann, Oxford University Press, 1998.

[SAL 89] SALAIS R., "L'analyse économique des conventions du travail", *Revue Economique*, vol. 40, 1989, pp. 199-240.

[SAL 93] SALAIS R., STORPER M., *Les Mondes de Production: Enquête sur l'Identité Économique de la France*, Editions de l'Ecole des Hautes Études en Sciences Sociales, Paris, 1993.

[SCA 79] SCANZONI J., "Social exchange and behavioral interdependence", in: BURGESS R., HUSTON T., *Social Exchange in Developing Relationships*, New York, Academic Press, 1979.

[SCH 85] SCHURR P.H., OZANNE J.L., "Influences on exchange process: buyers perceptions of a seller's trustworthiness and bargaining toughness", *Journal of Consumer Research*, vol. 11, no. 3, 1985, pp. 939-953.

[SEI 98] SEIDMANN A, SUNDARARAJAN A., "Sharing logistics information across organizations: technology, competition and contracting", in: KEMERER ED, *Information Technology and Industrial Competitiveness: How IT Shapes Competition*, Kluwer Academic Publishing, Boston, 1998, pp. 107-136.

[SER 97] SERVET J.M., "Les limites du partenariat dans la mise en place et le développement de systèmes financiers décentralisés au sud - modèle démocratique du marché versus hiérarchie", *Rapport Moral sur l'Argent dans le Monde*, AEF/Montchrestien, Paris, 1997, pp. 399-416.

[SHA 92] SHAPIRO D., SHEPPARD B.H., CHERASKIN L., "Business on a handshake", *Negoatiation Journal*, vol. 8, no. 4, 1992, pp. 365-377.

[SHE 96] SHEPPARD B.H., TUCHINSKY M., "Micro-OB and the network organization", in: KRAMER R.M., TYLER T.R., *Trust in Organisations: Frontiers of Theory and Research*, Sage, Thousand Oaks, CA, 1996, pp. 140-165.

[SIM 61] SIMON H., *Administrative Behavior*, 3rd edition, Macmillan, New York, NY, 1961.

[SOH 97] SOHIER J., *La Relation Inter-organisationnelle: une Approche Stratégique et Interactive*, Université du Languedoc-Roussillon, Nice, 1997.

[SUN 05] SUN S., YEN J., "Information supply chain: a unified framework for information-sharing", in: KANTOR P, MURESAN F, ROBERTS D, ZENG F-Y, WHANG H, CHEN H, MERKLE R. (eds), *Intelligence and Security Informatics*, Springer, 2005, pp. 422-429.

[SWA 85] SWAN J.E., TRAWICK I.F., SILVA D.W., "How industrial salespeople customer trust", *Industrial Marketing Management*, vol. 14, 1985, pp. 203-211.

[SWA 88] SWAN J.E., TRAWICK I.F., RINK D.R., ROBERTS J.J., "Measuring dimensions of purchaser trust of industrial salespeople", *The Journal of Personal Selling & Sales Management*, vol. 8, no. 1, 1988, pp. 1-9.

[TAN 01] TAN G.W., WANG B., "The relationship between product nature, demand patterns, and information sharing strategies", *Proceedings of the 22nd International Conference on Information Systems*, Washington, DC: IEEE Computer Society, 2001, pp. 543-549.

[TIR 98] TIROLE J., *The Theory of Industrial Organization*, MIT Press, Cambridge, MA, 1998.

[TYK 08] TYKHONOV D., JONKER C., MEIJER S., VERWAART T., "Agent-based simulation of the trust and tracing game for supply chains and networks", *Journal of Artificial Societies and Social Simulation*, vol. 11 no. 3, 2008.

[UZZ 97] UZZI B., "Social structure and competition in interfirm networks: the paradox of embeddedness", *Administrative Science Quarterly*, vol. 42, 1997, pp. 35-67.

[WAN 94] WANG Q., PARLAR M., "A three-person game theory model arising in stochastic inventory control theory", *European Journal of Operational Research*, vol. 76, no. 1, 1994, pp. 83-97.

[WEB 72] WEBSTER F.E., WIND Y., *Organizational Buying Behavior*, Prentice Hall, Englewood Cliffs, N.J., 1972.

[WIL 85] WILLIAMSON O.E., *The Economic Institutions of Capitalism*, The Free Press, New York, 1985.

[WIL 91] WILLIAMSON O.E., "Comparative economic organization, the analysis of discrete structural alternatives", *Administrative Science Quarterly*, vol. 36, 1991, pp. 269-296.

[WIL 93] WILLIAMSON O.E., "Calculativeness, trust, and economic organization", *Journal of Law and Economics*, vol. 36, no. 1, 1993, pp. 453-86.

[WIL 94] WILLIAMSON O.E., *Les Institutions de l'Économie*, InterEdition, Paris, 1994.

[WOO 87] WOODSIDE A.G., VYAS N., "Industrial purchasing strategies-recommendations for purchasing and marketing manager", *Industrial Purchasing Strategies,* Lexington Books, pp. 167-191.

[WOO 95] WOOLDRIDGE M., JENNINGS N.R., "Intelligent agents: Theory and practice", *The Knowledge Engineering Review*, vol. 10, no. 2, 1995, pp. 115-152.

[WOO 02] WOOLDRIDGE M., *An Introduction to MultiAgent Systems*, John Wiley & Sons Ltd, 2002.

[ZAH 94] ZAHEER A., VENKATRAMAN N., "Determinants of electronic integration in the insurance industry", *Management Science*, vol. 40, no. 5, 1994, pp. 549-566.

[ZUC 86] ZUCKER L.G., "Production of trust: institutional sources of economic structure, 1840-1920", in: STAW B.M., CUMMINGS L.L. (eds.), *Research in Organizational Behavior*, JAI Press, Greenwich, CT, Vol. 8, 1986, pp. 53-111.

Chapter 9

Value of Lead Time and Demand Information Sharing in Supply Chains

9.1. Introduction

In the current context of the competitive market, companies should increase their reactivity. One of the ways of doing so is through collaboration with the other members of their supply chain (SC), which usually involves information sharing (IS) among these members. Several kinds of information may be shared. Basically, upstream information (lead time, supplier capacities, etc.) is distinguished from downstream information (demand, demand forecasts, etc.) and IS may concern both. This paper studies the impact of lead time IS (i.e. upstream) and demand IS (i.e. downstream) in three different SCs. The impact of lead time IS as well as centralized decision making is investigated for the first two SCs (one SC with stock in the distribution center, another without). For the third SC, we compare replenishment policies with three different levels of demand IS (no IS, slow IS, and instantaneous IS).

The outline of this chapter is as follows. Section 9.2 reviews the literature on both upstream and downstream IS. A model for the first two SCs is developed in section 9.3 and another for the third SC in section 9.4. More precisely, we present models, experimental results and discussions about IS in these two sections. Finally, section 9.5 concludes this chapter.

Chapter written by Ali MEHRABI, Thierry MOYAUX and Armand BABOLI.

9.2. Literature review

Two major approaches are presented in IS literature: analytical and simulation [HUA 03]. Whereas the analytical approach investigates the value of the information in a system using mathematical theories such as probability and calculus, the simulation approach is based on a computer program that replicates the operations of a system [DAM 99]. Moreover, two classes of information are considered in the literature; namely, downstream information, such as demand information and forecasts of demand, and upstream information, such as capacities of suppliers, lead time information and production costs [CHE 03]. Hence, a SC may operate with upstream and/or downstream IS. In the following we present some studies, first on upstream and then on downstream IS.

9.2.1. *Survey of upstream IS*

The impact of both shipment and order lead times on the benefits of IS has been investigated in the literature [HUA 03]. The results show that the longer the lead time, the lower the benefit of (demand) IS. The variance in lead time has also been investigated, and a smaller variance has been proven to lead to more important IS benefits. Chen and Yu [CHE 05] studied the effects of replenishment lead time information in a single-location inventory model with random lead times. Their system is managed by a retailer and the stock is replenished by a single supplier who knows the lead time for every replenishment order. The customer demand arises periodically, with independent, identically-distributed demand (independent, identically-distributed random variable). These authors model the supply process with a finite-state Markov chain based on the work of Song and Zipkin [SON 96]. Using numerical evidence, they indicate that the value of lead time information is low for small-volume items, but significant for high-volume items where cost savings due to IS lead time can be as high as 35%.

Many studies have investigated the value of IS by means of an analytical approach. A comprehensive review can be found in Chen [CHE 03]. Chen [CHE 98], by considering a (R, nQ) replenishment policy and using the echelon inventory position concept and installation inventory position concept, investigates the value of demand/inventory information in a serial SC. This study shows that IS benefits the SC by an average of between 1.75 and 9%. Gavirneni *et al.* [GAV 99] consider a two-stage capacitated SC. They model three scenarios for presenting three information flows:

– no IS;

– the supplier knows the demand distribution; and

– the supplier has access to all information about the retailer's inventory position.

They show that the benefits are significant, with the average being around 14% and ranging from 1% to 35%.

Lee *et al.* [LEE 00] assess the value of sharing demand information in a supply-chain model with a non-stationary demand process. Cachon and Fisher [CAC 00] develop a model to assess the value of downstream inventory information in a one-warehouse multi-retailer system.

9.2.2. *Survey of downstream IS*

After upstream IS, we now turn our attention to downstream IS. The focus of this literature review reflects that of our research, on a comparison of several levels of IS-based replenishment policies, no IS, slow IS and instantaneous IS.

9.2.2.1. *No IS*

Basically, replenishment policies have to determine how much and when to order. Models without IS are called installation stock policies, in the sense that only the inventory system of the installation considered is modeled. Installation stock policies can be split into two families [SIL 98]:

– *continuous versus periodic review*: inventory levels are monitored all the time so that orders may be placed at anytime *versus* orders may only be placed at specific times;

– *fixed versus variable quantity*: ordered quantities are always the same *versus* orders are different.

For example, (s, Q) is a policy with continuous review (i.e. an order is issued whenever the inventory level becomes lower than s) and the quantity ordered Q is given by the EOQ (economic order quantity) model proposed by Harris [HAR 13]. On the other hand, (s, S) operates a continuous review (i.e. with the same level s firing new orders as (s, Q)) and variable quantity (i.e. the quantity ordered will increase inventory level to S). Conversely to the previous two continuous review policies, (R, S) works with periodic review (i.e. every R time period) and variable quantity (i.e. the quantity ordered is calculated as in (s, S)). These policies are developed with mathematical models of a greater or lesser degree of sophistication. For example, each parameter (e.g. demand, lead times, etc.) is constant or follows a statistical distribution. Interested readers can refer to textbooks such as [AXS 06] for more details on policies without IS.

9.2.2.2. Instantaneous IS

Such textbooks also develop models with IS, called echelon stock policies. IS in these policies does not deal with demand IS, as in the policies used in this chapter, but with inventory IS. Actually, these policies take account of both the inventory level of the company considered (as in the previous section), but also downstream stocks (e.g. those of clients). Consequently, IS of inventory levels is required to communicate the state of others' stocks to the company considered. After this information is known to a company, the company applies a replenishment policy similar to those described in section 9.2.2.1, except that the echelon stock level (i.e. the sum of the inventories considered and those downstream) is tracked, instead of the installation stock level. In addition to this teaching material, research on both demand and inventory IS has also been carried out, as illustrated below.

Instantaneous demand IS: Lee et al. [LEE 00] assessed the value of IS demand in a SC model with a non-stationary demand process. Aviv [AVI 01] then considered the same SC topology as we have here (dyadic with a retailer and its supplier) and compared three scenarios: (i) local forecasting; (ii) collaborative forecasting; and (iii) no forecasts. The reader is referred to the review by Chen [CHE 03] for additional investigations into IS demand.

We have naturally illustrated downstream IS with demand IS, although we could have outlined inventory IS. We nevertheless prefer to go directly to the IS of demand and inventory at the same time.

Instantaneous demand and inventory IS: Apart from his aforementioned review, Chen [CHE 98] also investigated the value of both demand and inventory IS in a SC by considering a (R, nQ) replenishment policy with both the echelon and installation inventory position concepts. He showed that IS benefits the SC by an average of 1.75 to 9%. Similarly, Gavirneni *et al.* [GAV 99] considered both demand and inventory IS in a two-stage capacitated SC. They modeled three scenarios for presenting three information flows: (i) no IS; (ii) the supplier knows the demand distribution; and (iii) the supplier has access to all of the information about the retailer's inventory position. These authors showed that the benefits are significant, with average savings of around 14% and ranging between 1 and 35%. Finally, Cachon and Fisher [CAC 00] studied IS of both inventory levels and demand. With IS demand, some authors [AGR 09, OUY 07] have focused on the impact of this kind of IS on the amplification of demand variability, also known as the bullwhip effect [LEE 97].

9.2.2.3. *Slow IS*

We shall see that, conversely to the aforementioned work, two of our replenishment policies differ by in IS speed: instantaneous, as in section 9.2.2.2, or slower. In fact, IS may not be instantaneous in practice when the different information systems along a SC are not connected (or companies do not want them to be connected), and/or information processing may be required before transmitting this information upstream.

For instance, electronic data interchange (EDI) architecture allows instantaneous IS, but the absence of EDI implies manual operations (e.g. fax sending), which reduce the speed of IS. In this respect, we have not found any paper in which information transmission may have different speeds; most papers assume it to be instantaneous.

After this overview of previous work on IS, we now present a first model on upstream IS.

9.3. Upstream IS

This section proposes a first model for IS. The purpose of this model is mainly to study upstream IS, but it also allows us to study downstream IS, which we do at the end of the section.

9.3.1. *Model*

The system studied, as shown in Figure 9.1, is a two-level divergent SC containing a central warehouse and several retailers. We suppose that demands at the retailers are variable and follow a normal distribution. The replenishment lead time to the warehouse is variable with a uniform distribution. We also suppose that the lead time between the warehouse and the retailers is constant.

We first present a basic inventory model of the SC studied that aims to minimize the total inventory costs of the system (warehouse plus retailers). We then explain the process adopted to integrate IS into this model. The last part of this introduction to the model is dedicated to various allocation hypotheses for which we analyze the effects of IS as well as the efficiency of different possible allocation hypotheses.

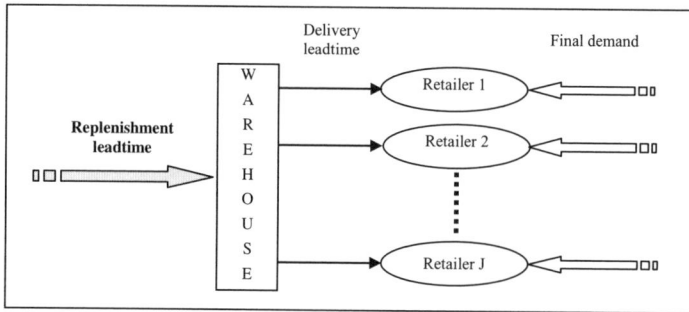

Figure 9.1. *Model considered for upstream IS*

9.3.1.1. *Basic inventory model*

The basic model represents the inventory costs of the system. The inventory costs of the warehouse only take holding costs into account, whereas for the retailers, both holding and shortage costs are taken into account. We assume one order per period and a negligible ordering cost.

The warehouse in this system is a decision center that has two decisions to make about inventory control and distribution. The first decision relates to replenishment, in order to satisfy the requests of all retailers. The second one concerns the allocation of available stock to the retailers. In other words, in each period the warehouse needs to determine: (i) an order quantity Q_t, readjusting its inventory to its optimal level; and (ii) the optimal quantities z_{jt} to transfer to the retailers.

The warehouse is the only decision-maker in the basic model. It minimizes the global inventory costs of all partners (its own as well as the total of those of the retailers) with a multi-echelon and centralized optimization approach. Consequently, an optimal inventory level at the warehouse optimizes the global inventory costs of the system. We suppose that all actions are performed at the beginning of a period, except the replenishment decision which occurs at the end of a period after the warehouse's inventory position is updated. We will now introduce the notations, followed by the model.

Indexes:

$j=\{1, 2,..., J\}$ – set of retailers,

$t=1, 2,..., T$ – timeline of planning periods.

Decision variables:

y^* – optimal inventory level of the warehouse,

z_{jt} – allocated quantity to retailer j by the warehouse in period t,

Z_t – sum of the quantities allocated (sent) by the warehouse to all of the retailers in period t,

Q_t – quantity ordered by the warehouse from its supplier in period t,

$AQ_{t,t+L_t}$ – quantity delivered to the warehouse in period $t+L_t$ (ordered in t as Q_t),

TAQ_t – sum of the quantities delivered to the warehouse in period t (ordered in any period before t),

X_{wt} – inventory level (in stock) at warehouse at the beginning of period t,

X_{jt} – on-hand inventory level of retailer j at the beginning of period t.

Parameters:

h_w – unitary holding cost to the warehouse (€.item^{-1}.period^{-1}),

h_j – unitary holding cost to retailer j (€.item^{-1}.period^{-1}),

p_j – unitary stock-out cost to retailer j (€.item^{-1}.period^{-1}),

D_jt – final demand at retailer j in period t. This demand follows the normal distribution $D_j = N(\mu_j, \sigma_j)$ with average μ_j and variance σ_j.

L_t – random lead time between the warehouse and its suppliers in period t,

l_j – constant lead time between retailer j and the warehouse,

TCW – inventory holding cost of the warehouse over the planning horizon considered T,

TCR – inventory (stock-out and holding) costs of all the retailers over the planning horizon considered T,

TCT – total cost of the system over the planning horizon considered T.

Objective function:

$$TCT = TCW + TCR \qquad\qquad [9.1]$$

$$TCW = \sum_{t=1}^{T} h_w (X_{wt} + TAQ_t - Z_t) \qquad\qquad [9.2]$$

$$TCR = \sum_{t=1}^{T} \sum_{j=1}^{J} \left[h_j \left(x_{jt} + z_{jt-l_j} - D_{jt} \right)^+ + p_j \left(D_{jt} - x_{jt} - z_{jt-l_j} \right)^+ \right] \qquad [9.3]$$

System dynamics:

$$X_{wt} = X_{wt-1} + AQ_{t-1} - Z_{t-1} \qquad \text{for } t = 1, 2, ..., T \qquad\qquad [9.4]$$

$$x_{jt} = x_{jt-1} + z_{jt-l_j-1} - D_{jt-1} \qquad \text{for } j = 1, 2, ..., J \text{ and } t = 1, 2, ..., T \qquad [9.5]$$

$$AQ_{t,t+L_t} = Q_t \qquad \text{for } t = 1, 2, ..., T \text{ and } t + L_t \le T \qquad\qquad [9.6]$$

$$TAQ_t = \sum_{n=1}^{t} AQ_{n,t} \qquad \text{for } t = 1, 2, ..., T \qquad\qquad [9.7]$$

Constraints:

$$Q_t = y^* - X_{wt} \qquad \text{for } t = 1, 2, ..., T \qquad\qquad [9.8]$$

$$Z_t \le X_{wt} + AQ_t \qquad \text{for } t = 1, 2, ..., T \qquad\qquad [9.9]$$

$$\sum_{j=1}^{J} z_{jt} = Z_t \qquad \text{for } t = 1, 2, ..., T \qquad\qquad [9.10]$$

$$z_{jt} \ge 0 \text{ and } y^* \ge 0 \qquad \text{for } j = 1, 2, ..., J \text{ and } t = 1, 2, ..., T \qquad [9.11]$$

9.3.1.2. *Decision on Q_t: replenishment policies for different levels of information accessibility*

We distinguish two scenarios here, namely, with or without IS. The difference between these two scenarios concerns their replenishment policies, which are adapted to the level of information accessibility. In the scenario with IS, the warehouse has full access to lead time information, whereas it ignores this information in the scenario without IS.

9.3.1.2.1. With IS

In the IS scenario, the decision maker (warehouse) receives the information concerning the actual replenishment lead time. This information allows this company to determine the optimal level of stock according to the known lead time. Song and Zipkin [SON 96] show that when the lead time is uncertain (random) and the decision maker has this information, thanks to IS the optimal policy is a variable stock level adjusted according to changes in the state of the system. (Here, this state is the variation in lead time.)

With the model corresponding to the IS scenario, it is possible to determine the optimal inventory levels of the warehouse for each period, according to the variations in lead time (y_t^* represents the optimal inventory levels of the warehouse in period t). Thus, in the scenario with IS and periodic rectification of the optimal inventory level, the inventory policy of the warehouse deciding on Q_t is a "state-dependent base-stock policy".

9.3.1.2.2. Without IS

When the warehouse has no access to lead time information, this company has to choose a single optimal inventory level. The model corresponding to this scenario without IS determines a single optimal inventory level for all periods (y^* represents a unique optimal inventory level of the warehouse, i.e. $y_t^* = y^*$ for any period t). In this scenario, the inventory policy choosing Q_t is a "simple base-stock policy".

9.3.1.3. *Decision on z_{jt}: different allocation hypotheses*

For the other decision to be made by the warehouse, different allocation hypotheses may be applied. An allocation hypothesis describes how the stocks available will be distributed between the retailers by the warehouse. We study various hypotheses in order to investigate the possible relations between different allocation constraints and the effects of IS. In fact, these allocation constraints make the allocation decision realistic and are unavoidable due to the usual agreements between partners in a SC. On the other hand, the hypotheses with supplementary constraints allow us to study the effects of real constraints on the efficiency of the allocation decision. For this we consider the following three hypotheses:

– *H1*: in the *constraint-free allocation*, the absence of constraints allows the warehouse to search for the optimal quantities z_{jt} to be sent to each retailer in each period. In other words, the warehouse determines the optimal allocation. Despite its lack of realism, this hypothesis should be the most efficient and thus act as a benchmark for the efficiency of more realistic hypotheses.

– *H2*: in the *final demand-dependant allocation*, the quantity z_{jt} allocated to each retailer is assumed to directly relate to the demands received from its customers. The model no longer optimizes the quantity to be sent to the retailers; it optimizes $Z_t = \sum_j z_{jt}$, i.e. the total sum allocated to all the retailers. On the other hand, this optimal total sum needs to be distributed according to another criterion, and an additional assumption is hence required to define this criterion. Obviously, this additional assumption allows us to analyze the effects of another type of IS, which is *final demand IS* – thus downstream IS in addition to upstream IS is considered so far – by defining the following two hypotheses:

- *H2_DS* (*H2 with demand IS*): the warehouse can access the actual final demand information of the retailers (D_{jt}) and uses this information to guide its allocation decisions:

$$z_{jt} = (D_{jt'}/\textstyle\sum D_{jt'}).Z_t \qquad\qquad \text{for } j = 1, 2, ..., J \qquad\qquad [9.12a]$$

– *H2_nDS* (*H2 without demand IS*): in this situation, the warehouse ignores the final demand information by the retailers and can only apply the average of this information (μ_j) to allocation decisions:

$$z_{jt} = (\mu_j /\textstyle\sum \mu_j).Z_t \qquad\qquad \text{for } j = 1, 2, ..., J \qquad\qquad [9.12b]$$

– *H3*: in the *equally shared allocation*, similarly to H2, by optimizing Z_t, the total quantity to be distributed is split equally among the retailers:

$$z_{jt} = Z_t/J \qquad\qquad \text{for } j = 1, 2, ..., J \qquad\qquad [9.13]$$

9.3.2. *Setting the parameters*

In all of the scenarios studied, the unitary holding cost is equal to 2 for the warehouse and 4 for every retailer. The delivery lead time between the warehouse and the retailers is considered to be negligible ($l_j = 0$). The final demand given by the customers follows a normal distribution with the different averages and variances for each retailer shown in Table 9.1.

Retailers j	1	2	3	4	5	6	7
Means of demand μ_j	100	150	200	150	170	250	120
Variances of demand σ_j	10	12	15	17	20	30	10

Table 9.1. *Averages and variance of final demands at retailers*

9.3.2.1. *Replenishment lead time (L)*

The duration L_t of the replenishment lead time between suppliers and warehouse seems to be another parameter with important effects on the value of IS lead time (according to the works described above). We consider that L_t follows a uniform distribution. To study the effect of the average as well as the dispersion of L_t on the value of IS, we consider three ranges of values: *L1* for the small range [5; 10] (thus, 7.5 ± 2.5); *L2* for the medium range [15; 20] = 17.5 ± 2.5 (thus, the same dispersion as *L1*); and *L3* for the wide range [1; 14] = 7.5 ± 6.5 (thus, the same average as *L1*).

	L1 (initial range)	*L2* (medium range)	*L3* (wide range)
Range of lead time L_t	[5; 10]	[15; 20]	[1; 14]

Table 9.2. *The three types of lead time studied*

9.3.2.2. *Shortage cost*

As in many industrial systems, shortages strongly affect the level of customer satisfaction and may have significant effects on the inventory costs and global efficiency of the overall system. When the level of customer service or the availability of stocks becomes critical, the unitary shortage cost also increases. To study the effect of unitary shortage costs, we make them take several values between 5 and 50.

9.3.2.3. *Number of retailers (J)*

As the number of retailers *J* may impact the global uncertainty of the system, we also study the effect of this factor on the value of IS. For this purpose, we consider three different numbers of retailers: $J \in \{3, 5, 7\}$.

9.3.2.4. *Customer behavior during the occurrence of stock-out*

Customers may display different behaviors when their retailers incur shortages. We call the case in which customers wait to receive the missing quantities "back-order". In this case, the retailer's stock position (X_{jt}) may be negative. If the customers do not wait to receive the missing quantities, what we call a "shortage" occurs in which the retailer's stock positions (X_{jt}) are never negative but are equal to zero. Consequently, we consider two models in which X_{jt} is either free (*back-order model*) or positive (*shortage model*).

9.3.3. *Results*

Considering a cycle of $T = 50$ periods, these models need to be run from five to 30 minutes in the LINGO 6 environment on a Pentium CPU at 2.67 GHz with 1.93 GB RAM, depending on the scenarios studied. We first present the experimental outcomes, then some sensibility analyses for all of the parameters introduced previously.

Tables 9.3 and 9.4 summarize the outcomes of the numerical experiments. Table 9.3 shows the costs when the end customer waits for the products sold by the SC considered to become available (back-order model). Table 9.4 summarizes the same costs when unsatisfied demand is not back-ordered but lost (shortage model). This corresponds to a situation in which the customer prefers not to wait (thus, does not buy at all or buys from a competitor).

			SOC 5	SOC 10	SOC 20	SOC 50
TCR	Shortage cost	nDS	44,535	169,094	344,541	487,362
		DS	27	15	76	88
		Saving	**99.9%**	**100%**	**100%**	**100%**
	Holding cost	nDS	145,290	112,254	100,752	92,963
		DS	1,174	1,060	1,144	1,125
		Saving	**99.2%**	**99.1%**	**98.9%**	**98.8%**
TCT	TCR	nDS	189,825	281,348	445,294	580,325
		DS	1,201	1,074	1,220	1,213
		Saving	**99.4%**	**99.6%**	**99.7%**	**99.8%**
	TCW	nDS	33,527	211,247	198,205	175,557
		DS	79,340	79,338	79,346	79,347
		Saving	**-136.6%**	**62.4%**	**60%**	**54.8%**
TCT		nDS	223,352	492,595	643,499	755,883
		DS	80,541	80,412	80,566	80,560
		Saving	**63.9%**	**83.7%**	**87.5%**	**89.3%**

Table 9.3. *Costs when unsatisfied demand is measured as back-orders*

Our model allows us to investigate the simultaneous sharing of upstream (lead time) and downstream (final demand) information by comparing the experimental outcomes obtained under *H2_DS* and *H2_nDS*. Specifically, the difference between *H2_DS* and *H2_nDS* is whether nor not final demand IS is used. *H2_DS* allows decisions to be made based on the actual demand of end customers, while *H2_nDS* replaces this information with its average.

9.3.3.1. Analysis of Table 9.3: unsatisfied demand is back-order

Our results seem to indicate that the benefit of downstream IS is related to whether or not upstream IS occurs. To see this, consider Table 9.5 more closely. In particular, *TCT* is lower for both values of stock-out cost (*SOC*) (5 and 50) under *H2_DS* when the information lead time is shared (case *DS*). In contrast, *TCT* under the other assumption *H2_nDS* is lower when the lead time information is not shared (case *nDS*). Consequently, when unsatisfied demand is back-ordered: (i) if the lead time information is shared (case *DS*), the demand information should also be shared (apply *H2_DS*); and (ii) if the lead time information is not shared (case *nDS*), the demand information should not be shared (apply *H2_nDS*).

			SOC 5	*SOC* 10	*SOC* 20	*SOC* 50
TCR	Shortage cost	*nDS*	20,295	70,429	162,794	398,587
		DS	51,258	67,454	113,155	281,685
		Saving	**-152.6%**	**4.2%**	**30.5%**	**29.3%**
	Holding cost	*nDS*	113,963	107,569	113,509	115,195
		DS	4,074	16,518	7,227	5,386
		Saving	**96%**	**85%**	**94%**	**95%**
TCT	*TCR*	*nDS*	134,258	177,998	276,303	513,782
		DS	55,332	83,973	120,382	287,071
		Saving	**58.8%**	**52.8%**	**56.4%**	**44.1%**
	TCW	*nDS*	35,819	44,879	31,092	36,442
		DS	64,328	78,767	110,576	105,527
		Saving	**-79.6%**	**-75.5%**	**-255.6%**	**-189.6%**
	TCT	*nDS*	170,077	222,876	307,395	550,224
		DS	119,661	162,740	230,957	392,598
		Saving	**29.6%**	**27%**	**24.9%**	**28.6%**

Table 9.4. *Costs when unsatisfied demand is measured as lost sales*

9.3.3.2. *Analysis of Table 9.5: unsatisfied demand is back-order*

Several calculations presented in Table 9.5 show the savings induced by final demand IS. This figure shows that this kind of IS always produces positive savings when lead time information is also shared and negative when it is not.

	SOC 5		SOC 50		Saving due to lead time IS	
	DS	nDS	DS	nDS	SOC 5	SOC 50
H2_DS (TCT)	**136,738**	293,386	**137,106**	1,106,864	53%	88%
H2_nDS (TCT)	158,427	**267,660**	173,348	**1,041,323**	41%	83%
Saving due to demand IS	14%	-10%	21%	-6%		

Table 9.5. *Effect of both types of IS in the case of back-ordering*

9.3.3.3. *Analysis of Table 9.6: unsatisfied demand is lost*

The previous conclusion does not hold when unsatisfied demands are lost. More precisely, the value of sharing demand information does not depend on sharing lead time information in the same way. In other words, demand IS is always cost-efficient, as shown by the fact that H2_DS induces a lower *TCT* than H2_nDS in all cases in Table 9.6.

	SOC 5		SOC 50		Saving due to lead time IS	
	DS	nDS	DS	nDS	SOC 5	SOC 50
H2_DS (TCT)	**136,223**	**196,444**	**462,871**	**551,121**	31%	16%
H2_nDS (TCT)	196,963	256,603	472,743	575,897	23%	18%
Saving due to demand IS	31%	23%	2%	4%		

Table 9.6. *Effect of both types of IS in the case of lost sales*

9.3.4. *Conclusion on upstream IS*

This first study on IS has considered a warehouse that stores products before delivering them to several retailers. The various scenarios considered in this section have allowed us to draw several conclusions.

Lead time IS has great impacts in all of the cases studied. This kind of IS positively or negatively impacts the performance, depending mainly on the type of behavior displayed by the end customer (back-order, i.e. patient customer, or stock-out, i.e. the customer does not come back). It also impacts on the cost of stock-outs, the number of retailers and the type of lead time:

– including allocation rules makes the model more realistic but does not reduce the performance;

– final demand IS does not always incur savings since it may also require lead time IS. In other words, final demand IS only has a positive impact when the lead time information is also shared.

Although we considered some upstream IS, this section has focused mainly on downstream IS. The next section studies the effects of downstream IS.

9.4. Downstream IS

9.4.1. *Model*

We now compare three replenishment policies, where two of them use downstream IS. This study is carried out in the context of the SC outlined in Figure 9.4. In this figure, two companies – the retailer r and wholesaler w – make replenishment decisions by applying one of policies α, β or γ. Table 9.7 outlines these strategies, which are summarized below (more details may be found in [MOY 09]).

Policy α is representative of traditional policies that are designed to be locally optimal. With this policy, the company orders (S-$InvPos$) items whenever its inventory position $InvPos$ is lower than some level s. When the demand O_t^{client} of the direct client is constant (thus, $O_0^{client} = O_1^{client} = \ldots = O^{client}$), and ordering and shipping lead times are ignored, the inventory system has the cyclic behavior shown in Figure 9.2. In particular, this figure shows that our simulation (dotted line) records the inventory level of a period as the level obtained at the end of this period in reality (continuous line). For instance, the company considered orders O^i items and instantly receives them, so that the inventory level is $s + O^i$ in reality, but only $s + O^i - O^{client}$ or $s + O^i - 2*O^{client}$ in our simulation.

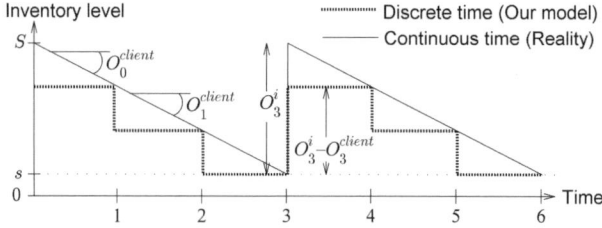

Figure 9.2. *Cycles for the inventory system of Company i when its supplier has no back-order and thus ships ordered quantity O_t^{client}*

The optimization of such an inventory system deals with the calculation of s and S. To calculate these parameters, first note that cycle [t = 0; t = 3] is identical to cycle [3; 6], etc. The duration of each cycle is O^i/O^{client} and a 365-day simulation thus has $365*O^{client}/O^i$ cycles. Next, the inventory level charged on the dth day of a cycle is $(s + O^i - d*O^{client})$, e.g. $s + O^i - O^{client}$ in [3; 4], $s + O^i - 2*O^{client}$ in [4; 5], and $s + O^i - 3*O^{client}$ in [5; 6] in Figure 9.2. Hence, the inventory on the dth day of a cycle costs $h*(s + O^i - d*O^{client})$, where h is the inventory carrying cost per item per day. Finally, the annual total cost (TC) of the inventory system is:

$$TC = 365\frac{O^{client}}{O^i}\sum_{t=1}^{O^i/O^{client}}h(s+O^i-tO^{client}) \qquad [9.14]$$

$$TC = 365\frac{O^{client}}{O^i}\left[h(s+O^i)\frac{O^i}{O^{client}}-hO^{client}\frac{\dfrac{O^i}{O^{client}}\left(\dfrac{O^i}{O^{client}}+1\right)}{2}\right] \qquad [9.15]$$

$$= 365h(s+\frac{O^i-O^{client}}{2})$$

Clearly, $TC = 0$ when $O^{i*} = O^{client}$ (the company orders what is ordered by its client) and $s^* = 0$ (no safety stocks necessary since demand is constant). Figure 9.3a shows the corresponding behavior, i.e. the demand is backlogged most of the time but this is ignored by discrete time. Figure 9.3b shows the same behavior when demand O_t^{client} is variable (e.g. $O_{t1}^{client} \neq O_{t2}^{client}$), and its forecast is perfect, and the ordering delay is two days. Other assumptions may be relaxed from Figure 9.2 in order to find the optimum of the model simulated.

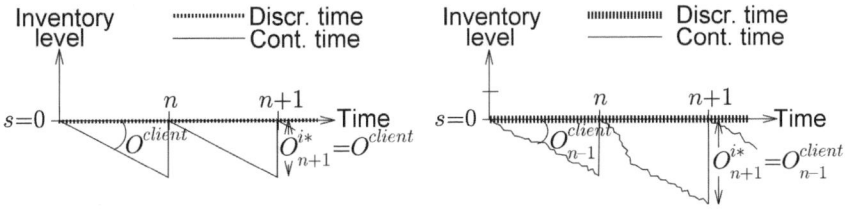

(a) O_t^{client} is constant ($O_t^{client} = O^{client}$) (b) O_t^{client} is variable and assumed to be

forecast without errors

Figure 9.3. *Optimal setting of Figure 9.2 for two assumptions about O_t^{client}*

In fact, the main reason for which the theoretical α presented in this section does not follow the simulated α is that we only model company *i* and assume that its supplier always ships O^i items when this quantity is requested. In other words, the inefficiency of the retailer's α is due to the wholesaler's back-orders, but these back-orders are not modeled in Figures 9.2 and 9.3. For instance, the wholesaler may not ship O^i items as expected in this figure, but, for instance, only $O^i/2$ now and $O^i/2$ later on. As a consequence, the retailer's inventory system does not always behave cyclically, as assumed in our figures.

Finally, Figure 9.3b shows why any order O_t^i placed on day *t* by following policy α may be calculated as in equation [9.16]:

$$O_t^{\text{direct\_client}} = \begin{cases} 0 & \text{if } InvPos_t^i > 0, \\ O_{t-2}^{\text{direct\_client}} - InvPos_t^{\text{direct\_client}} & \text{if } InvPos_t^i \leq 0. \end{cases} \qquad [9.16]$$

Policy β relies on a different paradigm than α, that is, on stream management (rather than optimization). More precisely, β has been designed to reduce the bullwhip effect as much as possible, rather than produce an optimal model. β also differs from α by its use of IS. Here, orders are now vectors of two orders (O, Θ), where *O* corresponds to market demand information (that is, all companies use the lot-for-lot policy to choose *O*, as illustrated in the first line of equation [9.17]), and Θ is chosen so that $O + \Theta$ corresponds to the quantity actually required by the company. If $\lambda = 4$ is a constant defined by the duration of the order and shipping lead times (see 2 days + 2 days in Figure 9.4), then equation [9.17] describes β:

$$\begin{pmatrix} O_t^i \\ \Theta_t^i \end{pmatrix} = \begin{pmatrix} O_{t-2}^{\text{direct\_client}} \\ \Theta_{t-2}^{\text{direct\_client}} + \lambda\left(O_{t-2}^{\text{direct\_client}} - O_{t-3}^{\text{direct\_client}}\right) \end{pmatrix} \qquad [9.17]$$

Policy γ is similar to β, except that IS is now assumed to be instantaneous, i.e. all companies are assumed to be connected to the same information system. As a consequence, companies can base their orders on the demand of the end customer and $λ = 2$ because only shipping lead times have to be taken into account, as shown in equation [9.18]:

$$\begin{pmatrix} O_t \\ \Theta_t \end{pmatrix} = \begin{pmatrix} O_{t-2}^{final\_customer} \\ \Theta_{t-2}^{direct\_client} + \lambda\left(O_{t-2}^{final\_customer} - O_{t-3}^{final\_customer}\right) \end{pmatrix} \qquad [9.18]$$

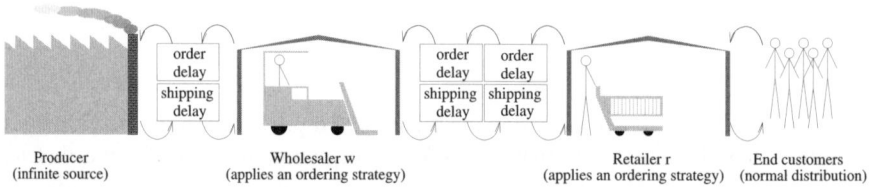

| | order delay | | order delay | order delay | | |
| | shipping delay | | shipping delay | shipping delay | | |

Producer (infinite source)   Wholesaler w (applies an ordering strategy)   Retailer r (applies an ordering strategy)   End customers (normal distribution)

Figure 9.4. *Structure of the SC in which downstream IS is studied*

Replenishment policy	Paradigm	Information sharing
α	optimization	none
β	stream management	slow
γ		instantaneous

Table 9.7. *Overview of the replenishment policies considered*

9.4.2. *Results*

Figure 9.5 shows the average over 15,000 simulations of the daily average on-hand inventory level in 365-day simulations, i.e. $AVG_{15,000simulations}$ $(AVG_{365days}$ *Inventory$_i$*), where *i* represents retailer *r* or wholesaler *w*. Note that the full shapes in Figure 9.5 are always above their empty equivalent, i.e. full squares above empty squares, full circles above empty circles, etc. This means that the wholesaler has higher inventory levels than its retailer, even if the same ordering strategy is used by both companies.

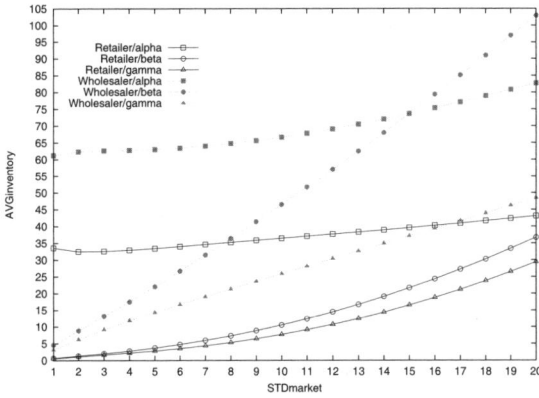

Figure 9.5. $AVG_{15,000simulations}$ ($AVG_{365days}$ Inventory$_i$) against the standard deviation STD_{market} of market demand with strategies α, β and γ (i ∈ {r, w})

Figure 9.6 shows $AVG_{15,000simulations}$($AVG_{365days}$ Backorder$_i$) where i represents the retailer or the wholesaler. Figure 9.6 cannot be described as easily as Figure 9.5. In fact, only full squares are always above empty squares, meaning again that the wholesaler has smaller back-orders than its retailer, but only when α is used. Things are less clear for circles (strategy β) and triangles (γ):

– empty circles are above full circles for STD_{market} ≤11, above for 12≥ STD_{market} ≥15 and below for STD_{market} ≥15;

– empty triangles are above full triangles for STD_{market} ≤8, above for STD_{market} = 9 and below for STD_{market} ≥10.

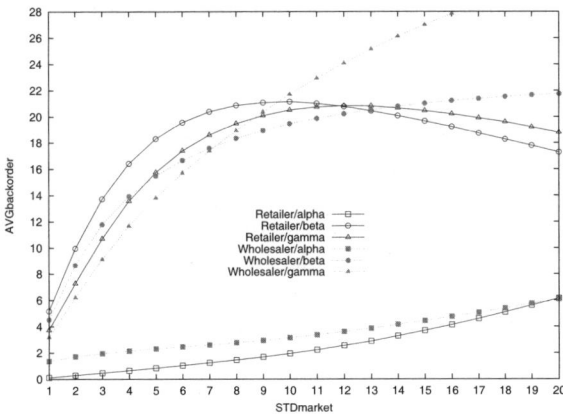

Figure 9.6. $AVG_{15,000simulations}$($AVG_{365days}$ Backorder$_i$) against the standard deviation STD_{market} of market demand with strategies α, β and γ (i ∈ {r, w})

In summary, the distribution of back-orders between the retailer and its wholesaler with β and γ depends on STD_{market}, while it does not with α (the wholesaler always has higher back-orders). Note that Figures 9.5 and 9.6 measure the consequences of the ordering strategy used on the dynamics of our SC. Of course, these dynamics include the bullwhip effect.

Next, we calculate the total daily cost of the entire SC as $cost_{sc} = cost_r + cost_w$ from Figures 9.5 and 9.6. Here, $cost_r$ and $cost_w$ are the logistic costs of the retailer and the wholesaler, computed as follows:

$$cost_r = \eta(Inventory_r + \varepsilon_r \, Backorder_r) \qquad\qquad [9.19]$$

$$cost_w = Inventory_w + \varepsilon_w \, Backorder_w \qquad\qquad [9.20]$$

In these definitions, parameter $\eta \geq 1$ measures the difference in costs, for the retailer and the wholesaler, in holding products in inventory. In fact, part of inventory holding cost depends on the value of the products stored, and this value increases along the SC. As a result, we assume that $Inventory_w$ represents both the daily average number of items in inventory for the wholesaler and the daily average cost of holding this inventory for this company. In other words, the cost of holding an item in inventory for one day is assumed to be €1 for the wholesaler. For the sake of simplicity, the rest of this section will consider $\eta = 1.37$ to reflect the fact that, in general, the annual inventory holding cost is 37% higher for the retailer than for the wholesaler. Next, $Inventory_r$ also represents the daily average number of items in inventory for the retailer, but this quantity has to be multiplied by η in order to obtain the average daily cost of holding this inventory for the retailer. The second parameter in the previous two equations is ε_i, which represents the pricing by i of its back-orders, e.g. $\varepsilon_i = 0$ means that i does not want back-orders and thus lets its clients wait for the products to become available, while a large ε_i denotes the fact that i prefers to have high inventory levels rather than back-orders.

Figure 9.7 shows the total cost of the SC against STD_{market} for ε equal to 0, 1, 2, 5 or 10. As may be expected without experimentations, the total cost of the SC increases as STD_{market}, i.e., the less predictable the market, the higher the inventory and back-order levels. Another point seen in Figure 9.5 and 9.6 is the fact that the three strategies induce different levels of inventory and back-orders. As a consequence, the total cost of the SC under a specific strategy is higher for some values of ε than for other strategies. What we mean here may easily be observed by comparing the upper left entry in Figure 9.7 ($\varepsilon_r = \varepsilon_w = 0$) with the lower right entry ($\varepsilon_r = \varepsilon_w = 10$): the strategy incurring the lowest cost in the former entry is α, and γ in the latter entry. This fact holds for any STD_{market}. Hence, the willingness to satisfy its direct client is better obtained by high values of ε.

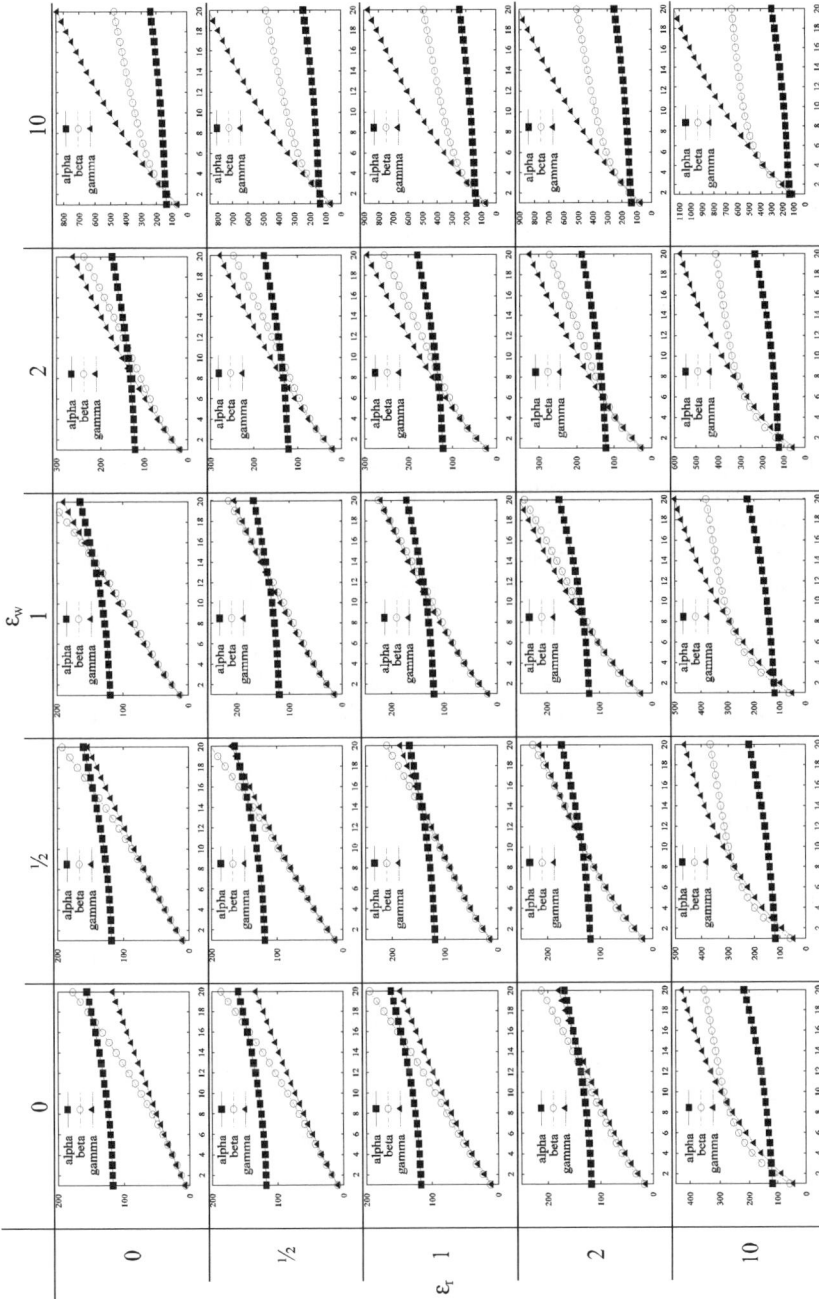

Figure 9.7. *Total cost of the SC with strategies α, β, γ against STD_market*

9.5. Conclusion

This chapter has presented two models for IS in SCs. The first model studies a mix of up- and downstream IS, i.e. lead time and demand IS, respectively. The second model deals with just downstream IS, i.e. demand IS. Both models show the value of IS measured as the savings allowed for by better information. To be precise, "better" may be understood as more accurate or earlier information about what happens in another part of the SC. Such information allows companies to reduce their costs. This cost reduction corresponds to the maximum price these companies are prepared to pay for such information, thus for IS.

Of course, we only considered the reduction of logistical costs, without paying any attention to the installation and operation costs of the information system needed to support IS. Depending on such installation and operation costs, IS is consistently the best strategy to increase the competitive advantage of a SC. In future work, we plan to extend the studies in this chapter in order to include costs incurred by connecting the different information systems along a SC. Chapters 5 and 6 indicate that such a connection of information systems is not trivial. Hence, the costs of installation and operation that are incurred may not be negligible.

Other extensions of the work in this chapter are possible. The next chapter presents the application of economic concepts to improve the analysis of the results obtained with our second model. More precisely, the SC structure and strategies α, β and γ will be studied when companies are autonomous (with game theory) and the decision-makers in these companies take risks into account (with the adaptation of a criterion called "value at risk").

9.6. Bibliography

[AGR 09] AGRAWAL S., SENGUPTA R. N., SHANKER, K., "Impact of information sharing and lead time on bullwhip effect and on-hand inventory", *European Journal of Operational Research*, vol. 192, no. 2, 2009, pp. 576-593.

[AVI 01] AVIV Y., "The effect of collaborative forecasting on supply chain performance", *Management Science*, vol. 47, no. 10, 2001, pp. 1326-1343.

[AXS 06] AXSÄTER S., *Inventory Control*, 2nd edition, Springer, 2006.

[CAC 00] CACHON G., FISHER M., "Supply chain inventory management and the value of shared information". *Management Science*, vol. 46, no. 8, 2000, pp. 1032-48.

[CHE 98] CHEN F., "Echelon reorder points, installation reorder points, and the value of centralized demand information", *Management Science*, vol. 44, no. 12, 1998, pp.S221-S34.

[CHE 03] CHEN F., "Information sharing and supply chain coordination", in: GRAVES S., De KOK, T. (eds.), *Handbooks in Operations Research and Management Science: Supply Chain Management: Design, Coordination and Operation, vol. 11*, North Holland, Amsterdam, 2003, pp. 341-422.

[CHE 05] CHEN F., YU B., "Quantifying the value of leadtime information in a single-location inventory system", *Manufacturing & Service Operations Management*, vol. 7, 2005, pp. 144-151.

[DAM 99] D'AMOURS S., MONTREUIL B, LEFRANCOIS P., SOUMIS F., "Networked manufacturing: The impact of information sharing", *International Journal of Production Economics*, vol. 58, no. 1, 1999, pp. 63-79.

[GAV 99] GAVIRNENI S., KAPUSCINSKI R., TAYUR S., "Value of information in capacitated supply chains", *Management Science*, vol. 45, no. 1, 1999, pp. 16-24.

[HAR 13] HARRIS, F. W. "How many parts to make at once", *Factory, The Magazine of Management*, vol. 10, no. 2, 1913, pp. 135-136, 152.

[HUA 03] HUANG G. Q., LAU J. S. K., MAK K. L., "The impacts of sharing production information on supply chain dynamics: a review of the literature", *International Journal of Production Research*, vol. 41, no. 7, 2003, pp. 1483-1517.

[LEE 97] LEE H. L., PADMANABHAN V., WHANG S., "Information distortion in a supply chain: the bullwhip effect", *Management Science*, vol. 43, no. 4, 1997, pp. 546-558.

[LEE 00] LEE, H., SO K., TANG C. "The value of information sharing in a two-level supply chain", *Management Science*, vol. 46, no. 5, 2000, pp. 626-643.

[MOY 09] MOYAUX T., LLERENA D., BABOLI A., "Choice of an ordering strategy taking account of risks about customer service levels and on-hand inventories", *Proceedings of the International Conference on Industrial Engineering and Systems Management* (IESM), Montreal, PQ, Canada, 2009.

[OUY 07] OUYANG Y., "The effect of information sharing on supply chain stability and the bullwhip effect", *European Journal of Operational Research*, vol. 182, no. 3, 2007, pp. 1107-1121.

[SIL 98] SILVER E. A., PYKE D. F., PETERSON R. *Inventory Management and Production Planning and Scheduling*, John Wiley and Sons, 1998.

[SON 96] SONG J. S., ZIPKIN P., "Inventory control with information about supply conditions", *Management Science*, vol. 42, 1996, pp. 1409-1419.

Chapter 10

Coordination of Replenishment Policies: Game Theory and Uncertainty in Supply Chains

10.1. Introduction

Replenishment policies are decisions at the operational level, on when and how much to order, while the choice of which replenishment policy to use is a strategic decision. These operational decisions on orders usually assume that the company considered is alone. However, most companies are embedded in (at least) one supply chain (SC), the different members of which are connected. Consequently, every order placed not only depends on the state (e.g. inventory level, products currently shipped from suppliers, etc.) and replenishment policy of the company, but also on the state and ordering policy of its clients and suppliers. A strategic decision on which ordering strategy to use must therefore take into account not only the internal constraints of the company, but also the constraints imposed by the rest of the SC. Game theory allows for such constraints to be taken into account in order to make this kind of strategic decision. It proposes tools to analyze the decision made by "players" (here, companies) when they take the decisions of the other players into account. Note that in this chapter we use "replenishment policy" and "ordering strategy" interchangeably. While the former corresponds to the terminology of SC management, the latter is characteristic of game theory and, more generally, economics.

Chapter written by Daniel LLERENA, Thierry MOYAUX and Armand BABOLI.

In addition to using game theory to study the multiple effects of choices made by the different companies in a SC, we investigate the impact of two of the parameters of these companies that may also impact on their choice of replenishment policy. These parameters are the corporate decision-makers' attitude towards risk, and the importance paid by these decision makers to the service delivered to their clients.

Attitudes towards risk are taken into account for the purpose of comparing the average μ and the dispersion σ (standard deviation) of the logistic costs incurred. Intuitively, the problem may be stated as follows: is it better to be sure to incur high costs (i.e. large μ and low σ) or, on the contrary, to take the chance of randomly incurring either low or very high costs (i.e. low μ and high σ)? We address this question by proposing a transformation of the value at risk (VaR) – a common way of comparing portfolios of financial assets in finance, taking the risk of loss into account – into a cost at risk (CaR).

The second parameter characterizing each of our companies is the attitude towards service delivered to clients. Here, the intuition is that some companies may not try to fulfill their clients' needs quickly in order to reduce their inventory holding cost. This reduces clients' satisfaction since they have to wait for the availability of products. (We consequently assume there are no lost sales since demand is back-ordered until products are available to satisfy this demand.) On the other hand, other companies may keep high inventory levels because they want to avoid any possible stock-outs so they can always satisfy their clients' demand. Hence, the stock-outs may be priced differently, depending on the importance given to the level of customer service. This chapter uses back-orders as a measure of customer satisfaction, i.e. as a measure of the time that the customer waited.

It is interesting to compare our approach to others. In fact, applying game theory to SC management and taking account of parameters such as attitude towards risk and customer service levels are not novelties. For instance, many papers on game theory have been reviewed by [LEN 05] but most of them deal with operational decisions, while the question addressed in this paper is at a strategic level where few papers are available. One example is the problem of location-allocation investigated by [SAI 08]. We do not know of any paper on strategic decisions that is similar to this chapter, i.e. analyzes choice of replenishment policy. Of course, applications of game theory to replenishment policies do exist and even account for most of the papers reviewed by [LEN 05], but these papers focus on the operational level, i.e. when and how much to order on a daily basis. For instance, [WAN 94] prove that the optimal order quantity of three retailers in the Nash equilibrium is larger than that under the classic newsboy problem. We do not know of any other work using game theory to study the replenishment policy chosen by companies in a SC. Nor do we know of any papers taking parameters, such as attitudes towards risk and customer service levels, into account.

One of the contributions of this chapter is a method based on game theory to study when companies prefer a replenishment policy. Technically, this chapter has several contributions, such as our method that depends on attitudes towards risk and client satisfaction, and the definition of a CaR based on a performance indicator called VaR. We also illustrate our method with a case study comparing three different replenishment policies. Here, α is a representative of traditional replenishment policies based on optimization and using no information sharing (IS), β is a policy designed to reduce the bullwhip effect by exploiting slow IS, and γ is an improvement on β in which IS is instantaneous. The main motivation for applying our method to compare α, β and γ is the comparison of two different paradigms: optimization and stream management. In fact, α is assumed to be locally optimal, i.e. each company decides on its orders without taking other companies into account, and thus ignoring their potential stock-outs.

On the other hand, β and γ were designed to reduce the bullwhip effect, i.e. the amplification of order variability that causes both the reduction of agility and increase in inventory levels in SCs [MOY 07]. Consequently, a company using β or γ acts as a "team player" by placing more stable orders; in other words, it helps upstream companies (suppliers, etc.) to reduce their logistic costs. Such a company thus tries to improve the overall efficiency (at least of the upstream part) of the SC, rather than just its own. We use our method to check whether it is rational for a company to use such behavior (i.e. to use β or γ), while this company could also opt for positive actions for itself and ignore the impact of its replenishment decisions on the rest of the SC (i.e. by using α). Of course, strong interdependencies among the members of a SC may induce harmful consequences, not only for the rest of the SC but also for a selfish company using α. Hence, another contribution of this chapter is the application of our method to study whether companies are better off being selfish (using α) or cooperative (using β or γ).

The outline of this paper is as follows. Section 10.2 details the proposed method. Section 10.3 then applies our method to compare policies α, β and γ, and presents our game theory analysis of the coordination of our three ordering strategies. Finally, section 10.4 discusses the results obtained with these three policies and section 10.5 concludes with some insights into our method.

10.2. Method of investigation

The method used in this chapter can be summarized in the following three steps:

– *Define the scope of the analysis*: we should first specify the question to be addressed, that is, choose the part of the SC to study and select the policies to compare before implementing them. At this stage, we should also make the replenishment policies compatible, e.g. adapt the strategy β applied by a retailer in order to make it usable with the γ followed by its wholesaler.

– *Run numerical experiments*: after the model has been programmed, numerical experiments are run in order to measure the efficiency of every combination of replenishment policies for every company. Different measures of efficiency may be recorded here. For example, our case study investigates the efficiency for retailer r and its wholesaler w when they use the three replenishment policies: α, β and γ. In this case, therefore, $3^2 = 9$ combinations of α, β and γ need to be run. We may also call each of these nine combinations "joint strategy" s or "configurations", e.g. $s = (α, γ)$ when the retailer applies $s_r = α$ and its wholesaler $s_w = γ$. Every joint strategy $s = (s_r, s_w)$ is run 15,000 times in order to measure the average μ and the standard deviation σ of the inventory i and back-order b. For instance, $μ_{i,r}(α, γ)$ is the average inventory level of the retailer when this company uses strategy α while the wholesaler uses γ. Here, each of the 9*15,000 simulations is repeated under 20 different values of standard deviation $σ_m$ of the market demand, so that the different μ and σ are functions of $σ_m$, e.g. $μ_{i,r}(α, γ, 1)$ when $σ_m = 1$ (see equations [10.8]-[10.47] for approximations of these functions obtained by regressions over simulation outputs in the appendix in section 10.6).

– *Analyze the experimental data*: the data collected in the previous step are used to build the companies' individual utility functions, which are then analyzed as games in the normal form. These utility functions are designed according to the question to be addressed and their analysis is the most important part of our method.

In our case study the utility functions will be based on the performance indicator CaR and will take customer service levels into account. The analysis of these functions is detailed in section 10.3.

10.2.1. *Model of SC studied*

Up to now, we have roughly described strategies α, β or γ, but have not specified these strategies or the model of SC considered. We now outline our model. Despite being a continuation of the fourth section in Chapter 9, this part of the chapter is intended to be self-contained. We therefore describe only the most salient elements of our simulation of a SC, especially the features of α, β and γ compared by our method. The reader is referred to the previous chapter of this book for additional details on the SC model and the three replenishment policies.

As noted above, we consider a SC in which the market m buys from a retailer r. This retailer orders products from a wholesaler w, and the wholesaler places orders with a supplier s. The first of these four participants is m, which is represented as a normal distribution of integers with mean $μ_m = 50$ and standard deviation

$\sigma_m \in \{1, 2 \ldots, 20\}$. The experiments are carried out over 365 simulated days. Ordering and shipping lead times last two days. The last participant, s, is an infinite source of products and does not place any orders.

r and w are the only members of the SC to make decisions. These decisions deal with ordering, which is achieved by implementing one of the following three policies (also called "replenishment policies"):

– *Policy/strategy α (optimization without IS)*: the first policy aims to minimize the operating cost of the inventory system of the company considered, assuming the direct supplier (i.e. w for r, and s for w) never incurs stock-outs. If we call $O_{d-2}^{direct\ client}$ the order O placed by the direct client of i two days earlier and arriving at i on day d, where $InvPos_d^i$ is the inventory position (defined as the sum of on-hand inventory plus on-order products minus back-ordered orders), then we can formally describe the order O_d^i placed by the company considered using strategy α as in equation [10.1]:

$$O_d^i = \begin{cases} 0 & \text{if } InvPos_d^i > 0, \\ O_{d-2}^{direct\_client} - InvPos_d^i & \text{if } InvPos_d^i \le 0. \end{cases} \qquad [10.1]$$

– *Policy/strategy β (point-to-point IS)*: strategy β does not aim to directly minimize the cost of the inventory system, but to reduce the bullwhip effect (i.e. amplification of order variability along a SC). For that purpose, this strategy replaces the single number of traditional orders by a vector (O, θ) so that it can share demand information and thus help companies to place orders that are closer to actual demand. This reduces the bullwhip effect. Technically, orders are vectors of the two components O (market demand transmitted from every company to its supplier) and θ (inventory adjustment) that enable the companies to share information, as shown in equation [10.2]:

$$\begin{pmatrix} O_t^i \\ \theta_t^i \end{pmatrix} = \begin{pmatrix} O_{t-2}^{direct\_client} \\ \theta_{t-2}^{direct\_client} + \lambda\left(O_{t-2}^{direct\_client} - O_{t-3}^{direct\_client}\right) \end{pmatrix} \qquad [10.2]$$

– *Policy/strategy γ (information centralization, i.e. instantaneous IS)*: in short, $\gamma = \beta +$ information centralization. More precisely, γ is very similar to β, except for the addition of information centralization (defined as the real-time sharing in of market consumption by the retailer with the rest of the SC). The difference between the IS in β and γ is its speed, which is as slow as orders with β, or instantaneous with γ. Consequently, equation [10.3] may rely on the market demand O^m, known thanks to actual point-of-sales data, which is the same information as O^{direct_client} without ordering delays:

$$\begin{pmatrix} O_t^i \\ \theta_t^i \end{pmatrix} = \begin{pmatrix} O_{t-2}^m \\ \theta_{t-2}^{direct\_client} + \lambda\left(O_{t-2}^m - O_{t-3}^m\right) \end{pmatrix}$$

[10.3]

10.2.2. Numerical experimentations

As r may adopt one replenishment policy while w applies another, we have to analyze $3^2 = 9$ combinations of the three policies in the two companies. Table 10.1 shows these combinations as a game in the normal form, e.g. the left entry of the third line corresponds to joint strategy (γ, α) in which r uses γ and w uses α. In each of the nine entries, market demand information O^m is transmitted by market m to retailer r, then orders O^r are placed by r to w, and O^w by w to the infinite source s of products. This table emphasizes the fact that the three policies considered differ not only in the paradigm they are based on (optimization *versus* stream management), but also by their type of IS (none with α, slow with β, and instantaneous with γ).

		Wholesaler w		
		α	β	γ
Retailer r	α	$O_t^r = \begin{cases} 0 \text{ if } InvPos_t^r > 0 \\ O_{t-2}^m - InvPos_t^r \text{ if } InvPos_t^r \le 0 \end{cases}$ *[graph: m r w s]* $O_t^w = \begin{cases} 0 \text{ if } InvPos_t^w > 0 \\ O_{t-2}^r - InvPos_t^r \text{ if } InvPos_t^w \le 0 \end{cases}$	$O_t^r = \begin{cases} 0 \text{ if } InvPos_t^r > 0 \\ O_{t-2}^m - InvPos_t^r \text{ if } InvPos_t^r \le 0 \end{cases}$ *[graph: m r w s]* $(O_t^w, \theta_t^w) = (O_{t-2}^r, \lambda(O_{t-2}^r - O_{t-3}^r))$	$O_t^r = \begin{cases} 0 \text{ if } InvPos_t^r > 0 \\ O_{t-2}^m - InvPos_t^r \text{ if } InvPos_t^r \le 0 \end{cases}$ *[graph: m r w s]* $(O_t^w, \theta_t^w) = (O_{t-2}^r, \lambda(O_{t-2}^r - O_{t-3}^r))$
	β	$(O_t^r, \theta_t^r) = (O_{t-2}^m, \lambda(O_{t-2}^m - O_{t-3}^m))$ *[graph: m r w s]* $O_t^w = \begin{cases} 0 \text{ if } InvPos_t^w > 0 \\ (O_{t-2}^r + \theta_{t-2}^r) - InvPos_t^w \text{ if } InvPos_t^w \le 0 \end{cases}$	$(O_t^r, \theta_t^r) = (O_{t-2}^m, \lambda(O_{t-2}^m - O_{t-3}^m))$ *[graph: m r w s]* $(O_t^w, \theta_t^w) = (O_{t-4}^r, \theta_{t-2}^r + \lambda(O_{t-4}^m - O_{t-5}^m))$	$(O_t^r, \theta_t^r) = (O_{t-2}^m, \lambda(O_{t-2}^m - O_{t-3}^m))$ *[graph: m r w s]* $(O_t^w, \theta_t^w) = (O_{t-4}^r, \theta_{t-2}^r + \lambda(O_{t-4}^m - O_{t-5}^m))$
	γ	$(O_t^r, \theta_t^r) = (O_{t-2}^m, \lambda(O_{t-2}^m - O_{t-3}^m))$ *[graph: m r w s]* $O_t^w = \begin{cases} 0 \text{ if } InvPos_t^w > 0 \\ (O_{t-2}^r + \theta_{t-2}^r) - InvPos_t^w \text{ if } InvPos_t^w \le 0 \end{cases}$	$(O_t^r, \theta_t^r) = (O_{t-2}^m, \lambda(O_{t-2}^m - O_{t-3}^m))$ *[graph: m r w s]* $(O_t^w, \theta_t^w) = (O_{t-4}^r, \theta_{t-2}^r + \lambda(O_{t-4}^m - O_{t-5}^m))$	$(O_t^r, \theta_t^r) = (O_t^m, \lambda(O_t^m - O_{t-1}^m))$ *[graph: m r w s]* $(O_t^w, \theta_t^w) = (O_t^r, \theta_{t-2}^r + \lambda(O_t^m - O_{t-1}^m))$

Table 10.1. *The nine combinations of ordering strategies considered*

Finally, running each of these nine configurations of replenishment policies generates the four aforementioned measures (i.e. μ_i, σ_i, μ_b, and σ_b,) per company and per joint strategy. Equations [10.8]-[10.47] in the appendix in section 10.6 provide polynomial approximations of the experimental outcomes. The rest of this chapter considers just these approximations.

Note that the five joint strategies covered by these 8*5 equations are enough to describe all of the nine joint strategies in Table 10.1. This is because some configurations induce the same behavior of the SC due to the similarity of strategies β and γ. For instance, Table 10.1 shows that (β, γ) and (γ, β) operate as (β, β) because O^m cannot be used by w, who can only use O^r. This is because: (i) O^m is not transmitted by r to w, and w only receives O^r in $(\beta, \gamma) - (\beta, \gamma)$ and thus operates as (β, β); while (ii) O^m is transmitted by r but ignored by w, who only uses O^r in $(\gamma, \beta) - (\gamma, \beta)$, and thus also operates as (β, β).

10.3. Game theory analysis of the coordination of ordering strategies

10.3.1. *Details on attitudes towards customer service levels and risk*

In this chapter we assume the inventory holding cost to be €1.day^{-1}.product^{-1} and the back-order cost to be €λ_k.day^{-1}.product^{-1} for company $k \in \{r, w\}$ with $\lambda_k \geq 0$. In fact, companies always have to pay for holding inventories and the cost depends on how many units there are and how long they are stored for. Companies may try to minimize the inventory holding cost by keeping as few items as possible, which often results in stock-outs.

In this chapter we assume no lost sales, so that stock-outs make the clients wait for the availability of products. Consequently, low inventory levels incur back-orders, which result in a decreased customer service level since clients have to wait for the products they have ordered. In addition, the utility of each firm will take inventory costs and back-order costs into account. Let us now introduce this utility function, called CaR.

According to the volatility of inventory σ_i and backorder σ_b performances, each joint strategy must be evaluated with a synthetic indicator. For this, we propose to use an adaptation of the VaR criterion. Investors, particularly financial institutions, often need to estimate the probability of "worst-case" scenarios.

In particular, VaR is a widely used measure of the risk of loss on a specific portfolio of financial assets. For a given portfolio, probability and time horizon, VaR is defined as a threshold value so that the probability that the market-to-market loss on the portfolio over the given time horizon exceeds this threshold value [JOR 06].

In other words, VaR estimates the largest loss that a portfolio would suffer with a (generally) small probability over a specified period [MCN 05]. Formally, if r is the financial output of the portfolio and *risk* the probability, VaR is defined as the value such that $\Pr[\text{VaR} < r] = risk$.

Since, in our study, the performances of joint strategies are inventory holding and back-order costs – and thus minimized by each company – we propose to transform this indicator into a CaR criterion with the formula in equation [10.4]. In this formula, company k plays strategy $s_k \in \{\alpha, \beta, \gamma\}$ while the other companies play joint strategy s_{-k}, i.e. s_{-k} is a vector of several individual strategies while s_k is a single individual strategy. In the case study illustrating this, $k = r$ implies $-k = w$ and *vice versa*, because we only consider two companies $k \in \{r, w\}$:

$$\Pr\left[C_T > CaR_k\left(s_k, S_{-k}, \sigma_m \right) \right] = risk \tag{10.4}$$

where C_T is the total cost of the strategy and $k \in \{r, w\}$.

If inventory and back-order performances are normally distributed, the CaR of a joint strategy is given by equation [10.5], which completes the basic form outlined in equation [10.4]:

$$\begin{aligned} CaR_k\left(s_k, s_{-k}, \sigma_m \right) = & \left[\mu_{i,k}\left(s_k, s_{-k}, \sigma_m \right) + \lambda_k \mu_{b,k}\left(s_k, s_{-k}, \sigma_m \right) \right] \\ & + t_{risk}\left[\sigma_{i,k}\left(s_k, s_{-k}, \sigma_m \right) + \lambda_k \sigma_{b,k}\left(s_k, s_{-k}, \sigma_m \right) \right] \end{aligned} \tag{10.5}$$

where t_{risk} is given by the standard normal distribution.

For a given joint strategy (s_k, s_{-k}) and a given volatility σ_m of market demand, the CaR indicator gives the threshold cost so that the probability of the total cost exceeding this value is *risk*. When comparing two joint strategies, the strategy with the lowest CaR – for a same probability *risk* – will be preferred by the company.

Let us illustrate the operation of our indicator by comparing two instances α and β in Figure 10.1. This figure shows the probability density corresponding to CaR(α) and CaR(β) incurred when strategies α and β are played, respectively (and the other players choose a joint strategy ignored in our example). We want to know when one CaR is better than the other.

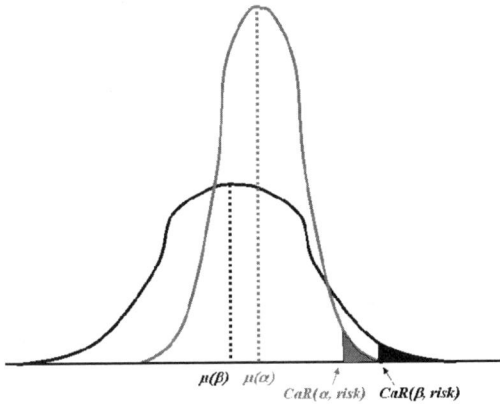

Figure 10.1. *How the CaR function models the dispersions of performances induced by two replenishment policies*

In this figure, two strategies α and β have average performances in terms of costs. β would be preferred to α because $\mu(\beta) < \mu(\alpha)$. Note that the dispersion of these performances is greater for strategy β than for strategy α. For a given *risk*, we can then deduce that the cost of strategy β has a probability *risk* of being higher than CaR(β, *risk*). On the other hand, the cost of strategy α has a probability *risk* of being higher than CaR(α, *risk*). In other words, one can note that CaR(α, *risk*) < CaR(β, *risk*). Hence, a participant afraid of incurring a high cost will choose strategy α, even if this strategy has a higher cost on average.

10.3.2. *Details on the application of game theory*

As a SC is a sequence of organizations that are involved in producing and delivering a product or service, each SC member's decision may impact the benefits received by other members. Because game theory applies to the analyses of multi-player decision problems, where the players behave in a conflicting situation to seek optimal solutions, this approach has become a primary methodological tool in SC analysis [CAC 04, LEN 05]. In fact, game theory deals with interactive and conflicting optimization problems. In our case study, the relationship between the ordering policies of two companies can be analyzed as a non-cooperative static game in which the strategic decisions of companies affect each company's payoff, which is the total cost evaluated with the *CaR* proposed in the previous section. In non-cooperative static games the players choose strategies simultaneously and are thereafter committed to their chosen strategies. The normal form of this game is given in Table 10.2. Note its specific form due to the similarity of strategies β and γ.

		Wholesaler w		
		α	β	γ
Retailer r	α	$CaR_w(α, α, σ_m)$ $CaR_r(α, α, σ_m)$	$CaR_w(α, β, σ_m)$ $CaR_r(α, β, σ_m)$	$CaR_w(α, β, σ_m)$ $CaR_r(α, β, σ_m)$
	β	$CaR_w(α, α, σ_m)$ $CaR_r(β, α, σ_m)$	$CaR_w(β, β, σ_m)$ $CaR_r(β, β, σ_m)$	$CaR_w(β, β, σ_m)$ $CaR_r(β, β, σ_m)$
	γ	$CaR_w(α, α, σ_m)$ $CaR_r(β, α, σ_m)$	$CaR_w(β, β, σ_m)$ $CaR_r(β, β, σ_m)$	$CaR_w(γ, γ, σ_m)$ $CaR_r(γ, γ, σ_m)$

Table 10.2. *General form of the non-cooperative game considered in this chapter*

For each company we can determine the best response to the other player's strategy. In a given two-player game, player k's best response to strategy s_{-k} of the other player is the strategy $s_k{}^*$, which that minimizes player k's *CaR*:

$$CaR_k(s_k{}^*, s_{-k}, σ_m) ≤ CaR_k(s_k, s_{-k}, σ_m) \quad \text{with} k ∈ \{r, w\} \qquad [10.6]$$

10.3.3. *Results of the coordination game*

According to the approximated performances of the joint strategies given in section 10.6, and for a fixed probability *risk* = 10% bilaterally (thus, t_{risk} = 1.65) and fixed back-order cost $λ_k$ = 1, we obtain Figures 10.2 and 10.3.

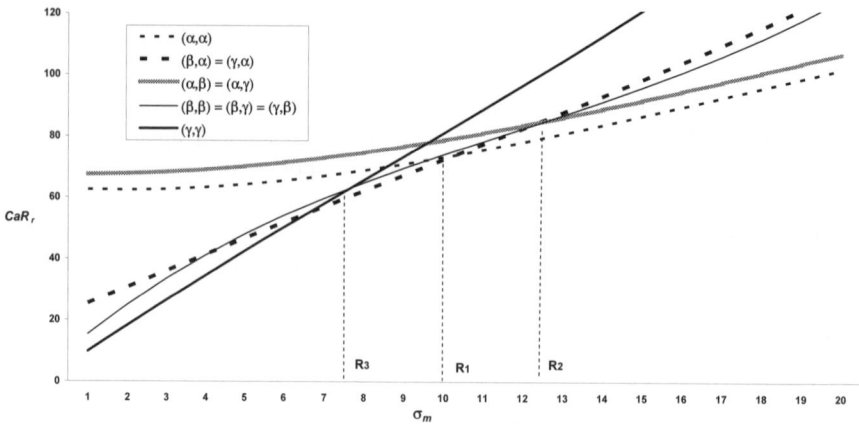

Figure 10.2. *Retailer's CaR functions against $σ_m$ for the different joint strategies*

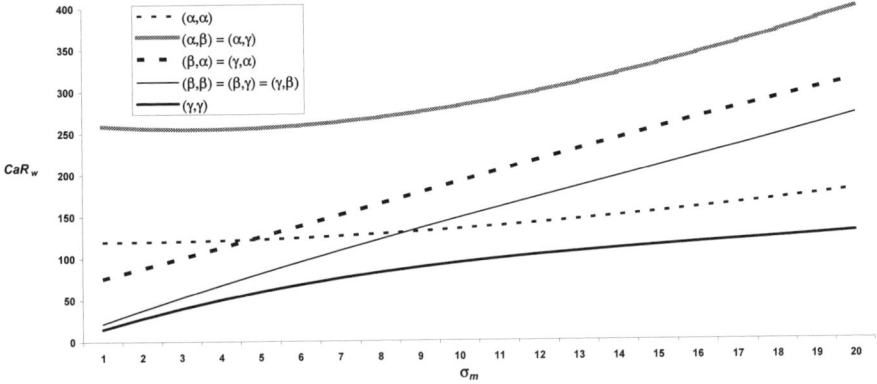

Figure 10.3. *Wholesaler's CaR functions against σ_m for the different joint strategies*

In Figure 10.3 we note that if the retailer chooses strategy α, then the best response of the wholesaler is α for any σ_m because the CaR of (α, α) is below the CaR of (α, β) – which is the same as the CaR of (α, γ). If the retailer chooses strategy β, then the best responses of the wholesaler are β or γ (without preference). If the retailer chooses γ, the wholesaler's optimal response is also γ. Note that these best responses, according to the strategy of the retailer, are identical for every value of σ_m.

The analysis of Figure 10.2 for the retailer's best responses is less obvious. In this figure, we observe that if the wholesaler chooses α, the best retailer's response depends on the value of σ_m:

– if $\sigma_m < R_1$, the best responses of the retailer are β or γ;

– if $\sigma_m > R_1$, the best response of the retailer is α.

If the wholesaler chooses β, the retailer's best response also depends on the value of σ_m:

– if $\sigma_m < R_2$, the best responses are β or γ;

– if $\sigma_m > R_2$, the best response is α.

Finally, if the wholesaler chooses γ, the retailer's best responses are:

– γ if $\sigma_m < R_3$;

– β if $R_3 < \sigma_m < R_2$; and

– α if $\sigma_m > R_2$.

$\sigma_m < R_3$		Wholesaler w		
		α	β	γ
Retailer r	α	$CaR_w(\alpha, \alpha, \sigma_m)$ $CaR_r(\alpha, \alpha, \sigma_m)$	$CaR_w(\alpha, \beta, \sigma_m)$ $CaR_r(\alpha, \beta, \sigma_m)$	$CaR_w(\alpha, \beta, \sigma_m)$ $CaR_r(\alpha, \beta, \sigma_m)$
	β	$CaR_w(\alpha, \alpha, \sigma_m)$ $CaR_r(\beta, \alpha, \sigma_m)$	$CaR_w(\beta, \beta, \sigma_m)$ $CaR_r(\beta, \beta, \sigma_m)$	$CaR_w(\beta, \beta, \sigma_m)$ $CaR_r(\beta, \beta, \sigma_m)$
	γ	$CaR_w(\alpha, \alpha, \sigma_m)$ $CaR_r(\beta, \alpha, \sigma_m)$	$CaR_w(\beta, \beta, \sigma_m)$ $CaR_r(\beta, \beta, \sigma_m)$	$CaR_w(\gamma, \gamma, \sigma_m)$ $CaR_r(\gamma, \gamma, \sigma_m)$

$R_3 < \sigma_m < R_1$		Wholesaler w		
		α	β	γ
Retailer r	α	$CaR_w(\alpha, \alpha, \sigma_m)$ $CaR_r(\alpha, \alpha, \sigma_m)$	$CaR_w(\alpha, \beta, \sigma_m)$ $CaR_r(\alpha, \beta, \sigma_m)$	$CaR_w(\alpha, \beta, \sigma_m)$ $CaR_r(\alpha, \beta, \sigma_m)$
	β	$CaR_w(\alpha, \alpha, \sigma_m)$ $CaR_r(\beta, \alpha, \sigma_m)$	$CaR_w(\beta, \beta, \sigma_m)$ $CaR_r(\beta, \beta, \sigma_m)$	$CaR_w(\beta, \beta, \sigma_m)$ $CaR_r(\beta, \beta, \sigma_m)$
	γ	$CaR_w(\alpha, \alpha, \sigma_m)$ $CaR_r(\beta, \alpha, \sigma_m)$	$CaR_w(\beta, \beta, \sigma_m)$ $CaR_r(\beta, \beta, \sigma_m)$	$CaR_w(\gamma, \gamma, \sigma_m)$ $CaR_r(\gamma, \gamma, \sigma_m)$

$R_1 < \sigma_m < R_2$		Wholesaler w		
		α	β	γ
Retailer r	α	$CaR_w(\alpha, \alpha, \sigma_m)$ $CaR_r(\alpha, \alpha, \sigma_m)$	$CaR_w(\alpha, \beta, \sigma_m)$ $CaR_r(\alpha, \beta, \sigma_m)$	$CaR_w(\alpha, \beta, \sigma_m)$ $CaR_r(\alpha, \beta, \sigma_m)$
	β	$CaR_w(\alpha, \alpha, \sigma_m)$ $CaR_r(\beta, \alpha, \sigma_m)$	$CaRw(\beta, \beta, \sigma_m)$ $CaR_r(\beta, \beta, \sigma_m)$	$CaR_w(\beta, \beta, \sigma_m)$ $CaR_r(\beta, \beta, \sigma_m)$
	γ	$CaR_w(\alpha, \alpha, \sigma_m)$ $CaR_r(\beta, \alpha, \sigma_m)$	$CaR_w(\beta, \beta, \sigma_m)$ $CaR_r(\beta, \beta, \sigma_m)$	$CaR_w(\gamma, \gamma, \sigma_m)$ $CaR_r(\gamma, \gamma, \sigma_m)$

$\sigma_m > R_2$		Wholesaler w		
		α	β	γ
Retailer r	α	$CaR_w(\alpha, \alpha, \sigma_m)$ $CaR_r(\alpha, \alpha, \sigma_m)$	$CaR_w(\alpha, \beta, \sigma_m)$ $CaR_r(\alpha, \beta, \sigma_m)$	$CaR_w(\alpha, \beta, \sigma_m)$ $CaR_r(\alpha, \beta, \sigma_m)$
	β	$CaR_w(\alpha, \alpha, \sigma_m)$ $CaR_r(\beta, \alpha, \sigma_m)$	$CaR_w(\beta, \beta, \sigma_m)$ $CaR_r(\beta, \beta, \sigma_m)$	$CaR_w(\beta, \beta, \sigma_m)$ $CaR_r(\beta, \beta, \sigma_m)$
	γ	$CaR_w(\alpha, \alpha, \sigma_m)$ $CaR_r(\beta, \alpha, \sigma_m)$	$CaR_w(\beta, \beta, \sigma_m)$ $CaR_r(\beta, \beta, \sigma_m)$	$CaR_w(\gamma, \gamma, \sigma_m)$ $CaR_r(\gamma, \gamma, \sigma_m)$

Table 10.3. *Equilibriums (gray entries) of the non-cooperative game against the value of σ_m*

These results show that an outcome of the game in which all players choose their best response simultaneously may be the solution. Each rational player aims to optimize its utility so, knowing that every other player will have the same incentive, such behaviors would lead to a solution from which nobody has any intention of unilaterally deviating. Such an outcome is called the Nash equilibrium of the game. The Nash equilibrium has a self-enforcing property: no player wants to unilaterally deviate from it since such behavior would lead to lower payoffs. Formally, we can define a Nash equilibrium as *a joint strategy (s_r*,s_w*) in which s_k* is a best response to $s_{-k}*$ for $k \in \{r, w\}$.*

Depending on the value of σ_m, and according to the CaR function of the two firms, we can transform the matrix presented in Table 10.2 into the four normal games in Table 10.3, in which the Nash equilibriums are written in gray.

Table 10.3 shows that there is no dominant strategy for both participants. In other words, depending on the strategy adopted by the wholesaler and the retailer, and on the volatility of market demand (σ_m), the best responses of the two participants may be α, β or γ. The analysis of the Nash equilibriums obtained is presented in the next section.

10.4. Discussion

Except for the case $\sigma_m > R_2$, we find two or three Nash equilibriums for each game in Table 10.3. The obvious problem with multiple equilibriums is that players may not know which equilibrium will prevail, and an inefficient outcome might occur not because of conflict between individual incentives but because there is more than one way to coordinate.

It is possible that a non-equilibrium outcome results because one player plays one equilibrium strategy while the second player chooses another. In fact, our three games above represent a Pareto coordination game. One method to rule out some equilibriums involves focusing on the Pareto optimal equilibrium alone. If there is an equilibrium preferred by every player, this equilibrium is Pareto optimal, and thus chosen by the players. Let us now describe how this applies to the four tables in Table 10.3.

In the first table in Table 10.3, and according to the two CaR functions in Figures 10.1 and 10.2, we note that the preferred equilibrium for both players is the same (this equilibrium is thus Pareto optimal), i.e. the equilibrium corresponding to joint strategy (γ, γ). For all $\sigma_m \leq R_3$ we have:

$$CaR_k\left(\gamma_k*,\gamma_k*,\sigma_m\right) \leq CaR_k\left(\beta_k*,\beta_k*,\sigma_m\right) \quad \text{with } k \in \{r,w\} \qquad [10.7]$$

Thus, for low volatility in market demand, even if the coordination of the two firms on joint strategy (β, β) is a Nash equilibrium (which means that no firm has incentives to deviate alone from this solution), joint strategy (γ, γ) is preferred. This is in line with the lower value of their corresponding CaR. In this case, both firms will centralize information, i.e. the retailer will share the market consumption in real time with the rest of the SC. Moreover, the wholesaler will also share this information in real time with its own supplier.

In the second table in Table 10.3, both equilibriums are equivalent for both players. Here we have:

$$CaR_k(\beta_k^*, \beta_k^*, \sigma_m) = CaR_k(\beta_k^*, \gamma_k^*, \sigma_m) \quad with \quad \in \{r, w\} \quad and \quad R_3 < \sigma_m < R_1$$

In other words, these two couples of joint strategies induce the same CaR. Thus, the Pareto optimal criterion is not useful. For all $R_3 < \sigma_m \leq R_1$, the retailer will play strategy β, while the wholesaler is indifferent about playing either strategy β or γ. Information centralization is costs money (although this not taken into account in our model), so we can expect that the wholesaler will choose strategy β in this case.

In the third table in Table 10.3, we obtain three equilibriums. Nevertheless, equilibriums (β, β) and (γ, γ) are always equivalent, as in the previous table. We may thus focus on the analysis of the dominance of (α, α) and (β, β). For the retailer, Pareto equilibrium (α, α) dominates (β, β) because CaR_r is lower over the range of σ_m between R_1 and R_2.

For the wholesaler, Figure 10.3 shows that $CaR_w(\beta, \beta) < CaR_w(\alpha, \alpha)$ for values of σ_m below a certain threshold, and then that $CaR_w(\beta, \beta) > CaR_w(\alpha, \alpha)$. Since this threshold is much lower than R_1, (α, α) Pareto dominates over $R_3 < \sigma_m \leq R_1$ for the retailer.

Finally, in the last table in Table 10.3, we have just one equilibrium: (α, α). In this configuration, the optimal strategy for both companies is identical, and consists of not sharing information and using a policy minimizing local inventory costs.

In short, all these results show that when the final market is characterized by a relatively low volatility (small values of σ_m), the best strategies for both firms is information centralization (γ), i.e. the real-time sharing of market consumption by the retailer with the rest of the SC. On the other hand, for higher values of σ_m, the best strategies for both firms are based on the local optimization of the operation of their inventory system (α). Between these two extremes, for $R_3 < \sigma_m \leq R_1$, there exist possibilities for slow IS (β) relevant for both companies.

More generally, we can conclude that IS (slowly or in real time) is not always the best strategy for the firms. Based on the specification of the firm's utility functions, which take into account the performances of joint strategies in terms of inventory holding and back-order costs, and their strategic behaviors, supported by game theory tools, we observe that firms only benefit from real-time IS when market demand is weakly volatile.

This result can be compared with those obtained with more classical and simple decision criteria. For instance, if the strategic decisions concerning replenishment strategies are based on the average inventory cost $\mu_{i,k}$ alone (or in the CaR criteria, $\lambda_k = 0$ and $t_{risk} = 0$), the normal form of the non-cooperative static game is given by Table 10.4.

		Wholesaler w		
		α	β	γ
Retailer r	α	$\mu_w(\alpha,\alpha,\sigma_m)$ $\mu_r(\alpha,\alpha,\sigma_m)$	$\mu_w(\alpha,\beta,\sigma_m)$ $\mu_r(\alpha,\beta,\sigma_m)$	$\mu_w(\alpha,\beta,\sigma_m)$ $\mu_r(\alpha,\beta,\sigma_m)$
	β	$\mu_w(\beta,\alpha,\sigma_m)$ $\mu_r(\beta,\alpha,\sigma_m)$	$\mu_w(\beta,\beta,\sigma_m)$ $\mu_r(\beta,\beta,\sigma_m)$	$\mu_w(\beta,\beta,\sigma_m)$ $\mu_r(\beta,\beta,\sigma_m)$
	γ	$\mu_w(\beta,\alpha,\sigma_m)$ $\mu_r(\beta,\alpha,\sigma_m)$	$\mu_w(\beta,\beta,\sigma_m)$ $\mu_w(\beta,\beta,\sigma_m)$	$\mu_w(\gamma,\gamma,\sigma_m)$ $\mu_r(\gamma,\gamma,\sigma_m)$

Table 10.4. *Equilibriums in the non-cooperative game with average inventory cost criteria*

With the average inventory cost criteria, strategy α is dominated by the other two strategies for both firms. We obtain two Nash equilibriums with no threshold value concerning market volatility. Applying the Pareto dominance criterion, joint strategy (γ, γ) will be preferred by both firms. In this game, the retailer and the wholesaler will both share market consumption in real time with the rest of the SC. This is consistent with the traditional finding that centralized control of the SC outperforms decentralized control in terms of inventory management.

In fact, by introducing the valuation of back-orders in the performance of joint strategies, we reduce the advantages of carrying out IS. This applies even more when both firms are sensitive to uncertainty about these costs, i.e. when they use the CaR function. The introduction of back-orders in the analysis modifies the performance of the SC in comparison with an analysis that considers just inventory levels. The joint strategies of both parties are then characterized by performances more sensitive to the volatility of market demand and to the bullwhip effect. In other words, for a given volatility of end demand, the costs incurred by back-orders may more than balance those incurred by inventory levels.

The originality of our model and results is also due to the recognition of the sensitivity of the firms' behavior in response to variations of costs generated by a joint strategy. Consequently, depending on the variability of end demand, performance in terms of inventory and back-order costs will be more or less variable as well. This is why the CaR function explicitly incorporates variations of performance in the choice criterion. Therefore, a high variation in performance may induce a choice of strategy that may not be that resulting from the simple minimization of average costs. Our simulations show that, for high values of variability in the end market, joint strategies consisting of sharing or centralizing information (slow or instantaneous IS) finally incur too many variations in terms of inventory and back-order performance, or at least many more than with a traditional flow management. For parties careful not to pay excessive costs, it is then rational to choose an equilibrium with a more stable performance, even when the equilibrium is not optimal in terms of average costs.

10.5. Conclusion

This chapter proposes a methodology based on game theory to explore the conditions under which different ordering strategies can be used in a SC. These conditions include the volatility of market demand and attitudes towards service levels (measured here as back-orders) and risks concerning total cost supported by the firms. This methodology is applied to a SC with two members who may use one of three strategies: strategy α, based on traditional concepts from optimization; and strategies β and γ implementing recent concepts from stream management. For companies' preferences considered over the valuation of their back-orders and attitude towards risk, we find that α is the only Nash equilibrium when market demand is highly volatile, while β and γ are beneficial to the companies when market demand is more stable.

Our analysis is based on concepts from both industrial engineering and economics. In fact, we think that concepts from economics may greatly improve the understanding of SCs by proposing new points of view. In particular, industrial engineering has mainly modeled inventory management as an optimization problem solved by isolated decision makers, while economics provides concepts such as Nash equilibrium, Pareto optimality and models of attitudes towards risk, in order to study the relationships between each individual decision and the overall performance of a SC.

10.6. Appendix: raw data obtained from numerical experimentations

The purpose of this chapter is the analysis of simulations detailed in previous papers, e.g. [MOY 09] or the previous chapter of this book. Hence, this chapter does not detail these simulations but describes the main features of our model, in particular the characteristics of the three replenishment policies considered. Nevertheless, we think it useful to provide approximations of the outputs of these simulations, so that the interested reader may reproduce the core of this chapter, i.e. our analysis, and even extend it to other values of the parameters.

Please notice that, for each of the following 40 polynomials, the determination coefficient R^2 measures the quality of the approximations; that is, the closer to 1, the nearer the corresponding approximation to the value actually obtained by simulation:

$$\mu_{i,r}(a,a,\sigma_m) = -0.0016\sigma_m^3 + 0.0629\sigma_m^2 - 0.1395\sigma_m$$

$$+ 32.903(R^2 = 0.9939) \qquad [10.8]$$

$$\sigma_{i,r}(a,a,\sigma_m) = -0.0023\sigma_m^3 + 0.1136\sigma_m^2 - 0.6157\sigma_m$$

$$+ 23.565(R^2 = 0.9999) \qquad [10.9]$$

$$\mu_{i,w}(a,a,\sigma_m) = -8*10^{-5}\sigma_m^3 + 0.0586\sigma_m^2 - 0.0885\sigma_m$$

$$+ 61.915 \ (R^2 = 0.9987) \qquad [10.10]$$

$$\sigma_{i,w}(a,a,\sigma_m) = -0.0017\sigma_m^3 + 0.1192\sigma_m^2 - 0.5127\sigma_m$$

$$+ 43.833 \ (R^2 = 0.9996) \qquad [10.11]$$

$$\mu_{b,r}(a,a,\sigma_m) = 3*10^{-4}\sigma_m^3 + 0.0017\sigma_m^2 + 0.1488\sigma_m$$

$$- 0.0052 \ (R^2 = 0.9999) \qquad [10.12]$$

$$\sigma_{b,r}(a,a,\sigma_m) = 3*10^{-4}\sigma_m^3 + 0.0058\sigma_m^2 + 0.597\sigma_m - 0.0081(R^2 = 1) \qquad [10.13]$$

$$\mu_{b,w}(a,a,\sigma_m) = 4*10^{-4}\sigma_m^3 - 0.0064\sigma_m^2 + 0.218\sigma_m$$

$$+ 1.2723(R^2 = 0.9986) \qquad [10.14]$$

$$\sigma_{b,w}(a,a,\sigma_m) = -2*10^{-4}\sigma_m^3 + 0.0244\sigma_m^2 + 0.2082\sigma_m$$

$$+ 7.1487(R^2 = 0.9999) \qquad [10.15]$$

$$\mu_{i,r}(\alpha,\beta,\sigma_m) = -7*10^{-4}\sigma_m^3 + 0.0377\sigma_m^2 + 0.1975\sigma_m$$

$$+ 32.97 \ (R^2 = 0.9982) \tag{10.16}$$

$$\sigma_{i,r}(\alpha,\beta,\sigma_m) = -0.0021\sigma_m^3 + 0.1081\sigma_m^2 - 0.5088\sigma_m$$

$$+ 23.503 \ (R^2 = 0.9999) \tag{10.17}$$

$$\mu_{i,w}(\alpha,\beta,\sigma_m) = -0.0052\sigma_m^3 + 0.5133\sigma_m^2 - 4.5834\sigma_m$$

$$+ 152.81(R^2 = 0.9969) \tag{10.18}$$

$$\sigma_{i,w}(\alpha,\beta,\sigma_m) = -0.0021\sigma_m^3 + 0.1674\sigma_m^2 + 0.0289\sigma_m$$

$$+ 81.699 \ (R^2 = 0.9993) \tag{10.19}$$

$$\mu_{b,r}(\alpha,\beta,\sigma_m) = 2*10^{-4}\sigma_m^3 + 0.0004\sigma_m^2 + 0.1192\sigma_m$$

$$+ 1.0895(R^2 = 0.9997) \tag{10.20}$$

$$\sigma_{b,r}(\alpha,\beta,\sigma_m) = 2*10^{-4}\sigma_m^3 + 0.0107\sigma_m^2 - 0.0175\sigma_m$$

$$+ 11.446 \ (R^2 = 0.9999) \tag{10.21}$$

$$\mu_{b,w}(\alpha,\beta,\sigma_m) = -5*10^{-6}\sigma_m^5 + 0.0003\sigma_m^4 - 0.0071\sigma_m^3 + 0.0819\sigma_m^2$$

$$- 0.4096\sigma_m + 2.9774(R^2 = 0.9751) \tag{10.22}$$

$$\sigma_{b,w}(\alpha,\beta,\sigma_m) = -6*10^{-4}\sigma_m^3 + 0.0203\sigma_m^2 - 0.1692\sigma_m$$

$$+ 18.441(R^2 = 0.9785) \tag{10.23}$$

$$\mu_{i,r}(\beta,\alpha,\sigma_m) = 8*10^{-4}\sigma_m^3 + 0.0327\sigma_m^2 + 1.0089\sigma_m$$

$$+ 0.891(R^2 = 0.9999) \tag{10.24}$$

$$\sigma_{i,r}(\beta,\alpha,\sigma_m) = 4*10^{-4}\sigma_m^3 + 0.0042\sigma_m^2 + 2.0883\sigma_m + 0.6849(R^2 = 1) \tag{10.25}$$

$$\mu_{i,w}(\beta,\alpha,\sigma_m) = -0.0017\sigma_m^3 + 0.0406\sigma_m^2 + 4.9204\sigma_m$$

$$+ 33.093(R^2 = 0.9999) \tag{10.26}$$

$$\sigma_{i,w}(\beta,\alpha,\sigma_m) = -0.0033\sigma_m^3 + 0.0807\sigma_m^2 + 4.6594\sigma_m$$

$$+ 21.93(R^2 = 0.9998) \tag{10.27}$$

$$\mu_{b,r}(\beta,\alpha,\sigma_m) = 0.0033\sigma_m^3 - 0.168\sigma_m^2 + 2.7501\sigma_m +$$

$$1.3075(R^2 = 0.9993) \tag{10.28}$$

$$\sigma_{b,r}(\beta,\alpha,\sigma_m) = -9*10^{-4}\sigma_m^3 + 0.0076\sigma_m^2 + 1.0138\sigma_m$$

$$+ 14.041(R^2 = 0.999) \tag{10.29}$$

$$\mu_{b,w}(\beta,\alpha,\sigma_m) = -1*10^{-4}\sigma_m^3 - 0.0007\sigma_m^2 + 0.7753\sigma_m$$

$$+ 0.3243(R^2 = 0.9998) \tag{10.30}$$

$$\sigma_{b,w}(\beta,\alpha,\sigma_m) = -0.0024\sigma_m^3 + 0.0914\sigma_m^2 + 0.589\sigma_m$$

$$+ 9.4998(R^2 = 0.9997) \tag{10.31}$$

$$\mu_{i,r}(\beta,\beta,\sigma_m) = 2*10^{-4}\sigma_m^3 + 0.0726\sigma_m^2 + 0.2618\sigma_m + 0.4934 \; (R^2 = 1) \tag{10.32}$$

$$\sigma_{i,r}(\beta,\beta,\sigma_m) = -1*10^{-3}\sigma_m^3 + 0.0699\sigma_m^2 + 1.2319\sigma_m + 0.4362(R^2 = 1) \tag{10.33}$$

$$\mu_{i,w}(\beta,\beta,\sigma_m) = -5*10^{-4}\sigma_m^3 + 0.0678\sigma_m^2 + 3.9635\sigma_m + 0.5934(R^2 = 1) \tag{10.34}$$

$$\sigma_{i,w}(\beta,\beta,\sigma_m) = -1*10^{-3}\sigma_m^3 + 0.0117\sigma_m^2 + 5.2792\sigma_m + 0.4969(R^2 = 1) \tag{10.35}$$

$$\mu_{b,r}(\beta,\beta,\sigma_m) = 0.0089\sigma_m^3 - 0.3878\sigma_m^2 + 5.0044\sigma_m$$

$$+ 1.3853(R^2 = 0.9894) \tag{10.36}$$

$$\sigma_{b,r}(\beta,\beta,\sigma_m) = 0.0056\sigma_m^3 - 0.2649\sigma_m^2 + 4.5621\sigma_m$$

$$+ 2.1428(R^2 = 0.9982) \tag{10.37}$$

$$\mu_{b,w}(\beta,\beta,\sigma_m) = 6*10^{-3}\sigma_m^3 - 0.2585\sigma_m^2 + 3.7752\sigma_m$$

$$+ 1.9329(R^2 = 0.9923) \tag{10.38}$$

$$\sigma_{b,w}(\beta,\beta,\sigma_m) = 0.0051\sigma_m^3 - 0.2399\sigma_m^2 + 5.082\sigma_m$$

$$+ 1.9993(R^2 = 0.9994) \tag{10.39}$$

$$\mu_{i,r}(\gamma,\gamma,\sigma_m) = 0.0011\sigma_m^3 + 0.039\sigma_m^2 + 0.2332\sigma_m$$

$$+ 0.463(R^2 = 0.9999) \tag{10.40}$$

$$\sigma_{i,r}(\gamma,\gamma,\sigma_m) = -3*10^{-5}\sigma_m^3 + 0.049\sigma_m^2 + 0.9621\sigma_m$$

$$+ 0.5393(R^2 = 0.9999) \tag{10.41}$$

$$\mu_{i,w}(\gamma,\gamma,\sigma_m) = 0.0065\sigma_m^{\ 3} - 0.308\sigma_m^{\ 2} + 4.5468\sigma_m$$

$$- 0.397(R^2 = 0.9984) \tag{10.42}$$

$$\sigma_{i,w}(\gamma,\gamma,\sigma_m) = 3*10^{-3}\sigma_m^{\ 3} - 0.1664\sigma_m^{\ 2} + 3.6395\sigma_m$$

$$+ 0.6878(R^2 = 0.9995) \tag{10.43}$$

$$\mu_{b,r}(\gamma,\gamma,\sigma_m) = 0.0017\sigma_m^{\ 3} - 0.0668\sigma_m^{\ 2} + 3.0595\sigma_m$$

$$+ 0.3759(R^2 = 0.9999) \tag{10.44}$$

$$\sigma_{b,r}(\gamma,\gamma,\sigma_m) = 0.0015\sigma_m^{\ 3} - 0.0982\sigma_m^{\ 2} + 4.2008\sigma_m + 0.0615(R^2 = 1) \tag{10.45}$$

$$\mu_{b,w}(\gamma,\gamma,\sigma_m) = 0.0027\sigma_m^{\ 3} - 0.1436\sigma_m^{\ 2} + 3.3396\sigma_m$$

$$+ 0.1745(R^2 = 0.9997) \tag{10.46}$$

$$\sigma_{b,w}(\gamma,\gamma,\sigma_m) = 0.0019\sigma_m^{\ 3} - 0.1127\sigma_m^{\ 2} + 4.1305\sigma_m$$

$$+ 0.3828 \ (R^2 = 0.9999) \tag{10.47}$$

10.7. Bibliography

[CAC 04] CACHON G. P., NETESSINE S., "Game theory in supply chain analysis", in: D. SIMCHI-LEVI, S.D. WU, Z. SHEN (Eds.), *Handbook of Quantitative Supply Chain Analysis: Modeling in the E-Business Era*, Kluwer, Boston, 2004, pp. 13-66.

[JOR 06] JORION P., *Value at Risk: The New Benchmark for Managing Financial Risk*, (3rd edition), McGraw-Hill, 2006.

[LEN 05] LENG M., PARLAR M., "Game theoretic applications in supply chain management: A review", *INFOR*, vol. 43, no. 3, pp. 187-220.

[MCN 05] McNEIL A., FREY R., EMBRECHTS P., *Quantitative Risk Management: Concepts Techniques and Tools*, Princeton University Press, 2005.

[MOY 07] MOYAUX T., CHAIB-DRAA B., D'AMOURS S., "Information sharing as a coordination mechanism for reducing the bullwhip effect in a supply chain", *IEEE Transactions on Systems, Man, and Cybernetics, Part. C*, vol. 37, no. 3, pp. 396-409.

[MOY 09] MOYAUX T., LLERENA D., BABOLI A., "Choice of an ordering strategy taking account of risks about customer service levels and on-hand inventories", *Proceedings of the International Conference on Industrial Engineering and Systems Management* (IESM), Montreal, PQ, Canada, 2009.

[SÁI 08] SÁIZ, M. E., HENDRIX E.M.T., "Methods for computing Nash equilibria of a location–quantity game", *Computers & Operations Research*, vol. 35, no. 10, pp. 3311-3330.

[WAN 94] WANG Q., PARLAR M., "A three-person game theory model arising in stochastic inventory control theory", *European Journal of Operational Research*, vol. 76, no.1, pp.83-97.

List of Authors

Blandine AGERON
University of Grenoble
CERAG, CNRS/UPMF
IUT Valence
France

Gülgün ALPAN
University of Grenoble
G-SCOP, CNRS/Grenoble INP/UJF
France

Sayed Hossain AKHTER
University Lumière Lyon 2
France

Armand BABOLI
University of Lyon
LIESP
INSA-Lyon
France

Emilie BAUMANN-CHARDINE
University of Lyon
LIESP
INSA-Lyon
France

Valérie BOTTA-GENOULAZ
University of Lyon
LIESP
INSA-Lyon
France

Xavier BOUCHER
Ecole Nationale Supérieure des Mines de St-Etienne
G2I Research Center
France

Patrick BURLAT
Ecole Nationale Supérieure des Mines de St-Etienne
G2I Research Center
France

Jean-Pierre CAMPAGNE
University of Lyon
LIESP
INSA-Lyon
France

Ludivine CHAZE
University of Grenoble
CERAG, CNRS/UPMF
France

Van-Dat CUNG
University of Grenoble
G-SCOP, CNRS/Grenoble INP/UJF
France

Carine DOMINGUEZ
University of Lyon
COACTIS
University Jean Monnet
Saint-Etienne
France

Alexis GARAPIN
University of Grenoble
GAEL, INRA/UPMF
France

France-Anne GRUAT LA FORME
Société BABOLAT VS
France

Olivier LAVASTRE
University of Grenoble
CERAG, CNRS/UPMF
IAE - Grenoble
France

Daniel LLERENA
University of Grenoble
GAEL, INRA/UPMF
France

Fabien MANGIONE
University of Grenoble
G-SCOP, CNRS/Grenoble INP/UJF
France

Ali MEHRABI
Golpayegan University of Technology
Iran

Pierre-Alain MILLET
University of Lyon
LIESP
INSA-Lyon
France

Thierry MOYAUX
University of Lyon
LIESP
INSA-Lyon
France

Gilles NEUBERT
Ecole Supérieure de Commerce de St Etienne
LIESP
France

Yacine OUZROUT
University Lumière Lyon 2
LIESP
France

Claude PELLEGRIN
University Lumière Lyon 2
COACTIS
France

Omar SAKKA
University of Lyon
LIESP
INSA-Lyon
France

Natallia TARATYNAVA
University of French West Indies and French Guiana
CEREGMIA
Martinique

Lorraine TRILLING
University of Lyon
LIESP
INSA-Lyon
France

Gonca TUNCEL
Dokuz Eylül University
Turkey

Ishraf ZAOUI
Ecole Supérieure de Commerce de St Etienne
France

Index